DIETRICH
A Biography

Printed in the UK by MPG Books Ltd, Bodmin, Cornwall

Published by Sanctuary Publishing Limited, Sanctuary House,
45–53 Sinclair Road, London W14 0NS, United Kingdom

www.sanctuarypublishing.com

Photographs from the private collection of Tobias Tak

Cover photograph © George Hurrell/Hulton Archive

While the publishers have made every reasonable effort to trace the copyright
owners for any or all of the photographs in this book, there may be some omissions
of credits, for which we apologise.

ISBN: 1-86074-409-5

DIETRICH
A Biography

E a n   W o o d

Sanctuary

Acknowledgements

Writing a book about anyone who led such a varied and complicated life as Marlene Dietrich involves gathering a lot of information. Quite apart from all the different social worlds she was a part of, in so many different countries and times, there are all the performances she has left us, on film, video and record. So I am grateful to many people for lending me books, videos, articles and records, for answering my puzzled questions, and for drawing my attention to many items I would have missed.

My thanks go especially to George Akers, Kevin Brownlow, David Evans, John Holmstrom, Linda McCarthy, Bernard Marlowe, Euan Pearson and Tom Vallance. In regard to the photographs illustrating the book, I am greatly indebted to Tobias Tak for allowing me to browse in his amazing collection of Marleniana, to Bryan Hammond, who pointed me towards it, and to Vic Bates, who transferred the images to disc with subtlety and taste. And finally, to Penny Braybrooke, Iain MacGregor, Alan Heal, Dan Froude, Michelle Knight and Gill Paul at Sanctuary Publishing for their customary help, hard work and patience.

Contents

Opening

The theme song is 'Falling In Love Again'. The house lights dim. Tall curtains part. Two brilliant streams of white light strike out from the follow-spots and begin hunting like searchlights over the stage.

For a while there is nothing but the criss-crossing lights and the music and the sense of breath-catching anticipation. Then she appears, swathed in a long cape of white swansdown, its train sweeping behind her from the wings. She bows deeply to the audience, then straightens. Her face – that perfect face, perfectly lit – is almost unbearably beautiful, with its finely modelled cheekbones and broad smooth forehead. Her eyes hold a knowing tenderness, her mouth a cool mockery.

As she allows the cape to part, there is the stunning body, clad in a figure-hugging translucent dress – a dress rendered opaque in discreet places by glittering swirls of sequin and rhinestone, and giving the illusion of nakedness. She is tailored to please, perfect from her trademark hairstyle to her elegant high heels. Her legs are, as ever, magnificent.

This is Marlene – the woman, the image, the icon – perfected over the years and still as perfect as ever. As the welcoming applause surges onwards, she surveys her audience with humorous acceptance – a complicity between herself and them that they all know how wonderful she is, while knowing that it is clearly ridiculous for anybody to be quite as wonderful.

She begins to sing, in that unmistakable voice, the foreignness of her accent underlining her air of sophistication and mystery. She has known exotic cities, both their opulence and their underside. She has experienced more of life and love, more of rapture and loss, than any woman who has ever lived, and yet she remains wry and detached, well in control of her life and herself. She is so magical in her beauty that she seems unapproachable in her person, and yet there is always perhaps the faint possibility that maybe, for some lucky man or woman...

As the show progresses she tells the story of her life (or as much of it as she cares to tell) and sings the songs she has accumulated, like experience, over the years. From *The Blue Angel*, her first major film success, made in the Berlin of her youth. From the Hollywood of the Thirties, in those glamorous days of the early talkies. From World War II, when she bravely toured the front lines, entertaining the troops.

Troops have been a key element in her life – her father was a cavalryman, and these live performances have an almost military precision – every gesture, every pause, every word, every whisper, every smile (and she has many different smiles) – all are immaculately delivered, and not one is wasted. The women in her audience feel more glamorous, the men more dashing and handsome.

Her presence is hypnotic. For as long as she holds the stage, her watching fans are living in her world, and as she makes her final bow, to rapturous applause, flowers rain down on the stage from all sections of the house. Whether this is carefully stage-managed or a spontaneous display matters not at all – it has become a traditional part of her performance, and her whole performance has once again been magnificent.

This is Marlene as she is remembered – as she is adored. Yet who was the woman who lay behind the image? Was she the passionate, disillusioned creature of the night she seemed? Certainly she was striking in her beauty, but was there more artifice in her stage and film appearances than there seemed? Was she clever as well as talented? Certainly the light of intelligence never seemed to recede from her features. Was she in private life (to the lucky few) the warm and compassionate woman one seemed to sense beneath the knowing mockery?

Who was Marlene Dietrich?

1 A Prussian Childhood

In 1898, in Berlin, Police Lieutenant Louis Erich Otto Dietrich married Wilhelmine Elisabeth Josephine Felsing. Josephine was twenty-two, Otto was thirty. A handsome man, stocky in build, he was of only medium height, but had the erect bearing of an officer and an upswept moustache resembling the one worn by the Emperor, Kaiser Wilhelm II. Josephine was a small pleasant-faced woman, slightly plump and with a smile that seemed to hint at some secret amusement. It was a smile that she would pass on to her daughter.

Otto came by his soldierly bearing honestly, because he had only recently completed five years as an officer in the lancer corps of the Uhlanen light cavalry. He had risen to the rank of Major, and had even been decorated, probably during the Kaiser's campaigns in the Far East in around 1896, attempting to expand the German trade area. He had an Iron Cross (second class), a medal from the Japanese Red Cross (second class), and a life-saving award. (He had not, as is sometimes said, fought in the Franco-Prussian War, which took place in 1870–71, when he was three years old.)

To enter the police force it was essential to have served in the army, and to become an officer in the police you had to have served for at least five years – Otto's father, Erich, had also been in the police but, as he had served in the army for only two years, he had had to be content as a patrolman.

It was after the Franco-Prussian War ended that the German Empire came into being, and Berlin, formerly the capital of Prussia, became the capital of the new country of Germany. It was a good time and place to be a police officer, because the two sections of society most respected by good Germans were the military and the police.

Nineteenth-century Germans, and Prussians in particular, valued order, respectability and correct behaviour. They felt comfortable in having their lives controlled and regulated, and had an immense respect for uniforms. It was in the little town of Köpenick, a few miles to the east of Berlin, that in 1906 a fifty-year-old shoemaker and ex-jailbird named Wilhelm Voigt, by the simple expedient of wearing an imposing army uniform bought from a second-hand shop, managed to commandeer a small detachment of soldiers and with their help arrested the burgomaster in his own town hall and impounded the municipal funds. Unfortunately he was soon caught, but the whole world (except the German military) laughed their socks off, and Voigt, after a short jail sentence, successfully toured the music halls as 'the Captain of Köpenick'. In Prussia, as one German newspaper observed, 'they will all lie on their bellies before a uniform'.

The Felsing family, from which Josephine came, was in trade, although it was definitely high-class trade. They were clock and watchmakers, and had been clock-makers for generations, beginning by making cuckoo-clocks in Giessen, on the edge of the Black Forest, at least as far back as 1733. In those early days the family name was Völtzing, but when they moved to Berlin in 1820, the then head of the family, Johann Conrad, changed it to the more sophisticated 'Felsing', giving the business the title 'Conrad Felsing'. 'Conrad' was spelt in the French fashion, not, as in Germany, with a K, and there may have been French blood in the family. Succeeding eldest sons, who inherited the business, adopted the first name 'Conrad', no matter what their actual Christian names were.

Eventually the family owned a small chain of highly successful shops, selling not only clocks and watches but also such things as jewellery, decorated picture frames, music boxes and statuettes (including model soldiers of every German regiment). From 1877 their leading shop, which was on the prestigious Berlin avenue, the Unter den Linden, had warrants of royal appointment from the first Kaiser (Wilhelm I) and his wife, the Kaiserin.

The head of the firm at that time (Albert Karl Julius, known as 'Conrad') eventually married three times. His third marriage was to a girl called Elisabeth Helsing, who at seventeen was less than half his age. It produced two children, Josephine in 1876 and her brother, Willibald Arthur Conrad, in 1878. When their father died, in January 1901, Willibald inherited control of the business (he owned eighty per cent of it – his mother Elisabeth, Marlene's grandmother, owned the other twenty per cent). To those in the clock-making trade, he in turn became known as 'Conrad', although to the Dietrich family he was 'Uncle Willi'.

Josephine, a strong-minded woman, married Otto Dietrich in the face of a certain amount of family opposition. The Felsings were not entirely sure that he was good enough socially, in spite of the respectability of his calling.

His surname 'Dietrich', for a start, seemed somewhat common (in German it means 'picklock' or 'skeleton key'). But she was determined. This may not have been because she was head-over-heels in love. At twenty-two she was, by the standards of the time, getting on a bit. She was a little too strong-minded for the taste of many young men, and the spectre of impending spinsterhood may have been rising in her mind.

The social problems on Otto's side were similar. In the strait-laced social world he lived in, no cavalry officer was allowed to marry until his commanding officer had vetted the prospective bride, principally with respect to the size of her dowry – after all, the character and solvency of an officer's wife would reflect on the honour of the regiment. There is a possibility that it was the disapproval of Otto's Commanding Officer of him marrying into trade that led him to leave the cavalry and join the police.

Police Lieutenant Dietrich was stationed in Schöneberg, a suburb of Berlin some 2.5km (1½ miles) south of the centre. In 1898, when the Dietrichs married, it had only just been officially declared a suburb, and still very much had the feel of a separate town. It had a strong military presence because many of the Kaiser's troops were garrisoned there but, as it was surrounded by farmland, it also had something of a rural atmosphere, quite different from the exciting cosmopolitan life of Berlin itself. Here, in this quiet and conventional place, the Dietrichs began their married life, in the station house of Precinct No 4, in the Sedanstrasse.

Their first child, a daughter they named Ottilie Josephine Elisabeth, was born on 5 February 1900. In the family she was known as 'Liesel'. Their second, another daughter, was born on 27 December 1901. They named her Maria Magdalene but, while still a girl, she would elide the two names and begin calling herself 'Marlene'. In spite of the somewhat Catholic sound of her given names, her parents were in fact Lutherans, and it was in that faith that she would be raised.

As to the name 'Marlene', nobody seems to know exactly when she adopted it. She was certainly using it by 1918, when she was sixteen. And she certainly did not invent it herself. Hans Liep, a German soldier, wrote the poem 'Lili Marlene' in 1917 (it wasn't turned into a song until 1938), and explained later that he based it on the names of two girls he knew. So the name, while uncommon, was definitely around.

Otto, in spite of being a cavalry officer and later a police officer, seems to have been a rather quiet and unassertive man. His personality left little impression on his younger daughter, who claimed in later life to remember him only as a 'shadowy silhouette'. She had vague impressions of the smell of leather from his uniform, the shine of his boots, the sound of him slapping his riding crop against the plum-coloured leg of his britches – but that was about all.

Certainly he was not very successful in the police. In a departmental examination at around the time she was born he was graded only *recht gut*, or 'quite good', and within a couple of years, in a similar exam, he had slipped to *ausreichend* ('adequate'). This was the third and lowest grade, and he came bottom in a list of twelve.

Possibly this poor performance was reflected in his pay, because the Dietrich family moved to different houses four times before Marlene was six. Possibly, too, it was partly caused by unhappiness in his marriage, because by that time he was living apart from Josephine and their two daughters, at a different address and with a different phone number. And within a year (by which time Josephine and her daughters had moved yet again), he was dead – Josephine was listed in the Berlin phone book as 'widow'. What he died of is not known – some accounts say it was influenza, most that he died from falling off a horse. There is also a strong possibility it was syphilis.

What is known is that the strong personality in Marlene's childhood was Josephine. She was an intelligent, active, well-read woman, with a taste for the German Romantics, and a great passion in her life was music. She was an accomplished classical pianist, and had a good voice – the songs she most liked to sing were madrigals and traditional German airs.

From early in their lives, before they were old enough to go to school, both daughters had a succession of governesses, although Marlene later liked to present these as rather grander than they were – in fact, they tended to be simple country girls, sent by their parents to get jobs in the big city so as to learn something of the ways of the world.

Above all, Josephine believed that the most important things in life were 'character' and 'good breeding' (terms she regarded as almost synonymous), and her children were raised to lives of discipline and duty. Duty she defined as fulfilling the day's demands. In Marlene's words: 'My mother was not kind, not compassionate, [but] unforgiving and inexorable... The rules were...ironclad, immovable, unalterable.' Obedience was drilled into her daughters, and praise for good behaviour or achievement was non-existent – they were simply what was expected. So stern was Josephine in her attitudes that within the Felsing family she was known as 'the Dragon' (although not to her face). Of her two daughters, Elisabeth tended to take after her, becoming a dutiful, obedient, earnest girl. Marlene was different. Although she absorbed (and would retain all her life) the lessons of hard work and discipline, and although in early childhood was quiet and obedient (even shy), there was within her a core of rebellion.

In spite of rebelling against the strictness of her upbringing, however, the young Marlene found it reassuring. The firm reliability of the rules made life predictable and safe. So, although there was little warmth in her relationship with her mother, Marlene would respect her all her life, praising her as 'a good General'.

On fine afternoons her mother would sometimes take her on social calls. The child was never told who they were to visit, and knew it was none of her business to ask. She was taught to accept kisses of greeting from half-known grown-up ladies, extending a formal hand and ritually reciting, 'Good day, Madame. I hope you are well.'

On one occasion, presented with a doll by one of her mother's friends, she was told to thank the woman with a kiss. Disliking the woman and finding her unattractive, Marlene refused. Her mother repeated the command, but Marlene still refused. At once her mother walked her home, rebuked her at some length and punished her. The child never again refused to give a polite kiss.

Josephine firmly believed that one sign of good breeding was never to display emotion, and Marlene learned never to complain of the cold, or of being thirsty. Later she recalled, 'My mother made acting difficult for me. My whole upbringing was to mask my feelings – the last slap I had from my mother was because of that. I was having dancing lessons, and had to dance with everybody in the room, including a young man I did not like. I made a long face. Mother saw it and slapped me as soon as we were alone. "You must not show your feelings, it is bad manners," she said.'

Before she went to school (at the age of six), her mother had already taught her to read and write German, as well as teaching her some French (regarded as the language of culture and sophistication), and a little English. Josephine was less fluent in this, but it was, after all, the native language of the Kaiser's mother (Queen Victoria's eldest child, Vicky).

She started school in the spring of 1907, at the beginning of the German school year, and was sent to the Auguste-Viktoria Schule (named for the

Kaiserin). It was a converted villa in Charlottenburg (a western suburb of Berlin), and a portrait of the Kaiserin hung in her classroom.

At school she was at first shy and retiring (one of her schoolmates remembered her as shrinking into the back row of the class 'like a little grey mouse'). She disliked losing her freedom and felt afraid of the teachers and their punishments. Her loneliness was increased by the fact that, although the youngest in the school, she was already able to read, write and count, and so was not put in the bottom class but in the one above, among girls who were a year or two older than she was. Holidays were more fun. She liked tomboyish games like marbles and roller-skating, and in her summer holidays enjoyed going to stay at her Uncle Willi's house in the country. Uncle Willi, head of the firm of Conrad Felsing, and then still a bachelor, lived in a grand apartment on the Leichtensteiner Allee in Berlin, but had a summer home at Wandlitz, some 25km (15½ miles) north of Berlin. It stood on the edge of a lake, where she enjoyed bathing.

As soon as she was old enough she had music lessons at school, first on the piano and then also on the violin. Music was one of the joys of her childhood, and soon she was also playing the lute (which she decorated romantically with bright ribbons) and singing – mostly sentimental German folk-songs. She was also given riding lessons. Through her father, her mother still had army connections, and she would ride through the Tiergarten in central Berlin, her horse guided on a leading-rein by an army private on another horse beside her. All these lessons – the French and English, the music, the riding, the dancing – were intended to give her useful social accomplishments that would in time enable her to meet an eligible young man and become his cultured wife.

She began to enjoy going to the theatre, and to the amazing new entertainment called the cinema. She had a family connection with this through her Uncle Willi. He had rented out space on the upper floors of the firm's figurehead store on the Unter den Linden to an optical instrument maker called Oskar Messter, who has a strong claim to be regarded as the founder of the German film industry.

In 1896, at a time when film would still remain for some years a sideshow novelty, he had opened Berlin's first permanent cinema (Messter's Biophon) next door to Uncle Willi's store, and from 1903 he began making his own films, using the store's flat roof. This was, in effect, Berlin's first working film studio, and Messter was even ambitious enough to attempt making short sound films – basically songs performed on film. (Josephine, as Willi's elder sister, rather disapproved of these goings-on as frivolous, especially as Willi was charging only a modest rent for the use of his roof and upper floor.)

Often when Marlene visited Uncle Willi at his Berlin apartment she would meet people from the world of the theatre. Her mother naturally disapproved of theatrical people in general, but as Marlene grew older she was beginning to develop an independent attitude towards her mother. While still looking up to her as stern and reliable, she began to feel that she herself more resembled her dimly remembered (and thus romantic) father. She certainly had his broad forehead and deep-set eyes.

Remembering herself when young, she once described herself as 'thin and pale as a child, with reddish-blonde hair and the translucent pallor that goes with ginger colouring, giving me a sickly look.' It distressed her to feel that the women of the Felsing family, including her mother, were all more beautiful than she was.

Her maternal grandmother, Elisabeth, she later recalled as 'not only the most beautiful of women, [but] also the most elegant, the most charming, the most perfectly complete lady anyone knew.' Her clothes were expensive – tasteful without concern for fashion – and even her gloves were made to measure. She wore pearl necklaces and ruby rings. Her shoes were French-made, and she would let the young Marlene balance them on her little finger to impress on her how light shoes must be. She would show her round the family shop on the Unter den Linden, explaining how important it was for a well-dressed woman to choose the correct jewellery and accessories. It was from her grandmother as much as anyone that Marlene began to acquire and educate a taste for elegance.

She felt that she herself was a Dietrich, inheriting her looks from her father, and not long after his death she adopted the odd habit, when alone with her mother, of calling herself 'Paul' (which she pronounced in the French fashion), and, in a half-comprehended way, she tried to replace him in her mother's life. In her own words, she wanted to take 'my father's place – against my mother's will.' Against her will or not, her mother indulged her in this role-playing, and it marked the beginning of a lifelong enjoyment of adopting male roles.

At school, she continued to feel isolated among her fellow-pupils. As she wrote years later: 'I remained lonely and was still excluded from their whispered secrets, their intimacies, and their fits of laughter. Yet I had no desire to know what they were keeping secret from me.' It may have been from these school years that she acquired her own lifelong habit of secretiveness – a secretiveness that went some way beyond a natural wish for privacy or a desire to present a calculated romantic image.

School life took a turn for the better when, at the age of ten or so, she was befriended by a teacher, Marguerite Breguand. Mlle Breguand taught French, and was French – the only non-German member of staff. As Marlene later described her, in almost obsessive detail, 'She had dark brown eyes, tied her black hair together in a loose knot, and always wore a white blouse, a black skirt, and a narrow soft leather belt around her waist.'

She took to conversing with Marlene every day during the lunch break, happy to talk to someone who by now spoke fluent French, and Marlene developed an intense schoolgirl crush on her. 'She banished my loneliness, my childish worries, my sadness. She embodied both my wishes and my fulfilment. I spent all my free time thinking up gifts for her: blue-red-and-white ribbons that my mother had once worn at a French ball; French landscapes I had cut out of magazines, a bouquet of lilies of the valley on the First of May, a cornflower, a daisy and a poppy on the Fourteenth of July. I bought Christmas and New Year cards made in France and even thought of giving her a French perfume, but my mother suggested that so expensive a gift might embarrass Mlle Breguand and that I should wait patiently till I got a little older... On the last day of school, before the holidays, she would never fail to give me her address, which she wrote down on a page torn from her notebook.'

This friendship helped Marlene's growing confidence, as did her growing musical ability. It became obvious to her mother that she had outstanding musical talent, and she bought her her own violin, spending the considerable sum of 2,500 marks for it. She began giving her daughter lessons herself, accompanying her at the piano, taking her through endless exercises, from beginners' pieces like Torelli's 'Serenade' and on to the more exacting Handel and Bach. 'Bach, Bach, Bach, always Bach!' Marlene complained, although from time to time she was rewarded by being allowed to play some Haydn or Chopin.

She adored playing the violin, and her now-ingrained habit of discipline and hard work meant that her playing progressed rapidly, developing good rhythm and an expressive tone. It was playing her violin in school concerts, she later claimed, that first awakened her desire to become a performer.

Her mother's lavishness in the matter of the violin indicates that her tastes in life tended to be expensive ones – tastes to which a police widow's pension did not really reach. This was possibly the reason why, when Marlene was nine or ten, Josephine took a job as a sort of 'glorified housekeeper' (as one of Marlene's classmates called her) to a First Lieutenant in the Grenadiers called Eduard von Losch. He came from a well-to-do family and, as a serving officer, was often away from Berlin on manoeuvres. When he was not, Josephine ran his household for him.

At school, Marlene was by now actually being taught by her Mlle Breguand, which she felt was bliss, and soon she also developed another crush on a somewhat more distant figure – the film actress Henny Porten.

Henny Porten was one of Germany's very first film stars, known popularly as 'the Mary Pickford of Germany', not for any facial resemblance to Pickford, but because she too had begun as a child star. Some of her early films had in fact been shot at the Messter studio on Uncle Willi's roof.

Growing into a handsome young woman, during the teens of the twentieth century she was turning out around a dozen short films a year, mostly of a rather sentimental nature, in which the innocence and purity of a young girl triumphs over adversity and brings her love. For Germans, a rather sentimental race, she had become a much-admired popular idol. Young women collected postcards of her and did their best to copy the way she dressed or did her hair.

Marlene was among her fans, but impulsively went further than most. In those early days of cinema, stars were still listed in the phone book, so she had no difficulty in finding Henny's address. Marlene started hand-colouring some of her postcards and sending them to Henny to wish her well for birthdays or film premières. She also took to shadowing Henny round the streets whenever she got the chance, lurking surreptitiously near Henny's front door on the offchance she would come out and, if she did, she would follow her through the streets, dodging behind kiosks and lamp posts – her shadowing was unsuccessful, however, as she did not go unnoticed by Henny.

Eventually she had another idea and, armed with her violin, turned up one day to stand in the foyer of Henny's front door and serenade her with a sentimental song – it was called 'Engelslied' ('Angels' Song'). Henny, peering out to see who was playing, was not too surprised to see it was 'the same sweet little girl with the blonde curls' who had been shadowing her.

Not long afterwards, however, Marlene did surprise her. Her school was taken on an excursion to Mittenwald, a German town on the border with the Austrian Alps. Like a true fan, Marlene was aware that Henny was on holiday with her husband in the larger town of Garmisch-Partenkirchen, some 15km (9 miles) away. So one evening she leant a ladder against the wall outside her bedroom window, and early next morning clambered down it, carrying her violin in its case. She took the first train to Garmisch, went to the hotel where Henny was staying, and began serenading outside her window.

Henny woke and heard the sound. She went to the window, opened the shutters and saw the same blonde girl again. Although admittedly flattered, she found this unnerving. Lost for words, she slammed the shutters closed again. Marlene was more delighted than disappointed – she had seen Henny, and Henny had seen and heard her, and that was something special.

And there was still Mlle Breguand in her life, a model to her of culture and gentleness who had given her what would be a lifelong love of France. Unfortunately things would soon change, and not only for the young Marlene. At the beginning of August 1914 the Great War began.

Later that month, when Marlene returned to school after the summer holidays, all the staff and pupils were assembled in the school auditorium. As the pupils were harangued by patriotic speeches relating to warfare, she was stunned and distressed not to find Mlle Breguand's face among the teachers assembled on the platform. The shock of suddenly realizing that she was not there, and would not be there, coupled with the realization that her own homeland, Germany, was now at war with her beloved France, actually caused her to faint (she related in her memoirs).

School again became like a prison to her, but (as she does not say in her memoirs) very soon she was to change schools. Eduard von Losch, her mother's employer, promoted on the outbreak of war from Lieutenant to Captain, felt it would be a good idea to move from Berlin and take a house in the city of Dessau, 100km (60 miles) or so to the southwest. Dessau was where the von Losch family came from, and his widowed mother still lived there.

He asked Josephine to come to Dessau as well, with her two daughters, to continue running his household for him. Josephine agreed, and by now it was becoming clear that there was (and maybe always had been) something more to their relationship than employer/housekeeper. Although there was never the slightest hint of any impropriety, he was after all a handsome, dashing officer, taller than Lieutenant Dietrich had been and of very good family, and Josephine was a good-looking and cultured widow, still only in her thirties.

She and her daughters moved to Dessau, and Marlene found herself at a new school there, the Antonetten Lyzeum. To her it felt just as much of a prison as the one she had left, bounded by rules and restrictions, and now, in addition, consecrated to the war.

The mood of the country was at first of jubilant patriotism (as it was in Britain and France). There was no idea of the prolonged horror to come. The war would be over, the Kaiser promised, 'before the leaves turn' (the British, a little less optimistic, had the phrase 'over by Christmas'). But Marlene, losing her friend and teacher, felt as if she was the first (of many future millions) to be bereaved.

School prayers were offered daily for the destruction of the enemies of the Fatherland (including Marlene's beloved France). Pupils were allowed a holiday if there was a death in the family, and if there was a German victory there was a day's holiday for the whole school. Lessons were often cancelled so that pupils could assemble in the school gymnasium and knit comforts for the troops – mostly gloves and socks. As food became scarcer, cookery classes became devoted to endless variations on ways of cooking potatoes and, when potatoes became scarce in their turn, of cooking turnips. A small personal trial for Marlene became the scarcity of sugar, because she had a sweet tooth and missed such treats as cream cakes.

Her life, in spite of the pervading presence of the war, remained in many ways normal. School still had its unvarying routine, so much so that she remembered in later years that, 'The fact that our education proceeded as in peacetime made us doubt the sanity of our elders.'

That wasn't the only doubt fostered in her by the war. At fifteen she was confirmed into the Lutheran faith, although even at that age she was beginning to feel unsure about the existence of a personal god. Surely a real loving God the Father (such as she had been brought up to believe in) would not permit such carnage and sorrow as the Great War had brought. And here again was a sign that grown-ups could be mad or mistaken. She was growing in independence.

By now she was also becoming an attractive teenager, and one day, again when she was about fifteen, a young soldier on leave, a guest in the von

Losch house in Dessau, kissed her. It wasn't just the delicious and awakening experience of being kissed by a man that affected her – she who at home and at school had had almost no contact with anything but women – but a feeling of the frailness of human life and the idiotic tragedy of war. As she recalled: 'This war, the one that I was living, had not made it quite clear to me until [then]. The soldier [visiting] in our house, the air he brought with him and then left with us, his steps echoing slowly through the hallways, the bigness of him, the danger he had left behind and the danger he went towards on leaving us, the kiss I had felt, his field grey shirts, the knowledge that he would never come back...made me see this war clearly for the first time.'

At around this time the war was brought home to her in another way. Late in 1916 Captain von Losch, fighting on the eastern front (possibly against Romania), was badly wounded, and Josephine was sent for to be by his bedside. She made the long wartime rail journey, and there, while he lay in his bed in a field hospital, she married him (this was unlikely to have been an impulsive decision on her part – there was little in Josephine that was impulsive). The Captain asked her to keep an eye on his mother in Dessau until he got home from the war, and she dutifully journeyed back to do so.

Marlene was disconcerted by this turn of events. Captain von Losch was another remote figure, as her father had been – one she barely knew because he had been so often away on manoeuvres. This turn of events would mean a new head of the family – a new senior officer to get used to.

As it turned out, she never had to. Within a week or so Captain von Losch died of his wounds, and Josephine took the train back to the front to reclaim his body and bring it home. His mother arranged for him to be buried in the family plot, and a few months after the funeral Josephine and her daughters moved back to Berlin, this time taking an apartment on the Kaiserallee.

Josephine got little out of her brief second marriage – an officer's widow's pension (which was at least a little more than a police widow's pension had been) and a new surname. The disappointment of her new loss made her even more emotionally constrained than she had been before. She became even more sharp-tongued and critical. The Felsings, while sympathetic to her misfortune, felt that her new name, with its aristocratic 'von', was a definite improvement on 'Dietrich'.

Liesel and Marlene were sent to a school near their home – the Viktoria-Luisen-Schule – enrolling there in April 1917. There Marlene would study

German, French, English, history, geology, religion, mathematics, physics, chemistry, music, gymnastics and homecraft (fortunately she liked, and would always like, cooking and sewing).

A couple of months later she gave what was in effect her first public performance, playing her violin in a pageant in aid of the Red Cross. The date was 19 June 1917, which happened to be the fiftieth anniversary of the day Emperor Maximilian of Mexico was shot by republican rebels. The pageant was given a Mexican theme, and Marlene played 'La Paloma', accompanied by girls dancing in Mexican skirts and rattling tambourines. She herself was dressed as a boy, wearing an embroidered jacket, knee-britches, and a sombrero. Whether or not this was her own idea is not recorded, but certainly as early as sixteen she was happy to perform in male costume.

She was also beginning to be interested in the idea of some day appearing in films, and had taken to pestering Uncle Willi to introduce her to his film friends. He asked her if he could bring some along to see her Mexican performance. He didn't in the end, but attended himself and, watching her, was amused.

The Marlene who had returned to Berlin was outwardly a considerably different character from the girl who had left for Dessau two years before. She had grown in confidence and was growingly aware that men found her attractive. Far from hiding away at the rear of the class, she now made sure to sit at the front. In spite of the war there were still a few male teachers, either too infirm, too old or too young to be called up, and she amused herself (and her classmates) by making eyes at them. She was beginning to enjoy having an effect on other people. One young teacher was so obviously intrigued by her that his interest in her was noticed, and he was dismissed. This her classmates found both shocking and exciting.

She now found it easy to make friends, and had one special friend, Hilde Sperling, who hero-worshipped her, imitating as far as she could her clothes and hairstyle, her gestures and mannerisms.

But in spite of finding school less forbidding than in childhood, to Marlene it was still a prison. Unlike her sister Liesel, two years older and boringly obedient, she wanted out, and the best way out seemed to be music. Liesel would dutifully remain at school till she graduated, and go on to become an earnest hard-working schoolteacher. Marlene, aged sixteen, would leave in the spring of 1918, at the end of the school year, and study to become a professional violinist.

Signing a friend's 'memory book', as was the custom, she wrote beside her signature, 'In the long run, happiness comes to the diligent.' Inside the flirtatious, restless and increasingly ambitious teenager there was still a solid Prussian upbringing.

2 Hello To Berlin

As the Great War ground to its end, life in Berlin (and in the whole of Germany) became harder and harder. Food and clothing became even more scarce, and the scarcities provoked strikes. The population was becoming bitterly distrustful of everything official – of military and government spokesmen, of newspapers, of the reason for being at war at all, and of money itself, which was steadily losing its value.

On 9 November 1918, two days before the Armistice, there was a general strike in support of a left-wing move to depose the Kaiser and abolish the Empire. In Berlin, hundreds of thousands of workers and servicemen rallied at the Reich Chancellery, and later that day the Kaiser, advised by his own generals to abdicate, abdicated, and went off into exile in Holland.

Almost at once Karl Liebknecht, a Social Democrat and anti-imperialist, and one of the few socialists who had opposed the war from the beginning, proclaimed from the balcony of the Imperial Palace that Germany was now a Socialist Republic. He was not officially in power – nobody was. Left-wing extremists occupied newspaper offices, government buildings, railway stations and the police headquarters. In response, private armies loyal to the old order took to the streets to oppose them, and bloody riots ensued.

Once the war ended, conditions in Berlin got even worse. Soon it would have a quarter of a million unemployed, and the victorious Allied powers, determined to punish Germany, imposed savage demands for financial reparation, plus a blockade around the country that made shortages worse than ever. Within six months, 700,000 Germans died from starvation and influenza, mostly children and the elderly.

Among those old people was Marlene's grandmother, Elisabeth, who died on 29 January 1919. The twenty per cent share she held in the firm of Conrad Felsing passed to her daughter, Josephine, who, with that and her military widow's pension, felt she at least now had some financial security.

Against this background of hardship and family tragedy, the seventeen-year-old Marlene, who by this time had left school, continued practising her violin. She loved music and loved performing, and this was to be her own passport to independence and security. As well as practising, she of course had lessons. Later in life she claimed she had even studied briefly at the Berlin *Hochschule für Musik*, although her time there must have been very brief, as there is no record of her name in its register.

Life in Berlin continued to deteriorate. There was increased rioting as politicians of all persuasions continued to struggle for power – republicans, socialists, communists, even anarchists. Early in 1919 Liebknecht (with Rosa Luxembourg among his colleagues) helped found the German Communist party and led them in a revolt. Both he and Rosa were killed. Speculators and black-marketeers began to flood into the city from all over Europe. They prospered, but most people starved.

Order began to emerge a little when, in February 1919, a conference in the city of Weimar drew up a new constitution. The new system of government became known as the Weimar Republic, but even this did not bring real stability – there was an uprising against the new government later the same year, and there would be another in 1920, which were both savagely put down by gunfire.

All in all, the city was becoming far too unstable for Josephine's peace of mind. She felt that her daughters would be safer elsewhere, and decided they should transfer their studies to respectable Weimar, some 200km (125 miles) to the southwest. Elisabeth, who had by this time left school and entered teacher training, begged to stay, so in the event it was Marlene only who went, in October 1919.

Weimar was the greatest centre of classic German culture, the city of Schiller and Liszt and, above all, Goethe, the greatest figure in the pantheon – poet, painter, playwright, novelist, theatre manager, politician, scientist and thinker.

Marlene was to lodge in a large boarding-house that in fact had a connection with Goethe. In the late eighteenth century it had been the home of Charlotte von Stein, a married woman whom he had met on coming to Weimar in 1775. She was then thirty-seven and he was twenty-six, and for the next eleven years they carried on an enthusiastic platonic relationship, mostly by correspondence. He called her his 'soul-friend' and modelled several of his heroines on her.

To Marlene, who worshipped Goethe's poetry, this was a very romantic idea. By this time, indeed, she was becoming considerably well-read. As well as Goethe, she liked (among others) the writings of Schiller, Heine and, rather surprisingly, Kant. She would quote passages of them from memory all her life.

At the boarding-house she shared a simply furnished room with five other girls and, like them, became a student at the *Musikhochschule*. It was run by a house-mother, Frau Arnoldi, and although it had many rules, it was far less of a prison than school had been. The disciplined Marlene practised her violin at least five hours a day, but she was pleased that, apart from attending her various lessons and being in her room every night at the appointed hour, her time was her own to schedule as she pleased. And every three weeks or so her mother came by train from Berlin, bringing hard-to-come-by supplies of soap and tinned food, to see that her daughter was looking after her health and behaving herself, to get a report on her progress and to give her hair a good shampoo.

At the end of each visit there was always an emotional farewell, with tears on both sides. In spite of Josephine's lectures about repressing feelings, lectures that had deeply influenced the young Marlene, both mother and daughter were at heart sentimental.

Marlene was also by now quite a lot of other things. From the moment she entered the boarding-house it was obvious to the other girls that there was something about this new arrival that set her apart. It wasn't only that she alone among them took private violin lessons in addition to her course work at the *Musikhochschule* – there was by now something in her manner that compelled attention. As one of them, Gerde Noack, recalled years later: 'As "the new girl"…stood there in the doorway in a pose that remains unforgettable to me, she fascinated us immediately as something special. It wasn't something made up, nothing "put on" – it was *in* her.'

She had become a lively and witty young woman, and a ringleader. She would lead her room-mates on expeditions from the boarding-house to buy sweets and cream-cakes (which were now available again, although very much in short supply). These expeditions were strictly against the rules, and back in their room the girls would shove a heavy armoire against the door (in case Frau Arnoldi made a round of inspection) before feasting on their illicit goodies. Marlene was not tall – she had by this time attained her adult height of 1.65m (5ft 5in) – and her sweet tooth caused her to become somewhat plump, which at that time in Germany, as in Edwardian England, was regarded as attractive.

As well as having an addiction to sweet things, she had now also become a smoker (her Uncle Willi, who liked Russian cigarettes, was a hundred-a-day man). At Weimar she was known among her friends for generously sharing her cigarettes.

More and more she was enjoying being the centre of attention. A regular performance she gave to amuse her room-mates was an impression of a Chinese pagoda, wearing only a bedsheet. This never failed to produce hysterical laughter, and it was obvious that she was developing a gift for subversive comedy as well.

At around the same time as she arrived in Weimar, so did another subversive phenomenon – the Bauhaus. This was an avant-garde teaching movement with new and disturbingly non-classical ideas, whose aim was to unify art, architecture, craft and design into an interrelated whole. Its leader was Walter Gropius, and it attracted young and vital members of the arts and crafts, many of a decidedly bohemian tendency. This tended to scandalise respectable Weimar, and the Bauhaus group became a fertile breeding-ground for scandal. It was rumoured, for instance, that its school used naked life-models (it didn't) and that they could be seen from outside through the windows.

The group came to contain such famous names as Wassily Kandinsky, Paul Klee, László Moholy-Nagy and Mies van der Rohe, and many members of it lodged or had studio space in Marlene's boarding-house, so she got to know some of them. One was the group's graphic and stage designer, Lothar Schreyer. She became friendly with both Schreyer and his wife and, with the instinct for celebrity that would become such a salient feature of her later life, used this friendship to contrive a meeting with the person who was perhaps the most striking personality associated with Bauhaus – Walter Gropius' wife, Alma Mahler-Gropius.

This formidable woman was the widow of Gustav Mahler and the former mistress of both Gustav Klimt and Oskar Kokoshka, and when Marlene learned that Alma was due to come from Vienna on a visit, and would be at the Schreyers' one evening, she asked Lothar if she could be present and be introduced. Lothar, seeing her as 'a kindly, quiet young girl', agreed she could be present, but advised her that her best course if she wanted to meet Alma would be to make herself quietly and discreetly visible.

Marlene placed herself, violin in hand, on the staircase leading into the Schreyers' apartment from their front door. As Lothar later recalled: 'The stairway was well-lit. Marlene Dietrich leaned there on the white-painted landing, violin in hand, gazing up with wide eyes. My wife introduced her. I should have done it, but I was too taken by the scene that now began.

'Marlene kept her violin in her left hand and sank almost to her knees. It seemed like the kind of court curtsy cultivated long ago in Vienna when there was still an Emperor Franz Josef. It was flawlessly executed, enhanced by the quite simple, *calculatedly* simple dress she wore.

'Frau Gropius performed wonderfully in turn: there stood a duchess in the Viennese Palace receiving a young lady-in-waiting... Radiantly restrained, she raised her hand with measured but imperious graciousness, and accepted the maiden's kiss.'

As Alma turned away, she whispered to Lothar, 'What eyes this one has! *What eyes!*' But Marlene did not learn this until years later when, world-famous and running into Lothar in Berlin she asked earnestly, 'What did she say about me?'

Undoubtedly, at the age of eighteen, she was searching avidly for some sort of role model. Not a respectable conventional woman like her mother, admirable though she might be, but a woman prepared (or driven) to seek a life richer and more rewarding than convention offered. And Alma was certainly unconventional – while not a creative artist herself, she was a powerful (even tyrannical) personality, and the sexual inspiration to a succession of male artists. Clearly to a girl of sufficient drive and ability, this was a viable way of life.

Even though Marlene still thought of herself as no great beauty, the shy mouse of early schooldays was now revelling in her ability to arouse admiration from both men and women. A piano student at the *Musikhochschule*, Wolfgang Rosé (who happened to be a nephew of Gustav Mahler) once commented that her beauty 'astonished us all. Young men were lining up to take her out.' This must have done a lot to help her already considerable confidence.

Marlene set out to try her seductive abilities on her private violin tutor, Professor Reitz, and would waft off to her lessons with him wearing chiffon so sheer it was almost transparent – 'sheerly obscene' *('geradezu obszön')* was Gerde Noack's comment. It became obvious to her fellow-students that she was now, as one might say, 'available', and quickly they came up with a pun on her tutor's name – '*Marlene reizt Reitz*', which roughly translates as 'Marlene makes Reitz rise'.

She certainly did. Professor Reitz, although married with children, was no model of marital fidelity (it wouldn't be long before he would leave his wife for another woman), and he undoubtedly became Marlene's lover. A curious aspect of her character all her life was an ability to become involved with lovers who would in some way also advance her career, and as a well-known and successful musician there was always the chance that Professor Reitz might be useful as well as exciting.

Her reputation in Weimar began to become scandalous. Tongues began to wag, not so much because of her relationship with Professor Reitz or because of her increasingly provocative behaviour, but for a reason more easily understood by the conventional. The gossip was that she was trying to marry for money. These rumours both unsettled her and made her angry. During the summer of 1921, on a four-week holiday back in Berlin, she had taken her violin for an overhaul to a violin-making friend of Professor Reitz, Dr Julius Levin. He and she got on well, and began a correspondence that would continue for years. In a letter to him she complained about the wagging tongues, protesting, 'It would be *unbearable* to me to have luxury in a marriage with a man I didn't love, that I can tell you!'

The rumours were possibly responsible for her life at this time taking a sudden turn. In October 1921, after she had been at Weimar for just over two years, her mother suddenly insisted she return at once to Berlin and continue her studies there.

This 'disaster', as Marlene later called it, seemed to her inexplicable, but it seems possible that Josephine, on one of her visits, had heard of the rumours surrounding her daughter from house-mother Frau Arnoldi. Also, what with the Bauhaus and all, Weimar seemed no longer the respectable cultural haven it had once been. At least in Berlin her unconventional daughter would be more under her eye.

There was also the matter of money. With inflation still rising, Josephine's income from her widow's pension and her share of Conrad Felsing was beginning to prove pitifully small, and perhaps she was finding Marlene's fees at Weimar beyond her means. If the problem was money, Marlene's claiming in later life that her removal from Weimar was inexplicable is perfectly explicable. She was not going to harm the image of her privileged upbringing by admitting her family was ever hard up.

Whatever the cause, back she came to Berlin, but she did not move back to live with her mother and sister. After the freedom of her Weimar life she wanted independence, and moved into the first of a succession of cheap lodgings. She continued her violin lessons, now with the renowned Hungarian, Professor Carl Flesch, who taught at the Berlin *Konservatorium* and had written an influential book on violin technique.

To support herself she took a succession of odd jobs – sometimes playing her violin in the bands of ratty night-clubs, sometimes working in even less glamorous places, such as a hat shop and a newspaper kiosk.

She also found she had another role model. While she had been in Weimar, her Uncle Willi had at last married. His wife was an elegant young Polish woman whose official forenames were Martha Hélène, but who was known to everyone as Jolly (meaning *jolie*, as in French). He had met her at a reception given for the ex-Kaiser's son, the former Crown Prince Wilhelm, who in spite of the fact that Germany had become a republic was still regarded as a social eminence.

Also invited had been a Hollywood businessman, a Mr McConnell, whose job was selling rides to amusement parks. In particular he was promoting something called 'the Devil's Wheel'. With him at the reception was Jolly, who was then his wife but who, within an amazingly short time, would be Willi's. From her marriage to Mr McConnell she had an infant son, named Rudolf, and now she was expecting another child by Willi – a son who would be born in 1922 and named Hasso Conrad.

Jolly was only a year older than Marlene, with the result that she became more of a friend to her than an aunt. In addition to her native Polish she spoke excellent German and a brand of Hollywood English that Berliners found amusing. And she was amusing herself, with a nonchalant cool that seemed to have been born with the Twenties. Much of her personality would bring out similar sides of Marlene's own.

Marlene once called her 'the most beautiful woman I've ever seen in my life' and she was the essence of international chic, wearing sables and foxes and jewelled turbans (the turban was very much the thing in the early Twenties). Generous by nature, she would happily lend turbans (and furs) to Marlene when she needed to make an impression at an audition or a night on the town.

Jolly herself was well aware of how to make an impression. Often she got Uncle Willi's firm to make up jewellery for her, such as necklaces or bracelets, and a trick she had was to ask them to mount gems of paste in among the real diamonds, thus achieving additional glitter at lower cost. This was a trick that Marlene would remember.

Jolly also grew her fingernails long, for elegance, and Marlene copied her, lengthening hands she felt were too short. (In America, in the early Thirties, her film appearances would spark a fashion for long fingernails – a fashion that has never entirely disappeared.)

With Willi's mother dead, Jolly became, in effect, the senior woman in the Felsing family. This was rather hard on Marlene's mother, Josephine, who disapproved of her. She also disapproved of Willi, whose enjoyment of the performing arts was, if anything, increasing. He continued to socialise with film and theatre folk, and in fact had let part of his vast villa on the Leichtensteiner Allee to the actor Conrad Veidt, who had recently become world famous as the star of the film *The Cabinet Of Dr Caligari*.

Marlene too was finding much in Berlin to enjoy. Now an increasingly confident twenty-year-old, she managed on her restricted budget to dress simply but fashionably (one account describes her as wearing cloche hats at around this time – a time when the cloche was very much the latest thing).

She became for a while the mistress of a wealthy businessman, accepting meals and trinkets from him (which helped her budget) until she found out that he had other mistresses besides her (and a wife and children), whereupon she dropped him instantly.

There was briefly said to be another man as well – a frail young man who before long was to die of dysentery – and this relationship was typical of many that Marlene would have throughout her life. She would always be attracted by men who were in some way ill or frail or displaced. Their weakness would bring out in her an irresistible urge to mother them – to express pity and tenderness.

Then there was Gerda Huber. Gerda was a would-be writer of about her own age – dark-haired, confident, earnest and intelligent. One day late in 1921 she was having lunch in a small, cheap, crowded restaurant when she was asked, 'May I sit here with you?' It was Marlene. She was, as Gerda recalled, somewhat plump, and had dark gold hair screwed up into a bun at the nape of her neck.

They got into conversation and, by the end of their meal, each was feeling she'd met a kindred spirit. Marlene was having trouble making ends meet, and that same day (at Gerda's insistence) she moved in with Gerda at her *pension.* For several months they remained inseparable, and Gerda became Marlene's first serious female lover.

Marlene also endeared herself to Gerda's amiable landlady, Trude, and to Trude's fat, striped cat, Puck. She liked cats, believing they brought luck, and Puck would sit happily by her in the *pension* while she read or mended Gerda's stockings in a housewifely manner. She also used her skill at needlework while at the *pension* to make a little money sewing gloves together for an outside contractor, working on a piece-work basis. And she took to helping Trude prepare meals for the other tenants. In return Trude gave her a helpful reduction in rent.

Marlene was attracted by Gerda's education and eloquence – her conversation was peppered with quotations from Marx and Goethe – and Gerda, herself somewhat quiet and bookish, admired Marlene's carefree attitude to life. She noted that Marlene's attitude to her music career was by now somewhat offhand, and she was amused by the mock-serious intensity about it that Marlene affected when visited by her mother. Marlene, she felt, was more interested in enjoying life than in spending hours practising.

Gradually a new Berlin was emerging. In 1920 an ordinance had absorbed a number of surrounding towns and districts (including Schöneberg), making them suburbs and creating 'Greater Berlin'. This, with a population of almost four million, was now the third largest city in the world (after London and New York). It was also becoming regarded as the most exciting city in Europe, its population swollen by immigrants from all over the world looking for stimulation and opportunity (and attracted too by its immensely favourable exchange rate as the mark continued to devalue).

In 1918 one dollar had been equivalent to eight marks. By 1922 it was equivalent to fifty marks, and it would get much worse. Saving was becoming pointless. Those who had money elected to spend it instead, and a frantic disillusioned night-life came into being. Clubs and cabarets opened by the hundred, offering a brightly lit world of sensation and cynicism. Life was pointless. The old pre-war certainties of an ordered society with a God-ordained right and wrong had led to destruction, slaughter and defeat, so now nothing seemed certain, or even worthwhile.

In the absence of any meaning in life, surface show became everything. For women in particular, the essential thing came to be to present a chic image to the world, hiding nothing because there was nothing inside to hide. The importance of presenting a good public image was not lost on the young Marlene, although she was too young and resilient to be as disillusioned as those older than her.

In spite of all the poverty, violence and disillusion, the arts flourished (which, as Harry Lime pointed out, they tend to do in such times). Painting, music, film and theatre all entered a period of energetic change and creation.

The night-life of 1921 was beginning to be fuelled by the new music, jazz, that was developing in America. Americanism was fast becoming the fashion of the day all over Europe. In Berlin, among artists and intellectuals especially, America was becoming seen as the promised land. People read American writers – Edgar Allan Poe, Mark Twain, Walt Whitman, Herman Melville – and shows based themselves on American models, with lavish spectacles and showgirl revues.

One American export that was slow to arrive in Germany was cinema. Film as a serious medium had still been in its infancy when the war broke out. Although America had remained neutral until 1917, Germany saw few of its films during the war, during those boom years when men such as D W Griffith and Thomas Ince were developing the technique of the feature-length film, and others, such as Mack Sennett and Charlie Chaplin, were taking screen comedy to new heights. Some Chaplin films did get through and, in Germany as everywhere else in the world, he was adored, becoming part of the country's love of all things American.

Even after the war, for several years, Germany saw little American cinema. This was because of the continuing loss in value of the mark – it simply wasn't worthwhile for American companies to distribute their films there. As a result, the German film industry was rather isolated, and this helped it to develop a strong style of its own, building partly on the imaginative strength of German theatre. In the Twenties its films were more individual than those of any other non-American country, including even the film-loving Soviet Union.

The dominant organization in German film-making at this time was the state-run *Universum Film Aktiengesellschaft,* known as UFA (pronounced 'oofa'). Although it did make films itself, mostly it controlled a group of semi-independent production companies, and concerned itself mainly with distribution and exhibition.

It had been founded towards the end of 1917, as part of the German war effort, by General Ludendorff, the army's quartermaster-general and next in rank to commander-in-chief Hindenberg. He ordered the merging of a number of German film companies into one, secretly under state control, with the aim of making the production of propaganda films more efficient.

Continuing after the war, it began to move into feature film production, and took over even more independent companies, including the one owned by Uncle Willi's colleague, Oskar Messter.

It was UFA that gave Marlene her first job connected with the cinema. Films, then still silent, needed musical accompaniment, and UFA maintained a pool of musicians to supply this in its various cinemas. The leading conductor of film-orchestras was the composer Dr Giuseppe Becce, and he not only hired Marlene to play her violin in one of his orchestras, he was also sufficiently impressed by her talent to make her his concert-mistress, with responsibility for rehearsing and leading the other musicians. As all the other musicians were men, this was a tribute to her ability as well as to the open-mindedness of the Berlin music world in the matter of sexual equality.

Unfortunately, her sex proved her downfall. After only four weeks Becce was obliged to dispense with her services, on the grounds that her legs were proving too much of a distraction to her male fellow-musicians. As there must have been easy ways to get around this problem, it seems likely that by now she was finding it impossible to resist the urge to be coquettish.

During this brief period working as an UFA pit-musician, she had continued her lessons with Professor Flesch, but it wasn't long before she abandoned both them and her ambition to become a concert violinist.

In later life she gave conflicting reasons for her change of course. One was that from practising too long and too hard she strained a finger-ligament in her left hand, and that her tutor advised her to give up. Another was that the over-practising had caused a permanently swollen ganglion on the primary nerve of her left wrist, with a similar result. At other times she mentioned a broken ring-finger and a diseased muscle.

It has also been suggested that her ceasing to pursue a musical career was dictated by the simple need to earn a living. This probably had some truth in it, but her strongest motivation by now was the urge to perform – not simply as a musician, but as herself, and if possible in films – she wanted to be seen, to be known, to be adored.

This is obvious from the fact that, after her return to Berlin, as well as studying with Professor Flesch, she began taking singing lessons from one of the city's leading operatic voice coaches, Dr Oskar Daniel. Dr Daniel's lessons didn't come cheap but, in spite of the fact that he thought her voice was weak, he thought highly enough of her instinct for music to let her pay for them when she could.

He was a cheerful, lively man, and his teaching methods were somewhat unorthodox. According to actress Lotte Andor, who was one of Marlene's fellow-pupils, 'He made us run, make faces, jump around, do all sorts of tricks. This was his method of improving voice projection, and Marlene and I obeyed without question. She was remarkably anxious to please.'

This anxiety to please apparently didn't extend to being punctual, which is unusual because for most of her life she was noted for being unfailingly on time. In fact she was so late for so many of her lessons that she was told that if she couldn't show up at the appointed hour she needn't show up at all. But then, as she entered her Twenties she was still in the process of discovering herself – rebelling still further against the strict rules of her childhood, deciding that the classical violin was not for her, in spite of her years of hard work, and beginning a period when her moods would swerve from elation to despair, from burning ambition to depressed acceptance of failure.

By now Marlene had started dressing strikingly so as to be noticed. Lotte Andor recalled her coming to voice class wearing bright red hats with long plumes, or a large bow in her hair, or a feather boa. Or she might wear a striking mix of brightly coloured clothes, or arrive with a borrowed dog – a borzoi or a poodle. (Her friend Gerda, who had less drama in her soul, felt that Marlene simply had no dress sense, and that her taste in hats was terrible.)

In the spring of 1922 Gerda managed to land a job in journalism, in the editorial department of a Hanover newspaper. This of course meant that she had to move to Hanover, and her *ménage* with Marlene broke up. Gerda worried about what would happen to her, feeling that Marlene was too gentle and sensitive to survive successfully in the harsh world of Twenties Berlin. Marlene tearfully saw her off on the train, and for weeks they exchanged letters (Marlene stopped first). She also continued to lodge with Trude.

It was at around this time that, in order to make some money, Marlene sold her violin, thus finally renouncing her musical career, as well as upsetting her mother.

Her respectable sister Elisabeth was rebelling in a small way too. In spite of their mother's mistrust of theatricals, she married a man named Georg Will, who was the manager of a basement cabaret, the Theater des Westens (which continued operating for decades). It was Georg Will who gave

Marlene the break of her first stage appearance, as one of a short line of chorus-girls at the club. (It wasn't only her fellow-musicians who had noticed the beauty of her legs, and Marlene herself was beginning to realise they were pretty good – in fact for some years she was to believe that they were her only really attractive feature.) Many other people claimed in later years to have given Marlene her first break, but Georg's claim is better than most.

This was the beginning of a year or so in which she worked from time to time as a chorus-girl. For a while she was one of the twelve 'Thielscher-Girls', a chorus-line backing the highly popular and long-established singer Guido Thielscher, whose songs were either tuneful and sentimental or tuneful and slightly naughty. The girls who backed him needed to do little but have good legs, wear feathered and sequinned costumes, and move reasonably well in time to the music.

After touring for a while with Thielscher, playing night-clubs in several German towns and cities such as Hamburg, she returned to Berlin and got a classier job in one of the revues written and presented by Rudolf Nelson at his theatre on the Kurfürstendamm. These were cheeky and stylish productions, aimed predominantly at titillating men but also attracting Berlin's flourishing lesbian set. Marlene would go on to appear in several of them, not only dancing but also occasionally singing.

A song Nelson wrote, called 'Peter', may have been in one of these shows. Marlene did not sing it then, but over the years would record it four times – three times in German and once in English. The Berlin songwriter, Peter Kreuder, who was one of her lovers in the Twenties, believed she had asked for a song of that title to be written as a loving gesture to him.

By 1922 she was supplementing her income by a little modelling in advertising photographs, usually featuring the legs that she knew were good, and between dancing engagements, like other struggling performers, she took to scouring the call-sheets for the film studios, hoping for even a bit part. She also pestered Uncle Willi to use his contacts in the film world to help her, and eventually, to shut her up (he said), he phoned a production company called Decla and spoke to an executive he knew there called Horstmann, asking if his niece could be given a screen test.

Horstmann agreed, and gave the job of testing her to a young Hungarian cameraman who was then working for Decla. His name was Stephan Lorant, a brilliant, volatile man who would emigrate to England in the Thirties and found in succession the highly successful illustrated magazines *Lilliput* and *Picture Post*. He would later go on to America and write an acclaimed life of Lincoln.

Lorant was not pleased to be given the job. It would have to be done at the end of a long, hard day filming under hot studio lights. When she showed up (one day in April 1922) to be tested he tried to discourage her. But he didn't know Marlene. She was not to be discouraged, and as she pleaded with him he realised she was 'prepared to wait till midnight, if necessary'. He asked her why being filmed was so important to her, and she replied, 'Because... That's what I was born to do.' (Although Lorant did not see it, this might well have been a practised response.)

Giving in, Lorant decided to film the test outside in the daylight, rather than in the exhausting heat of the studio. He set up his camera facing a fence that he'd decided would be a useful prop and, rather in a spirit of revenge, directed her to climb on and off it, jump over it and crawl under it, watched by the camera and several of his colleagues on the film he was shooting.

'Marlene must have been made to get up on this fence some fifteen times, and jump down again,' he recalled in an interview years later, 'and while doing this she had to laugh, cry, grimace, scream, sob. But [she] didn't mind at all. She jumped down from the fence, she jumped into the ditch, she hopped and skipped and shouted for joy... After we had made her jump enough, I took a really serious shot of her, a close-up of her head. There was something menacing about the broad, high Slavonic cheekbones... She turned her head from left to right like a mannequin at a fashion parade. When her eyes met the lens of the camera, she had to laugh. She screwed up her mouth, then she turned her head round into profile.'

Having an audience excited her, and she threw herself into her performance. But the test was a disaster. Studio staff viewing it all had a good laugh. In Lorant's words, 'In the close-up, the girl, who was quite pretty in real life, looked distinctly ugly. Broad face, expressionless eyes, uncouth movements. The opinion was unanimous: no talent whatever.' She was not even recommended to Horstmann as an extra.

But Lorant was wrong in one thing – opinion had not quite been unanimous. Among those watching her hopping around the fence had been a young and highly respected actor with ambitions to become a film director. Then aged twenty-nine, his name was Wilhelm Dieterle, and he would eventually succeed in his ambition, going in time to America and changing his first name to 'William'.

He was already trying to get together a team and enough money to make a film, and in Marlene, no matter how inept and comical she appeared, he saw a genuine and strong personality. He decided he would ask her to become involved in his project when he got it together.

Marlene, not knowing of this solitary vote of approval, but undaunted, continued to try and improve. Shortly after her abortive screen test, she applied for admission to the drama school run at the famous Deutsches Theater by Professor Max Reinhardt. Reinhardt (whose real name was Maximilian Goldmann) was a cyclone of Viennese energy who had come to Berlin in 1894 and for years was probably the most respected stage producer in the world. In fact it was he as much as anybody who raised the role of the producer (or director as he or she is now more commonly called) to the dominant position it still holds today.

Professor Reinhardt's approach to acting and staging was expressionistic. He moved acting away from the more naturalistic style that had been in vogue, in favour of a more stylised performance, symbolizing hidden feelings, and his staging took two main forms – vast spectacular productions, with sets that owed more to architecture than to painting, and chamber productions, small-scale and intimate, developing a detailed subtlety in his actors. These intimate productions took place in another of his theatres (he ran four in Berlin), the Kammerspiele, next door to the Deutsches Theater. This small theatre seated only two hundred, while the Deutsches Theater held a thousand.

Auditioning for the Reinhardt school had originally been suggested to her by Gerda Huber, and it took considerable chutzpah for Marlene to even attempt such a thing because, apart from her appearances as a chorus-girl, her theatrical experience was precisely nil. She had no acting training, only a good memory for lines (especially poetry, which she adored) and a passionate desire to be a success as a performer.

Her audition took place in May 1922, and Reinhardt himself was not present – he didn't audition students himself, and in any case was away in Vienna at the time – and in it she delivered a speech from *Der Tor Und Der Tod (Death And The Fool)*, a mystical verse drama by Hugo von Hoffmansthal, the Austrian poet who most famously wrote librettos for Richard Strauss, among them *Der Rosenkavalier*.

It was doubtless no accident that she chose a piece from a play that had been produced by Reinhardt, but it is also a romantic and melancholy piece that appealed to her sentimental side (the speech is given by the spirit of a dead girl speaking to a dying nobleman). She delivered it well enough to be shortlisted from the scores of fellow-applicants and asked to come back for a further audition, this time to perform a piece chosen not by herself but by the examiners.

She was lucky with their choice as it was a passage by her beloved Goethe – 'Gretchen's Prayer' from *Faust* (which had also been a famous Reinhardt production). This, although quite short, is a tough piece. Using deceptively simple language (Gretchen was a simple girl), but with complex rhythms and powerful emotional undertones, it requires simplicity in performance. 'Less is more', as the Bauhaus architect Mies van der Rohe liked to say.

In later life nobody was better than Marlene at playing emotionally complex scenes simply, but at this second audition her inexperience let her down. In Goethe's play Gretchen delivers her prayer to an image of the Virgin Mary grieving over the body of Christ, and Marlene, giving her performance all she'd got, fell to her knees with a thud. Not only that – at some point she rose to her feet, shedding real tears, and then again fell thud to her knees, and was startled when one of the examiners in the darkened auditorium tossed a cushion onto the stage beside her.

The failure of this audition did not deter her long. Looking for someone to help her gain admission to the Reinhardt school, she approached one of Berlin's most popular cabaret stars, Rosa Valetti. Having prevailed on a friend of Valetti's to give her an introduction, she presented herself at the star's dressing-room at the Grössenwahn (Megalomania) cabaret.

Valetti, a short square-built woman with bushy red hair, a squat mug of a face and a tough, no-nonsense manner, spotted Marlene at once as a mere beginner with a lot of work to do. But she was impressed by the timbre of Marlene's voice (as millions would be later), by her personality, and by her determination. Valetti was having cabaret songs written for her by a young but highly successful composer, Friedrich Holländer, who happened to be the nephew of one of Reinhardt's administrators, the amiable and amusing Felix Holländer, known as Fritz. She recommended Marlene to him.

Holländer, when Marlene presented herself to him, was equally impressed by her distinctive voice and her determination, and arranged for her to be tutored by Dr Berthold Held, who was the administrator in charge of the entire Reinhardt school.

Marlene now embarked on a serious course of study. She was still taking voice lessons from Dr Daniel, managed to talk Rosa Valetti into giving her a few informal lessons in cabaret performance, and with Dr Held began studying the basic Reinhardt disciplines of fencing, elocution, voice projection and rhythmic movement.

At these lessons she had a fellow-pupil, Grete Mosheim, who would go on to great success in German plays and films, and neither Marlene nor Grete thought too much of Dr Held, who was rather pompous and a poor teacher. But the important thing for Marlene was that she was now inside the Reinhardt organization – not simply as a member of the school, but as a private pupil to one of the management's most important members. And in due course, like most Reinhardt students, she could expect to be given small roles in various productions.

Marlene also continued to pester her Uncle Willi, and at around the time she began her studies at the Reinhardt school, he spoke to Georg Jacoby, a director he knew who was then working for the newly founded company EFA (European Film Alliance). This company had been founded specifically to make films aimed at the American market, in the hope of earning some reliable dollars.

A film made in 1919 by the German director Ernst Lubitsch, *Madame Bovary* (retitled *Passion* in the States) had done well there, and in the hope of emulating its success Jacoby was preparing another costume drama – a comedy about the amorous adventures of Napoleon's younger brother, Jérome, who became king of the German province of Westphalia. It eventually had various titles, including *The Little Napoleon, Napoleon's Little Brother* and *That's How Men Are*.

Uncle Willi asked Jacoby to give his persistent niece a role in it – any role. His rather optimistic hope was that once she had made an appearance in a film she would be satisfied and have no craving to make another. Jacoby amiably agreed, and cast her in the small role of Kathrin, maid to the leading lady, who coincidentally was also named Dietrich – Antonia Dietrich (an actress whose career never really prospered). In the film Kathrin helps her mistress, Charlotte, to evade Jérome's lecherous advances.

Marlene was delighted to be cast, and her performance shows it – it is full of a sort of naïve giggly pleasure at being in front of the camera at all. There is personality there, but not a sign of the magnificent stage repose she would soon come to possess, and no understanding that the camera magnifies gesture and expression. Nor does she look much like her later famous self – her face is plump and broad, closely framed by curly hair squashed down on her head by a mob cap. When she saw herself, months later, her shocked reaction was, 'I look like a potato with hair!'

As the months went by she began getting the expected roles in Reinhardt productions. The Reinhardt system was to have several plays in production at the same time, presenting each for a day here and a day there, interspersed with others, and Marlene's first appearance on the legitimate stage took place on 7 September 1922. On that day, in the intimate Kammerspiele, she played the vivacious, depraved Ludmilla Steinhertz in Wedekind's 1904 play *Die Büchse Der Pandora (Pandora's Box)*. The piece was directed by the man who had accepted her into the Reinhardt organization, Fritz Höllander. As well as being an administrator and a director, Fritz was also a musician and composer, and from time to time she took singing lessons from him. (Her voice at the time was a little uncertain in its register, with a tendency to veer between soprano and a rather husky baritone.)

It was at about this time that, after a gap of some months, she wrote again to Gerda, saying: 'Gerda, do you remember me? I'm still continuing my theatrical career, but without hope of getting much further in it, without hope of ever becoming a good actress. I might as well try to reach the moon. I suppose the life itself is neither better nor worse than lots of others, but it's so different from the one I ought to have chosen for myself... You can imagine the kind of people and the surroundings with which I am involved. I feel so miserable, so sick of everything. I have a part in a play at the moment, a better one, although it is very small. I'm not living with Trude any more – I've found a *pension* that is more central, nearer the theatre. Puck is with me, and we're going to live like this for ever and ever...'

Gerda found this letter depressing, and began worrying about her friend. But it reveals a side of Marlene's character she would carry with her all her life – a tendency to become, if only for a brief while, the sort of person people wanted her to be. Dr Levin is a serious and respectable musician, so in letters to him she complains about the sexual faithlessness of the people of Weimar. When she has an ailing young man as her lover, she becomes a devoted nurse. To Gerda she is the gentle feminine lover, the housewife. Gerda herself is quiet and cultured, so Marlene regrets to her the crassness of people she meets in the theatre world, and appears almost helpless.

Helpless she wasn't. In September 1922 she managed to get herself a part in another film. The prolific producer/director Joe May was planning a major production starring one of Germany's leading stage and film actors, the heavily built Emil Jannings. It was to be called *Tragödie Der Liebe (Tragedy Of Love)*, a violent story of lust, jealousy and revenge. It would be released in two two-hour parts, and in it Jannings would play a brutal wrestler who is tried for the murder of his mistress, played by Erika Glässner (he throws her off the roof of an apartment building). This was a fairly typical part for Jannings, an excellent actor who tended to specialise in tragically sentimental pieces about pompous characters brought low by fate. His co-star would be Mia May, wife of Joe.

An open casting call was advertised to select extras for the picture, and Marlene answered it, along with a number of her fellow-drama students, including Grete Mosheim. When they arrived at the studio they found an enormous throng of applicants. In the words of the young assistant director Fritz Maurischat, 'a line formed that went all the way down the corridor and down the stairs. In this line was a tiny, fragile creature, dressed in a loose wrap almost as intimate as a negligée. Despite this revealing garment, she could easily have been overlooked, since most of the girls were trying to attract attention by throwing their breasts or legs at me... But she had with her a puppy on a leash, and none of the other girls did... Marlene picked it up and... Came to my desk. As she did so, there was something about her movements that made me say to myself, under my breath, "My *God!* How attractive she is!"'

Fritz drew the attention of Joe May's assistant, Rudolf Sieber, to this heady combination of seductiveness and innocence, and Rudolf quickly rushed her into May's office. May, auditioning her, asked her to stand, to sit, to turn her head this way and that, to smile, to nod slowly. Marlene obeyed, but with a sort of offhand puzzlement. All this fuss seemed unnecessary to cast a small anonymous crowd role. Indeed, with her growing Berlin sophistication, she found it boring.

This offhandedness may have helped, for she was cast as an extra, to be a party girl in some scenes set in a casino. This was a small triumph.

Next day, however, Rudolf Sieber came looking for her. He tried the Reinhardt rehearsal hall at the Deutsches Theater, but learned she was not there as she had no class that day. Eventually he tracked her down at her mother's apartment, where she was temporarily living due to a lack of money. He had good news – Joe May wanted to give her an additional and more prominent role. He wanted her to play Lucie, the insolent, spoiled mistress of the presiding judge in the film's big courtroom scene.

Naturally she accepted and offered to make Rudolf a cup of coffee. He had been as bowled over by her as Fritz Maurischat, and made the counter-offer of taking her to lunch at a nearby café. Rudolf was twenty-five with blond hair and brown eyes. He was handsome and charming and smartly dressed, and Marlene accepted. Over lunch they found they enjoyed each other's company, and although when they met he was engaged to be married to Joe May's daughter Eva, Marlene soon told her mother that he was the man she wanted to marry. It turned out his full name was Rudolf Emilien Sieber (known to everyone as 'Rudi') and he was born in Aussig, not far from Prague, in 1897. He was bright, he was ambitious and he had something of a reputation as a ladies' man.

While *Tragedy Of Love* ground its way towards the actual filming, Marlene's theatre life continued. On 2 October 1922, in another Reinhardt theatre, the enormous Grosses Schauspielhaus, with a capacity of three thousand, she appeared in a German translation of *The Taming Of The Shrew*, playing the witty but unnamed widow who appears in the last scene, betrothed to Bianca's ex-suitor, Hortensio. (Reinhardt believed that nobody could be called an actor until he or she could play Shakespeare.)

The role of Kate, the play's heroine, was taken by the tiny, pretty Polish-born actress, Elisabeth Bergner. She was highly talented, although somewhat restricted in her range of roles, best at playing perky boyish girls, and more at ease with tenderness and gaiety than with tragedy. She was four years older than Marlene, and Marlene, always easily starstruck, was so in awe of her poise and beauty that she rather muted her own tiny role and made little impression. Ironically, it wouldn't be long before Bergner would remark, somewhat waspishly, 'If I were as beautiful as Dietrich, I wouldn't know where to begin with my talent.'

Marlene's next play was a flop. It was called *Timotheus In Flagranti*, written by Hennequin and Weber, and it was removed from the Reinhardt repertory after only twelve days. In it, however, Marlene had the useful experience of playing three different small roles in turn, sharing them with two other actresses. Slowly but surely she was learning her trade.

Towards the end of 1922, shooting began on *Tragedy Of Love*. As Lucie, Marlene had one short scene making a phone call from her bed, but her main appearance was as a member of the general public attending the trial. Her function was to provide comic relief in the tense drama by fluttering, giggling, yawning and generally being insolent.

Rudolf suggested that Marlene wear a monocle, so as to stand out better among the other extras (the monocle was a popular fashion accessory among Berlin women who wished to appear decadent), and she did, allegedly using one that had belonged to her father. This worked well with the frivolous sexiness of her character (among other things, she flirts with another lawyer to make her lover, the judge, jealous), and she improved on it in her final scene by replacing the monocle with opera glasses – an idea of her own.

This was her first good screen performance, and it delighted crew and cast as well as the film's eventual audiences. Although she was at this time still somewhat plump, she was becoming less so, and hints of the famous Marlene features were beginning to emerge.

Early in 1923 she was on stage again as the bridge-playing Mrs Shenstone in a translation of Somerset Maugham's *The Circle*, which played for twenty-three performances between 24 January and 5 March. The part was small, and mainly exposition, but again the leading lady was Elisabeth Bergner, and again Marlene was able to study her successful technique.

In February, while still playing in *The Circle*, she was also in Heinrich von Kleist's epic verse tragedy, *Penthesilea*, set in the time of battles between the Trojans and the Amazons, and performed on a vast revolving stage. This ran for nine performances and she played an Amazon warrior. Again here she had a major star to watch, because the title role of the Amazon general was played by Agnes Straub.

Straub was so admired that before long Berlin would name a theatre after her, and the starstruck Marlene was lucky that the great actress was cripplingly short-sighted. As Amazon generals do not wear spectacles, this meant that she was almost blind on stage, and it became Marlene's job to take her hand in the darkness as the stage revolved and lead her to her next position.

Young Wilhelm Dieterle, who alone had seen something in her abortive screen test, and who was also a Reinhardt actor, watched several of her stage performances. He remained impressed and, now having scraped together enough money to make his film, asked her to be in it.

The film was to be based on a Tolstoy short story, a variation on the parable of the Good Samaritan, and it was to be called *Der Mensch Am Wege (The Man By The Wayside)*. As Dieterle later said of his team, 'We had no money. We were just four [or] five very young, enthusiastic, and revolutionary [Reinhardt] people who wanted to do something different. We brought it out; it didn't make any money, but was shown, and it was a very interesting experiment.'

The way in which it was experimental was that Dieterle felt the films being made in Germany at the time (quite a few of which he had had major roles in) were studio-bound and stagy. He wanted to shoot more realistically, in real locations, and he himself starred in the film, as well as writing and directing it.

The Man By The Wayside was shot mostly on location in Schleswig, and mostly out of doors (which was of course also cheaper), and in it Marlene played a peasant girl, wearing a dirndl, with her hair pulled back off her face into coiled plaits. This revealed her face better than either of her previous films, and as she continued to lose weight (some of which was late-adolescent puppy fat), she continued to become more beautiful.

Rudolf Sieber, who was by now her constant companion, frequently escorted her to the filming. But her relationship with him was causing her some anxiety. She was well aware that he was a catch for any woman – being fairly well established in the film industry wasn't doing him any harm. And although their relationship had developed into a sort of courtship (in spite of the fact that he was still technically engaged to Eva May), there were still problems. One was the fact that she was still living with her mother, who did not approve of Marlene's busy social life, and thought Rudi was encouraging it. It was typical of Josephine, having reconciled herself to the fact that her daughter was determined on an acting career, to feel that it should be approached with Teutonic thoroughness, putting duty before pleasure.

Once, when Rudi came to call for Marlene, Josephine told him flatly that she disapproved, and shortly afterwards he said to Marlene, 'This is too boring for me. I can't come to your house because of your mother. Why? I can have any of the most beautiful Russian girls in Berlin – any of them I please. We need to stop this, it just doesn't please me any more.'

He was also, in spite of his reputation as something of a Lothario, not as sexually open as she was. He was even slightly strait-laced. He disapproved of her sleeping around with women, which she disdained to conceal and showed no sign of stopping.

At the same time she was desperate that he should love her. A woman should have a husband. She found him sexy and loving, and thought him dependable, which was perhaps most important of all. At last she seemed to have in her life a man who was as dependable as her mother had been in her childhood – as neither her father nor her stepfather had turned out to be.

To try and make herself as attractive to him as possible, she took to going (with Grete Mosheim) to exercise classes, which were given by a powerful female Swedish gymnast, Ingrid Menzendick. As Grete recalled: 'The realization that he might marry another girl just about drove her to suicide. Finally she stole some coal and food from her mother and one winter night she went through the snow to his house. She gained access to his quarters, laid on a hot meal and waited for him to return.'

From that moment on, their affair took on a new momentum. The next day Rudi gave her enough money to take a flat of her own. She took one in an apartment block at 54 Kaiserallee, which was quite close to where Josephine lived but at least meant that Marlene was no longer under her mother's roof. A near neighbour who became a friend was Leni Riefenstahl. Only a few months younger than Marlene, she was then an idealistic painter and dancer. Later she would become a film-maker, notoriously and naïvely in support of the Nazi party.

Shortly after filming on *The Man By The Wayside* was completed, and very suddenly, they married. He was of a Catholic family, and she was technically a Lutheran, so the wedding was a civil one, at the town hall of the Berlin suburb of Friedenau. It was a quiet ceremony, with few present, and the date was 17 May 1923.

Rudi's best man was his closest friend, the actor Rudolf Forster (who had appeared in *Tragedy Of Love*), and the witnesses were Josephine and one Richard Neuhauser, described in the register as a salesman, who may have been courting Josephine at the time. Marlene signed her name as 'Maria Magdalene Dietrich'.

Shortly afterwards, Eva May attempted suicide by slitting her wrists. She failed, but during the following year succeeded, shooting herself through the heart. Rudi ceased to be Joe May's assistant.

3 Married Life

After their marriage, Marlene and Rudi moved into her apartment in the Kaiserallee, and for a while she entered enthusiastically into the role of *hausfrau*, cooking and cleaning and looking after her handsome husband.

It wasn't a long while. Soon it became clear that she had no intention of being a conventional wife. Shortly after she and Rudi returned from their honeymoon she signed a three-year contract with the theatrical producers Carl Meinhard and Rudolf Bernauer. They didn't have the class of the Reinhardt organization, but they were active and successful, running a number of Berlin theatres. As soon as the contract was signed she began appearing in what would be a succession of their plays.

In June 1923, a month after her marriage, she made her first appearance for them, as the daughter in *Between Nine And Nine*, described as a 'backstairs tragicomedy'. In July, while still appearing in this she made two brief appearances in the potboiling film *Der Sprung Ins Leben (The Leap Into Life)* – once as a bathing beauty and once attending a circus, as a girl in love with one of the acrobats. The producer of this film was Erich Pommer, who in 1920 had famously produced *The Cabinet Of Dr Caligari*.

Her next play was Björnsterne Björnson's *Wenn Der Junge Wein Blüht (When The Young Vine Blooms)*. In this, she and Hilda Hildebrandt played sexually awakening teenage sisters who are the daughters of sexually arid parents (who eventually stop being arid and get it together just as the vines are coming symbolically into bloom).

As well as playing her role, Marlene also sang as a member of the chorus that accompanied the piece. The chorus was drilled by the actress Erike Meingast, who at the time had as her lover the Franco-German chanteuse, Marianne Oswald. Marlene became friendly with Erike, who frequently came to her and Rudi's house as a guest, sometimes bringing Marianne Oswald with her. Years later Marianne would remember Marlene at the time as a 'plump but promising girl'.

Erike was not the only woman connected with the play to be attracted to another woman. Marlene developed a crush on a young fellow-actress in the cast, from the moment she saw her at rehearsal. She made no secret to Rudi of her infatuation, and he took to delivering her to the theatre personally, then hanging round backstage during the performance till it was time to bring her home again. The infatuation soon ran out of steam.

In another play, soon after *When The Young Vine Blooms*, she again played a sexy schoolgirl. But this was a much more dangerous and controversial piece – *Frühlings Erwachen (The Awakening Of Spring)*, written by Frank Wedekind as far back as 1897 and probably the first play to depict masturbation and homosexuality on stage. Late in her life Marlene claimed to have loathed the piece, but late in her life she was somewhat given to editing her past to protect the smooth surface of her image.

In September 1923 she appeared in a farce called *My Cousin, Edward*. This would run for almost a year, but long before its run ended Marlene had left to again play an Amazon – this time in a more distinguished piece, even if her role was not a large one; she played Hippolyta, Queen of the Amazons, in a translation of *A Midsummer Night's Dream*.

Somewhere around this time she also played a maid in Molière's *Le Malade Imaginaire*. There was a reason for all this activity on her part. Quite apart from wishing to build her reputation and advance her acting career, her and Rudi's financial situation was distinctly rocky. He was finding little film work since he had stopped working for Joe May, and the two of them had got married when inflation was sky-rocketting. In 1922 the situation was bad enough, with the exchange rate standing at fifty marks to the dollar, but by 1924 it would soar to the unbelievable rate of 2.5 million million to the dollar. A barrowload of banknotes would barely buy a loaf.

Fortunately, America stepped in to help. In 1923 a Republican politician, Charles Gates Dawes, was appointed to look into the situation, and towards the end of 1924 he had hammered out a plan of action – known, naturally enough, as the Dawes Plan. Implemented in November 1924, it restored the mark to more or less its pre-war value by simply lopping twelve zeros off the exchange rate (it settled at 4.2 marks to the dollar). The USA also gave Germany a loan of $200 million to help it pay off the war reparations demanded of it.

It was fortunate for Marlene and Rudi that this happened when it did, because on 12 December 1924, after taking several months off from acting, she gave birth (with some difficulty) to their daughter. The child was named Maria Elisabeth, although for some years from the beginning of her life she would be known affectionately as 'Heidede'.

Marlene was delighted with her, and for a while eagerly adopted the new role of motherhood. But soon her ambition to succeed as an actress reasserted itself.

Her theatre career had suffered a slight setback during her accouchement. Carl Meinhard and Rudolf Bernauer had turned all their theatres over to Victor Barnowsky, a Viennese producer whose reputation in Austria and Germany was second only to Reinhardt's. He wished to build up in Berlin the same sort of large and active organization as Reinhardt had. He had even used several of Reinhardt's stage stars in Vienna – Elisabeth Bergner and Wilhelm Dieterle among them – as well as Rudi's friend, Rudolf Forster. But he had reservations about Marlene, thinking she was more beautiful than talented, and was not eager to use her.

Her mind reverted to her other ambition – film. At around the time of Heidede's birth an event had occurred in the film world that had reinforced to her the possibility of stardom. A young Swedish actress had been brought to Berlin to make a film for the famous director Pabst. The film was called *Die Freudlose Gasse (Joyless Street)* and the actress was Greta Garbo – both it and she were such successes that as soon as it was released (in December 1924) she was summoned to Hollywood by Louis B Mayer to be one of the stars of the recently formed Metro-Goldwyn-Mayer.

There was for many years a legend that Marlene herself had a small role in *Joyless Street*, but she didn't. The confusion seems to have risen from a resemblance between herself (as she looked in 1924) and another actress, Hertha von Walther. Hertha, who lived until 1988, rather resented this confusion all her life.

From 1925 on, Marlene became an active part of Berlin's club and cabaret scene. This was partly because it was a good way to publicise yourself and partly because she just plain enjoyed it. One of her favourite haunts was the Eldorado Club, on Martin Lutherstrasse, where every waitress, barmaid or hat check girl was a man in drag, but she was also frequently to be seen (with or without Rudi) in similar places such as The White Rose or Le Silhouette.

Joe May's wife, Mia, recalled her being 'very amusing and diverting and attractive and original... She was irresistible to men [and] usually wore a monocle or a feather boa, or sometimes as many as five red fox furs on a stole. On other occasions, she wore wolf skins, the kind you spread on beds. People used to follow her through the streets of Berlin, they would laugh at her, but she fascinated them; she made them talk.'

She also made them talk, according to actress Elisabeth Lennartz, by appearing in restaurants and cafés 'wearing neither bra nor panties'.

The stabilizing of the currency had given a new impetus to Berlin's night-life. While attitudes retained an undercurrent of disillusion, shows from 1925 on became even brighter and brassier. The music played in the clubs received quite a lift when, for the first time, real American jazz began to be heard. In May 1925 a show called *Chocolate Kiddies* arrived from New York, with music by a black band led by pianist Sam Wooding. Not only was this show greeted rapturously by a large section of the public, but it also influenced young Berlin composers such as Kurt Weill and Ernst Křenek.

Max Reinhardt had failed to make his productions at the Grosses Schauspielhaus pay, and in around 1924 he had turned this vast theatre over to the dancer and choreographer Erik Charell. Charell mostly produced lavish revues and musicals (in later years he would have enormous success with the spectacular *White Horse Inn*), but early in 1926 he briefly presented the most famous American band of the Twenties, Paul Whiteman's.

His competitor, Rudolf Nelson (for whom Marlene had danced as a chorus-girl), retaliated a short while later by booking the show *La Revue Nègre*, which had just created a sensation in Paris and which starred the charleston-dancing Joséphine Baker.

Berlin night-life of the late Twenties had a flavour all its own. There were the world-weary cynical songs and sketches of its cabarets, and there were numerous clubs featuring sexual deviation (as it was then known). There were clubs for sado-masochists, fetishists, transvestites, and homosexuals of both sexes. This was another rebellion against the conformity of the past, and many Berliners adopted perversions with enthusiasm, or at least dressed and talked as if they had – those in the fashion threw about words like 'urnings', 'algolagnia', 'podexfetichism' and 'necrophagy'.

Many early sexologists, like Stekel, Hirschfeld and Krafft-Ebing were German, or at least German-speaking, and Marlene like many Berliners of her generation (including Billy Wilder) read their books avidly. A term she learned at this time was 'penis envy', and for the rest of her life she would use it to shock and disconcert people she wanted to dominate in argument –

usually men who seemed to be admiring other female performers too much, a habit that men could not often be accused of when she was around.

A few people were appalled by the prevailing sexual attitudes and behaviour. The Austrian author Stefan Zweig wrote, 'Along the entire Kurfürstendamm powdered and rouged young men sauntered and they were not all professionals; every high school boy wanted to earn some money and in the dimly lit bars one might see government officials and men of the world of finance tenderly courting drunken sailors without any shame. Even the Rome of Suetonius had never known such orgies as the balls of Berlin. Hundreds of men dressed as women and hundreds of women as men danced under the benevolent eyes of the police.' But poor Zweig was rather given to taking a gloomy view of life. He was expelled from Germany by the Nazis in 1934, and he and his wife committed suicide in Brazil in 1942.

A more cheerful observer of the scene was Anita Loos. Passing through Berlin and alluding to her most famous book, she observed that if gentlemen preferred blondes then 'the prettiest girl on the street was Conrad Veidt'.

A light-hearted approach to sexual activity was thought to be the ultimate in chic, and Marlene adopted this attitude enthusiastically. The writer and producer Geza von Schiffra, who knew her in her night-clubbing days, said, 'She was quite boyish, with her masculine buddy-like behaviour. She readily joined us at tables where several of the patrons were homosexuals, for in fact she was much more interested – though not exclusively – in women.'

She would continue an active and varied sex life for years. In the Nineties her grandson Peter revealed that she had kept a diary in code and that when it was deciphered by his mother (Heidede, by then long known by her real name of Maria), it revealed that she often had sex with three different people in one day. Her preference, as several of her ex-lovers noted, was for oral sex. It took less effort and, more importantly, allowed her to keep control. As Maria later noted, it gave her 'the power to direct the scene'.

But in spite of her enjoyment of sex (and her intellectual interest in it), it seemed to be for her more of a way to establish friendships, to reach out for closeness, than anything else. Almost all her lovers, male and female, remained lifelong friends, to the extent that she could become upset and even angry if one of them married. And several described her love-making, although enthusiastic to the point of almost being aggressive, as being at the same time somehow clinical and detached. Sex was another way of being what people wanted her to be, without giving anything of herself, and in the famous TV documentary about her, made late in her life by Maximilian Schell, she admitted that she had never understood eroticism, that her attitude to sex was to be 'cheeky' about it.

As well as appearing slightly masculine, and having a carefree attitude to sex, it was chic to smoke, and Marlene, who had started smoking at seventeen, at around the time she went to Weimar, remained a heavy smoker almost all her life. A cigarette became part of her sophisticated image.

Curiously, while on the club scene she was noted for her firm dislike of people who drank too much, or who took drugs at all (cocaine in particular seemed to be everywhere – in sophisticated circles it was even acceptable as a friendly party gift). This stern disapproval reveals the respectable Prussian side of her upbringing that never entirely left her.

In March 1925 she was with Rudi in a night-club when she was spotted dancing by a young film-worker called Skutesky. He was bowled over by her (especially by her legs). As he was then working as assistant to the director E A Dupont, who was preparing a film called *Variety*, he suggested the next day to Dupont that she might be an attractive addition to the cast. *Variety* was to be set largely in Berlin's Wintergarten, which was a sort of combination night-club, theatre and circus, and Skutesky thought that maybe she could play something like a trapeze artist.

Dupont was dismissive, saying, 'Maybe someday *you* can give her a chance, if you ever have a bit part that needs a mini-vamp with beautiful legs.'

Three months later, however, in June 1925, she did get another film role. It was again for Erich Pommer, who had cast her in *The Leap Into Life*, but this was a much more prestigious production, with elaborate sets by the famous designer Paul Leni, and Marlene's role was considerably bigger. The film was *Manon Lescaut*, and she was to play Micheline, the second female lead. The female star was Lya de Putti, fresh from making *Variety*.

Micheline is a Parisian courtesan, flirtatious, flippant and self-centred, and although in her performance Marlene was still rather inclined to overact, she was definitely becoming more beautiful. She was one of those women who tend to lose weight following a pregnancy, in both face and body, and in *Manon Lescaut* she was at last beginning to resemble her later famous self.

The film was such a success that Hollywood snapped up Erich Pommer, Paul Leni and Lya de Putti – but not Marlene, even though the film would be the first of hers to be shown in America. As soon as Lya de Putti arrived in Hollywood, she starred in D W Griffith's *Sorrows Of Satan*, and the

American public were so taken with her that in 1926 *Manon Lescaut* was shown there as well. As was *Variety*, which so impressed Paramount that they not only distributed it but showed it to its employees as an example of how movies should be made. German film-makers were, by the mid-Twenties, assured that the cinema world held them in awe.

At around this time Marlene wrote a letter to her old friend Dr Levin, bemoaning the fact that she was having little success in becoming a serious actress, and regretting both the sort of work she was having to do and the fact that she was getting a reputation for being frivolous. In other words, writing to him as exactly the sort of person a serious classical musician would sympathise with.

In the autumn of 1925 she did manage (after getting a little promotion done on her behalf by Rudolf Forster) to audition for the ambitious Victor Barnowsky. The piece was a translation of Bernard Shaw's 1921 play (or series of plays) *Back To Methuselah* – an attempt on his part to breathe new hope into a world demoralised by the Great War. It is enormously long – Shaw had intended it to be read rather than performed – and Barnowsky intended to present it in two parts, running simultaneously in two theatres.

Of Marlene's audition for *Back To Methuselah*, he recalled: 'When I first met her, Marlene was very young, dazzlingly fresh, elegant, supremely good-looking, and with a touch of "feyness" that made her slightly mysterious. But she lacked self-confidence, and seemed unaware of her many attractions – except, perhaps, of her legs... I can see her now, in a copper-coloured dress, leaning against the wall of my office...reciting lines from some sentimental play, the name of which I've forgotten. It was an arresting sight – but could she have been aware of the effect she was creating?... Her first audition for me was successful, and when she began rehearsals for *Back To Methuselah* she threw herself heart and soul into the part. Even so, she seemed sadly lacking in that inner fire which should have been the complement of her physical charms. She was in sharp contrast to Elisabeth Bergner, who as a beginner displayed apparent physical helplessness, and yet seemed to hold something ultimate, something mysterious in reserve.'

He cast Marlene in both Part One and Part Two. In Part One she played Eve, and that opened in September 1925. Part Two opened in November.

Rudi, who was unemployed when rehearsals began, took on the role of house-husband and stayed at home to look after Heidede. But shortly after the run of Part One began he got film work again, as production manager for a Hungarian producer-director who had been in Berlin since shortly after the war and whose original name had been Sandor Laszlo Kellner. Now it was Alexander Korda (his last name adapted from that of his wife, the actress Maria Corda), and he was making a picture called *Der Tänzer Meiner Frau (My Wife's Dancing Partner)*. Marlene, while still appearing in *Back To Methuselah*, played a small role in it as an extra in a dance scene, possibly out of gratitude to Korda for employing Rudi.

A friend of Rudi's (and of Marlene's) was also working on the picture. His name was Alexander Choura, later to become a famous photographer of celebrities in Paris. During the shooting he introduced Rudi to a Russian dancer he knew. Her real name was Tamara Nikolaeyevna, but she danced under the somewhat simpler name of Tamara Matul. Marlene already knew her from the world of Berlin theatre, and indeed may have shared the stage with her in her chorus-girl days, but Choura's introduction of Tamara to Rudi would put an end to his friendship with Marlene, as Rudi and Tamara would eventually become more than just friends.

Barnowsky continued to use Marlene in his plays, although confessing himself puzzled that she repeatedly begged to be cast as either an ingenue or a tragedienne – neither of which roles he thought she was exactly fitted for. When *Back To Methuselah* finished, he cast her in a farcical satire on modern manners, set in Venice and called *Duell Am Lido (Duel On The Lido)*. It was written by Hans Rehfisch and was not to be directed by Barnowsky himself, but by Leopold Jessner.

Marlene turned up for the first rehearsal straight from partying all night at a transvestite bar called Always Faithful. She was wearing silk trousers, a dark jacket and a monocle. Leopold Jessner told her that the outfit was just right, and that she was to wear it for her role. Which she did, playing a decadent Parisienne called Lou Carrère.

Such young women were known in Paris at the time as *garçonnes*. The word came from the title of a 1923 novel, *La Garçonne*, written by Victor Marguérite. Its heroine, Monique Lerbier, is a student at the Sorbonne who cuts her hair short, wears a man's jacket, joins in orgies, has a child out of wedlock, and flirts with lesbianism. Marlene played her role well enough, but with a hectic gaiety that did not quite come off. As one reviewer, Fritz Engel, wrote, 'The role should have been acted by Marlene Dietrich not in a demonic revelry but icy-cold.' Whether or not she ever read that review, it would not be long before she learned that that was the way to do it.

By the time *Duel On The Lido* opened, in February 1926, another strand was appearing in the fabric of Berlin – a strongly right-wing movement bent on purging decadence in any form from German society, aiming to bring into being a nation that was healthy, fit and strong. This was, of course, the infant Nazi movement, known in its mid-Twenties infancy as the Brownshirts.

At first it was perceived by many as some sort of youth movement, but there were several in the cast of *Duel On The Lido* who would later become heavily involved in it. One was an actor called Veit Harlan, who would enthusiastically direct the most viciously anti-Semitic film ever to arise out of the Nazi movement – *Jew Süss (Sweet Jew)*, based cynically on the pro-Jewish novel by Lion Feuchtwanger. Another was Rudolf Forster, who after making an unsuccessful attempt to establish himself in Hollywood would return to Germany and happily work for the Third Reich.

So Marlene was aware of Nazism quite early on, and disliked it from the start. Ironically, the Berlin world in which she was immersed in the Twenties bore some responsibility for helping Hitler come to power. Respectable people all over Germany, away from the bright lights of Berlin, felt that the highly visible decadent night-clubbers (and the artists, writers and musicians) were destroying even such shreds of decent ordinary life as the war had left. And Hitler was the most respectable man who ever lived (which is quite apart from his monstrous actions as a dictator) – he liked respectable painting and sculpture and music, and nostalgic landscapes, and convention in matters sexual. He neither smoked nor drank.

The American columnist, Dorothy Kilgallen, interviewing him in 1932, was stunned by his 'startling insignificance', finding him 'the very prototype of the Little Man'. No wonder so many voted for him.

From *Duel On The Lido* Marlene went straight into another Barnowsky play, a drawing-room comedy called *The Rubicon*. This was directed by its leading man, Ralph Arthur Roberts. Marlene had worked with him three years before in *Between Nine And Nine*, in which she played the daughter. In *The Rubicon* she played a Frenchwoman, and seems to have played the part well, because her Uncle Willi felt it was her best-ever stage performance.

Rudi continued to work for Korda as his production manager, and in the late spring of 1926 Marlene got a small role in his film *Eine Du Barry Von Heute (A Modern Du Barry)*. Intended as a social satire, its star was Korda's wife, Maria Corda. Marlene played a spoilt, petulant Parisian playgirl. She had three short scenes and a small sub-plot of her own. She orders an expensive new dress and leaves it at the shop to be altered. At an elegant restaurant that evening she is outraged to see a flower girl from the shop (Maria Corda) wearing it, and insists to her escort they leave. Next morning, from her bed, she phones the shop to demand the girl be dismissed, only to learn that she has already quit because the dress made her an instant social success. (The main plot of the film concerns the attempts by the flower girl to attract a king – the satiric angle shows how merely wearing the right clothes can gain a person admission to the highest circles.)

Marlene underplayed her scenes with telling comic effect (gradually perfecting one of the main weapons in her future armoury), and in the restaurant scene danced a brief charleston in loose imitation of Joséphine Baker, who had recently been all the rage in Berlin. But the film itself was poor, unable to sustain the cynicism it started out with, and suffering further from being over-produced. As one reviewer wrote, 'The decor [was] worth more than the film.'

At around this time, fighting fiercely to advance her film career, Marlene went to photographer Elli Marcus, famous for her portraits of celebrities, and bluntly demanded, 'Take some pictures of me that will make me a star.' She paid for three days of sittings, and while the results were pleasing, they failed to have the desired effect.

Rudi was still with Korda, and in August 1926 Marlene again performed as an extra in one of his films. This one, another comedy of modern manners, was called *Madame Wünscht Keine Kinder (Madame Wants No Children)*. Again its star was Maria Corda, and Marlene appeared in several party scenes, this time dancing a spirited black bottom.

Theatre for the moment seemed to be offering her more than film. Towards the end of August she was hurriedly summoned by dancer-choreographer-producer Erik Charell, who had taken over the Grosses Schauspielhaus from Reinhardt. He was producing another lavish revue, called *Von Mund Zu Mund (From Mouth To Mouth)*, and only a few days before it was due to open his mistress of ceremonies, Erika Glässner, had suddenly fallen ill (it was Erika Glässner who had been thrown off a roof by Emil Jannings in *Tragedy Of Love*). Would Marlene take her place?

Marlene didn't much like Charell, referring to him late in her life as a horribly flamboyant and extremely promiscuous homosexual, but the opportunity was too good to miss. The show was to be divided into two halves, with four scenes in each. In the first half, five children, played by five stars of theatre and cabaret, are in the Garden of Eden, fantasizing about Things to Come. In the second half the same five, now grown up, meet in Marienbad to review how the world has gone since the Fall. There was also, of course, a chorus of beautiful showgirls.

The book for the show was provided by humourist Hans Riemann, and its songs came from a variety of composers, including Jerome Kern, Irving Caesar, Rudolf Friml and Friedrich Holländer (the young cabaret composer who had written songs for Valetti and whose uncle Fritz had brought Marlene into the Reinhardt organization).

Marlene herself, as well as acting as compere, was to sing three songs. This she approached with some misgivings, since she hadn't paid much attention for a while to developing her singing. But during the brief time she had for rehearsal she was coached by the show's musical director, composer Herman Darewski, which helped allay her nervousness. For the rest of her performance she was coached by Charell himself, who decided that she should be dressed to resemble the famous French performer, Gaby Deslys. Accordingly he had her costumed in a buttercup-yellow dress with a long train (and a slit in the side to show off her glamorous legs) and trimmed around the neck with a ring of artificial pink roses. He also fitted her out with what she remembered as 'the most ridiculous lampshade head-dress imaginable'.

Ridiculous or not, the head-dress did not prevent her from making a considerable sensation. At her own suggestion she stood perfectly still to sing her songs, barely acknowledging the sumptuous staging behind her or the vast audience in front. As the rest of the show was lively and fast-moving, the contrast made her stand out all the more. On opening night the second of her songs even earned her a standing ovation. She was fast refining her style, and another element of the patent Dietrich image was emerging.

Among the cast of *From Mouth To Mouth* was one of Berlin's favourite cabaret entertainers, Claire Waldoff. A short, stocky, square-faced woman with bright red hair, then forty-two, her stage persona was that of a rasping-voiced comic provincial and outrageous lesbian. As was her private persona. When she first saw Marlene it was reported she exclaimed, 'How bee-oo-tee-ful the child is!', a remark that became a Berlin catchphrase for a season.

Waldoff was fearless as a comedienne. Recently she had run into heavy criticism from the conservative press for singing a number called 'Willy, Don't Talk So Much', which poked fun at the deposed Kaiser (in the Thirties she tried a similar trick in a comedy routine mocking 'Herman' – this did not go down well with Goering and soon led to her losing her life).

For the brief duration of *From Mouth To Mouth* she and Marlene were lovers and Marlene became quite besotted with her. After the show they would often dine together (sometimes with Rudi in tow) at such places as the Eldorado Club, and in the small hours of the morning could be heard singing together along the Kurfürstendamm. And Marlene learned a few things about singing from Claire – she learned how effective it could be to be wittily outrageous in a song, mocking both her audience and herself. She began to learn how to dominate audiences instead of simply appearing before them, and she learned the trick of suddenly dropping her voice half an octave at certain points in her songs, a trick she would continue to use all her life.

While still appearing in the show she had parts in several films. *Kopf Hoch, Charly! (Chin Up, Charly!)* was a comedy about the changing sexual attitudes of the Twenties. The film was produced by its star, Ellen Richter, and directed by her husband, Dr Willi Wolff, and yet again Marlene was cast as a Frenchwoman (even in Germany there seemed something about her that was exotic). Again she played a *garçonne* and again she found herself wearing a monocle.

Chin Up, Charly! was not very subtle (or very successful), but her performance impressed Dr Wolff enough for him to offer her the female lead in his next film (in which his wife was not to appear), starring opposite the actor Reinhold Schünzel. He would have first billing, she would have second.

The film, set in the present day (although based on an operetta) was entitled *Der Juxbaron (The Bogus Baron)*, and it told of how the young Sophie (Marlene), abetted by her parents, sets her sights on trapping the rich but crass Baron von Kimmel into marriage. Unfortunately for her he is smart enough to skip out before she arrives at his castle and a passing tramp (Schünzel) is hired to impersonate him. The rest of the film of course tells how romance eventually blossoms between herself and the tramp.

Although the film was tosh, Marlene delivered her best performance to date. Playing a good-natured but empty-headed girl of the Twenties, again she wears a monocle. She also smokes cigarettes, drives recklessly, wears short skirts to show off her legs, and is totally charming and amusing (if still a trifle overweight compared to her later image). But again the film as a whole was dismissed by critics and public as a trifle, and her performance did little to help her career.

Meanwhile, Rudi's film career had suffered a setback when Alexander Korda, at the end of 1926, had decided to go with the flow and hit the road to Hollywood. He did manage to get another job almost at once, but it was as assistant to a much poorer film-maker.

This was Harry Piel, self-billed as 'the Douglas Fairbanks of Germany'. Whatever else can be said about Piel, he was both popular (although his films do not play well today) and prolific – by the time Rudi joined him he had made over fifty films, and he would go on to make over a hundred. He both starred in his films and directed them, and like the films of Fairbanks, they tended to be swashbuckling comic adventures, with romantic plots and plenty of acrobatic stunts.

No sooner was Rudi working for him than he managed to get Marlene a role in one of them. It was called *Sein Grösster Bluff (His Biggest Bluff)*, a farce about jewel-robbers, in which Piel played identical twins (giving many opportunities for risible misunderstandings) and Marlene, in a relatively minor role, played a French (again) woman of easy virtue with an extensive wardrobe and a mania for jewellery.

Unfortunately, in such a riotous setting, she rather lost her bearings, and played her role all out for broad comedy (in spite of gradually learning assurance in her playing, she was still not quite sure about what played well for her and what didn't). By now, however, she was seen by her fellow-performers as a total professional – always punctual and always well-prepared. She would remain so all her life, and by now had also developed a habit she would also retain – that of generosity with little gifts, giving cakes or trinkets to colleagues in celebration of birthdays or anniversaries. This was another way of pleasing people while contriving to stay detached.

His Biggest Bluff was to be the last time she and Rudi would work on the same production. He hadn't proved to be as able to help her in her career as she might have hoped. Fortunately, however, with her increasingly high profile on the Berlin scene, there were other avenues open to her. One was Betty Stern.

Betty Stern was starstruck. She loved celebrities of the performing world, or those who she felt were about to become celebrities. The wife of a buyer for a textile firm, she devoted her life to knowing and encouraging them, holding court in the modest two-room apartment on Barbarosse Strasse where she lived with her husband and their young daughter, and where she kept in a glass case a costume that had been worn by Elisabeth Bergner. She loved bringing together people she thought were on their way up, sharing their ambitions and fears and secrets, and bringing journalists to meet them. She became so successful a hostess that it was said that if you weren't invited to Betty Stern's you'd never make it in Berlin.

Marlene was of course invited. In fact she became one of Betty Stern's very favourites. And it was at Betty Stern's apartment that she met the Viennese actor Willi Forst. He was a handsome matinée idol who embodied the very essence of Viennese sophistication, and Marlene fell for him.

He had been in Berlin, appearing to great acclaim in Rudolf Nelson revues, but when she met him was shortly to return home, lured back to Vienna to appear in a film, *Café Electric*. They embarked on a passionate affair, and Marlene decided that if he was going back to Vienna then she would go there too. *From Mouth To Mouth* had by then finished its run, and Vienna had a flourishing theatre world where she might find work. This would mean leaving Rudi and their daughter Heidede, but Heidede was by now two-and-a-half and had plenty of relatives to take care of her, among them her grandmother Josephine, her aunt Elisabeth, and her great-aunt Jolly.

Marlene did find work in Vienna, in an intimate revue called *Three's Company*, whose star was the popular comedian Max Brod. That had a short run, after which she started rehearsing for a German version of the American musical *Broadway*, originally written by George Abbott and Philip Dunning, which had been a major hit on Broadway. Its setting was a jazz-age world of gangsters, speakeasies, bootleggers and vaudeville, and Marlene played Ruby, one of the six lightly clad chorus-girls. Although there was no dancing in the show, she made sure that her skirt was always a couple of inches shorter than anyone else's, showing off the only glamorous asset (or assets) she felt entirely sure of.

The show opened at the Kammerspiele Theater on 20 September 1927, and another point of interest in the production was that a waiter in it was played by a young Hungarian actor who had changed his name from Laszlo Loewenstein to Peter Lorre.

During the run of *Broadway* Marlene's performance was seen by Dr Robert Klein, newly appointed as artistic director of the Reinhardt theatres. He had come specially from Berlin to Vienna to see the show – not to see Marlene but to appraise the young actress who was playing the part of the ingenue, Billie. Once he had seen enough of Billie to decide that he wasn't interested, he was about to leave the theatre when Marlene caught his eye. Finding something fascinating about her, he stayed for the rest of the performance and, after it was over, went backstage and offered her a three-year contract with Reinhardt in Berlin. She didn't sign immediately, unsure if this might not be some elaborate come-on, but agreed to consider his offer.

Café Electric, now well into pre-production, was being produced by the only major film-company Austria had. It was called Sascha-Film, and was headed by the rich and flamboyant Count Alexander Joseph Kolowrat-Krakowsky, or 'Count Kilowatt' as he was known to his admirers. An enormous man, weighing over 160kg (25 stone) and the owner of palaces in Vienna and Prague (as well as several small castles elsewhere), he was devoted to building up an Austrian film industry to rival Germany's.

Count Kilowatt had been to *Three's Company*, had seen Marlene, and had been deeply smitten by her. And the executive producer of *Café Electric* had been to the first night of *Broadway*, and had also been impressed (although not as impressed as Count Kilowatt). So when Willi Forst arrived to begin work on *Café Electric* and demanded she be given a screen test, he received no opposition (it helped too that, like *Broadway*, *Café Electric* had an underworld setting – a world of pimps and prostitutes).

Marlene was nervous about her screen test, fearing at this time that she looked better on stage than she did on the screen, and indeed the first test she made for Sascha-Film was not especially good. But Forst agreed to appear with her in a second one, this time playing a love scene. Given their passionate involvement, it is perhaps not surprising that this did the trick.

She was given the role of Erni, the well-behaved daughter of a businessman, who turns bad after being seduced by Ferdl, a young pimp (played by Willi Forst). This strand of the plot counterpointed another in which the love of a young man for a bad girl transforms her to goodness, and this young man was played by a handsome Bavarian actor called Igo Sym, who would have a curious influence on Marlene's performing life.

Among the first of many homosexual men to be charmed by Marlene, he was also a musician, and during lulls in the filming he expressed his admiration by teaching her to play the musical saw. This instrument is shaped like a conventional saw, but toothless, and it is played by grasping the handle between the seated thighs, holding the blade upright and playing it with a bow, like a cello. The pitch of the note is varied by bending the blade, and the sound produced is ringing and ethereal.

She would go on playing this unlikely instrument from time to time during her live shows for years, performing on it with the solemnity of a concert violinist. The effect this produced was complex – the contrast between her high glamour and the somewhat ludicrous instrument was comical, but this was offset by her solemn concentration and by the sexual overtones of her gripping what appeared to be a simple tool from a carpenter's shop between the most glamorous legs in show business.

She made no secret of her affair with Willi Forst. News of it reached Berlin, and during the filming her husband Rudi made a special trip to Vienna to demand that she end it. Which of course made her more determined than ever to continue it. In her early life she had had enough of submitting to the wishes of others, and had now grown enough in confidence never to do so again, except in the necessary case of stage and film directors (although at the end of her life she claimed never to have enjoyed obeying them, saying that she always thought of directors as her 'dictators'). Rudi had to content himself with pointing out that he too had an affair ready and waiting, if he chose to take it up. This was with the dancer Tamara Matul.

Marlene cheerfully told him to go right ahead. As she said a little while later, 'I haven't a strong sense of possession towards a man, perhaps because I am not particularly feminine in my reactions.'

Rudi returned to Berlin, and did begin a relationship with Tamara. It was more than just an affair, and would continue for decades. Tamara became his constant companion, and even acted as a sort of substitute mother to Heidede during Marlene's frequent absences. Over the next few years, whenever Marlene was in Berlin, she would spend some of her nights with Rudi (although they rarely made love), but after 1930 she ceased to do even that, although she never divorced him. She was not about to be owned by anybody, and having a living husband somewhere in the world was useful for keeping lovers from becoming too serious. Also she was fond of Rudi, as she would be fond of all her lovers, and reluctant to let them go completely.

Café Electric turned out to be an ill-starred venture. For a start the film itself was nothing exceptional. Although it contained many shots of Marlene's legs as she danced the charleston (in the low-down Café Electric) or stretched out in Willi Forst's bed, she mainly acted in the over-energetic mode she would soon learn to abandon.

Worse, however, for hopes of the production company, Sascha-Film, was that during the shooting of *Café Electric* Count Kilowatt fell seriously ill. He was diagnosed with leukemia. His weight dropped rapidly from 160 to 35kg (25 to 5½ stone) and, although he lived to see a print of the film projected in his hospital room, he died in December 1927, shortly after it opened.

There was a story that on seeing Marlene's legs in the film he expressed a dying wish that she come and visit him so that he could once more see them in the flesh. Which, according to the story, she did, quickly raising her skirt by his bedside and then leaving. Whether or not this harmless story is true will never be known. Marlene late in her life dismissed it as rubbish (but she would, wouldn't she?) and Willi Forst denied it, pointing out that the dying count wanted no-one to see him in his sad emaciated state. But the young Marlene, with her free sexual attitudes, was undoubtedly capable of such a generous act.

After the film was shot, Marlene was begged by Willi to stay on a bit longer in Vienna, so she got herself a small role in the play *Die Schule Von Unzach (The School Of Unzach)*. This was another satire on high society and was written by Germany's leading comic dramatist, Carl Sternheim. It opened towards the end of November 1927 at the small but elegant Theater in der Josefstadt (one of Max Reinhardt's theatres). Marlene played an up-to-the-minute young miss attending a progressive school, and she played the part well. Reviewer Felix Salten (who would go on to write *Bambi*) said, 'Among the girls Marlene Dietrich expressed most honestly what the type should be: a beautiful, sensual, unthinking young chatterbox.'

The School Of Unzach alternated at the theatre with another play, a version of the runaway (and notoriously dreadful) Broadway success *Abie's Irish Rose*. This gave Marlene a certain amount of time to herself. Some of this time she spent in the company of a twenty-one-year-old stage director who in time would also go to Hollywood and make a reputation there – his name was Otto Preminger. Whether or not she had an affair with him is not clear, but he was sufficiently taken by her to try and persuade her to remain in Vienna, and to take her to meet his family. He also tried to get her work, but his producers thought she had limited talent and no real future.

She continued in *The School Of Unzach* through Christmas 1927 (and her birthday on 28 December) and, tearing herself away from Willi, returned to Berlin early in 1928, bearing an armful of belated Christmas (and birthday) presents for Heidede, who had just turned three.

For two weeks she devoted herself to the child, throwing herself heart and soul into the role of mother. Then, on 9 March, she began rehearsals for the

Berlin production of *Broadway*, presented by Viktor Barnowsky. The cast for this was almost completely different from the one she had been part of in Vienna. Apart from her, the only actor to appear in both productions was Harald Paulsen, who played a slow-witted vaudeville dancer called Roy. (In a year's time he would rise to fame by originating the role of Mack the Knife in *The Threepenny Opera*.)

Paulsen was to play Roy in both Vienna and Berlin, but in Berlin Marlene hoped to change her role. Even in Vienna she had wanted to play Billie, the innocent ingenue, which was a bigger and more rewarding part, and to try and land this she got Rudi's friend Rudolf Forster to have a word with Barnowsky. Barnowsky thought about it, and for a moment hesitated, but eventually decided, as the Viennese producer had done, that she was best suited to play the wisecracking chorus-girl Ruby.

Marlene was disappointed by this, but set herself to shine in the part she did have. She had put on a little weight while in Vienna (she adored Viennese pastries and gâteaux), and embarked on a strenuous course of exercises to reduce. The course she took before and during the run of *Broadway*, a course which even included boxing lessons, was from a famous and somewhat ruthless Berlin instructor, Sabri Mahir, known as 'the Terrible Turk'. In fact he was from Cologne and his real name was Sally Mayer, but he certainly knew his stuff. Among his clients were successful bankers and businesssmen, and as actress Elisabeth Lennart, also a chorus-girl in *Broadway* and a fellow-client with Marlene, remembered: 'What he could do to a body! [Marlene and I] were his most faithful followers. He was insane and took no care of our nerves. But he knew what a body *was*.'

Unfortunately, while exercising too vigorously, at one time Marlene cracked a bone in her arm. Like a true trouper she said nothing about it and went on stage anyway. As Elisabeth Lennartz recalled, Marlene draped her arm 'very elegantly in a chiffon shawl. This looked fantastic, and only later did she mention her extreme pain. We hadn't known anything.' (This would turn out to be the first of many fractures in her long career. The dietary deprivations of her wartime childhood, especially a shortage of milk, had left her with permanently weakened bones.)

One of the exercises she did was lying down and bicycling her legs in the air, and this routine found its way into *Broadway*. Positioned close to the front of the stage, she gave her bicycling all she had, and it turned into a major piece of scene-stealing. As the Reinhardt actress Käthe Haack recalled, she 'acted very close to the audience, right at the front of the stage. She was very, very sexy. She was lying on the floor and sort of bicycled with her breathtakingly beautiful legs...we all talked...*every*body talked...Marlene's name had already become a byword for sexiness, for beauty.'

Her piece of scene-stealing paid off. It so happened that Dr Robert Klein, who had offered her the three-year Reinhardt contract, was preparing an intimate revue, to be called *Es Liegt In Der Luft (It's In The Air)* and he had a problem. As he recalled, 'There wasn't enough sex appeal on the stage and I remembered Marlene. We called her and I asked if she had any special talents that might be used in a revue. She said she could play the violin and the saw. I had never heard anyone play the saw and I asked her to display this art for us [the] next day... She took her legs apart, put the saw in between and played.' He hired her.

The revue, scheduled to open at the Komödie Theater in June 1928, was a somewhat surreal piece set in a big department store. Some children, visiting the store with their parents, get lost in it, and grow up in it, raised by the store's employees among the ghosts of people who have died there. As they age, they find themselves mindlessly happy in a consumer paradise. They themselves marry and have children, and when their parents find their way back, after years, they mistake their grandchildren for the original children.

The show was divided into twenty-four scenes, and Marlene, as one of the three stars of the show, appeared in seven of them. Her two co-stars were Margo Lion and Oskar Karlweis, and also in the cast were Hubsie von Meyerinck and the black American tap-dancer Louis Douglas, who had come to Europe in the show that electrified Paris (and Berlin) in 1925, *La Revue Nègre*, featuring Joséphine Baker.

There was also a line of ten chorus-girls (one of whom was Tamara Matul) and a jazz band, and the show featured (on record) the voice of the popular American singer Whispering Jack Smith. Now unjustly forgotten, Jack Smith was one of the very first crooners, using the newly invented microphone to sing in a subtle, quiet, slightly hoarse voice (some said he got this voice from being gassed in the war). Marlene adored his singing all her life, and some of the quality of his delivery passed into hers.

As did the delivery of her co-star, Margo Lion. The show had basically been written for Margo Lion, by her husband Marcellus Schiffer. He was not interested in women (as she was not really interested in men) and he was an extraordinary character even by the standards of Twenties Berlin. A goth before there were goths, he painted his face dead white. He was a cocaine addict, who would soon commit suicide, and had recently achieved notoriety by publishing a book of 'immoral and unsavoury' fairy tales. An image in it of two nuns ascending to heaven with crucifixes between their legs had been regarded as particularly scandalous.

Margo Lion herself was French. Tall, slender and boyish, she spoke perfect German and was at the time extremely popular. Her husband Marcellus wrote a song for the show to specially feature her and Marlene in duet. It was called 'Wenn Die Beste Freundin' and was a wicked parody of the then-fashionable sort of friendly girls' duet sung by performers such as The Dolly Sisters. It was all about two girls, who escaped from their boyfriends and bought lingerie together for themselves and each other. The lesbian undertones were clear from the start, but after the show was a week or so old, Marlene emphasised them further by pinning bunches of violets on each of their chic outfits.

Her excuse was that the outfits were too dark and needed a dash of colour, but to those in the know bunches of violets were a lesbian symbol. This had begun with the popular German poet Stefan Georg, who had established the colour lavender as a symbol of homosexual love. This symbol had been emphasised further when, in 1925, the French dramatist Edouard Bourdet wrote a play *La Prisonnière*, in which bunches of violets were an explicit lesbian signal. When the play opened on Broadway the next year, under the title *The Captive*, it was vigorously attacked by guardians of public morals, and the ensuing publicity caused sales of violets in New York to plummet.

Wearing their violets, and singing their song, Marlene and Margo strolled hand-in-hand across the stage, giving an impression of dazed infatuation for each other. They were an enormous success. Margo sang in a high falsetto, Marlene used her laid-back smoky lower register, and their two voices complemented each other perfectly (the suggestion that Marlene use her lower register came from the show's composer, Mischa Spolianski). Towards the end of the song their two voices were joined by that of Oskar Karlweis, enlarging on the pleasure to be gained from watching beautiful women buy enticing underwear.

The song would be Berlin's greatest hit until 'Mack The Knife' arrived later in the year, and it led Marlene into the world of professional recording (she had made a private recording a couple of years earlier of her duet with Claire Waldoff). In June 1928 she went into the Telefunken studios with other members of the cast and, as members of the show's chorus, they recorded a medley of songs from *It's In The Air*, covering two sides of a 78rpm record.

They were accompanied by the band from the show, led by Mischa Spolianski, and a few days later Marlene went back to the studios with Margo and with Oskar Karlweis, and recorded 'Wenn Die Beste Freundin', this time accompanied only by Spolianski at the piano. The record became a great hit.

Marlene had another good song in the show. It was called 'Kleptomaniacs', and in duet with Hubsie von Meyerinck she sang of the health-enhancing benefits of shoplifting. It even included the line 'We do it for sexual kicks'. She was now finding her way, and *It's In The Air* allowed her to give her most successful performance so far. One of Berlin's leading dramatic critics, Herbert Ihering, after referring to her 'delicate carriage and weary elegance' wrote, 'This was perfection: an event.'

A person who was stunned by her performance, but in a rather unexpected way, was Professor Max Reinhardt. He was taken to see *It's In The Air* by his friend and long-time colleague, Dr Karl Vollmöller (author of Reinhardt's nun-laden and world-wide success, *The Miracle*). Dr Vollmöller who had a keen eye for beautiful up-and-coming actresses, had noticed Marlene, and wanted Reinhardt to see her. Reinhardt was bowled over by her beauty, elegance and sexy wit, almost to the point of infatuation, and it gave Dr Vollmöller a wicked pleasure to let him know that the sensual creature showing her legs up there, singing depraved songs and playing the musical saw, was not only a contracted Reinhardt actress but had been working for him on and off for some five years.

As a result of her success, in the summer of 1928 Marlene found herself playing a courtesan (again French, and this time called Chicotte) in a romantic film comedy called *Prinzessin Olala (Princess Olala)*. It was directed by the UFA writer and director Robert Land, and although Marlene had the title role ('Princess Olala' being Chicotte's *nom de guerre*), its stars were Walter Rilla, who played a prince, and Carmen Boni. Much of the plot tells of how they are innocents in the art of love and are instructed by Chicotte, who knows all about it.

Although the piece was based on an operetta, it had a present-day setting, and Marlene wore the fashionable bobbed hair and short skirts of the Twenties. She gave a good performance, mixing seductiveness and self-mockery, and many people commented on her increasing resemblance on screen to Greta Garbo, who by 1928 was almost the biggest star in the world.

Marlene adored Garbo, virtually to the point of hero-worship. She had by this time seen her in three films (*The Saga Of Gösta Berling*, *The Torrent* and *The Temptress*) and the growing resemblance between them was by no means accidental. Marlene had observed that they shared similar colouring, and that both were effective at being aloof (although her aloofness was more mocking than Garbo's).

At the time *Princess Olala* was released there was a well-publicised search on to find a star to appear as the heroine, Lulu, in a film of Wedekind's famous play *Pandora's Box*. Several reviewers, after seeing Marlene's performance as Chicotte, suggested that she might be ideal for the role, and indeed the director (Pabst again) did seriously consider her.

He knew who he really wanted for the role – the dark-haired, vivacious, sexually aware American actress Louise Brooks, whom he had seen in the Howard Hawks film *A Girl In Every Port*. She was only twenty-two, while Marlene was twenty-six, and there was an innocence and vulnerability in her that Marlene lacked. But Pabst had tried to hire Louise from her studio, Paramount, and had had no response.

Reluctantly, he decided that probably Marlene was the best available, and had a contract drawn up for her to sign. But before she could, he heard from Louise that she was prepared to abandon her Paramount contract and would be available after all.

This was a blow for Marlene. Lulu was an exceptionally good role in an exceptionally good piece. But from Pabst's point of view his decision was obviously the right one. As he said himself at the time (according to Louise's later recollection), 'Marlene was too old and too obvious – one sexy look from her and the film would become a burlesque.'

Having lost out on *Pandora's Box* she went back to the theatre – to Reinhardt's Komödie Theater – to play Hypatia Tarleton in a translation of Bernard Shaw's play *Misalliance*, retitled *Eltern Und Kinder (Parents And Children)*. It was directed by Heinz Hilpert, and Marlene's part was well suited to her, because Hypatia is described by Shaw as having 'movements that flash out of a waiting stillness, boundless energy and audacity held in leash'.

She played the part with little movement and with quiet authority. As her co-star in the piece, Lily Darvas, said she 'had a quite rare ability, the ability to stand completely motionless on stage and still draw the audience's attention to her... Marlene simply placed herself on the platform and smoked a cigarette – very slow and sexy – and the audience forgot there were other actors there. Her pose was so natural, there was so much melody in her voice, her gestures were so sparing, that she fascinated the audience as if she were a painting by Modigliani... She possessed the most important quality for a star: she could be great without doing anything at all.'

It also helped that she had great legs to draw the audience's eyes to her. Even in Shaw she wore extremely short skirts, leading one reviewer to report that she had 'a way of sitting that one certainly cannot characterise as discreet. If she showed less it would still be enough.'

Although she was growing in assurance in her performances, and was having increasing success, she was still not achieving the grand success she yearned for, and continued to be subject to fits of depression. During these moods she was given to saying things like, 'Nothing's ever going to happen to me. No-one wants to know about me, not in Vienna and not now in Berlin.' She would talk darkly (but not entirely convincingly) about giving up performing and finding some other career.

While still playing in *Parents And Children* she got another film role from director Robert Land. It was called *Ich Küsse Ihre Hand, Madame (I Kiss Your Hand, Madame)*, and in it she was to co-star with the extremely handsome and likeable Harry Liedtke, who had been the star of her very first film, *The Little Napoleon*. She was to play a society woman who has just got divorced and falls for a man (Harry Liedtke) whom she takes to be a Russian nobleman. He turns out to be a head waiter – but later on it is revealed that as well as being a head waiter he is also an exiled Russian nobleman.

Again she got good reviews; a typical one, in the *Hamburger Anzeiger*, said, 'And now we come to what makes the film finally so indisputably piquant. It presents... A medium-blonde woman, with somewhat tired eyelids and a beautifully feminine mouth: Marlene Dietrich. She is, in short, the "Madame" whose hand is kissed. Her performance is not bad... To have to be erotic and yet have style, to have to be "Madame" and yet be able to run off with other men: this is a new type of woman, if you believe Robert Land.'

In this film for the first time her thinning face shows those hollows under the cheekbones that would be so much a part of her eventual image, but there was another first in it that was to prove of even more importance – it had sound. Not the sound of Marlene's voice, nor sound all the way through, but sound nonetheless.

Talkies, the biggest single revolution in the history of the cinema, had appeared on the American scene towards the end of 1927, with Al Jolson's performance in *The Jazz Singer*. It was immediately obvious to everyone in the industry (and in the audiences) that talkies would be the way of the future. Production companies were reluctant to invest the considerable sums necessary to convert shooting-stages, cutting-rooms and cinemas to the new process, but gradually, from 1928 onwards, the changeover began all over the world.

Even partial sound attracted audiences, and *I Kiss Your Hand, Madame* was Germany's first film to have any sound at all. Which wasn't much – it simply had a title song, which was mimed by Harry Liedtke to the voice of the great tenor Richard Tauber. To publicise the film Marlene was photographed with Tauber for the front cover of the new magazine *Film Und Ton (Film And Sound)*. Rumours went around at the time that she and Tauber were lovers.

Silent films continued to be made for a while, and after spending the Christmas of 1928 with Rudi and Heidede, Marlene found herself immediately filming another. Called *Die Frau, Nach Der Man Sich Sehnt (The Woman One Longs For)*, it was adapted (considerably) from a novel by the Czech writer Max Brod (best known as Franz Kafka's executor), and was directed by the twenty-nine-year-old Kurt Bernhardt.

Marlene was to be its female star, although Bernhardt had a hard time convincing his company, Terra Films, that she was established enough. They claimed nobody had ever heard of her.

Bernhardt won, however, and she was cast, to co-star with Fritz Kortner (an actor she had worked with several times on stage). The film tells of how Stascha (Marlene) has a lover, Dr Karoff (Kortner), who murders her husband. They flee together to a luxurious resort on the Riviera. But on the train taking them there they encounter a young man, Henri, en route for his honeymoon with a wealthy woman he has just married (Henri was played by a Danish actor, Uno Henning, who closely resembled Gary Cooper).

Henri falls madly in love with Stascha on sight, abandons his bride and begins to pursue her at the resort. Eventually the complications of the plot, and Sascha's intriguing, lead to Dr Karoff shooting her stone dead.

Marlene gave an assured performance, and the first that embodies much of her later famous image and mystique. She is cool, mocking and manipulative, and extremely beautiful. This beauty was partly due to experiments she had been making with lighting. On her own initiative she went into a Berlin photo booth and discovered that a dominant overhead light defined her cheekbones, darkened her pale blue eyes, and straightened a nose whose slight upturn at the end (like Gloria Swanson's) had always disconcerted her.

She insisted on this style of lighting during the filming, and became so obsessed by it that she irritated both her co-star and her director. As Bernhardt later wrote, 'She drove Kortner crazy (although he would have loved to go to bed with her). She never moved her head from the spotlight over the camera, facing forward and refusing to move her head to speak with other actors – she simply looked at them out of the corner of her eye. I wanted her to turn to Kortner, to be natural with him, but she wouldn't do it. She was completely aware of the lighting and how it hit her nose. Marlene looked fantastic, but as an actress she was the punishment of God.'

She was also trouble in another way. Immersing herself in her manipulative role in the film, she became manipulative herself, using Kortner's infatuation for her to fuel disagreements between him and Bernhardt, disagreements which gave her an edge over both.

In spite of all this (or maybe because of it) her performance in the film was outstanding. For almost the only time in her life she got to play the sort of tragic role she craved, and playing it she learned how to appear enigmatic instead of simply detached and aloof.

While she was filming it, her theatrical life took another turn. Dr Robert Klein, who had cast her in *It's In The Air*, decided he would like to break from the Reinhardt organization and produce plays for himself. Marlene heard about this and wrote him a letter saying that she would rather work under his management than stay with Reinhardt. Dr Klein was agreeable, and that evening they met in a *chambre séparée* in the famous Restaurant Horcher, where she signed a new three-year contract with him.

At around the same time, but not for Dr Klein, she appeared on stage in a one-night-only production of Wedekind's *Der Marquis Von Keith*, presented by Leopold Jessner (who had directed *Duel On The Lido*) as a tribute to the recently deceased theatrical giant, Albert Steinrück. It was a star-studded occasion, both on stage and off, and a mark of how Marlene's star was now rising (even if Terra Films hadn't heard of her).

She was rising so fast, in fact, that a film was being prepared especially to star her. It was to be called *Das Schiff Der Verlorenen Menschen (The Ship Of Lost Men)*, and it would be directed by the great pioneer director, Maurice Tourneur, who began making films as far back as 1912. He started his career in Paris, and had a lengthy and successful career in Hollywood before falling out with his studio (MGM) when they insisted he not only have a producer on his 1927 film *The Mysterious Island*, but actually pay attention to what that producer said. This would soon become the standard pattern of film-making, but it was anathema to an old individualist like Tourneur. He quit and came to Berlin.

Again a silent film, *The Ship Of Lost Men* was an attempt to attract the international market, using the one great advantage that silent films had over talkies – the ability to play anywhere in the world without language problems (title-cards were relatively simple to change). Its plot, however, was considerably dodgy. With an all-male cast (apart from Marlene), it was set on an outlaw ship, filled with sexually frustrated sailors and doomed to sail endlessly from port to port under its depraved captain (again Fritz Kortner).

Marlene was cast as an American aviatrix (a deeply fashionable role in the Twenties and Thirties) who crashes into the sea near the ship while attempting to fly solo across the Atlantic (Lindbergh had made his wildly popular first solo crossing in 1927), and, when she is taken aboard, arouses lust and dissension among the crew. At first she is taken by them to be a man (because of her flying-suit), but once her sex is discovered she has a narrow escape from being gang-raped.

Unfortunately the film had more visual imagery than plot. Tourneur had, after all, begun his career as a painter, and he insisted on endless expensive detail. Marlene's leather flying-suit was a real one, found in London, that had been actually worn. Beer mugs for a waterfront bar scene were sought from actual dives in Hamburg. A real sailing ship, built in 1856 to sail from Brazil to Chile round Cape Horn, was bought, and when it proved impractical to film on was reproduced with meticulous exactness in a studio.

The whole thing took four months to shoot and cost 600,000 marks, an astronomical sum for a 1929 silent movie. All in all it was an unsatisfactory experience for Marlene, who got on even less well with Fritz Kortner than she had on *The Woman One Longs For*. She spent most of her between-scenes time socializing with a British actor, Robert Irvine, who was playing the one likeable character on the ship, a young doctor who has been shanghaied.

Her next film, *Gefahren Der Brautzeit (Dangers Of The Engagement Period)* was another turkey, although again it was an attempt to create a film deliberately to feature her. Its poorness is hinted at by the fact that it was one of those films that was given a succession of titles before the final one was settled on (which is never a good sign). In turn it had previously been called *One Night Of Love*, *From The Diary Of A Seducer*, *Love Letter* and *Night Of Love*, and it seems quite clear that Marlene made it only because it offered her a chance to co-star with her lover, Willi Forst, who was back in Berlin from Vienna.

It was made in the summer of 1929, and mainly tells of how the lecherous Forst, travelling to the home of a friend, falls in with and seduces Marlene, unaware that she is the fiancée of that very friend. When, at the friend's house, this all eventually comes out, Forst is shot by the friend. Dying, he redeems himself somewhat by considerately arranging to make his death appear a suicide. Marlene faints. The End.

The whole piece has a distinctly debauched feel, and there is even a scene in it where Marlene and Willi appear to be masturbating each other under the table they are sitting at. Marlene, late in her life, claimed this scene was added later and filmed, without her knowledge, by stand-ins.

After her part in the filming finished she took Heidede, now four-and-a-half, for a short holiday on the island of Sylt, up in the North Sea alongside the border between Germany and Denmark. It would be the last holiday she and her daughter would have together for a considerable time.

Also in the summer of 1929 (possibly just before her holiday with Heidede), she took the step, unusual at the time, of undergoing slight cosmetic surgery to correct the tip-tilted nose that had always bothered her. It wasn't quite a large enough alteration to be called a nose job, but at least her nose would now be straighter, and easier to light.

She also attended the première of *The Ship Of Lost Men*, presented at the UFA Pavillon in Berlin. There she and Fritz Kortner suffered the mortification of being booed off the stage by the disappointed audience.

Fortunately, there was more theatre work for her, as Dr Robert Klein was putting together a new musical called *Zwei Krawatten (Two Bow Ties)* at the Berliner Theater. This would be her first performance for him under her new three-year contract, and she would have a leading role (although, for some reason, in her memoirs she claims to have had only one line in it). Another headliner in it would be her old friend and mentor, the cabaret star Rosa Valetti.

Marlene played Mabel, a rich American jazz baby visiting Germany. Mabel meets a waiter, played by Hans Albers, who, after winning a lottery, dons white tie and tails and passes himself off as a gentleman. They sail to America on a luxury liner and, following a shipboard romance, she decides she is in love with him. They visit the exotic and gangster-filled city of Chicago, then go on to Miami, where they get engaged. But eventually he decides to leave her and return to a fiancée he already had in Germany, whereupon he discovers that the fiancée has become an heiress and now has more millions than Mabel.

Marlene was to appear in virtually every scene, and sing several songs, and the whole production around her was to be lavish, with fifty charlestoning chorus-girls and a lively jazzy score. The book and lyrics had been written by the highly successful Expressionist playwright Georg Kaiser, and the music was again by Marlene's old acquaintance, Mischa Spolianski, who had composed the score for *It's In The Air*. An expensive production, *Two Bow Ties* was for a while the hottest show in Berlin, knocked off the top only by the famous *Threepenny Opera*, which opened a few months later.

It opened on 1 September 1929, and Marlene played her role well, shifting easily from flirtatiousness to world-weariness to cynicism. It was perhaps fortunate for her that she had such a showpiece to appear in, because, during the first week of its run, an American film director, brought to Berlin to show UFA how sound films should be made (by making one), came to see it. His name was Josef von Sternberg.

4 The Blue Angel

Von Sternberg was a film director of enormous imagination and style, and he would have more influence on Marlene's career than anyone else she ever met. For the rest of her life she would always praise him for bringing her career to life.

Although in 1929 he came to Berlin from Hollywood, he was actually born in Vienna, in 1894. The first child of his parents, he was given the name Jonas – his real name was Jonas Sternberg (without the 'von').

His childhood was not often happy. Although his father, Moses Sternberg, was a handsome and intelligent man (in his younger days he had written a textbook on simple mathematics), he was a dictatorial Orthodox Jew with Teutonic ideas about discipline. Jonas' mother, whose maiden name was Serafin Singer, had been a circus performer. In spite of his orthodoxy, Moses had gone against his family wishes in marrying her, and as a result he had been financially cut adrift by them.

What made things worse was that he turned out to be an ineffective businessman, so he and Serafin were poor, and Moses, who was strong and pugnacious to begin with, expressed his frustration at life by becoming bad-tempered and brutal.

Much of his aggression was taken out on his eldest child, Jonas, who recalled in his memoirs, 'I was beaten and pounded until I howled like a dog. After each beating, the punishing hand was extended to be kissed, in the noble tradition then prevalent.'

Fortunately, when he was three his father went to America, hoping to earn enough money there to bring his wife and family after him – at that time it consisted of Jonas, a second infant son, and a baby (who would turn out to be a girl) on the way.

With Moses gone, they were left in even worse poverty than before, dependent for their food mainly on the generosity of Serafin's relatives. Jonas, ill-nourished at this vulnerable stage in his life, grew up slightly stunted, reaching an adult height of only 1.63m (5ft 4in) – a couple of centimetres shorter than Marlene.

School, too, proved an ordeal for him, even though he turned out to be extremely bright. He went to a Jewish school at the age of six, and there he was hounded through learning the Hebrew alphabet and language by a bullying master who held his young charges in a state of terror.

Nonetheless, Jonas' infancy was not without its pleasures. There was music in the streets, from calliopes, hurdy-gurdies and music-boxes; there was the nearby Danube, bordered by sweet-smelling trees; there was an amusement park, where there were puppet-shows, shooting-galleries, sword-swallowers, contortionists, midgets, magicians and bearded ladies; and near his home there was a permanent circus, where his mother had once appeared as Snow White in a tableau, and where he could see acrobats, jugglers, clowns and performing animals. All these images would later find their way into his films, as would the uniformed soldiers he saw on the streets, and the ladies of easy virtue.

He attended the Jewish school for only a year. When he was seven his father sent a letter summoning his wife and family to join him in America – without, however, sending either money or tickets. Somehow Serafin contrived to get them there (possibly, Jonas thought later, through money from relatives glad to get rid of them), and they settled in New York City, in an area that was then largely German-speaking.

Their tenement lodgings were poor, and up five flights of stairs, but it did have hot and cold running water, and a bathtub. Young Jonas was handed two large volumes of American history by his father, and told they would be his to keep as soon as he learned English. He soon learned a little, and got to keep the books, although for years his father would take all other books away from him on the grounds that no book would ever help him earn a living.

Life in New York remained hard. Moses earned a living as best he could – one of his jobs was at a Coney Island funfair, controlling the flow of water that propelled boats through the Tunnel of Love. There were epidemics of scarlet fever and chickenpox. Young Jonas was unfortunate enough to catch both at the same time, and for once his father was kind to him, caressing his feverish head tenderly. Maybe this tenderness was a side-effect of his own discouragement, because by the time Jonas was ten his father abandoned trying to make it in America and transported himself and his family back to Vienna.

This was not to be for long, however. Soon he decided to try once more and again left his poverty-stricken family (which by this time had acquired a second daughter and a third son) to go back to the States. Sternberg continued his education, reading the German classics, and learning something of Latin and French, as well as some more English. And when he was fourteen his father sent for his wife and children again, bringing them to live in Long Island. Jonas stayed at school there for only a year (mostly struggling to learn more English), before he was forced to leave and earn enough money to eat properly.

With no clear aim in life, his first jobs were in shops selling millinery and lace (his knowledge of fabrics would also become a prominent feature of his films), but by the age of seventeen he was not of work and homeless – his mother had had enough of his father and left home, and shortly afterwards Sternberg followed suit.

For a while he slept rough and took what odd jobs he could – shovelling snow, driving a team of horses delivering bolts of paper, selling rhinestones door to door – and enlarged his education by sheltering in libraries and museums. He began to develop a deep interest in painting.

Then he met a boy whose father had invented a contraption for cleaning films. He got a job helping with this, and over the months also learned to repair film and to operate a projector. Eventually his employer got the job of maintaining films for an early production centre, the World Film Corporation, which was situated in Fort Lee, New Jersey, and made dozens of films (of various lengths) each year. But he fell out with them (for taking too many kickbacks from his employees), and Sternberg, rather to his surprise, was given the job instead. In time he would graduate to writing silent-film titles, and even to doing a certain amount of re-editing.

Cinema at this time, around 1914, was entering a stage of rapid development, but Sternberg was contemptuous of most of the celluloid that passed through his hands (like many assertive small men, he was fast developing a tendency to arrogance). He was impressed by D W Griffith, however, whose films *The Birth Of A Nation* and *Intolerance* showed him to be 'the first master to use scope and spectacle, and to be in full control of his work'. He admired Chaplin (as a director) for 'his pictorial sobriety and his skill in dealing with the most primitive emotions'.

Very few directors, he thought, 'developed a style distinct enough to classify their work as unique'. But gradually his interest in cinema was growing, and his instinct was to approach it as a genuine art form, in which the director was the artist whose vision was to be expressed. This was a common attitude among the best early directors – not only Griffith and Chaplin (and Maurice Tourneur), but those who came a little later, like the magnificently obsessive Erich von Stroheim (whose aristocratic 'von' was also fake). It was an attitude, however, that became increasingly difficult to sustain in Hollywood by the end of the Twenties, as studios gave increasing authority to supervising producers.

After America entered the Great War in 1917, Sternberg was called up and given the job of making training films for the army signal corps, but his depiction of the horrors of war turned out to be a little too graphic, and he was reassigned to the medical corps. The war ended in November 1918 but, as often happened, he was kept in the service for some months after the Armistice. Eventually he appealed for help to the head of the World Film Corporation, William A Brady, who used his influence to get Sternberg out and re-employed him.

In 1919, while working for the World Film Corporation, he was offered the job of assistant to the Paris-born Emile Chautard on a film called *The Mystery Of The Yellow Room*. Chautard liked to use French-speaking actors and technicians, and everyone spoke French on his set, which was a problem for Sternberg because his French was decidedly on the shaky side. Nonetheless, he learned several things from the kindly Chautard, including the value of inspecting each scene through the camera to make sure that every detail was correct, and appraising the impact of light and shadow.

He assisted several other directors (by now feeling that he knew how to direct better than they did) and in 1921, believing his career was getting nowhere fast (he was now twenty-six), he made his way to Vienna, where he tried to find work, claiming to be already a director. After failing to sell himself in this role, he spent a short time adapting into English a short Austrian novel by Karl Adolph (whom he may have known from his boyhood). It was published as *Daughters Of Vienna*, and he may have written his adaptation as a means of building up his artistic reputation.

He made his way to Britain, and got a job on a film shot on location in Wales, assisting another director he said 'did not know how to direct' (he later claimed that working for such directors helped his confidence, making him feel that directing needed no special skill).

By 1923 he was back in America, in Hollywood, and after being there only a week was lucky enough to get a job assisting director Roy William

Neill on a film called *By Divine Right*. It was on the credits of this that his real name, Jo Sternberg, was expanded into the aristocratic 'Josef von Sternberg'. He always claimed that this was done without his knowledge, but whether that was true or not, he adopted the new name enthusiastically – after all, 'von' implied aristocracy (as well as having echoes of the now-famous von Stroheim), and after all the famous Emperor of Austria was called 'Franz-Josef'.

On the set of the film he had noticed a pretty extra reading a book, and was flattered to see that it was the book he had translated. Her name was Georgia Hale. A little while later he was approached by a Scottish actor, George K Arthur, who had already appeared in several films, notably in the title role of *Kipps* (which was why he was generally known as 'Kipps'). Kipps claimed to have $6000 in the bank, and he wanted to use it to make a film, starring himself, based on a story he had written, and directed by von Sternberg.

Von Sternberg agreed to direct the film, but told Kipps his story was rubbish, and undertook to write a better one himself. This he did, carefully planning one that could be made for the minute budget available (which it turned out didn't exist anyway). In writing the script he made visual use of a dredger he had seen removing mud from San Pedro Harbor in Los Angeles. And as his female star he cast Georgia Hale.

Somehow the film got made (Kipps proving to be a talented hustler who got 16 people to put up about $350 each), and when it was completed Kipps proved an even better hustler by bribing Chaplin's Japanese major-domo, Toraichi Kono, to project it 'by accident' at the nightly film-show in Chaplin's private cinema.

The film was called *The Salvation Hunters* and it was set in the squalid world of the poor and underprivileged. The frequent shots of dredging for mud symbolised futility, and Georgia Hale, as John Baxter says in his book *The Cinema Of Josef Von Sternberg*, was 'brooding and self-destructive...the prototype Sternberg heroine'.

Chaplin was impressed enough by the film to immediately (that same midnight) show it to Douglas Fairbanks, and together they agreed to buy it for $20,000 and distribute it through their company, United Artists. It was early in 1925, and von Sternberg was an overnight sensation at the age of 30. Briefly he was hailed by many in Hollywood as a 'genius'. (Georgia Hale did well out of the film too. Chaplin hired her at once to be the leading lady of his next, and possibly best, film, *The Gold Rush*.)

Chaplin hired von Sternberg at once to make another film, *A Woman Of The Sea* (nothing to do with the famous Ibsen play, *The Lady From The Sea*). It was to star Chaplin's former lover Edna Purviance, who had appeared with him in thirty-five of his films, starting in 1915. Chaplin felt she was beginning to appear old-fashioned (she had a sad romantic beauty that was somewhat out of place in the bright hectic Twenties), and he hoped she might give her career a lift by appearing without him and developing herself into a dramatic actress.

Von Sternberg was delighted, feeling his career was at last taking off, and he enthusiastically began to act the role of film director. Uneasily aware of his short stature, he developed a personality of scornful arrogance. He began wearing jodhpurs and eye-catching headgear (a white cap, a beret, a turban, a sola topee), and to carry an officer's swagger-stick. He practised a cold-eyed stare and cultivated a curious thick down-turned moustache that he conceived of as sinisterly oriental. 'The only way to succeed is to make people hate you,' he once told actor Clive Brook. 'That way they remember you.' (Which may not be the best advice.)

The film did his career no good. Although he had financed it, Chaplin simply screened it, buried it in his vaults, and eventually destroyed it. He did send von Sternberg to direct a film for another of his partners in United Artists, Mary Pickford, but she didn't like his proposals for the script and the project came to nothing.

He was hired by MGM to direct Mae Murray in *The Masked Bride*, but found the plot and setting so tedious that he tilted his camera to the rafters of the ceiling, claiming that they were more interesting than anything he saw on the set. He was dismissed.

Going to Paramount, he did odd directing chores for the studio's head of production, B P Schulberg – he reshot some scenes for *It*, the film that gave the studio's popular sexpot Clara Bow her publicity tag, 'The "It" Girl', and then did the same for another of her films, *Children Of Divorce*, which also starred Gary Cooper, then near the beginning of his long career.

He helped re-edit the second part of Erich von Stroheim's *The Wedding March* – which was designed to be released in two parts, and which, like all of von Stroheim's films, was impressively imagined and shot, and much too long to be commercially released. As von Stroheim was almost the only director that von Sternberg wholeheartedly admired, he asked his approval before beginning his re-edit, but his politeness did him little good – from that time onwards von Stroheim viewed him with contempt as one of the studio's hired butchers.

But his diligent work was winning the approval of B P Schulberg, who rewarded him with a cheap film to direct. Based on a story by newspaperman Ben Hecht, called *Underworld*, it was the first film to feature gangsters (although not properly a 'gangster film'). It made a star of the actor George Bancroft, and was an enormous and unexpected (to the studio) success.

By this time (1927), the great German actor Emil Jannings had joined the flood of actors and technicians coming from Berlin to Hollywood. He too had joined Paramount, making a film version of Samuel Butler's novel *The Way Of All Flesh*, and the studio, in the wake of the success of *Underworld*, assigned von Sternberg to direct him in a film called *The Last Command*.

This had a good plot, telling of a general in the imperial Russian army who, after the revolution, winds up in Hollywood working as a film extra and finds himself cast as a general in the imperial Russian army. Naturally, as it is a Jannings piece, he is ultimately degraded and humiliated.

The plot had been contrived by von Sternberg himself, based on an anecdote he had heard from Ernst Lubitsch, another immigrant German, who had come to Hollywood in 1923, and was welcomed there in the wake of the American success of his film *The Merry Widow*; in 1927 he was directing for Warner Brothers.

On set, von Sternberg was arrogant and domineering (the amiable William Powell, who played the role of the film director within the film, specified in his next studio contract that he was never to be directed by von Sternberg again), and Emil Jannings was spoilt and temperamental, demanding constant attention and reassurance. Even so, he respected von Sternberg's Teutonic direction, and expressed a wish to work with him again some time. This time it was von Sternberg who balked, saying 'under no circumstances, were he the last remaining actor on earth, would I ever again court the doubtful pleasure of directing him.'

In spite of all this bickering, *The Last Command* turned out to be a fine film – von Sternberg's best to date. In May 1929 it won Emil Jannings the first-ever Oscar for Best Actor (for his performance in that and also in *The Way Of All Flesh*).

It was as a result of this collaboration that Jannings suggested to UFA that von Sternberg be brought to Berlin to direct him in a prestigious German talkie, which was then being planned and aimed partly at the American market. This would be Germany's second-ever, all-talking picture – the first was *Dich Hab' Ich Geliebt (You I Have Loved)*, made by another, smaller studio, AFA. Jannings had by 1929 made a talkie in Hollywood, a Paramount film called *Betrayal*, but his German-accented English proved so impenetrable that the studio was forced to insert titles and release it as a silent (this effectively ended his Hollywood career).

Von Sternberg too had made one talkie, a gangster drama called *Thunderbolt*, again starring George Bancroft, as well as several more silent pictures, all for Paramount. His reputation as a director was now fairly solidly established, although not as solidly as that of Ernst Lubitsch, who in 1928 had also joined Paramount. In fact it was Lubitsch whom UFA had first approached to help them make what would be their own first talkie. They wanted to make it in two languages, a German version and an English version, and sensibly felt that an English-speaking director whose first language was German would be an ideal choice.

Unfortunately, Lubitsch wanted too much money ($60,000). Not only was this a large proportion of the film's proposed budget ($325,000), but Emil Jannings had protested that this was more than the $50,000 fee that he was getting, and he was the star, so if Lubitsch were to get that much, then he must have $75,000. So the idea of hiring Lubitsch was dropped and von Sternberg was approached. He was offered $30,000, held out for $40,000, and got it.

He had to arrange with Paramount for leave of absence, which they granted him on condition he extend his contract with them for two additional years, and that he be away for no longer than five months, returning by 14 January 1930. For every week longer he stayed in Germany, UFA would have to make penalty payments to them.

The most important person involved with UFA at this time was the press baron Alfred Hugenberg. During the Twenties a distribution company called Parufamet had been set up as part of an agreement between Paramount and MGM in Hollywood, and UFA in Berlin, to distribute German films in America and vice versa. Unfortunately, this had not quite worked out – far more American films got into German cinemas than German into American. In fact, there seemed a real danger that the German film industry would be swamped. So Hugenberg, rabidly right-wing and politically ambitious, assembled a consortium of businessmen to buy out the Paramount and MGM interests in UFA.

To recoup their investment, they wanted to make a big film that would do well in America, and what was more natural than to use sound and to star Germany's own Oscar-winner, Emil Jannings? And as he had won his Oscar playing a Russian, what could be better than to choose a Russian story (this would also help to explain his thick accent)? Rasputin, they felt, might be the ideal subject.

Von Sternberg arrived in Berlin on 16 August 1929. With him was a wife he had acquired in between directing films. Her name was Riza Royce, and she was a somewhat temperamental ex-actress. The marriage was not going entirely smoothly; in fact, not long before they set sail they went to Mexico and got a quickie divorce, which may or may not have been legally valid. Valid or not, when the Berlin trip became a possibility, they hastily re-married so as to go there together.

The producer of the proposed film was to be Erich Pommer and, in spite of his vast experience and considerable success, he was somewhat taken aback when, as soon as von Sternberg arrived, he announced that he had not the slightest interest in making a film about Rasputin. He felt the story of Rasputin was too well-known, offering no surprises in its plot and little to explore in the way of character.

Taken aback or not, Pommer was slightly relieved. He had become aware that there might be legal problems surrounding the Rasputin story, as turned out to be the case a few years later when MGM made a film called *Rasputin – The Mad Monk* and were successfully sued for libel by various exiled members of the Russian nobility. He was also somewhat disarmed when von Sternberg went on to say how much he had always admired Pommer's film *Variety* (starring Emil Jannings) and wouldn't it be nice to use Jannings again in some sort of entertainment setting – a circus, maybe. He knew quite a lot about circuses.

At this point Emil Jannings reminded Erich Pommer that he himself had a novel in mind that might fit the bill – a novel they'd already discussed and that he'd wanted to be filmed in for years. It was called *Professor Unrat* (which roughly translates as 'Professor Shit'), and it was written by Heinrich Mann, brother of the much more famous Thomas Mann. Its main plot involved a respectable schoolteacher whose career is ruined when he becomes infatuated by a cabaret singer, and who takes revenge on bourgeois society by running a gambling den, for which he is eventually imprisoned. Cabaret wasn't the circus exactly, but surely there were enough similarities?

Von Sternberg liked the idea. Pommer liked the idea, and also liked the fact that the screen rights to *Professor Unrat* might come cheap – for one thing, it had been out for some years, and for another, he knew that Heinrich Mann was somewhat hard up. He set about acquiring the rights in a cunning and roundabout way. He had an assistant who was living with a dancer called La Jana, then working in an Erik Charell show. Also in the show was a cabaret singer, Trude Hesterberg, who was Heinrich's Mann's mistress. So via his assistant and La Jana and Trude he transmitted a hint to Heinrich Mann that UFA might be interested in his book.

The word came back that that was just fine by Heinrich Mann, and exactly one week after von Sternberg had arrived in Berlin the screen rights to the book were bought. Pommer at once hired screenwriter Robert Liebmann and playwright Dr Karl Volmöller to write the screenplay. Volmöller was the man who had written Reinhardt's *The Miracle*, and who had taken Reinhardt to see Marlene in *It's In The Air*.

The next day Pommer also hired a third writer, the playwright Carl Zuckmayer, and on that same day Alfred Hugenberg hit the roof. He had just read the contract to buy the film rights to the book, and until that moment had been under the impression that UFA was buying a novel by Heinrich's famous brother Thomas, who only that year had won the Nobel Prize for Literature. Not only was Heinrich much less esteemed, *Professor Unrat* was an attack on the hypocrisy and corruption of respectable society – the very section of society that the right-wing Hugenberg held most dear.

For a moment he and his business colleagues considered cancelling the contract on the grounds that UFA had been defrauded, but soon they settled on demanding that Pommer and his team 'completely rework' the story of the book.

As it happened, this suited von Sternberg perfectly. The more he thought about the book, the more he realised that the main female character in it, the cabaret singer who causes the Professor's downfall, was more interesting to him than the Professor himself. After all, a pompous and respectable professor whose life crumbles round him due to an unsuspected weakness in his character was the sort of role Emil Jannings had already played a dozen times.

This meant that the entire latter part of the book, where the ruined Professor attempts revenge on society, could be dropped. And if the Professor was no longer the absolute centre of the plot, the title should be changed as well. Von Sternberg decided to call his film by the name of the cabaret where the singer sings – *Der Blaue Engel (The Blue Angel)*. And he decided to rename the singer herself, who in the book was called Rosa Fröhlich. The name he invented for her was 'Lola Lola', a deliberate echo of the heroine of Pabst's famous film *Pandora's Box*, whose name was Lulu. Lulu too was a sexually knowing young woman inhabiting a seedy underworld.

The question was, who was to play Lola. For a while von Sternberg considered some of the American stars he knew, such as Gloria Swanson or Phyllis Haver, but with an American star there would be the problem of filming in German. He decided he would have to find his actress in Germany.

Naturally word soon spread in the tight world of Berlin theatre that this plum role in Germany's prestigious new talkie was available. It was quite obvious to everybody that this was not going to be just another movie. For a start there was the glamorous involvement of an important Hollywood director. Rumours flew. Almost every actress even vaguely suitable was said to have been considered, or auditioned, or tested, or even been offered the part. With one exception. Nobody discussing the rumours, including herself, mentioned Marlene.

Von Sternberg ran into trouble at this time when he went to meet author Heinrich Mann and his mistress, Trude Hesterberg. He went because he was under the impression that Trude might have been the model for the singer in the book, and that meeting her would give him a clearer idea of the woman he was looking for, but it turned out he was mistaken. Worse still, because of the way Heinrich had been approached by UFA (via Trude), she was under the impression that the role in the film would be hers.

Von Sternberg hastened to assure her that for a start she was too old, and left with both Heinrich and Trude furious with him.

Another actress who inwardly believed the role was hers was Leni Riefenstahl, who by late 1929 had starred in three films, all directed (or co-directed) by Dr Arnold Fanck. His films made much use of mountain scenery, and tended to have a somewhat mystical tone, and his directing style would greatly influence her when she later became a director herself.

Von Sternberg, still searching, did consider Leni Riefenstahl, to the extent of inviting her to meet him for dinner at the Hotel Bristol. But it turned out that her chances had only ever been slim. As they dined, he asked her what she knew of an actress called Marlene Dietrich. Riefenstahl's reply was cautious, omitting all mention that she knew Marlene rather well, and subtly dismissive. 'Marlene Dietrich?' she said. 'I've seen her only once, and was struck by her. She was sitting [in a café] with some young actresses, and my attention was drawn by her deep, coarse voice. Maybe she was a little tipsy. I heard her say in a loud voice, "Why must we always have beautiful bosoms? Why can't they hang a little?" With which she lifted up her left breast and amused herself with it, startling the young girls sitting around her. She might be a good type for you.'

Several people had mentioned Marlene to von Sternberg, and not just to gossip about her. One was Erich Pommer's wife, Gertrud, who knew her from Betty Stern's salon. Another was Karl Volmöller's mistress, Ruth Landshoff (another woman given to wearing a tuxedo and a monocle), who had acted with Marlene in Vienna in *The School Of Unzach*. He was also aware of her from America. Just before he passed through New York en route to Berlin her film *The Woman One Longs For* (retitled *Three Loves*) had opened there to enthusiastic reviews, the *New York Times* calling her 'a rare Garboesque beauty'.

He had even looked at a rather flat and uninteresting photo of her in a casting catalogue, and had asked one of his assistants what he thought. 'The behind is not bad,' said the assistant, 'but don't we need a face as well?'

So in spite of his awareness of her existence she was by no means in his mind as a possible Lola when he went to see *Two Bow Ties*. He had in fact almost decided that the best actress available was Lucie Mannheim, and had even made an appointment to film a test of her singing. He went to see *Two Bow Ties* mainly to observe the performances of two actors he had already cast in minor roles – Marlene's co-stars Hans Albers and Rosa Valetti.

When he saw Marlene he knew at once he had found his Lola. He had been looking for a woman whose physique resembled the chic Parisiennes in the erotic etchings of the Belgian artist Félicien Rops, and he had found one. But he could also see ways in which to bring out the striking contours of her face and was bowled over by the mocking insolence of her performance. As he wrote in his memoirs, 'Here was the face I had sought, something that told me my search was over. She leaned against the wings with a cold disdain for the buffoonery, in sharp contrast to the effervescence of the others.' At the same time she managed to give the impression that if you pushed the right button she could be more fun than any of them.

Von Sternberg was so taken by Marlene that whenever she was on stage he found it impossible to take his eyes off her, to such an extent that Hans

Albers said jealously, 'If he'd been seated a little nearer the footlights I'd have peed on his head.'

Marlene too knew that he was in the audience, and of course coveted the role of Lola Lola, but her on-stage indifference could be useful off stage as well. It even fooled von Sternberg, who wrote, 'She had heard that I was in the audience, but as she did not consider herself involved, she was indifferent to my presence.'

He did not go backstage to approach her. That was not his style. But he had her summoned to the UFA studios for an interview. Here she carried her indifference to amazing heights. For a start she gave him the impression that she believed he was only considering her for a minor role (like Hans Albers and Rosa Valetti). When he asked why he had heard such poor reports about her film career, she replied that she photographed badly, had been poorly reviewed, had made only three films and was no good in any of them.

She couldn't have been cleverer. The was exactly the sort of arrogant, self-confident behaviour to appeal to von Sternberg, who had a strong masochistic streak in his character that attracted him to beautiful, indifferent women. Furthermore, it was very much the character he wanted for his Lola.

He told Marlene he would like to make a screen test of her singing. There was no real need for this, as he had already made up his mind that the part was hers. Shrewdly, he wanted to make it so as to show it to the powerful Jesse L Lasky, co-founder (with Adolph Zukor) of Paramount, and to Lasky's head of production, B P Schulberg, who at that moment was on his way to Berlin aboard the *Île De France*. Both, he was sure, would be extremely interested in a 'rare Garboesque beauty', not to mention the director who had discovered her and who would be her mentor and guide.

She agreed, but only on condition he would also view her 'three films'. These, it turned out, were *I Kiss Your Hand, Madame*, *The Woman One Longs For* and *The Ship Of Lost Men* (in each of which she was the female star). She also took it on herself to point out that she'd seen some of his films and didn't really think he was any good at directing women.

One more thing was necessary before von Sternberg filmed his test – he had to get Marlene approved by Erich Pommer and Emil Jannings. So after interviewing her he took her to meet them. Pommer asked her to remove her hat and walk up and down, and she did so (according to von Sternberg) 'with bovine listlessness, a study in apathy, her eyes completely veiled'. Pommer was not sure she was right for the part, feeling she was somewhat overweight and far too casual. Jannings, aware of the sexuality she projected, and protective of his own role as the star, was completely against casting her.

Von Sternberg, increasingly smitten with her, and aware he could transfer her attraction to the screen, was adamant. He threatened to leave the film and go back to America if he were not allowed to film her test. Pommer and Jannings gave in.

He did watch her films, and of course attributed any failings in her performance to the fact that her directors, unlike himself, were rubbish. 'Never before,' he wrote, 'had I met so beautiful a woman who had been so thoroughly discounted and undervalued.'

At the same time he felt there was nothing to be lost in carrying out his planned screen test of Lucie Mannheim. This turned out to be plain sailing (apart from the fact that Lucie was not going to get the part), and provided a bonus for von Sternberg in that she brought as her accompanist the composer Friedrich Holländer, who had contributed songs to *From Mouth To Mouth* (among many other shows) and was by now enormously successful. Hearing him play, von Sternberg knew at once that he had found the composer for his film.

Marlene's test was not plain sailing (even though she was going to get the part). She made sure of that. She showed up with no accompanist and no songs prepared. Von Sternberg sent for a pianist, got her into a spangled costume, frizzed her hair with a curling iron, had her sit on top of the upright piano, and arranged her lighting.

He filmed her singing a German song, 'Wer Wird Denn Weinen' ('Why Cry? There's Another On The Corner'), and then asked if she would sing an American song. She and the pianist agreed that she should sing 'You're The Cream In My Coffee' (although in her live shows later in her life she often claimed it was 'My Blue Heaven').

The filming went well, and von Sternberg was just as enraptured by the way she responded to his direction as he had been by the lady herself. 'She came to life and responded to my instructions with an ease that I had never before encountered,' he recalled.

Word that von Sternberg had found his Lola swiftly travelled round the Berlin theatre world. When Leni Riefenstahl learned from a phone call that she had missed out, she was so distraught that she threw the young man for whom she had been preparing a goulash dinner out of her apartment, and dumped the goulash. Lucie Mannheim, as a front-runner who had actually been screen tested, was formally notified by UFA that she had lost the race. Friedrich Holländer learned the news when the studio told him he was to compose songs to suit Marlene's voice, not Lucie's.

Marlene learned the news late in the day, and it was from Holländer she learned it. The waiting had been nerve-wracking for her. Cool and self-confident she may have appeared in front of von Sternberg, but inwardly all her uncertainties and worries about her career were still there. After performing as usual in *Two Bow Ties* she had gone to one of her favourite clubs, Le Silhouette, after the show and it was there that Holländer ran into her. He saw, as he said, 'two question marks in two worried, wide-open eyes', and could not resist giving her the news. When he told her, he said, 'she ordered so much champagne you could have bathed in it.'

All the same, she still felt some disquiet, telling one friend that all this was happening too late. After all, she had wanted to be a big star for such a long time, and now was nearly thirty. As years went by she would increasingly insist on the story that she had been cast in *The Blue Angel* almost straight from drama school, and had never made a film before it.

Erich Pommer, who had never been totally against casting Marlene, was mostly relieved that a Lola had at last been found. Emil Jannings, who had never felt she was right, continued to be hostile to her. 'You'll rue the day,' he told von Sternberg.

Marlene was given a contract by UFA, hiring her for the film for a fee of 20,000 marks (around a tenth of what Emil Jannings was getting) and giving them an option on her services for further films if they liked *The Blue Angel* once it was shot. She was also approached by Hollywood's Universal Studios. Universal had a tie-in with the company Terra Films, for which she had made *The Woman One Longs For*, now running in New York, so they were well aware of her. They sent their man in Berlin, Joe Pasternak (later to become Universal's top producer), to discuss things with Marlene. She received him, he said, 'wreathed coolly in a sheer peignoir and nothing else', and told him how grateful she was to hear of Universal's interest.

Of course, Pasternak had to get von Sternberg's permission to approach his star, and while von Sternberg gave permission, and was pleased for Marlene, it made him uneasy. If Marlene went to Universal, and he was still tied to Paramount, it might mean the end of their working together.

Swiftly he wired Paramount executive Jesse Lasky, enthusing about his discovery. Lasky was cautious. He ordered a Paramount sales manager in

Berlin, Sidney Kent, to have a look at Marlene and report back to him, just in case von Sternberg was simply infatuated. Kent did so and his wire to Lasky read: 'SHE'S SENSATIONAL. SIGN HER UP.'

Within days, B P Schulberg, also of Paramount, arrived in Berlin. Von Sternberg showed him Marlene's film test, and Schulberg himself offered her a contract. She declared herself agreeable, but unfortunately was unable to sign one, because of the clause in her UFA contract giving them an option on her further services. She did, however, say that if they did not exercise their option, then she would be happy to accept Paramount's offer.

During September and October of 1929 the three writers, plus von Sternberg and Erich Pommer, continued to work on the script, with occasional conferences with Emil Jannings about the development of his character, the Professor – a role that was increasingly based on the book's author, Heinrich Mann, and on the bullying teacher von Sternberg remembered from his boyhood at the Jewish school in Vienna. It was decided that at the end of the film, instead of running a gambling den and going to prison, the Professor would go out of his mind with despair, have a heart attack, and die.

Marlene's character, Lola Lola, was to be younger than she had been in the book, and was no longer to have a child. The story thus became almost totally a tale of sexual obsession, paralleling von Sternberg's own growing obsession with his star. Many elements in his films, especially those he would make with Marlene, echoed elements in his own life.

Shooting began (on UFA's Stage Five) on Monday 4 November 1929. Every shot in it involving dialogue was filmed in German first, then in English. In the German version, all the characters would be German. In the English version, the Professor would speak English because he taught it in school, and Lola would be a foreign woman who spoke only English, demanding that those who wanted to communicate with her use that language.

During the shooting, Emil Jannings was a little less difficult and temperamental than von Sternberg had found him during the making of *The Last Command*. Possibly this was because *The Blue Angel* was being shot with sound, and Jannings found the new medium somewhat unnerving. Used to delivering dialogue to audiences in the live theatre, he was disconcerted by the silence and lack of response of a film set (he had also had the chastening experience in Hollywood of having his only previous attempt at a talkie released as a silent).

Marlene, on the other hand, took to the microphone like a cat to cream. Her distinctive voice was one of the talents she was surest of, and now she would be able use it in films. She also had enormous confidence in von Sternberg as a director. His infatuation with her was obvious and flattering, and she was reassured that he seemed to know exactly what he was doing. Among other things, he understood how to light her properly. As a painter he could see the underlying structure of her face – the strength of her cheekbones and the beauty of her broad forehead – and he quickly devised a style of lighting that was similar to the one she had been groping towards herself.

It is a tribute to von Sternberg's strength as a director that in spite of his adoration of Marlene he was able to film her well. Many directors, even great ones, who were smitten by their leading ladies have not filmed them well. The difficulty for them is that everything their beloved does seems wonderful – François Truffaut rather failed with Julie Christie in *Fahrenheit 451*, as did the young Jean Renoir with his wife Catherine Hessling in *Nana*. Maybe the fact that von Sternberg believed (or hoped) that women were always able to dominate men gave him the necessary detachment.

While working, he masked his infatuation at all times behind a bullying and peremptory manner, and this made Marlene feel completely at home. She was, after all, both the daughter and the step-daughter of Prussian officers (as well as of a mother who had deliberately concealed her feelings).

His direction consisted mainly of abrupt orders – as he himself explained, they went something like 'Turn your shoulders away from me and straighten out… Drop your voice an octave and don't lisp… Count to six and look at that lamp as if you could no longer live without it… Stand where you are and don't move, the lights are being adjusted.'

This style of directing was entirely in line with his conception of the director as artist. In his view, his actors were simply there to embody the story he was conceiving and bringing to the screen. Not that he viewed them merely as puppets – they must be able to portray exactly the subtlety of emotion he wished in each shot. But he directed them piecemeal, from shot to shot, rather than in the film as a whole.

This had been a fashionable philosophy among some leading stage directors for a number of years. The influential designer Gordon Craig, for instance, had argued that the conventional stage actor should be replaced by what he called the *Übermarionette*: 'a supremely beautiful creature –

something like a Greek statue' who could be completely controlled by the director in the interest of the work.

Jannings was an able and experienced actor who worked out his performance as a complete unity anyway, developing his character smoothly as the story progressed – moving from pomposity to fascination (with Lola Lola) to shock (at being dismissed from his post for marrying her) to degradation and total despair.

Marlene was not as talented as a straight actor, and her acting performance in *The Blue Angel* does not always hang together. Why, after roaring with incredulous laughter at the Professor's proposal does she almost at once agree to marry him? And why does she marry such a man at all? Is it a desire for respectability? If so, why does she go through with the marriage after he has lost his job? Does she perhaps wish to escape from her life in a seedy cabaret and attain respectability as a *hausfrau*? There is never any sense in her performance that she feels hemmed in by her cabaret world, or doomed to remain in it – she seems alive and at home there.

Her songs are a different matter. For a start Friedrich Holländer did her proud (he also performs them in the film, taking the role of the club's pianist), giving her 'Nimm' Dich In Acht Vor Blonden Frauen' ('Blonde Women'), 'Ich Bin Die Fesche Lola' ('Naughty Lola'), 'Kinde Heut' Abend, Da Such Ich Mir Was Aus' ('A Regular Man') and of course the splendid 'Ich Bin Von Kopf Bis Fuss Auf Liebe Eingestellt', which translates directly as 'I'm Designed For Love From Head To Foot', but which in its English version became 'Falling In Love Again' – a song that would be associated with Marlene for the rest of her life, in spite of her latter-day assertion that she hated it and wished she'd never heard of it.

The German lyrics for these songs were written by Walter Rillo and Robert Liebmann, and their English versions by Jimmy Connelly.

Von Sternberg filmed them simply, and with subtle changes in their presentation. When she is first introduced she is singing in a high brassy voice, and surrounded by a swirling mass of performers and club-goers. Gradually over the course of the film her voice becomes deeper, and there are fewer people around her, until when we last see her, after four years are supposed to have elapsed, she is alone in shot, top-hatted, and singing more slowly and reflectively, using her smoky lower range. Her whole performance during this rendition of the song is subtle and stunning, the first performance recorded on film of the mature and assured Marlene.

The top hat is an important symbol in the film. Von Sternberg quickly seized on the aura of sexual ambiguity surrounding her. Not only does Lola dress in an increasingly masculine way on stage as the film progresses, but throughout the film she is also a more active character than the Professor. By the end she is almost totally dominant and he is reduced to almost total passivity.

The shooting proceeded quite smoothly. Some problems were caused by von Sternberg's decision to shoot it as far as possible in script order, meaning that sets such as the Professor's school-room, unseen for much of the middle of the film, had to be left standing until they were needed again. And Marlene, while her English was passable, did have some difficulties in pronunciation.

One word, 'moths', in the song 'Falling In Love Again', gave her particular trouble. She kept pronouncing it as 'moss', and it has been said that von Sternberg bullied her through two hundred and thirty-five takes of the song in two days to try and get the word right (in those early days songs were recorded live), until he had to concede defeat. Finally he arranged for an extra to shout out 'Give me a beer!' to cover her mispronunciation.

With such perfectionism on his part, the shooting began to run a little behind schedule, and the situation was not helped by the fact that important visitors were welcomed on the set (von Sternberg enjoyed letting people see the genius director at work, although he insisted on quiet), and Stage Five became one of the fashionable places in Berlin to have visited.

One of the first famous people to visit was the American star, Buster Keaton. Later came other film people, like the Russian director Sergei Eisenstein, the Berlin director Kurt Bernhardt, the actor Conrad Veidt, who had starred in Erich Pommer's *The Cabinet Of Dr Caligari*, and the American actor George Bancroft, who had starred in von Sternberg's films *Underworld* and *Thunderbolt*. B P Schulberg paid a visit, as did Max Reinhardt and the satirical artist George Grosz. Even Leni Riefenstahl came by, accompanied by her director, Dr Arnold Fanck.

They happened to be present for the filming of 'Falling In Love Again', when Lola sings it to the besotted Professor sitting in her audience. This is the scene from which Marlene's most famous still is taken, as she sits, top-hatted, on a barrel, wearing only frilly knickers and suspendered stockings below the waist, and clutching one raised knee. In that still, the woman standing looking at her legs is her old friend and mentor, Rosa Valetti, who continued to coach her in cabaret presentation during the making of the film.

Although in later life Marlene claimed to have disliked playing 'a whore', at the time the film was made she seemed completely at ease with being outrageous. To the extent that (according to Dr Fanck) von Sternberg at one point admonished her, 'You sow! Pull down your pants! Everyone can see your pubic hair!'

A problem that grew as shooting progressed was Emil Jannings' jealousy of Marlene. As he saw it, this film, which was meant to feature him and be a major advance in his career, was being stolen by a jumped-up nobody.

He began to behave almost as badly as he had on *The Last Command*, needing endless reassurance from von Sternberg before he would emerge from his dressing-room, keeping the crew and the rest of the cast waiting, sometimes for a couple of hours. He kept urging Marlene to ignore von Sternberg's direction, telling her that if she performed as he instructed her then her acting career would be over. He demanded that lines of hers be cut (which von Sternberg of course refused to do), and eventually became so exasperated by her that in the scene near the end where the Professor is driven to desperation and attempts to strangle Lola, he actually did almost strangle the real Marlene, not so violently as to seriously injure her, but badly enough for filming to be delayed while the make-up department worked to hide the bruises on her neck.

Marlene for her part disliked and despised him, seeing him as gross and brutish. But in spite of having to work with someone she found personally so unpleasant, and in spite of the exhausting nature of the filming, she was full of high spirits. Von Sternberg noted that the calm knowingness of the character she was playing – and would continue to play – was considerably different from the ebullient and sparkling woman she was in private life.

She knew that this was a much better film than any she had previously been in, and that she was performing better, and looking better, than she had ever done. She was a little alarmed at how much von Sternberg was basing the character of Lola on aspects of her own character (as he saw them) and she was not a hundred per cent sure how much of a success the finished film would be, or how she might fare if UFA took up the option on her contract and she had to work with a different director. But there was always the chance that they might not, and that she might get her promised Paramount contract, and then would be able to work with von Sternberg again.

She worshipped von Sternberg. It was he who had improved her lighting and make-up and hairstyle, and he was a man of a type she was used to, who was not only in control but totally domineering on the set. She went into her motherly mode during the shooting. As von Sternberg recalled: 'Her attention was rivetted on me. No property master could have been more alert. She behaved as if she were there as my servant, first to notice that I was looking for a pencil, first to rush for a chair if I wanted to sit down.'

She took to preparing lunches at home and bringing them in to the studio, so that she and von Sternberg could share them in her dressing-room, and gradually their relationship ripened into an affair. They were discreet about it, and nobody could do more than suspect. She even introduced him to her husband Rudi, saying that she hoped one day Rudi in turn would be able to meet von Sternberg's spouse, Riza.

But suspicion was soon quite enough for Riza who, while shooting was still in progress, abruptly packed her bags and headed back to her married home in Hollywood. The event did not go unnoticed by the press, causing Marlene to utter one of the very few unguarded statements of her life, when she told a journalist from Vienna, Dr Sandor Incze, that Riza's going had nothing to do with her, because von Sternberg wanted to be rid of his wife anyway. This remark, published in the *Neues Wiener Journal*, would in due course cause her trouble.

Once Riza was gone, Marlene took to visiting von Sternberg in his hotel suite – sometimes in the mornings before the day's filming, sometimes in the evenings after it.

What with one thing and another the shooting of the film went slightly over schedule. Instead of taking ten weeks it took twelve, which gave producer Erich Pommer a considerable headache. Expenses were rising, partly caused by the unfamiliar difficulties of using sound and the need to shoot versions in two different languages. Added to his outlay was the fact that he was obliged to make his penalty payment to Paramount for every week von Sternberg stayed on after 14 January 1930. Eventually the film's budget rose to two million marks (nearly $500,000), more than any sound film made anywhere in the world so far had cost, and certainly the most expensive that he (Pommer) had ever been concerned with.

One way to keep costs from running any further away was, of course, to get rid of von Sternberg as soon as they could after shooting was over. Fortunately, helped by the fact that he was mostly shooting the film in script order, von Sternberg had been able to edit it (the German version, that is) as he went along, and his editor, Sam Winston, would be able to do any fine-cutting necessary after he left. On 30 January, he sailed back to America on the *Bremen*.

While waiting for *The Blue Angel* to be released, UFA arranged that Marlene should go into the recording studios and make records of her songs from the film, accompanied by an orchestra led by Friedrich Holländer. This she did towards the end of January, recording 'Falling In Love Again', in English; 'Blonde Women', first in German, then in English; 'Naughty Lola', first in German, then in English; and 'A Regular Man', in German.

Some days later, in February, she went back to the studios and recorded the German version of 'Falling In Love Again' and a song by Holländer not from the film, 'Wenn Ich Mir Was Wünschen Durfte' ('When I Thirst For What I Wish'), on which last she was accompanied simply by Holländer's piano.

At around the end of the first week in February, Alfred Hugenberg and the UFA top brass viewed the film. They were appalled, and demanded that its première, planned for later that month, be delayed. They felt that not enough had been done to soften what they saw as the un-Germanness of the original book. They felt they had made a mistake in entrusting its direction to an Austrian-American, especially in view of the way he had exaggerated the story's atmosphere of seediness and sexuality – why, it even had hints of fetishism, of voyeurism, of sado-masochism.

It undermined the high ideals of the German educational system, and worst of all, it wasn't made clear enough at the end that the Professor, slumped over the teacher's desk from which he once lorded it over his pupils, had paid the price for his moral frailty and died.

Nonetheless, the money they had invested in the film must be recouped somehow, even though they were sure it would be found so offensive to public taste that it would do poorly. Their solution was music. Over the last shot, when the camera slowly pulls back from the dead Professor to reveal the whole empty classroom – a shot which von Sternberg had wanted to have played in total silence – they overlaid a sonorous and funereal chunk of Beethoven. (This was removed in later releases of the film, which is as well, as there is no music remotely resembling Beethoven anywhere else in it.)

Hugenberg and his colleagues also decided not to exercise their option on Marlene's contract. Within hours of learning of this she was in the office of Paramount's representative in Berlin, Ike Blumenthal, signing a two-picture contract at a salary of $1,750 per week. The contract also guaranteed that her sole director would be Josef von Sternberg.

She omitted to mention to Ike Blumenthal that she was also bound by her three-year theatre contract with Robert Klein. Klein, learning of her deal with Paramount, was furious, and announced his intention of enforcing his own contract. Marlene, uncertain what to do, phoned von Sternberg, who told her to get in touch with Dr Vollmöller, who he was sure would sort things out. Vollmöller did, although Paramount had to pay Robert Klein a settlement of 20,000 marks (almost $5,000). She was now completely clear to go to America.

In spite of her excitement at being on the road to stardom, leaving for Hollywood was a big decision. It would mean leaving Berlin, with the theatres, clubs and cafés where she now felt so at home. But already these were beginning to lose some of their lustre – the Twenties were over, and while the recession of the Thirties was not yet making itself felt (Wall Street had only recently crashed), there was a growing reaction among many of the general public against the decadent excesses of Berlin night-life. Things were not what they were.

Also there was her family. Rudi was a good man, always willing to discuss her plans with her and offer what advice he could, but they were no longer anything more than good friends, and he was happily involved with Tamara. So she need not worry about him.

Leaving Heidede, now just turned five, would be much more of a wrench. Should she take her daughter with her? No, it would be unfair to uproot her child from the home she knew. Even though she and Heidede would miss each other, Rudi and Tamara (and her mother Josephine) would look after the child. And besides, she was only contracted to make two films in America – she would very likely be back within a year. Her eventual decision was that she would go alone. It would be a kind of reconnaissance, she told Rudi, to see what kind of opportunities Hollywood could offer her.

On Tuesday 1 April 1930 *The Blue Angel* was given its première, at the Gloria-Palast on the Kurfürstendamm. The film had been widely publicised for weeks beforehand, and in any case was Germany's first really important (and most expensive) sound film. Anyone who was anyone was there – not just film and theatre people, but artists, writers, politicians, businessmen.

Before the film was shown, most of those there expected this to be Emil Jannings' great evening. Typical was Heinrich Mann's mistress, Trude

Hesterberg, who confided to a young actress, Dolly Haas, seated beside her, that this would be 'Emil's evening', that everybody knew Marlene hadn't much to offer.

One who already knew differently was Emil himself. He had seen a press show of the picture that afternoon and, self-centred as he was, knew star quality when he saw it. Maybe he even remembered telling Erich Pommer and von Sternberg that if they cast Marlene they'd rue the day. He didn't watch the film again at the première, but sat alone in the cinema's coffee-bar, drinking endless cups of coffee.

Marlene, on the other hand, was extremely visible. After the film finished, clad in a long white gown and furs, she took curtain call after curtain call from the stage, and accepted a giant bouquet of roses as the many cameras flashed.

On von Sternberg's firm instructions, she had already lost weight during the three months since the end of shooting, and looked even more elegant than she had on screen. Jannings was barely noticed.

Taking the roses with her, she went from the Gloria-Palast to Uncle Willi and Aunt Jolly's villa on the Leichtensteiner Allee, where a party in her honour was to be held. It wasn't only to celebrate her success at the première, but to wish her bon voyage, as she was leaving that very night to sail away on the *Bremen*.

As it happened, Rudi could not be present, because he was working on a film in Munich as a production assistant, so when she left the party to catch the midnight boat train she was escorted by Willi Forst. Nor was she to travel alone. Rudi, still solicitous for her, even though absent, had insisted she take as companion the woman who had been her dresser on *The Blue Angel*. Her name was Resi. They sailed on 2 April 1930 and Marlene now had a new role in life. She was to be a star.

5 Paramount Star

Once Marlene was under contract, Paramount Studios wasted no time in publicizing their new star. The *Los Angeles Times* even announced that she had arrived in Hollywood five weeks before she left Berlin. And, also before she set off, von Sternberg had started briefing the studio's publicity department about her, telling them a series of stories about her age, her background and her acting experience that were so inaccurate and conflicting they would have done credit to Marlene herself. All of which tended to build up an image of her as someone tantalizing and mysterious.

Her crossing was fairly rough and took a day longer than scheduled. Resi, a poor sailor, was so seasick that on the first day out she threw up her false teeth over the side, and spent most of the rest of the trip lying miserably in her cabin. Marlene, on the other hand, was not only a good sailor but also buoyed up by euphoria. Following her across the sea came a stream of telegrams celebrating the success of her performance in *The Blue Angel* and relaying complimentary reviews.

The *Lichtbildbühne*, for example, described her as 'fascinating, like no other woman before on film, [with] the silent, narcotic play of her face and limbs, and her dark, exciting voice.' Reviewer Herbert Jhering, in the *Börsenkurier*, wrote, 'She sings and performs almost phlegmatically, but this she does in an exciting way. She is common without being common, and altogether extraordinary.' The *Berliner-Zeitung* called *The Blue Angel* 'the first work of art in sound film', and Hans Sahl, in *Der Montag Morgen*, said, 'Marlene Dietrich has already gone to America; German film is one artist poorer.'

She carefully kept all the telegrams for Resi to paste into a scrapbook and continued enjoying her voyage. She played table-tennis, and she socialised. Among the people she met were a young New York couple with a show-business connection. Their names were Jimmy and Bianca Strook, although in his business life as a theatrical costumier Jimmy called himself James Brook.

She liked them both, but especially the pretty and stylish Bianca, who was touched and a little surprised when a bunch of fresh violets started to be delivered to her every morning. The symbolism of this escaped her until one day Marlene invited her to her cabin, gave her a glass of champagne, showed her an illustrated book on the techniques of lesbian lovemaking, and made a certain suggestion. Bianca, surprised but relieved (having had an uneasy feeling that Marlene was after Jimmy), declined, and Marlene in turn was surprised. 'In Europe,' she explained, 'it doesn't matter if you're a man or a woman. We make love with anyone we find attractive.'

The *Bremen* docked in New York in the early morning of 9 April 1930. Marlene was at once gathered up by a publicity team from Paramount's east coast office, and by a troop of reporters and press photographers they had gathered (who as yet had little idea who she was).

The publicity men advised her to say as little as possible (partly in order to conceal her still somewhat shaky English, and partly so as to foster an air of Garbo-like reticence and mystery) but she was photographed sitting on top of a pile of her luggage – twelve cases, including a portable record-player and two violin-cases (one containing her saw).

She was then rushed to the Ritz, where, at a breakfast press conference, she was introduced to another group of reporters by Jesse Lasky himself. Here she was allowed to answer a few questions and almost at once appalled the Paramount personnel present by admitting, in slow and careful English, that yes, she was married, and that she had a baby who she missed desperately.

This sort of information was anathema to studio publicity departments in 1930. Received wisdom was that the public preferred to think of their stars, especially their new stars, as single (and thus in a sense available). Marlene was one of the first to break the taboo, even if it was done in ignorance, and on the whole the revelation of her marriage soon turned out to be to her advantage – any scandalous whispering about her sexual goings-on could be counteracted by pointing out her respectable married and maternal state. (S J Perelman, in his wonderful piece *Scenario*, which parodies Thirties screen dialogue mingled with front-office discussions, has a passage that sums up the studio attitude perfectly – 'I ask you confidentially, Horowitz, can't we get that dame to put on women's clothes, a skirt or something? The fans are getting wise, all those flat-heeled shoes and men's shirts like a lumberjack. Get me Gerber in publicity, he'll dish out some crap about her happy home life.')

Marlene was booked (with Resi) into the famous Algonquin Hotel, and stayed in New York making publicity appearances for several days before heading west for Hollywood. Between these appearances she diverted herself in various ways, frequently to the alarm of von Sternberg.

On her own initiative she booked a portrait session with the photographer Irving Chidnoff, and when von Sternberg heard he hit the roof. He had a contractual agreement with Paramount that 'his' star was not to be formally photographed except under his supervision. He furiously phoned Marlene from Hollywood, and demanded that all Chidnoff's photographs and negatives be instantly destroyed. Which she sort of did. She had the photographs safely removed from America by signing them (in flamboyant green ink) and sending them to newspapers and magazines in Berlin and Vienna, which duly published them, often on their covers.

Then she took to going out dining and dancing with Paramount's east coast head of production, the educated but lecherous Walter Wanger. He took her to speakeasies (Prohibition was still in force), and introduced her to bootleg hooch, and she was incautious (or innocent) enough to tell von Sternberg about all this. Knowing Wanger to be a notorious wolf, and no fit companion for a respectable married lady, von Sternberg ordered her to leave New York and take a train to Hollywood as soon as possible.

Before she left on 12 April, she had one major publicity exercise. She was interviewed on the ABC radio programme *Paramount-Publix Hour*, which was transmitted coast-to-coast. The radio microphone emphasised her still-shaky and heavily accented English, but again she spoke slowly and carefully, and the results were gratifying – all across the country members of the American public found her fascinating, and thousands of intrigued letters flooded in to the station.

Taking no chances with the handling of her publicity as she arrived in California, von Sternberg arranged to take a train to meet hers in New Mexico, and then travelled with her to her eventual destination, the city of Pasadena, just outside Los Angeles.

With him he had a screenplay for what would be her first Hollywood film, and its origin was curious. The story, as von Sternberg told it, was that when he sailed from Germany Marlene had sent him a *bon voyage* basket of goodies, and that in it was a novel called *Amy Jolly*, written by Benno Vigny.

Its heroine was a Parisian cabaret singer (and whore and cocaine-addict) who abandons Paris, adopts the false name of 'Amy Jolly' (pretty friend) and moves to North Africa, where she gets a job working in a brothel run by a lesbian pimp. There she falls for two men, a young soldier in the French Foreign Legion and an older man who is both a painter and a millionaire. But she loses them both and at the end of the book sails bravely and hopefully off to take up a cabaret engagement in Buenos Aires.

Reading it during his voyage, von Sternberg realised that, like the soldiers of the Foreign Legion, there was 'a foreign legion of women, so to speak, who also chose to hide their wounds behind an incognito', and that the book would make an excellent film for Marlene. When he told her this, he claimed, she protested, saying that the book was *schwache Limonade* (weak lemonade), and that surely he could find a more suitable subject for her.

This is all rather fishy. Marlene prided herself on being well-read, and knew that von Sternberg was himself a literate man, and *Amy Jolly* sounds too much like Twenties romantic tosh (albeit rather on the saucy side) to be the sort of book she would give him as casual shipboard reading. It is at least conceivable that while in Berlin they had discussed possible projects, and when she found a book set in an exotic location (she knew she was good at being exotic) and with a woman as the central character, she thought it might be suitable.

Whatever the truth of the matter, von Sternberg decided to use it and commissioned a screenplay from the writer Jules Furthman (who had worked, uncredited, on his film *Underworld*) and they gave the piece the more romantic title of *Morocco*. He knew that Foreign Legion films were popular (they had been so since the runaway success of *Beau Geste* in 1926) and he also had a hidden reason for choosing it – it needed little dialogue. This would not only be an advantage in selling a sound film around the world (film-makers were still a little unsure, in those early days of talkies, about how to get over the language problem), but it would also mean that Marlene would not have many lines.

He was worried about her English (then more heavily accented than it soon became) because for years American vaudeville comedians such as the famous Weber and Fields had made a German accent an almost automatic trigger for laughter. To deal with this problem, he insisted that she embark at once on a course of voice lessons.

This would only be part of his grooming her into a full-blown Hollywood star. She would also continue to diet (and have a masseur), and the studio would arrange for her to have thorough lighting and make-up tests, including hairstyling. And in order to keep an eye on her (as well as to stop her from feeling homesick and isolated in this new country) he had her move into an apartment in the same block as the one he shared with his wife, Riza – in fact on the same floor, and right across the hallway.

The studio furnished her apartment for her in true film-star style, with overstuffed chintz-covered sofas, a wall of mirrors and a leopardskin carpet. And at von Sternberg's insistence they also allotted her a lavish wardrobe.

All this somewhat impersonal pampering naturally did little to help her undoubted feelings of homesickness, both for Berlin and for her husband and daughter. Although she was kept so busy being groomed as a star that she had time to see little of the world but her apartment and Paramount Studios, she did find time to send chatty notes and little gifts to Rudi and Heidede every few weeks.

Moving Marlene into an apartment so close to his own was not perhaps the most diplomatic thing von Sternberg could have done, as far as his rocky marriage was concerned. Although he and she were no longer lovers (he wasn't really her type), he still adored her and she depended on him a great deal to guide and reassure her in the new environment she found herself in.

In fact he spent so much of his spare time conferring with her in her apartment (as well as sometimes escorting her out to fashionable eating-places) that Riza demanded bitterly 'Why don't you just marry her? Maybe that will make her happy.' To which von Sternberg replied wryly, 'I'd as soon share a telephone box with a frightened cobra.'

This reply, and others like it, failed to reassure Riza. The marriage became stormy, and on Sunday 11 May 1930 von Sternberg ejected her from their apartment 'with force'. Two days later she obtained a legal separation, and on 2 June would sue him for divorce, citing cruelty.

Meanwhile the important work of preparing films went on. The make-up artist assigned to give Marlene a makeover was Paramount's outstanding Dottie Ponedell (supervised, of course, by von Sternberg). It was she who raised Marlene's eyebrows at the outer corners, made her eyes seem larger by lightening her lower eyelids, and, perhaps most importantly of all (at least to Marlene), drew a fine silver line down the centre of the nose she had always felt was too broad, slimming it and giving it an elegant shape.

Paramount also continued to do everything to make her name known. When she joined the studio it had almost finished assembling a feature-length compilation film, called *Paramount On Parade*. The idea of this was to make the cinemagoing public even more aware of the studio's impressive array of stars – among its roster at the time were Clara Bow, Fredric March, William Powell, Maurice Chevalier, the Marx Brothers, Jean Arthur, Jack Oakie, Kay Francis, Fay Wray, Adolphe Menjou and Gary Cooper.

Various Paramount directors had been employed to shoot the sections of the compilation, and the company, wanting to include their new star (at least for showing to their German audience) decided that a section showing her singing a song should be hastily added. She would wear top hat and tails, the song would be written by Friedrich Holländer, and the section would be directed by their star German director, Ernst Lubitsch.

Von Sternberg again hit the roof. By the terms of Marlene's contract, he was to be her sole director, and he had his own strong ideas of how best to create her image. He wanted the general public to be aware of her first as seductive and vulnerable, softer and more romantic than she had been in *The Blue Angel*. While discussions raged, Lubitsch had to content himself with directing a photo session of her. She wore top hat and tails, but von Sternberg was able to prevent the resulting pictures from being released in America, and again Marlene got hold of a handful of them, signed them 'Vati Marlene' ('Daddy Marlene') in green ink, and sent them to Germany to amuse her old night-life friends.

Von Sternberg was then allowed by the studio to take over her publicity, and he in turn supervised a series of portraits of her, taken by the Paramount photographers Eugene Roberts Richee and Don English. Marlene was stunned by how beautiful her face looked in them, and later said to a friend that it was 'the most beautiful thing I've ever seen in my life' (possibly meaning: 'Is that really me? Can I be that beautiful?' Yes she could, and she owed her new image to von Sternberg and to Hollywood).

Von Sternberg also took over the booking that Lubitsch had arranged for filming her, and made a short publicity film (called *Introducing Marlene Dietrich*) in which she did appear in top hat and tails, but that was for showing to Paramount sales staff only.

Her first big public appearance in America was orchestrated by Paramount's B P Schulberg. It so happened that his assistant, the fast-rising David O Selznick, had just become engaged to Irene Mayer, the daughter of MGM's chief executive, Louis B Mayer. This proposed union of young people from the two most prestigious studios had almost the status of a royal wedding in the enclosed world of Hollywood, and Schulberg capitalised on it by arranging a splendiferous engagement party for the pair, held in the ballroom of the Beverly-Wilshire Hotel.

Everyone who was anyone was there. They dined and danced, and at the height of the festivities the high double doors at the end of the ballroom opened. A silence fell, and through the doors Marlene made her entrance. As the newly engaged Irene Mayer recalled years later: 'No one had ever laid eyes on her before. She entered several hundred feet into the room in this slow, riveting walk and took possession of that dance floor like it was a *stage*. I can't think of any greater impact she ever made. It was something out of a dream, and she looked absolutely sensational.'

'Ladies and gentlemen,' announced B P Schulberg, 'Paramount's new star, Marlene Dietrich!'

Of course, this was a direct challenge to the MGM executives present, including Louis B Mayer. MGM might have had in Garbo the most prestigious female star in Hollywood, but her throne was no longer secure.

The Paramount publicity machine ground relentlessly on. Stills from the photo session with Eugene Roberts Richee plastered walls and billboards and magazine covers. She was photographed in her film-star apartment and photographed visiting Charlie Chaplin on the set of his film *City Lights*. She was photographed dining out with von Sternberg and photographed talking on the phone to her daughter Heidede in Berlin (transatlantic phone calls were at that time an enormous novelty). Marlene fan clubs were formed, and encouraged by the studio, for an actress that most Americans had still never seen in a film.

But her first American film was still firmly on course. The plot of the book *Amy Jolly* had been drastically pared down by Jules Furthman and von Sternberg. Amy would no longer have a drug problem, or work in a brothel (instead she would perform in a North African cabaret), and at the end she would find love (or at least the chance of love) with the handsome young legionnaire, struggling gamely and barefoot out into the burning desert to follow him wherever his regiment might take him.

Her other lover, the older and devoted painter-millionaire, would renounce his love of her (although he would always love her), wanting her to have whatever would make her happiest, no matter how much pain it cost him – just as von Sternberg had given up all hope of ever being Marlene's true love, but would live for ever with the pain of remaining her devoted (and amused) admirer.

When it came to casting the millionaire he was lucky that Paramount had Adolph Menjou among its star players. Menjou was cultured and debonair, with a certain air of emotional detachment, and he bore a resemblance to von Sternberg himself – he was even short with a moustache.

For the legionnaire von Sternberg first wanted John Gilbert, the handsome romantic silent star whose career was just beginning its disastrous slide – either because he had difficulties with dialogue once sound came in, or because he had made an enemy of Louis B Mayer. But Gilbert was under contract to MGM, who would not release him.

Von Sternberg's second choice was Paramount's Fredric March, but producer David Selznick wanted to use him at the same time in the comedy *The Royal Family Of Broadway* – scripted by George S Kaufman and Edna Ferber – in which he would impersonate (rather well) the famous actor John Barrymore.

Meanwhile, Selznick was being lobbied for the part in *Morocco* by another Paramount contract star, Gary Cooper. Cooper pointed out that not only had he already played a legionnaire successfully in the 1928 film *Beau Sabreur* (an attempt to cash in on the success of *Beau Geste*), he had also worked with von Sternberg a year before that when reshooting scenes for the Clara Bow film *Children Of Divorce*.

Cooper was suggested to von Sternberg, who agreed to use him, thinking he was 'harmless enough not to injure the film'. What he did injure, however, were von Sternberg's feelings, because very quickly Gary Cooper and Marlene Dietrich became lovers, and he was a frequent visitor to her apartment.

Sexually he was almost as freewheeling as she was, except that he was totally heterosexual. At the time they met he was still working his way out of an affair with the tempestuous Mexican star Lupe Velez, which he was finding too tempestuous to be wholly enjoyable.

Shooting began on 30 July 1930, and the first day did not go easily. Marlene had trouble with her English pronunciation, even though carefully coached by von Sternberg before each shot. In particular she had trouble with the word 'help', seeming to put a vowel between the last two letters, so that it came out something like 'hellubh'. Von Sternberg, the domineering perfectionist, kept her repeating the line for more than forty takes, and finally had the inspiration to tell her to think of the word as written in German. This helped her to get it right.

When directing her, he spoke in German, which soon caused friction between him and Gary Cooper, who felt excluded. Von Sternberg might have done this deliberately, partly out of jealousy of Cooper for having an affair with Marlene, and partly because he was uneasy around tall men (in many of Cooper's scenes in *Morocco*, von Sternberg has him seated). In any case it did cause friction. On one occasion Cooper became so annoyed that he grabbed von Sternberg by the neck of his coat and lifted him off the ground, saying, 'You goddamned Kraut, if you expect to work in this country you'd better get on to the language we use here.' Von Sternberg left the set and did not return that day. According to screenwriter Jules Furthman, Marlene watched him go with 'a kind of Mona Lisa smile'.

In spite of the on-set atmosphere, the film that was being shot was magnificent. Marlene, lit by von Sternberg's cameraman, Lee Garmes, to bring out the fine modelling of her face, and slimmer than she had ever been, looked ravishing. B P Schulberg, seeing the rushes, hastened to acquire the American rights to *The Blue Angel* – not to release it at once, but to keep it off the screen until after *Morocco* was released because *Morocco* had the more romantic image of her they wished to publicise. And before shooting was finished he offered Marlene a further two-picture contract, the two pictures to be made in a year at a vastly increased salary of $2,500 a week. This would keep her working for them until February 1933.

Again she insisted that the new contract stipulate that von Sternberg was to continue as her director. She knew how magnificent he was making her look. Even if their aims were different, they worked together well; he regarded the film as an end in itself, expressing his personal vision; she considered it more as a vehicle in which the world could see and admire her.

He worked her hard, but she was never afraid of hard work, and regarded his bullying directorial style with some amusement. When filming the scene that ends *Morocco* – a scene shot in the Mexican desert, in which she sets off barefoot across the burning sands to follow her legionnaire wherever he may go – she passed out from the heat. When she woke up on a stretcher to find von Sternberg beside her, her professionalism made her ask him if he needed another 'cloze-up'. 'Close-up' he corrected her at once and she told the story delightedly all over town.

Aware of how much they had spent on publicizing her, Paramount were anxious for her to make the second film in her first contract as soon as possible, and even before *Morocco* was edited they made her begin filming.

They knew that she and Gary Cooper were having an affair, and felt that their on-screen chemistry had profited from it, so they wanted to pair them again. Accordingly they gave the task of preparing a script to writer Daniel N Rubin, who the year before had written the screenplay for the Gary Cooper picture *The Texan*.

Rubin duly wrote one, basing it on an original story provided by von Sternberg, set in 1915, in wartime, in his native Vienna. Marlene is the widow of an Austrian army officer (called Kolowrat as a tip of the hat to 'Count Kilowatt' who had wanted to establish an Austrian film industry, and who produced *Café Electric*). For reasons never clearly explained, she has become a whore, and near the beginning of the film announces fatalistically that she is afraid neither of life nor of death. This remark is overheard by the head of the secret service, and it leads to his co-opting her as a spy.

During her spying activities she constantly tangles with a spy for the other side, a Russian airman and officer, and eventually, when he has been captured, helps him to escape, her love for him having overtaken her love of her country. For this she is shot as a traitor, to the sadness of the head of the secret service, who sees in her a true nobility.

Von Sternberg wanted to call the film *X-27* (the widow Kolowrat's code name as a spy), thus emphasizing her anonymous and mysterious past – it is made clear in the film that it is difficult for the authorities to find out anything at all about her history. But the Paramount front office disliked the title, and instead the film ended up as *Dishonored*, a title with a dated silent-movie feel about it even in 1930.

Nor did the casting end up as originally planned. Gary Cooper, who was to have played the Russian officer, joined the list of actors who refused ever again to be directed by Josef von Sternberg. Instead the role went to another actor on the studio payroll, Victor McLaglen. Which was a pity because, in spite of his long career in films, he had almost no sexual magnetism, so there turned out to be no real tension between Marlene and himself in their scenes together. Cooper's refusal did have one benefit for Marlene, however. It meant that in *Dishonored* she would have top billing.

It began shooting early in October 1930, and Marlene's appearance and character in it were subtly different from the way she had been in *Morocco*. Her hairstyle was softer and her lip make-up was more defined (Dottie Ponedell again). As well as her mocking smile, she had learned a more open one, in which her mouth looked even prettier. Overall, she less resembled

Garbo. The character she played, the widow Kolowrat, alias X-27, was darker than Amy Jolly in *Morocco*. X-27 is more sophisticated, more disillusioned, and half in love with death from the beginning. Nor does she sing. Instead, she frequently plays the piano, von Sternberg wickedly hiding from the audience till almost the end of the film that Marlene really can play it herself, and confidently.

During shooting, von Sternberg adopted his usual domineering and temperamental manner, which Victor McLaglen found unpleasant, but which he observed, seemed to bother Marlene not at all, even when von Sternberg went into one of his rather calculated rages. 'To look at those two gives me a temperature,' he once remarked.

Shooting continued until almost the end of November, by which time, in the middle of that month, *Morocco* had had its première, at the Rivoli cinema in New York.

It was a stunning success there, breaking box-office records, and the reviews were ecstatic. The *Los Angeles Times*, for instance, said that Marlene was 'distinguished by provocative poise and beautiful economy of expression', and the magazine *Photoplay* observed that von Sternberg 'not only gave the picture to Marlene; she took it.'

And no wonder. She was by now slender and chic – more mysterious than Lola Lola, and with a greater stillness and intensity. She was now as beautiful on screen as she could ever have hoped to be.

Her fan mail at once became prodigious. She began receiving so much mail from adoring fans, both male and female, that Paramount had to allot her two secretaries to help deal with it.

It was not entirely surprising that some of her adoring fans were female, because early in the film von Sternberg had given her what was then an outrageous piece of cross-gender mockery. As a cabaret performer, singing the first of her two songs in the film ('Give Me The Man Who Does Things'), and dressed in top hat and tails, she first subdues a critical audience, then, strolling among them, asks a pretty girl for the flower she is wearing. The girl gives it, and Marlene gives her a mocking kiss full on the lips. Then she strolls further round the cabaret and bestows the flower on legionnaire Gary Cooper, who tucks it behind his ear.

The timorous and interfering Hays Code, Hollywood's attempt to avert censorship by imposing its own, was then just coming into force, and how such a scene evaded their vigilance can only be explained by naïvety. A detail during her second song, a little later in the film, was, however, censored. During that song ('What am I Bid for My Apple?'), wearing a short frilly skirt that showed the whole length of her famous legs, she carried a tray of apples around her neck for members of the audience to buy, and she was to have concluded by auctioning her room key. But that was forbidden. Instead she had to slip it to Gary Cooper surreptitiously.

The Hollywood première of the film took place two weeks after the New York première, on 24 November 1930. At Grauman's Chinese Theater on Hollywood Boulevard. Which was a sign of what a runaway success the film was. Sid Grauman, the proprietor of the Chinese Theater, had had a long-standing feud with Paramount, refusing ever to showcase their films. This policy changed abruptly when he was shown a print of *Morocco*.

The première at the Chinese Theater, which took place at midnight, was a glittering occasion. B P Schulberg was there, as was his co-founder of Paramount, Adolph Zukor (who mostly spent his time with the studio money-men in New York). MGM's legendary executive producer Irving Thalberg was there, with his wife, the star Norma Shearer. Douglas Fairbanks and his wife Mary Pickford were there, as were Joan and Constance Bennett.

Marlene arrived with von Sternberg, and with them came Charlie Chaplin, accompanied by his co-star in *The Gold Rush*, von Sternberg's discovery Georgia Hale. Gary Cooper arrived separately, bringing Lupe Velez with him.

In Hollywood, too, *Morocco* was a success. During its run at Grauman's Chinese it again broke box-office records, and again the reviewers showered it, and Marlene, with praise. The only thing that disturbed her was how many people commented on her resemblance to Greta Garbo, which of course Paramount had deliberately contrived. She complained to the press that it was 'cruel' to harp on this resemblance, and that if people had been allowed to see *The Blue Angel* first they would have seen her as more like herself.

At the same time, in interviews (her English was now good) she assured journalists that she was Garbo's greatest fan, and that there was no way in which she, a mere newcomer, could possibly dream of rivalling her.

The reticent Garbo (who was less good in interviews), when asked if she herself felt there was a resemblance between them, is said to have simply replied, 'Who is Marlene Dietrich?'

The day after the Hollywood première of *Morocco*, with filming on *Dishonored* complete, Marlene set sail back to Berlin, where was met off the boat-train by Rudi and Heidede, by her mother, by delighted members of the press, and by her old friend and flatmate, Gerda Huber. Gerda and Rudi were not prepared for the new, slim, Hollywood Marlene. As Gerda recalled: 'It was our own Marlene, and she looked like a convalescent after a long and serious illness... She was no longer beautiful – in fact, she seemed almost plain. Her cheeks were hollow, her eyes looked sunken without their artificial shadow.'

Marlene would remain in her native city for over four months, from early December 1930 to the middle of April 1931, celebrating Heidede's sixth birthday, followed by Christmas, her own twenty-ninth birthday, and the New Year. She would share the money she had earned in Hollywood with Rudi and Heidede (and Tamara, who by now was well-established as Rudi's woman, although they prudently still lived separately), and she would stay in Berlin until after Heidede began school at Easter.

She enjoyed this brief spell of family life, seeing her daughter, her husband, her mother, and her Uncle Willi, although she was sorry not to see her Aunt Jolly, who had taken off with the famous German air ace of the Great War, Ernst Udet, to fly all over Africa (coincidentally, Udet had also done aerial photography for Leni Riefenstahl's mentor, Dr Arnold Fanck, for their 1929 mountain film *Die Weisse Holle Von Piz Palu/The White Hell Of Pitz Palu*). Aunt Jolly would never return to Uncle Willi, and Marlene would never see her again.

Early in 1931 Marlene also resumed an affair with an old flame, the composer Peter Kreuder, a witty and attractive man with a slight air of romantic boredom, and it was often with him that she attended plays and concerts.

Her public life at this time was one of high-scale celebration – she visited favourite clubs and friends and theatres, and everywhere was fêted as the major celebrity she had now become. While flattering, she learned this could also be wearing. When she attended a Friedrich Holländer revue, the audience demanded she take to the stage and sing 'Falling In Love Again' before they would allow the show to proceed. In clubs she was mobbed, and on an evening at her friend Betty Stern's she felt so crowded in by well-wishers that she took refuge for a moment on a hall stairway. There she was joined by a journalist she knew well. He asked her how it felt to be so famous, and she replied thoughtfully that the funny thing was it didn't make her as happy as it might once have done. 'Naturally it's very nice, and I'm not ungrateful,' she said, 'but it came too late.'

This might have been momentary fatigue talking, because her fame would go on for years, for far longer than she could then have believed, and the longer it went on the more she would revel in it.

What was apparent though was that the city was no longer 'her Berlin'. She was too much of a celebrity now to have the freedom of the streets. No more would she be able to parade along the pavements in her wild wolf-skins, or ramble along the late-night Kaiserallee singing songs with Claire Waldoff.

There was another disturbing change too. The political party that called itself the National Socialists had grown from a fringe movement of brown-shirted youths to a noisy and active voice of protest. Even as she set sail from New York they were holding a widely reported meeting in Bayreuth, at which they demanded the banning of *The Blue Angel* from German cinemas, calling it 'mediocre and corrupting *Kitsch*'.

Part of the reason why the National Socialist Party was gaining such power was that many Germans were still suffering from unemployment and poverty, and it was offering them hope of a prosperous new future. This background of poverty also roused resentment in certain quarters against Marlene herself, with her much-publicised salary of a quarter of a million dollars a year. Why was she working in Hollywood in any case? If she was a good German, why wasn't she working in Germany, instead of in America (and furthermore playing the part of a Frenchwoman)?

More and more it was becoming obvious to Marlene that Hollywood was now the place for her to be. Her exploratory trip had turned out better than she could ever have expected – it was Hollywood that had brought out her great beauty and turned her into a star.

In between being fêted and enjoying friends and family, she found time to make several short trips away from Berlin. She visited Prague (near to where Rudi had been born), and travelled to London in order to attend the British première of *Morocco*.

Learning that her dinner-companion from the Hollywood première of *Morocco*, Charlie Chaplin, was himself visiting Berlin, she went to the Hotel Adlon, where he was staying, steamrollered her way past his security guards, and arranged to have a convenient photographer take pictures of the two of them together – her seated and the polite but somewhat shy Chaplin standing beside her with a bemused smile. These pictures she immediately sent to one of her secretaries at Paramount for distribution to the American press.

All was not plain sailing for Paramount at this time. Following the Wall Street Crash of October 1929 came the Depression. It came gradually, not overnight, but by the beginning of 1931 it was definitely there, and while the film business survived it better than most (people needed somewhere to forget their troubles), even their revenues were suffering.

Morocco helped Paramount's finances, earning a more-than-respectable two million dollars as well as being nominated for four Oscars – for Best Direction, Best Photography, Best Sound and Best Actress (Marlene's only-ever Oscar nomination). Of the four nominated, the sound recordist, Harry Mills, was the only one who actually won an award. But the prestige caused by this success did little to help the studio's suffering revenues, and even the two million earned was a drop in the ocean.

Furthermore, *Dishonored* did less well than Paramount had hoped. Partly this was because many people went to *Morocco* simply out of curiosity, to see what this much-publicised new star was like, and now they had seen her. Nor had *The Blue Angel*, to which Paramount owned the American rights, done all that well, although critics praised the freshness and vitality of Marlene's performance in it.

The financial pressures the studio was feeling led to jockeying for power among the executives, especially in the New York head office (most of the major studios had their financial administrations in New York – only the executives involved in the actual film-making were based in Hollywood). A voice that was growing in power and increasingly making itself heard was that of Jesse Lasky's assistant, Emanuel 'Manny' Cohen.

Lasky enjoyed, and would long continue to enjoy, his position as co-founder of Paramount, but what Manny Cohen liked was being in charge – he was a small man, once described by Dorothy Parker as a 'pony's ass'. Wires from him assessing the performance of Marlene's pictures began arriving in torrents on B P Schulberg's desk in Los Angeles.

One read: 'ALL OF THIS MYSTERY AND GLAMOUR WERE NOT ENOUGH TO GIVE THE PUBLIC COMPLETE SATISFACTION STOP IT IS TRUE THAT MOROCCO WENT OVER BIG BUT WITH THE MYSTERY OF THIS PERSONALITY IN HER FIRST PICTURE IT HAD AN OPPORTUNITY OF MAKING A MUCH MORE TREMENDOUS

SUCCESS THAN IT ENJOYED AND ESTABLISH HER ON A MUCH LARGER SCALE THAN SHE ENJOYS EVEN NOW.' Another, referring to *Dishonored*, called it 'A FAIRLY COMPLETE FLOP'.

On reflection, Cohen came to the conclusion that the trouble was that in neither picture did the Dietrich character get her man (in *Morocco* there is a chance she might, although we never see it, and in *Dishonored* she winds up dead). Artistic success was all very well, but if she got her man, at the same time as retaining her mystery and glamour, she might do better at the box office.

These communications were passed on by B P Schulberg to von Sternberg, who was well aware that he had better co-operate. Not only had *Dishonored* flopped, so too had another film he had made in Marlene's absence – *An American Tragedy*, starring Paramount newcomer Sylvia Sidney. What was more, the author of the original novel, Theodore Dreiser, felt that they had turned the social comment of his book into romantic tosh, and sued the studio.

So von Sternberg set to work on a script for Marlene in which she would get her man. He decided to base it on a twenty-two-page outline by writer Harry Hervey, which had a suitably exotic location – it is set in China during the revolution of 1911, and takes place almost entirely on a train travelling from Peking to Shanghai which is hijacked by a rebel army. He enlisted Jules Furthman again to write the script, which was to be called *Shanghai Express*, and sailed for Berlin with the outline in his luggage to discuss it with Marlene.

While in Berlin, Marlene was developing a story-line for herself. She wanted her public to know how deeply she felt about her role as a mother, and she was keen to appear in a film in which she played one. When von Sternberg arrived she told him about this idea, and he agreed that he would consider it, but what had begun to concern him (and Paramount) more was her role as a real-life mother.

America, moving from the hedonistic Twenties into the grim Thirties, was entering a period of increased moral rectitude, and certain pressure groups were objecting to a woman who not only seemed to spend her life playing hookers, but who also seemed to have abandoned her child in a country that only recently had been America's enemy. The fact that the child was living with a father who was having an adulterous relationship with another woman was fortunately not generally known, but Paramount knew, and felt that something should be done to defuse the situation.

After some discussion between Marlene, von Sternberg and the Paramount front-office, it was agreed that several steps would be taken. First, Heidede would not start school in Berlin but come with Marlene to America when she returned. This, of course, was a delightful idea to Marlene, immersed as she then was in the role of mother.

Furthermore, it was agreed that if Rudi (and Tamara) would move to Paris, Paramount would give him a job supervising the dubbing of their films into other languages for the European market. He might even supervise some of the European films they occasionally made there.

Von Sternberg set off back to America to continue preparing *Shanghai Express*, and Marlene began making her revised arrangements. She cancelled Heidede's enrolment in the Berlin school (making an announcement to the press that this was not a criticism of Germany, that it was all down to maternal feelings), and she hired Gerda Huber to be Heidede's governess in America. Heidede, she furthermore decided, would no longer be known by her childhood pet name, but by her real name, Maria. Maria would be sent to a private school in Hollywood, attended mostly by the children of celebrities.

During March and April 1931, before Marlene left Berlin, Rudi arranged for her to go into the recording studios several times. At the first session, accompanied by an orchestra led by Mischa Spolianski, who had written the scores for *It's In The Air* and *Two Bow Ties*, she recorded 'Leben Ohne Liebe Kannst Du Nicht' ('You Can't Live Without Love'). At her next, with an orchestra led by Peter Kreuder, she recorded 'Quand L'Amour Meurt' and one of her songs from *Morocco*, 'Give Me The Man Who Does Things'. And at a third session, with the same accompaniment, she recorded 'Peter', the Rudolf Nelson song that Kreuder believed had been written for him in the early Twenties, and two different arrangements of the Friedrich Holländer song 'Jonny', which Friedrich had written back in 1920 as a birthday present for his friend Jonny Soyka (at the time Marlene made *The Blue Angel*, Jonny Soyka was her agent).

Marlene, Maria and Gerda, accompanied by two German maids Marlene had also hired, set off from Berlin on 16 April 1931, seen off by Rudi, Willi Forst, and a brass band conducted by Peter Kreuder.

They reached California on 24 April, and moved into a large house that von Sternberg had rented for them, at 822 North Roxbury Drive, in Beverly Hills. Situated on the northwest corner of Sunset Boulevard, it was ten years old, built in a Mediterranean style, and had a swimming pool in its back yard. Waiting for Marlene in the front drive, as a present from the studio, was a car that had been used in the closing scenes of *Morocco*. It was a Rolls-Royce convertible, and it came complete with chauffeur. Von Sternberg had arranged for it to be given to her, but at the same time he was still a martinet. Observing that while away in Berlin she had put on around 6kg (1 stone) in weight, he ordered her to lose it again. She obeyed, living for three weeks or so on tomato juice and soda biscuits.

As she and Maria and their entourage settled in, and preparatory work continued on *Shanghai Express*, Paramount continued to worry about her life causing scandal. What was now bothering them mainly was the attitude of von Sternberg's ex-wife, Riza Royce. She was furious about Marlene, about von Sternberg, and about the way she had been treated and was being treated. In particular she was annoyed that, now she and von Sternberg were properly divorced, he was dragging his feet about sending alimony cheques. The reason he was dragging his feet was, to him, quite simple. He felt she'd already given him enough trouble.

At the same time, Riza increasingly believed that it was Marlene who had been responsible for von Sternberg throwing her out. After all, hadn't Marlene, back in Berlin at the time of *The Blue Angel*, said to the journalist Dr Sandor Incze that von Sternberg wanted to get rid of his wife? What made this worse was that his article had since been translated and published in an American magazine.

In order to try and deal with this situation, Paramount decided that the more emphasis they could place on Marlene's happy family life, the better. So they arranged for Rudi (now a Paramount employee) to be flown from Paris for a reunion with his wife and child.

He arrived in late July, and was met off the train at Pasadena by Marlene, Maria, von Sternberg, and a horde of invited reporters and photographers. Pictures and interviews celebrating the happy family reunion, with Maria clinging round her father's neck, were widely published. But the immediate result of all this hoopla was not at all what the studio hoped for. On 6 August Riza, through her lawyers, slapped Marlene with not one lawsuit, but two – one for 'alienation of affection', for which she wanted $500,000, and one for libel (in the Incze interview), for which she wanted $100,000.

The money was the least part of Paramount's problems. It was the possibility of scandal that scared them. Rudi was despatched back to Paris, as Riza had implied that he was all too complaisant a husband, as you could see by how friendly he was with von Sternberg. And Marlene publicly announced that she had been misquoted by Dr Incze. But Riza's lawsuits continued to hang over both her and her studio.

Shooting on *Shanghai Express* began late in September 1931. The male star was the English actor, Clive Brook, who had worked with von Sternberg on his silent film *Underworld*. Also in the cast was the Los Angeles-born Chinese actress, Anna May Wong, whom Marlene had met socially a couple of years before in Berlin (Anna May, four years younger than Marlene, who had been in movies for years, was one of the first globe-trotting film stars).

Werner Oland, who had played a treacherous Austrian officer in *Dishonored*, was cast as the villain in *Shanghai Express* – a passenger on the train who turns out to be the Anglo-Chinese leader of a rebel army.

But the star of the film in a way was the train (von Sternberg felt so himself). Most of the action takes place aboard it, with a multi-national collection of passengers – American, English, French, German – each of whose characters is gradually revealed during their journey. Von Sternberg filled his screen with a swirling kaleidoscope of railway images – smoke, steam, pistons, connecting-rods, driving wheels, carriage wheels, train windows, corridors, compartments, as well as a constant montage of Chinese lettering passing by on goods waggons, station signs and platform furniture.

The images are among the richest and most striking in any of von Sternberg's films and cameraman Lee Garmes' black-and-white (strongly black-and-white) photography is magnificent. As the Scottish documentary-maker and film theorist John Grierson wrote: 'The scenes of Chinese life are massive, painstaking to the point of genius in their sense of detail...the rest is Dietrich. She is shown in seven thousand and one poses, each of them photographed magnificently.'

It is true that, springing from severe Scotch Calvinist stock, he did go on to say: 'For me, seven thousand poses of Dietrich (or seventy) are Dietrich *ad nauseam*', but the truth is that most of the film is Marlene's, and she is photographed magnificently (and lovingly), often in almost unmoving close-ups that resemble the most glamorous studio portraits. Her hair was now marcelled, and less soft than it had been. Her eyebrows had been raised even further at their outer ends, giving them an amused lift, and her fingernails were elegantly longer. It was a journalistic cliché at this time to say she looked more beautiful in every film she made, but it was true.

Her character is less mysterious this time round. Although she is bruised and disillusioned, this time we are told exactly why she is disillusioned. She plays a young woman (named Magdalene) who has been deeply hurt by the abrupt ending of a love affair between herself and an English army doctor (Clive Brook). Over the five years (and four months) since their break-up she has become a courtesan along the China coast, so notorious that she has earned the sobriquet 'Shanghai Lily'.

He and she meet again aboard the train, setting off on a three-day journey from Peking to Shanghai. They had fallen out because she foolishly tried to make him jealous, to test his love, and he became so jealous he left her (although when they meet he is still wearing a watch she gave him, with her portrait in). He is rational and sceptical, she is intuitive and emotional, and it will take the whole film for them (especially him) to learn to trust their love.

They will also have to undergo adventurous and purifying hardship, as Werner Oland reveals himself to be not just a passenger but also a revolutionary commander. He and his small army hijack the train, and hold it up at a wayside station they have commandeered. Clive Brook is seized as a hostage, but not before he has punched Oland for laying hands on Marlene. As a result, Oland threatens to blind him, and is prevented only by Marlene offering to become his mistress. She is saved from this fate by Anna May Wong (playing a lower-grade whore) who stabs him to death after he rapes her (off screen).

Clive Brook is insensitive enough to believe she really intended to go off with Oland, but eventually all is explained to him, and on Shanghai station they embrace.

Unfortunately, Clive Brook is a somewhat wooden actor, which detracts rather from the film, because it is hard to see why anyone as desirable and intelligent as Marlene would be so passionately in love with him. Nor was he one of those leading men with whom she had an affair. During the filming she had found another lover – her fellow-Paramount star Maurice Chevalier.

He was then Paramount's most successful male star, as she was their most successful female, and (perhaps for this reason) they had adjoining dressing-rooms. He had been at Paramount since 1929 and had, of course, been aware of Marlene since she arrived there in April 1930. But over the following year-and-a-half their friendship had grown only slowly, even though he later admitted he had found her 'ravishing'.

As they got to know each other better he found her to be 'an extraordinary comrade, a woman of great intelligence and sensitivity, spiritual, charming, kind, amusingly and charmingly unpredictable'. They were also sharing the experience of being expatriates in America, and he was able to sympathise with her in her moments of homesickness. It was hardly surprising that they became lovers. She often invited him to her house and cooked him meals, and she took to dining out with him around town, which she also sometimes did with Gary Cooper. Or with both together. Or with von Sternberg as well, which was intended to give the impression that all this was really business, although it didn't quite. Which again gave Paramount something to worry about.

She was also at this time increasingly given to going out clubbing wearing a man's tweed suit. She took to frequenting a club for lesbian transvestites (one not often visited by famous stars who should be careful of their image), on several occasions accompanied by a dancer, singer and star of Spanish films called Imperio Argentina. Marlene began courting her with bunches of violets, and soon their evenings, back at Marlene's house on Roxbury Drive, became more intimate. This went on until Argentina's husband, the Spanish director Florian Rey, arrived at the house equipped with a couple of steamship tickets and ordered his wife to pack her bags, as she and he were leaving Hollywood. Which they did.

It says something about how highly Paramount rated Marlene that they went to such great lengths to protect her image. Many stars were bounced for lesser indiscretions.

One step they did take in 1931 was to put another famous female star under contract, mostly of course in the hope that her films would make money, but partly in the hope that the existence of a rival might encourage Marlene to act more discreetly. Unfortunately, the star they chose was the bisexual Tallulah Bankhead, who thrived on being outrageous and didn't give a damn about Hollywood because her heart was with the stage, on which she was a success in both New York and London. She stayed with the studio for only a couple of years, making six forgettable films, and was something of a worry to them all the time.

Her first three films were made at Paramount's Astoria Studios, in Long Island. Then she was brought to Hollywood. At that time the publicity machine was trying to drum up an imagined feud between her and the more famous Marlene, but there was never anything in it, and the story soon ran out of steam. Marlene was courteous and polite towards her and, as Tallulah recalled in her memoirs: 'I first saw Marlene in the commissary at lunch. In a flame-coloured tea gown she was presiding at a table over which hovered the flower of Paramount. I was snookered behind a pillar. On seeing me she came over and welcomed me to the studio, was all candour and charm. When asked if I might come and watch her work, she readily consented.'

When *Shanghai Express* was released it was a great success with reviewers and public alike. It made more money than any film Marlene and von Sternberg would ever make, and was nominated for Oscars for Best Picture, Best Director and Best Photography (it won only the last, Lee Garmes collecting the award).

While pleased by this success, Paramount had yet another headache. They were worried about the story that Marlene had written and wanted von Sternberg to direct her in. Although it would give her the chance to play a mother (with a small son, not a daughter), it seemed that there was somehow too much sex in it.

They assigned the reliable Jules Furthman (who had to keep working for the studio because they had paid off a lot of his gambling debts), and gave him as co-writer, a young New York playwright called S K Lauren.

In the plot they came up with, based on Marlene's original and developed by von Sternberg, she was to play a German former night-club singer who has come to New York, retired from singing and married, whose scientist husband falls seriously ill with radium poisoning. While he is away in Europe recovering, she goes back into the entertainment business to earn money for his cure and to support their child. But she falls in love with a handsome young patron of the club, who happens to be extremely rich, and becomes his mistress. He begins paying the bills, but her husband finds out on his return. He divorces her and obtains custody of their son on the grounds of her 'immoral conduct'. She is forced to kidnap the child and take to the streets as a hooker. He kidnaps the child back and she, after considering suicide, returns to entertaining (in Paris) and becomes an international star.

Although this contained many elements of Marlene's own life – she was a German entertainer, loved her child, loved more than one man at the same time, and desired stardom – the script gave the Hays Office fits. They told Paramount that they hoped they'd 'forget the story altogether'.

Paramount, in turn, told von Sternberg they wanted the script heavily sanitised. To the extent that it would become almost meaningless. Von

Sternberg refused, and to show them he meant it, took a train to New York instead of reporting on the scheduled first day of shooting, 25 April. Immediately the studio suspended him, suing him for $100,000 for breach of contract ('Is that all?' he said. 'I valued myself higher than that. I think they are trying to humiliate me by asking so little.') The studio reassigned the picture to journeyman director Richard Wallace, and Marlene, whose contract specified von Sternberg as her director, refused to work with him. So she in turn got suspended.

To try and put pressure on the studio, she announced publicly that although she had been happy in Hollywood, she was thinking of going back to Germany to work. There was a small grain of truth in this – UFA had been attempting to entice Rudi to return to Germany and work for them, the unspoken underpinning being that this might entice Marlene to do the same. That she would do this, however, was becoming more and more unlikely. In January 1931 the Nazis (not yet in power) had announced a party ban on *Dishonored* – their reason for this was that it seemed critical of war as an instrument of policy. Marlene was increasingly aware that any film she might make in Germany in the future would be severely constrained by right-wing policy.

Riza Royce, reading Marlene's announcement, and believing that Marlene might escape her by leaving America, intensified pressure on both her and her studio. Paramount had managed to get a co-operative statement from Dr Sandor Incze, saying that he might have somewhat misquoted Marlene in his published interview. But that wasn't enough for Riza. She wanted his statement to be published, and in addition wanted a letter of apology from Marlene, to which she herself would be permitted to reply, the whole correspondence also to be published.

To add to Marlene's problems, Maurice Chevalier's wife, who had remained in Paris, had heard whispers and believed them, and was now threatening Maurice with divorce, citing Marlene as the reason.

Threats were by now flying in all directions. Paramount was suffering financially from the Depression – their profits were falling heavily, and so was their quoted price on the stock market. Hollywood executive B P Schulberg was under pressure from those even higher up in Paramount than himself, such as Manny Cohen in the New York head office, to turn out good pictures as fast as possible and with the minimum of trouble. As a result he was forced to tell von Sternberg (even though he'd always admired and encouraged him) that if he didn't co-operate by directing Marlene's picture, then he'd be prevented from ever working for anyone in the film business, anywhere in the world, ever again.

To try and help sort things out, Rudi was again summoned from Paris, and miraculously acted as catalyst to solve some of the problems. Von Sternberg gave in and agreed to direct the picture, which made Marlene happy and allowed the studio to remove her suspension. This happened even though neither of them were yet happy with the script, which was still undergoing revision.

One thing among many that disturbed them was the studio's insistence that it be given a more domestic happy ending in which, as well as Marlene becoming an international star, her rich young lover reappears on the scene, she marries him, and together they return to New York, where her new husband is understanding about her loving not only him but also her son and her scientist ex-husband.

The title had been changed from *Deep Nights* to *East River* to *Song Of Manhattan* to *Velvet* to (finally) *Blonde Venus*. It had also acquired a further problem – it was by now April 1932, and a few weeks earlier, on 1 March, the twenty-month-old son of the famous aviator Charles Lindbergh had been kidnapped (he would be found in a shallow grave on 12 May). Thus the whole of America was kidnapping-conscious. Kidnappers were villains, and the moment in the script when the heroine kidnaps her son might not look as much like maternal love as villainy. The scene would have to be handled with great care.

Naturally, after the Lindbergh kidnapping all the high-profile stars in Hollywood who had children began worrying. Marlene had iron bars fitted to the windows of Maria's room.

One night Groucho Marx, who happened to live next door to her, and who had two young children himself, was alarmed to see a black limousine pull up in the night outside his house. It stayed there for a long time, its motor idling, and at last he was sufficiently concerned to phone Marlene. As a result of their conversation, each hid their children in a safe place until the morning, by which time the black limousine had vanished. It wasn't for two years that Groucho discovered the whole thing had been a rather poor practical joke by lyricist Lorenz Hart.

Not long afterwards, however, on Friday 13 May, Marlene began getting genuine letters threatening to kidnap Maria. These drove her almost frantic with worry. Made up of words and letters cut out of newspapers and magazines, they demanded $10,000 or Maria would soon be dead. They contained instructions to leave the money outside the house on the running board of a car, with the usual warnings not to inform the police.

Rudi, however, did so at once. Private detectives were hired, some of them disguising themselves as gardeners or servants, and the police co-operated in setting a trap – Marlene, Rudi, von Sternberg and Maurice Chevalier were to be inside the house armed with rifles, while members of the Beverly Hills police force concealed themselves outside.

Nobody arrived, and next day Rudi set off back to Paris (and to maybe discuss things further with UFA). But the letters continued to arrive, and it turned out that a Mrs Egon Muller, the wife of a German linen importer, had been getting similar ones. She had been asked to leave $500 in a designated place, but had compromised by leaving $17.

Marlene was naturally somewhat surprised then to receive a letter demanding 'the $483 you forgot to leave'. Mrs Muller, the same day, received this:

> You Marlene Dietrich, if you want to save Maria to be a screen star, pay, and if you don't she'll be but a loving memory to you. Don't dare to call detectives again. Keep this to yourself. Say, what's the big idea! Attention! Is the future of your girl worth it? Wait for new information. $10,000 or pay heavily later on. You'll be sorry. Don't call for police or detectives again.

That one Mrs Muller gave to the press, which could have been a mistake, but as it happened, once their existence was made public, the letters stopped. Nobody was ever arrested, but the police eventually announced they believed that the sender had been an aggrieved ex-employee of Paramount, angry at having been laid off (they were cutting back on staff to reduce expenses).

All the same, the experience did little to calm Marlene's fraught existence. Shooting on *Blonde Venus* began on 26 May and the script was still being interfered with.

Her scientist husband was played by the English actor Herbert Marshall, fresh from starring opposite Claudette Colbert in the successful *Secrets Of A Secretary*, and the second male lead was the young Cary Grant, then just moving up from playing supporting roles – handsome enough, but not yet in control of the wonderful Cary Grant persona of later years. (Marlene wasn't particularly struck by him, but during the following year his potential would be spotted by a recent arrival at Paramount, Mae West.)

For the first time since *Morocco*, Marlene would sing. In the finished film she has three songs, 'Hot Voodoo', 'You Little So-And-So' and 'I Couldn't Be Annoyed', and they are by far the best part of the film (even though the Hays Office kept asking for revisions in the lyrics right into the last week of shooting, and requesting that they be reshot in less provocative costumes). None of the actors, including Marlene, seem very involved in the plot, although in her scenes with her son, played by the six-year-old Dickie Moore, she manages to combine glamour and maternal tenderness in a way that is both unselfconscious and convincing. (Dickie Moore would shortly become a leading member of Hal Roach's 'Our Gang', and once recalled of *Blonde Venus*: 'I still remember every detail. Marlene and Sternberg – how they screamed and laughed... They yelled at one another constantly in German, but always ended up laughing and embracing.')

Von Sternberg in fact screamed so much during shooting (at others as well as Marlene) that he lost his voice. Production manager Sam Jaffe (not the actor of the same name) suggested he use a megaphone, and von Sternberg improved on his suggestion by hooking up a microphone for himself to the public-address system.

Of Marlene's songs, the most wittily staged is 'Hot Voodoo', in which she begins concealed inside a gorilla costume, emerging unexpectedly to don a silver-blonde afro wig, wearing a short black shimmering costume trimmed with feathers, and showing plenty of leg. Her last number in the film, 'I Couldn't Be Annoyed', takes place when she is a howling success in Paris. She is in white tie and white tails, singing in French (in her own translation of the lyrics), and declaring her independence from anyone and everyone. Which makes the tacked on happy ending seem even more ludicrous than ever.

Shooting, which had suffered many delays from script problems and other problems, finished at the end of August. During it, another problem had been resolved, when Paramount agreed a settlement with Riza Royce and her lawyers. The sum was never disclosed, but was said to be $100,000. Riza disappeared from the scene.

Blonde Venus was hurried into the cinemas, opening in the autumn of 1932 without a formal première at the Paramount Times Square Theater in

New York. The critics disliked it, but the public took to it and it earned an unexpected three million dollars during its initial release.

This, however, was not enough to rescue the ailing Paramount, who by the end of the year would be sixteen million dollars in the red. Changes would have to be made.

6 The End Of A Partnership

At the beginning of 1932, Franklin Delano Roosevelt became president of the United States, and under his energetic administration the country would gradually haul its way out of the Depression. But 1932 would turn out to be the worst year.

Like many businesses, Paramount was still having financial difficulties. These were caused more by poor investments than by the quality of films their Hollywood studio was turning out. However, those in charge in New York decided that heads would have to roll, and some that did were those in charge of film production. Top executive Jesse Lasky, although a co-founder of the studio, was bounced, and he moved to Fox Studios to work as a producer. And the head of production in Hollywood, B P Schulberg, was involved in negotiations to have his contract bought out (although this would take some time).

This disturbed von Sternberg. Schulberg had always been his protector and encourager, and his position, he felt, would be less safe and less powerful with Schulberg gone. Also he had been annoyed by the studio's interference in the script of *Blonde Venus*. His contract with Paramount was due to run out at the end of December 1932, and he began to wonder whether he should renew it.

He was by now a highly respected director, and perhaps might be better off at some other studio, especially if he could take Marlene with him – her contract was due for renewal at the end of February. He had an idea for another film for her, to be set in Spain, and with this in mind he had discussions with Charlie Chaplin at United Artists, and with Jesse Lasky in his new position at Fox. Both seemed interested.

But von Sternberg needed time to think, and after several meetings with Manny Cohen in New York it was arranged that, to work out the end of his contract, he would go with a cameraman to the West Indies to collect footage of hurricanes, for use in a proposed film to be set in the South Seas.

Paramount were only too well aware that their major star's contract was due to end in February, so they were anxious to rush her into another film as fast as possible. Meanwhile, to keep her happy they raised her salary to $4,000 a week, simply as a retainer. They searched through the vast archive of stories to which they had the rights, and settled on a script for her called *Song Of Songs*. This was something of an old warhorse. It was based on a play based on a famous German novel of 1908, and Paramount had already filmed it twice, most recently with Pola Negri in 1924 (they had also recently considered it as a vehicle for Tallulah Bankhead).

Marlene was reluctant to appear in it, but before he left for the West Indies, von Sternberg encouraged her to accept it, and she did. He had no intention of directing it, because that would mean renewing his contract with Paramount, but he realised that if another director made a picture with Marlene that was a flop, then it would underline his own genius at working with her; and if it was a success then it would make her an even more attractive proposition if they approached some other studio.

Now arose the problem for the studio of who would be her director. A natural choice, as the original story was German and the story was set in Germany, would have been her fellow-Berliner Ernst Lubitsch. But von Sternberg was jealous of Lubitsch, who was two years older than he was, similar in height and appearance, and always just ahead of him in reputation and salary, so the studio knew that von Sternberg would not recommend him to Marlene, and that she would not accept any director he did not recommend. Furthermore, the man who now had effective control of Paramount, Manny Cohen, was not at ease with creative decisions, and thus was depending more and more on Lubitsch to advise him, so he had less time to do much directing.

Instead they settled on Reuben Mamoulian. Aged thirty-four, he was part Russian and part Armenian. Born in Tiflis, the capital of the republic of Georgia, he had left in 1917, at the time of the Russian Revolution, and become a respected stage director, first in London, then in America. He was one of many theatre directors snapped up by Hollywood when talkies came in and the need was felt for people who could direct dialogue.

He had already made several successful films – his most recent was the 1932 version of *Dr Jekyll And Mr Hyde*, for which Frederic March would win the Oscar for Best Actor, and Mamoulian was rightly regarded as a director of taste and sophistication. It was also common knowledge around

Hollywood that he had been chosen by Greta Garbo to direct her the following year in her film *Queen Christina*. But Marlene was wary of him. She still wanted von Sternberg.

Von Sternberg returned from the West Indies, where the hurricane season had failed to provide a decent hurricane, and announced that he felt he had had enough of the film business, and was seriously thinking of retiring. This did not make Marlene any happier. His announcement came during December, just as Paramount scheduled a production meeting for *Song Of Songs*. Marlene did not show up for it.

Rudi had just come over again, to spend Christmas and New Year with his wife and daughter, and had brought with him a script from UFA. It was called *Liebesgeschichte (Love Story)*, based on a short novel by Carl Zuckmayer, and Rudi hoped that she and von Sternberg might be interested. Von Sternberg thought he might well be, and started making plans to go to Berlin and discuss the matter.

Paramount scheduled a second production meeting for *Song Of Songs*, and again Marlene did not show up for it. So they stopped paying her her salary of $4,000 a week. She decided that this constituted breach of contract, and let them know that she now considered herself a free agent (as von Sternberg would also soon be).

In return, Paramount filed a breach of contract suit against her, suing her for the amount her behaviour had already cost them in delaying *Song Of Songs*, which they put at $184,850 (and six cents). Within a few days they were in court, where they asked the judge to issue an arrest warrant, fearing that she might try to flee the country (von Sternberg's secretary at Paramount, Eleanor McGeary, had testified to hearing him and Marlene discussing the UFA film in his office). This the judge refused, although he did issue a restraining order, forbidding her to work for any other studio, and demanded she appear again in court in a week's time.

Over the following weekend, relaxing with Maurice Chevalier at a beach house she had rented on Ocean Front Boulevard (later renamed Pacific Coast Highway), she gave him the appearance of being airily unconcerned. Her attorney, Ralph Blum, however, was not. He phoned her repeatedly, pointing out the wreck her behaviour might make of her career. She remained inflexible, and the situation was eventually resolved by von Sternberg, who promised that if she made *Song Of Songs* with Mamoulian, he would direct her again at Paramount in her next picture.

So on 5 January Eleanor McGeary informed the heads of the studio that Marlene would be available for work. Paramount immediately withdrew legal action, and offered her a new contract, for five years at a salary of $4,500 a week. This was not pure generosity. Ernst Lubitsch, just back from a fact-finding trip to Europe, had informed them that the three most popular Hollywood stars there were Dietrich, Garbo and Jeannette MacDonald.

On Monday 9 January, she joined Reuben Mamoulian in the studio commissary to discuss her first scenes in *Song Of Songs* over lunch. She was wearing a man's tweed suit, with a tie and a beret, and this would be the year in which male costume became her almost invariable public attire.

In *Song Of Songs* (which she told the press she regarded as 'one of the great works of fiction') she was to play Lily Czepanek, a shy and pious country girl, whose mother had died and whose father is dying. On his deathbed he insists that she read to him the more respectable passages from Solomon's 'Song Of Songs'.

After his death, now an orphan, she comes to Berlin to work in her drunken aunt's bookshop. She meets a handsome young sculptor called Richard Waldow, who talks her into posing nude for a sculpture he wants to make symbolizing 'Song Of Songs' (which he has heard her reciting bits of). He makes the sculpture and she falls in love with him, but he values his freedom, and when the rich and licentious Baron von Merzbach, who is one of his clients, admires both the sculpture and Lily, he makes no effort to stop the baron marrying her (her aunt also connives in the marriage).

She goes to live with him in his castle, but in spite of the life of riches he provides for her, and the education he gives her in aristocratic behaviour, he is cold and sadistic (his household includes a jealous former mistress). The Baron's handsome but susceptible young farm manager gives her riding lessons, and one afternoon she thrashes him with her whip for presuming to express love for her.

That evening, feeling she has perhaps been too hasty, she makes her way to his cottage, where he is about to presume some more when the cottage accidentally catches fire and burns down. The baron throws her out, and she goes on the streets of Berlin to make ends meet, also making some money on the side by singing. The sculptor runs into her again, realises how beautiful she is with her clothes on, and begs her forgiveness for letting her go.

Now truly loved, her virtue reawakens. Seizing a convenient crowbar, she smashes the nude statue into fragments as an act of repentance (to the strains of Tchaikovsky's symphony number six, the *Pathétique*), and tearfully she and her sculptor again recite from the 'Song Of Songs'.

It was a good job that Mamoulian had taste because Paramount certainly didn't. To publicise the film they would have thousands of life-sized reproductions of the nude statue made, sending them to cinemas right across America and fuelling endless speculation as to whether Marlene had really posed naked for it herself. (She had, for the sculptor S C Scarpitta. The statue depicts her standing on tiptoes with her hands, palms forward, by her sides. Her head and shoulders are back, her legs together and her breasts thrust forward.)

In the role of the baron, Mamoulian cast the cultured English actor Lionel Atwill, whose stock in trade was playing mad doctors or scientists, but who at other times performed well in more prestigious films.

Fredric March had turned down the part of the young sculptor, and instead Mamoulian cast Brian Aherne (who had been appearing on Broadway with Katherine Cornell in *The Barretts Of Wimpole Street*), thus giving him his first major film role. 'Why have you come to do this silly picture?' Marlene asked him. 'I have to do it because of my contract, and because Mr von Sternberg has walked out and I am left without any protection, but you are the great actor from New York and can do what you like? Are you crazy?'

Silly picture or not, its script bothered the Hays Office, who warned the studio they were aware that the stage version of *Song Of Songs* had been the success it was partly because the public knew it had had censorship problems. Mamoulian was forced to exert all his artistic prestige to reassure them that not only would the whole film be done in the best possible taste, it would also be crammed with culture – the soundtrack would feature music by Tchaikovsky, Beethoven, Bach and Brahms, and Marlene would sing 'Heideröslein' with words by Goethe and music by Schubert. There would be the poetry of the Old Testament, and there would be paintings and sculptures all over the place.

This reassured the Hays Office enough for filming to begin in mid-January, although as it proceeded a succession of writers continued to modify the script.

Marlene, Mamoulian recalled, was disciplined and professional on the set, although he felt that her performance was more calculated than spontaneous, and he was a little annoyed at her always overseeing her own lighting. She had begged von Sternberg to come onto the picture as her lighting supervisor, but he had refused, partly because he was sure that Mamoulian would (rightly) object, and partly because he was going off to Berlin to talk to UFA. And as it turned out, Marlene need not have worried.

She was by now, and would remain all her life, an expert in how she should be lit, insisting on having a full-length mirror beside the camera so that she could check the lamps were correctly positioned, the key-light always to be about 2.5m (8ft) above her and a little to her right. She had become so skilful that by simply wetting a finger and holding it up she could tell from the warmth of the light whether it was the correct distance from her.

In Berlin, von Sternberg had encouraging discussions with the head of UFA, the right-wing press baron Alfred Hugenberg, who by now was Minister for Economics in the increasingly powerful Nazi party (in 1932 it had become the party with most seats in the German parliament, the Reichstag). At that time the aging Hindeberg was still Chancellor, but in January 1933 Hitler ousted him, using a devious Nazi-Nationalist coalition.

These events indirectly caused von Sternberg's discussions to come to nothing. On 27 February, on the day he travelled by taxi to the airport to fly back to Hollywood, the Reichstag burned down. His taxi passed the still-smouldering ruins, and the taxi-driver cynically remarked that he believed it had been set on fire deliberately by the Nazis in order to create some kind of a scapegoat.

He was perfectly correct. The next day Hitler, blaming Communist agitators, suspended the constitution and assumed power as the absolute dictator of Germany. Although von Sternberg would take a moment to realise it, this meant that there would be no chance of a Viennese Jew directing pictures for UFA. When Marlene learned of events in Germany, she understood the situation at once.

For the time being, however, she was still at work on *Song Of Songs*, and while Mamoulian was not entirely pleased by her directing her lighting, he was if anything less pleased by her constant refrain that she missed von Sternberg. Each day, at the beginning of her first shot, she had taken to ritually whispering into the microphone, 'Oh, Joe – why hast thou forsaken me?' She genuinely did feel lost without him, and her behaviour reached a climax on 28 March, during a shot for which she had to ride a horse. She fell off deliberately (but carefully) and lay where she had fallen, weeping for von Sternberg to come to her aid. He was hastily summoned and took charge at once, accompanying her as she was taken to her home, where she stayed for three days, recovering.

He was not, however, the only man in her life at this time. She had swiftly embarked on an affair with Brian Aherne (beginning it by baking him a cake), and occasionally with Reuben Mamoulian as well. And of course there was still Maurice Chevalier, although at around the time of the shooting of *Song Of Songs*, their relationship cooled off somewhat.

This came about partly because of her now almost always wearing male clothing in her private life. This made Chevalier uncomfortable. He disliked taking her out dining or dancing in such attire, and frequently asked her to wear something more feminine. But she refused, and there was (as he knew) a reason. She had just embarked on what would be a long relationship with the stylish Spanish playwright and screenwriter Mercedes de Acosta, then working for MGM, and described by actress-writer-photographer Jean Howard as 'a little blackbird of a woman, strange and mysterious, and to many irresistible'.

In 1933 Mercedes was forty, and had mingled for years with the leading lights of the artistic world, in both Europe and America. She knew Picasso and Stravinsky and the renowned actress Eleanora Duse, and among her friends had been such performers as Sarah Bernhardt, Mrs Patrick Campbell and Isadora Duncan. With a lively and curious mind and a strong personality, she was part Buddhist and part spiritualist, a vegetarian and an active lesbian (Alice B Toklas is rumoured to have said, 'Say what you like about Mercedes, she's had the three most important women of the twentieth century', which led a Thirties humourist to remark that, given two of them were Dietrich and Garbo, who was the third? Gertrude Stein? Eleanor Roosevelt? Shirley Temple?)

At the beginning of 1933 she was still heavily involved in an affair with Greta Garbo. But Garbo had gone back to her native Sweden for a holiday when Marlene attended a dance concert being given by Berlin's Harald Kreutzberg and noticed Mercedes sitting behind her in the audience. She had been escorted there by Cecil Beaton, whom Marlene knew. She greeted him, and gave Mercedes a shy smile.

The next day she showed up at Mercedes' home, wearing slacks and carrying armfuls of white roses. As Mercedes wrote in her book of reminiscences, *Here Lies The Heart*, published in 1960: 'As she entered, she hesitated at the doorway and looked at me in the same shy way [as the evening before]. I asked her to come into the room and put out my hand. She took it in an almost military manner, bent over it and [explained], "I hope you will forgive me. I noticed you last night in the theatre and wanted to meet you. I know very few people in Hollywood and no-one who could introduce us, so I just found out where you live and I came myself."'

Their relationship soon blossomed into romance – a much deeper affair than any she was having at the time with any man. They enjoyed candlelit evenings, had long, late pillow conversations, and the occasional lovers' quarrel. Marlene began cooking for Mercedes, and bombarding her with flowers – as Mercedes wrote, 'sometimes twice a day, ten dozen roses or twelve dozen carnations... We never had enough vases and when I told Marlene this, as a hint not to send me any more flowers, instead I received a great many Lalique vases and even *more* flowers. The house became a sort of madhouse of flowers.' Their affair would continue, quite openly, right through the Thirties.

Song Of Songs finished shooting in early April. After this, the studio allowed her to go to Europe for a holiday before beginning her next film, which was to be directed by von Sternberg. Following his trip to UFA, and his rapid realization of how impossible it would be to work there now the Nazis were in power, he had, within a few weeks, signed a new contract with Paramount – a contract that gave him almost complete directorial control over his pictures.

Marlene and Maria set off for Europe, taking with them Marlene's new car, a huge sixteen-cylinder Cadillac, for which she had recently traded in her Rolls. They travelled via New York, where Marlene had a brief reunion with Maurice Chevalier, who had now, after a couple of rather mediocre films in succession, left Paramount to go and work for MGM. Then she and her daughter boarded the German ship *Europa*, and set sail.

She was anxious to discover for herself how things were in Germany under the new regime, but she would not go there. Many of her old acquaintances seemed to be fleeing the country. One old friend, the actor Hans Heinrich von Twardowsky, had been among the first to arrive in America, but others were settling in such non-German cities as Paris. She would go there to see what she could find out.

Marlene and Maria arrived in Paris on 19 May, and at last, for the first time in her life, she was in the city that she had heard about and adored ever since her schooldays.

Rudi met them at the Gare St-Lazare. Marlene got off the train wearing a man's chocolate-coloured polo coat over a man's pearl-grey suit, a tie and a felt hat. To her surprise and dismay the crowd that had turned up to see her arrive burst into noisy jeers – jeers that followed her to her hotel, the Hotel Trianon in Versailles. What she had failed to realise was that in France cross-dressing was illegal, even in Paris. A magistrate there suggested she should be arrested.

When she wore female dress, however, she was greeted everywhere with delight. She attended cocktail parties and the Baron de Rothschild's ball, and she visited her old friend Margo Lion, now in exile. Margo had just appeared in a film made in Paris, directed by G W Pabst, who was also in exile but would soon return to Germany. It also starred another old Berlin friend and exile, Peter Lorre, who would not. It also had in it a young French actor, Jean Gabin, then just beginning to make his reputation in films.

Marlene had a little film work of her own to do in Paris. At the Paramount studio where Rudi was based she spent a week recording her dialogue for a proposed French version of *Song Of Songs*.

Her old friend and musical director, Peter Kreuder, was now also in Paris, and it seemed to her a good idea for them to make some more records together. She would act as her own producer, Rudi would help arrange things, and together they began hunting down songs that she could sing. Rudi located another Berlin exile, Kurt Weill, and asked him to write a couple of songs, which he did, but they turned out to be unsuited to Marlene's voice (a failure that would come to obsess Weill). He also went around town trying to track down a song she had been sent by a Berlin journalist friend while she was in Hollywood. She had liked it, but, not expecting to need it, had left it behind.

It had been composed by two Berliners – the music by Franz Wachsmann and the lyrics by Max Colpet, and both of them were now in Paris too. Rudi set out to find them, with the help of other refugees, and quite soon got hold of Colpet's phone number and address – the inexpensive Hotel Ansonia, at 8 Rue de Saigon. He phoned, telling Colpet that Marlene Dietrich wanted him to come to her at the Hotel Trianon. Colpet, thinking it was a joke, put the phone down on him.

This was repeated several times, and eventually the only thing to do seemed to be for Marlene to send her Cadillac to collect him. Which she did, to Colpet's astonishment. He and a friend got into the car and were driven to the Hotel Trianon. She explained to Colpet that she wanted to record his song, but poor Colpet had to admit he no longer remembered the words.

That was no problem, she explained. She knew the words. It was the music that was the problem, and where was Franz Wachsmann? Colpet indicated the friend he had brought with him. 'This is Wachsmann,' he explained. (Wachsmann was also living at the Ansonia, along with several other exiles, many of them people Marlene had known in Berlin – such as his fellow-composer Friedrich Holländer, Peter Lorre, and a screenwriter called Billy Wilder.)

The song Colpet and Wachsmann had written was 'Allein In Einer Grossen Stadt' ('Alone In A Big City'), and at her recording session, on 19 July, with a small orchestra directed by Peter Kreuder, Marlene recorded it. On the same day she recorded 'Assez', 'Je M'Ennuie', 'Ja, So Bin Ich' and two songs co-composed by Kreuder, 'Wo Ist Der Mann?' and 'Mein Blondes Baby' (which was accompanied only by Kreuder at the piano). But of all the songs, by far the best was 'Allein In Einer Grossen Stadt'. A haunting, lonely song, Marlene would go on singing it for the rest of her life, although for the record to be sold in Germany the composer and lyricist had to give themselves assumed names, 'José d'Alba' and 'Kurt Gerhardt'.

From Paris, she and Maria and Rudi (and Tamara) motored to Vienna, where she looked up her old friend, co-star and lover, Willi Forst, who had just switched careers to become a director, and was making his first film, *Leise Flehen Meine Lieder (The Unfinished Symphony)*, which, unsurprisingly, was a biography of Franz Schubert.

This time Willi was not to be Marlene's lover. Her eye immediately fell on the handsome twenty-eight-year-old actor playing Schubert. His name was Hans Jaray, and during her stay in Vienna he and she became inseparable, though often accompanied in public by the understanding Willi Forst or the even-more-understanding Rudi.

But Marlene's trip to Vienna was not entirely to visit old friends, or the city that was among her favourites. Since 'Count Kilowatt' had died, the old Sascha-Film Company had been reorganised under Kurt Hartl (who had been a production assistant when she and Willi Forst had made *Café Electric* back in 1927), and was prospering. It seemed to her that with Berlin off-limits to von Sternberg (and he a Viennese), Sascha-Film might prove a useful place for him and her to work. It did not occur, even to her, that in a short while Austria would become as anti-Semitic as Germany.

In July, while she continued to tour Europe, *Song Of Songs* opened in America. It was well-received by the critics, many of them pointing out how much better she performed when not directed by von Sternberg. They preferred her not to be so knowing and disillusioned, and indeed she had acted her role with grace and simplicity, but her performance has not lasted well. It is too simple and safe, and even in its day the plot of the film was already old-fashioned.

From Vienna she and her family went to Salzburg, then to the Cap d'Antibes, and briefly back to Paris, staying this time at the Plaza Athénée. She was now on her way back to Hollywood, but just before she left Paris she received an unexpected visit from a group of German film distributors who had been authorised to ask her to come back home to Germany and resume her film career there.

She indignantly refused, berating Germany for forcing so many of its talented people into exile. On 10 May the infamous book-burning had taken place in the Berlin Opernplatz where the works of such 'decadent' authors as Heine, Marx, Freud, Brecht, Remarque, Stefan Zweig, and both Thomas and Heinrich Mann had been singled out for destruction.

Marlene and Maria sailed back to America aboard a French liner (which may have been purely by chance, although some newspapers thought it 'significant'), and soon Marlene was back at Paramount where von Sternberg, secure in the power his new contract had given him, was completing the screenplay for her next picture.

It was to be based on the early life of Catherine the Great, who, although born into a rather impecunious royal house in Pomerania (in 1729), became Russian by marriage and eventual Empress of Russia, reigning for thirty-four years. Although her life was romantic and dramatic in itself, von Sternberg took considerable liberties with the truth, planning a film that would be lavish, highly imaginative, and certainly the most extraordinary film that Marlene would ever make. He himself described it as 'a relentless excursion in style', and assured her, 'If this film is a flop, it will be a grandiose flop.' The credits on the finished film claim that it is based on Catherine's own diary, but that is pure von Sternberg invention – everything in it except its remote historical origin came from his vivid imagination.

He planned it almost like a silent film (although there are many passages of dialogue). Its scenes and sequences are linked by titles, each baldly setting down the next piece of exposition as the story progressed, and he thought of each sequence almost in musical terms, as a prelude, a rondo, a scherzo, a fugue, an allegro, a largo.

The whole thing would depict Catherine's life as it moved from childhood to teenage romanticism, to awakening desire, to amused disillusion and the lust for power. He had hoped to call the film *Her Regiment Of Lovers*, a title the Hays Office refused to allow, and, after a brief period of using the working title *Catherine The Great,* it eventually became, and remained, *The Scarlet Empress.*

Once again, as in all of von Sternberg's film with her, many elements in the character of the heroine are based on the character of Marlene herself – she had an 'army' of lovers, a great and growing desire for power (over audiences, over lovers and ex-lovers, over the sick or suffering who might need her help, over the presentation of her image), and she loved to take a male role (at the end, dressed in an elegant white hussar's uniform, she effectively becomes not Empress of Russia, but Emperor).

A curious point about the real Catherine was that the Earl of Malmesbury, writing home from her court, expressed the opinion that, in spite of her many lovers, she died 'a stranger to the tender passion'. It is likely that in this too she resembled Marlene.

The film begins with a short sequence of Catherine's childhood in her home court in Pomerania, and the role of her as a child was played by Marlene's daughter Maria, then aged nine. She looks pretty, and reasonably assured, and after only a couple of years in America had acquired a natural-sounding American accent, with no hint of the German that was her native tongue until the age of six.

The young Catherine's family, especially her mother, are determined that she shall marry into a grand royal house, possibly that of Russia, so she is to be taught about Russia, and the transition from her childhood to her youth is accomplished by a long montage showing the barbaric tyranny of Russian history. This montage, feverishly imagined by von Sternberg, contains a sort of lexicon of sadomasochistic images, with whippings, beheadings, brandings, bondage and near-naked women.

The National League of Decency, formed by America's Roman Catholic bishops, was about to come into being, and in response to it (and similar organizations) the film industry's own censorship body, the Hays Office, was busy drawing up its imposing Motion Picture Production Code. *The Scarlet Empress* would be one of the last films made before the Code was enforced, and for years afterwards such images as it contained would be disbarred. Even images of naked babies would be banned, as would an endless list of other things, including long kisses, adultery and double beds.

In the film, we emerge from the montage of Russian history into a scene of girlish innocence, with the young Catherine (now played by Marlene) on a garlanded swing in a garden. She never looked lovelier or more youthful, and von Sternberg, by now a virtuoso in bringing out her beauty, lit her with a flat white light. As the film continued he would gradually increase the shadowing of her face, bringing out its modelling along with her character's growing disillusion and determination.

An emissary, Count Alexei, comes from the Russian court to take her back there with him as the prospective bride of Peter, the heir to the Russian throne. Count Alexei is tall and dark and strikingly handsome, and the young Catherine is rather taken with him, but he reassures her that Peter is taller and more handsome, and can even read and write.

He is lying. After an arduous seven-week journey by coach and sledge the young Catherine discovers Peter to be a dwarfish half-mad imbecile, with a manic grin and a passion for playing with toy soldiers. Count Alexei apologises for his fib, saying that he could not bear the thought that Catherine might not come to Russia if she knew the truth, because he has fallen madly in love with her.

The Russian court, and indeed the whole of Russia, as imagined by von Sternberg, is shadowed and nightmarish – a delirious riot of vast doors (which take half-a-dozen servants to push them open), icons, flags, hangings, banners, balustrades, stairways, candelabra, Russian crosses, censers, asperges, bells and vast crude carvings of heraldic symbols and devils. As much as anything *The Scarlet Empress* is a film of (and about) excess – the decadent excess of too much food, too many furs and jewels, too much sex, too much cruelty.

Catherine, brought to Russia by the reigning Empress to provide her son (and thus the country) with an heir, gradually shifts from disappointment in her husband to desire for the soldiers surrounding her (she mostly fancies Count Alexei, but is further disillusioned to discover that in spite of his declared love for her he is also secretly the lover of the Empress herself).

She bears a son (by one of the soldiers), earning the enmity of her husband (who has never liked her anyway and knows it cannot be his) but the delight of the Empress.

The Empress dies and Catherine's husband becomes Tsar Peter III; he embarks on a campaign of brutality and repression. He lets Catherine know that he plans to have her killed and, partly out of self-defence and partly out of growing ambition, she assembles an army of her beloved officers and has him killed instead, declaring herself (somewhat unconstitutionally) Empress. We end on her in her white hussar's uniform, smiling triumphantly as the '1812 Overture' rings out on the soundtrack. This was probably the most incandescent smile Marlene ever gave in any of her films – a smile of almost insane joy. At last she has power over a whole empire.

To play the part of Count Alexei, von Sternberg cast John Davis Lodge, a tall, dark, handsome actor who looked convincingly Russian. In fact he was one of the socially prominent Lodges of Boston, and shortly afterwards left the acting profession for politics, becoming in turn a congressman, governor of Connecticut and the United States ambassador to Spain. Von Sternberg, describing him as 'one of the most intelligent performers', praised him as one of the few actors who recognised that an actor is simply there to be manipulated by the director into creating something beyond what is in him and congratulated him for having the wit to leave the profession.

The intelligent Marlene continued to be manipulated by von Sternberg, but by this time there appeared to be some stress in their relationship. He seemed to be becoming even more tyrannical, perhaps because he was still smitten by her and wanted some revenge for his unhappiness at her string of other lovers. He had her repeat one long walk down an imperial staircase forty-five times. On that occasion she made no complaint. But when, in another scene, he had her repeatedly blow out some candles, she eventually walked off the set and was only persuaded back with great difficulty.

Mercedes de Acosta sometimes dropped in from MGM to watch the filming, and recalled that although Marlene still viewed von Sternberg as a friend, 'he was often very difficult and explosive on the set. One day they had a violent quarrel and Jo refused to speak to her except when directing her in front of the camera. After three days of this she hit on a solution.' Her solution, as she explained privately to Mercedes, was that she was again going to fall off a horse, as she had done during the filming of *Song Of Songs*.

Mercedes was present to see this, and recalled, 'The moment came, and I saw her, every inch an empress, high up on the horse before the camera... She quietly tumbled off the horse, slipping to the ground as though it were a feat she often performed. The cameras stopped grinding and everyone, stagehands, grips, assistant directors, and Jo, rushed in wild confusion to her side. Marlene lay as though she were dead. Jo picked her up in his arms and screamed for a doctor, who appeared in an unnaturally short time.' (He was Mercedes' own doctor, providentially present). 'Luckily, Jo was too beside himself to notice this. He kissed Marlene's hands and begged her to forgive him, as if she were dying and they were parting forever.'

Mercedes was not von Sternberg's only reason for jealousy. Encouraged by the active lesbian milieu in which Mercedes moved, Marlene herself was by now openly pursuing any woman she found attractive, usually actresses. At Paramount she made overtures to both Frances Dee and Carole Lombard, sending them notes and flowers and making intimations. Both were unrepentantly heterosexual (Lee was the wife of Joel McCrae, Lombard of William Powell) and she got nowhere with either.

In spite of the lavish visual excesses of *The Scarlet Empress*, it had in fact not been quite as expensive to make as it looked. Von Sternberg was extremely talented at making a little look like a lot. He made use of model work, giving the impression of vast sets, and for the sound of great church bells tolling he recorded a small table-bell, slowing and distorting the sound to give it a sonorous deepness. Also, for many of the crowd scenes in the film, he made use of footage of hundreds of extras taken from a silent film, *The Patriot*, directed for Paramount in 1928 by Ernst Lubitsch.

This would lead him into trouble. Lubitsch, increasingly involved as a supervisor of the studio's productions, viewed the cutting-copy of *The Scarlet Empress* and became seriously concerned at what he saw as reckless expenditure. With Paramount's financial situation still shaky, he felt that von Sternberg (whose pretensions to artistry he had always disliked) was endangering the whole studio. In particular (according to von Sternberg) he complained about the extravagance of the crowd scenes, not recognizing them as originally his own.

Whether or not this was true, Lubitsch came to the conclusion that von Sternberg would have to go. He knew that his contract called for him to make one further film, again with total artistic control, and decided to let von Sternberg get on with it. If von Sternberg would, as Lubitsch saw it, indulge himself in such a way again, losing the studio vast amounts of money, it would then be a simple matter to get rid of him. For the moment, however, it was simply agreed between von Sternberg and the studio that he would make just one more picture with Marlene, to which he agreed happily, feeling that he had made as much use of her as he could (at least for the moment), and that, in view of the slight distance beginning to grow between them, such a move would be good for both their careers. For his own part, he feared he was becoming known in the business as simply Marlene's director. Directors too can become typecast.

The Scarlet Empress turned out to be a box-office disaster. It had its world première in London, and both there and in America it appealed to neither the critics nor the public. (It was at this point that Paramount announced to the press that their next film would be the last that Marlene and von Sternberg would make together.) Ornate and obsessive, it suffered from comparison with a film that had been released just before it – *Catherine The Great*, produced in London by Alexander Korda and starring Marlene's old Berlin acquaintance, Elisabeth Bergner. That film was by comparison conventional and unthreatening, and did well.

After shooting on *The Scarlet Empress* finished, in the early spring of 1934, Marlene set sail again for Europe, this time to visit Berlin briefly. She felt it was time to see the situation there for herself, to find out if there was after all any chance of her working there, and to visit her mother and other relations. Her Uncle Willi, she knew, was in poor health, and indeed he would die later that year, leaving his shares in Felsing & Co to his (and Aunt Jolly's) son, Hasso. As Hasso was then only twelve, Marlene's mother Josephine would, for the time being, become the effective head of the family firm.

On 14 March, shortly after Marlene had arrived in Berlin, it was announced in the German press that she had donated 'a considerable sum' to a Nazi-run film welfare fund, as a 'reconciliation'. She may well have been pressured into doing this, but her gesture did her little good. Almost immediately – indeed, only two days later – it was announced that the Nazis had banned her film *Song Of Songs*, thus letting everybody know they were not for sale. The reasons given were that original novel had been written by a Jew, that it had been financed by Jewish money, and that in it Marlene had besmirched the moral purity of the German people by playing a role in which a German adulteress went unpunished.

In future, as long as the Nazis remained in power, Germans would hear little and see nothing of their most famous film actor – any news of her was filtered for public consumption by the Ministry for Propaganda, headed by Josef Goebbels. She would be condemned for having too often played whores, and reports would start to appear that would imply she wasn't

German at all, but the daughter of a Russian army officer and that she had come to Berlin after dancing in Paris at the notoriously lewd Folies Bergère.

Goebbels' propaganda, however, did not much reflect his private feelings and opinions. An obsessive film-goer since his boyhood, since long before he came to power, he adored films (including American films), and his favourite German performer was Marlene. (She, for her part, regarded him as 'that grotesque dwarf'.) He loved entertainment, and believed that making entertaining films that contained subtle hints of propaganda was a much better way of controlling people's minds than crass bullying polemics. Film, he believed, was the most powerful medium that existed for tapping into the subconscious.

It was at around the time of her Berlin visit that Thomas Mann, now in exile in Zurich, wrote a letter to a fellow-writer, René Schickele, who was also in exile in France:

> I often envy Hesse, who has been out of Germany for so many years, but for whom Germany is not closed. My abhorrence of the conditions there, and my ardent desire to see the gang there go to Hell one way or another in the shortest possible time, has not changed in the slightest...
>
> Do you believe in the likelihood of a collapse in my lifetime or yours? The discontent is vast; there is a great deal of vigorous and open grumbling; the outlook for the economy is bad (although certain industries are thriving); a fall of the mark and ersatz goods are in the offing...
>
> Added to that is the regime's vast apparatus for deceiving, stupefying, and brutalizing them. The intellectual and moral level long ago sank so low that the spirit necessary for a real uprising simply cannot be summoned up. And at the same time they have, in that debased state, the heady sense of representing a new world – which indeed it is; a world of debasement.

Marlene's trip back to the city of her birth, where she encountered such a forbidding atmosphere of repressive change, was on the whole an unpleasant one, but her voyage back to America on the *Île De France* did bring her one golden present. She met a man on board who would remain a staunch lifelong friend – Ernest Hemingway. Already an established writer, having published, among other things, his novels *The Sun Also Rises* and *A Farewell To Arms*, he later recalled meeting Marlene ('The Kraut', as he affectionately tagged her) for his biographer, A E Hotchner:

> I was crossing cabin on the *Île*, but a pal of mine who was traveling first loaned me his reserve tux and smuggled me in for meals. One night we're having dinner in the salon, my pal and I, when there appears at the top of the staircase this unbelievable spectacle in white. The Kraut, of course. A long, tight white-beaded gown over *that* body; in the area of what is known as the Dramatic Pause, she can give lessons to anybody. So she gives that Dramatic Pause on the staircase, then slowly slithers down the stairs and across the floor to where Jock Whitney was having a fancy dinner party. Of course, nobody in that dining room has touched food to lips since her entrance. The Kraut gets to the table and all the men hop up and her chair is held at the ready; but she's counting. Twelve. Of course, she apologises and backs off and says she's sorry, but she is very superstitious about being thirteen at anything and with that she turns to go, but I have naturally risen to the occasion and grandly offer to save the party by being the fourteenth. That was how we met. Pretty romantic, eh?

Their friendship would last for years, mostly via correspondence, and would ripen into a sort of fierce protectiveness of each other. But by some sort of unspoken mutual agreement, they never became lovers. On Hemingway's side this was possibly due to his lifelong uncertainty about women – he found them fascinating, tending even to idealise them, but at the same time he resented and almost feared them (his aggressive preoccupation with having a macho image was a response to these feelings). And Marlene of course had something masculine in her manner, to which he could respond. To him she became one of his 'buddies'.

Although he was only a couple of years older than she was, she quickly came to regard him as a sort of father-figure in her life – a sturdy, intelligent counsellor and guide. As he called her 'the Kraut', she came to call him 'Papa' (in the same way that many others around him did). And there was something else about him that attracted her – he was a celebrity. She retained for years the sort of hero-worship that had caused her to stalk

Henny Porten in her youth, and now that she was an international celebrity herself, she would increasingly use that to make the acquaintance of other celebrities – not just from the worlds of film and theatre, but from many other worlds. Also, of course, being photographed with fellow-celebrities, or mentioned in the gossip-columns as mingling with them, adds to one's own sense of celebrity.

Not that all her friends were celebrities (or even lovers). At around this time a young Scottish actor, an ex-army officer, came to Hollywood to try his luck. His name was David Niven, and as he later wrote:

> When I first arrived I knew nobody in the film world and I had never acted in my life. Consequently I sat around for quite a long time looking hopeful but getting more broke by the minute. Marlene was then the glamour queen, and was driven round in the biggest private automobile ever built... I was lucky enough to meet Marlene at a party and, of course, have loved her deeply and devotedly ever since. Once in those early days I got ill. I got 'flu or something. I was living in a room over a garage in Hollywood, and I was now broke and very miserable. At my lowest ebb, the biggest automobile ever built suddenly glided up and Briggs [Marlene's chauffeur] came staggering into the room carrying food and medicine and champagne and caviar, and even a huge cake which Marlene had made herself. She happens to be a sensational cook, too.
>
> That was a typical act of impulsive kindness and generosity – she had heard that someone she hardly knew was ill and lonely and miserable, and she reacted in what I now know to be typical Dietrich fashion.

David Niven was only one of many. As well as subsidizing her family, including her mother and her husband (and Tamara), she would be endlessly generous to the increasing stream of German exiles coming to work in America. She was never one to hoard her income.

Marlene, returning to Hollywood, moved into a new home – a large house in Bel Air, which was previously owned by the silent-movie star Colleen Moore. Then just entering a long and prosperous retirement, Colleen had been the top box-office attraction in America in 1927, earning $12,500 dollars a week.

Back at Paramount, things had continued to change. B P Schulberg had finally had his contract bought out and moved to Columbia Pictures to work – his post as head of production was taken by Ernst Lubitsch. Von Sternberg had been developing the Spanish story he had had in mind for Marlene for some time. It was based on a novel by Pierre Loüys, called *La Femme Et Le Pantin* (*The Woman And The Puppet*), and versions of it had already been successful twice for Paramount, in 1920 and again in 1929. He had prepared a first draft script with the American writer John Dos Passos, and his proposed title for it was *Caprice Espagnol*. Lubitsch, however, on reading the draft, decided it should be given the more dramatic title *The Devil Is A Woman*.

Before filming began, von Sternberg told Marlene that in this, their last film together, she would look more beautiful than ever. And so it turned out.

The story of it, as reworked by von Sternberg, more closely paralleled their relationship than any they had ever made. In it, the beautiful but heartless Concha Perez breaks the hearts of not just one man, but hundreds. Much of the plot is told in flashback, during fiesta time in a Spanish city, by a former army officer, Don Pasqual, to a younger fellow-officer, Antonio Galvan. Don Pasqual, who has been in a state of unrequited love with Concha for several years – during which she has milked him for cash, caused him to lose his commission, and caused him endless distress (alternating with brief hope) – tells Antonio, who has just become smitten with her, the story of their relationship.

But Antonio will not be dissuaded, and she treats him nearly as badly, agreeing to go off with him on a train to Paris at the end of the film, then capriciously letting the train leave without her. She is going (she says) back to Don Pasqual.

Don Pasqual is patently modelled on von Sternberg himself, in both character and appearance, and more openly so than any character since Adolphe Menjou in *Morocco*. The part was taken by Lionel Atwill, who had appeared with Marlene in *Song Of Songs*, and his moustache, as Menjou's had been, was modified to resemble von Sternberg's.

The role of the younger officer, Antonio, was given to Joel McCrae, but a few days after shooting started (on 10 October 1934) he was replaced. Accounts of what happened vary. Von Sternberg claimed in his memoirs that McCrae was so scared of his reputation as a martinet that he 'fled in terror after his first scene with me', and he is inclined to ascribe part of the blame to McCrae's wife, Frances Dee (to whom Marlene had made advances).

A more likely version is that he was fired for insubordination – Marlene claimed that after about five days of filming he objected strenuously to the number of takes von Sternberg was forcing him to do. He was replaced by another young actor, Cesar Romero, who as it happened was an improvement – he looked more convincingly Spanish than the very American McCrae would have done, as well as having a much stronger air of sexuality.

Not that he liked von Sternberg any more than McCrae had done, later referring to him as 'a mean man, a little Napoleon'. He was annoyed that after all the takes the actors were made to do (sometimes up into the forties), often it was take one or take two that got used. He was also appalled at the way von Sternberg treated Marlene on the set, often reducing her to tears.

It seems likely that by now in their relationship there was a certain amount of revenge in the way he treated her. After all, he had been deeply in love with her for five years (the same period as Don Pasqual in the film), and knew that after this film was over they would drift even further apart. And for all his arrogant bluster, he was inside a vulnerable and sensitive man, and much more easily hurt than Marlene could ever be. He did manage to hurt her, however, when, as soon as the last shot of the film was completed, he dismissed the crew, turned, and strode off the set without giving her a look or a word.

But he had done what he said. In *The Devil Is A Woman* she looks more beautiful than ever (even if her character, Concha, is rather too broadly coquettish than Marlene was good at being, and far too often).

The film too is beautiful. Almost as stylised as *The Scarlet Empress* (although much lighter in mood), it is a riot of streamers, balloons, confetti, and grotesque masks (much of the film takes place during fiesta time). There are palms, railings, ornate ironwork, fans, baskets and slatted shutters. But in spite of the beauty there is a bitterness in it. Concha is totally mercenary and heartless (albeit entrancing), and Lionel Atwill gives a fine performance as a dignified and well-mannered man hiding inner pain.

Interestingly, in this film for the first time Marlene does not play a whore. This was of course because of the newly introduced Motion Picture Production Code. Although she is seen being coquettishly friendly with several handsome young men, and we are told there have been hundreds more, there is never much hint that there has been any sexual intimacy between her and them. Nor even with Don Pasqual, who is characterised as an experienced man about town.

The film may have squeezed past the Hays Office, but the studio was worried about its commercial potential. As part of their attempt to sell it to the public they made a ten-minute film called *The Fashion Side Of Hollywood*. In fact what it showed was the fashion side of Paramount, parading its stars (Mae West, Claudette Colbert, Carole Lombard) in costumes from their forthcoming films. Especially it paraded Marlene, who is presented at both the beginning and the end of the film, with her designer Travis Banton, in what is described in the narration as a 'costume test', but which in reality was shot after the film was made.

Such measures didn't help. From the moment *The Devil Is A Woman* was premièred – on 3 May 1935, at New York's Paramount Theater – it was clearly going to be a critical and box-office disaster. Typical was the review in the magazine *American* – 'the delightful Dietrich pouts and poses through dreary, repetitive reels of dull story clumsily told, and the boresome botch makes even the magnificent Marlene appear amateurish and almost ridiculous.'

In America, only the *New York Times* found something to praise in it, saying, 'The uninformed will be bored by *The Devil Is A Woman*. The cultivated filmgoer will be delighted by the sly urbanity which is implicit in Mr von Sternberg's direction, as well as excited by the striking beauty of his sets and photography.' Unfortunately, the uninformed were in the majority, and the *New York Times* also reported (on the day of the première), 'The future of Josef von Sternberg appears to have been settled. Following the preview the other evening of *The Devil Is A Woman*... The studio indicated that no attempt would be made to hold Mr von Sternberg and that, in spite of certain financial loss, the film would be released in its present form, without retakes... [Lubitsch's] production regime was described as favoring the immediate departure of the director, with the whole thing charged off to experience.'

When it came to foreign distribution, the film ran into a serious (and totally unexpected) problem. The Spanish government took exception to the way their country was depicted in it (although von Sternberg's Spain was no more like the real thing than his Russia or his China). In particular they objected that government officials were portrayed as weak and corrupt in the film (mainly in a typically jittery performance from Edward Everett Horton as the town's mayor), and they announced that if it were not instantly withdrawn from exhibition, and all prints and negatives destroyed, they would ban all Paramount films from being shown in Spain, and close the Paramount office in Madrid.

By November 1935, when it became clear that these protestations were no joke, it had long been apparent to the studio that *The Devil Is A Woman* was a commercial disaster anyway. Nobody much liked it, and so the studio obediently burned prints and negatives. Fortunately a few good prints did survive. Marlene had one (it would remain her favourite of her films), and so did von Sternberg. After a gap of almost quarter of a century the film would be seen again when his print was shown in 1959 at the Venice Film Festival. It was hailed as a lost masterpiece.

It is only a pity that, due to pressure from the Hays Office and other self-righteous organizations, about seventeen minutes of the film had by then been censored, including Marlene's second (and better) song, 'If It isn't Pain (then It isn't Love)'. Her record of it, however, made in 1935, does still exist.

After *The Devil Is A Woman* was finished, a stage in Marlene's life was over. Never again would she work as closely and intensely with a director as she had with von Sternberg.

That the film remained her favourite is not surprising. By now the Dietrich image, reaching its full realization in *The Devil Is A Woman*, was firmly established, and it was this that she would preserve and exploit for the rest of her life. As her daughter Maria remarked, she would never again act as well as she had in *The Blue Angel*, the powerful image that was her face taking over from her talent as an actor.

The image would turn out to have power not only over her audiences, but over Marlene herself.

7 The Highest-Paid Woman In The World

During the spring and summer of 1935 Marlene had several months of freedom from film-making, and went into her domestic mode. She looked after Maria, she baked and did housework, and she gave small dinner-parties (doing the cooking herself) for friends. Often Mercedes de Acosta was there, and the two felt no need to conceal their emotional involvement with each other – it was always easier in those days for two women than for two men as their relationship was seen by the uninitiated as simply a warm friendship.

She and Mercedes spent several days together each week. They would go hiking in the canyons near Pacific Palisades, or motor north along the coast to Santa Barbara for lunch, or sometimes simply sit quietly at home (either one of their homes), reading.

Although Mercedes was at this time the most important woman in her life, there were occasional others. She attended a 'come-as-the-person-you-most-admire' costume party escorted by the young English actress Elizabeth Allen, both in costumes that would have done justice to the sensuous and highly charged imagination of von Sternberg himself. Marlene was dressed as both Leda *and* the swan (she loved the Rilke poem), while Elizabeth was dressed as Marlene, in top hat and tails.

Rudi came over from Paris on a visit, and while in Hollywood continued to involve himself in Marlene's business affairs, discussing them with her tax advisers and with her agent, Harry Edington. Edington, who was also Garbo's agent, was a shrewd operator. In March he had renegotiated Marlene's contract with Paramount, the new contract stipulating that in return for making two pictures over the period of a year (under the 'personal supervision' of Ernst Lubitsch), she would receive a total salary of $250,000. This was quite an achievement, considering that her popularity with the public had severely declined after *The Scarlet Empress* and *The Devil Is A Woman*. He managed it mainly by convincing the studio that now she was free from the malign influence of Josef von Sternberg, her career would flourish.

Indeed, she was in something of a curious situation. Not even close to being one of the top box-office attractions in America, she was one of the most famous stars. She was so famous that, like Garbo, she was billed by her surname only – she was 'Dietrich'. Garbo, in fact, was in a very similar situation at MGM – the studio's most prestigious star, but nowhere near the top of the industry's money-makers.

When the *Motion Picture Herald* started compiling its annual list of the ten biggest stars at the box office, at the end of 1932, Garbo was fifth (the top three were Marie Dressler, Janet Gaynor and Joan Crawford), and for the rest of her career, in spite of her superstar reputation, she never again appeared in the top ten.

Marlene did even less well, but by this time she felt secure in her fame, widely publicised as 'the most glamorous woman in the world', and now accepting of the fact that, for the time being at least, her main career must be in Hollywood. Which was no bad thing. A star in Hollywood was a lot more famous, and more glamourised, than a star anywhere else in the world. She was no longer the young girl who somehow wanted success as an actress on stage or screen. Now her face was on cigarette cards.

Germany, she knew, was lost to her. Above all, her Berlin of the Twenties could now be nothing but a memory. More and more she was coming to despise her fellow-Germans for voting in the Nazis, causing so many of her friends to become refugees. And after all, had not Germany declared war on her beloved France back in 1914? She was happy to relax in Hollywood while Paramount's production head Ernst Lubitsch sorted out a new script for her.

Lubitsch's plan was to make her on-screen character more approachable: to do away with much of the wry Berlin mockery that von Sternberg had always found so tantalizing and appealing, and to make use of her wittiness without making it seem cold and reserved.

At the same time, he had to preserve her exotic quality, so what was needed was another story set somewhere abroad. Sorting through European properties that Paramount had acquired the rights to, he unearthed a recently made German film about a lady jewel thief reclaimed from her life of crime by the power of love. It had been called *Die Schönen Tage Von Aranjuez (The Beautiful Days Of Aranjuez)* – a line from Schiller's *Don Carlos*, but Lubitsch planned to give it the snappier title *The Pearl Necklace* (after the item the heroine steals). It would be shot in the glamorous new process, Technicolor. The first-ever Technicolor film, *Becky Sharp*, was even then in production at the studio, directed by Reuben Mamoulian, but Lubitsch intended to direct *The Pearl Necklace* himself.

Marlene was happy enough with the story, partly because it would have a role in it that would suit a recent acquaintance, the famous film actor John Gilbert. He was only thirty-eight, but his career was already in disarray, partly caused by his drinking and partly the cause of his drinking.

Gilbert had been Garbo's lover, and in 1926 they had decided to get married. It was to be a double wedding – the other couple were director King Vidor and actress Eleanor Boardman. Except it didn't turn out like that because the capricious Garbo changed her mind at the last minute and left Gilbert standing humiliated, drink in hand. The story goes that Louis B Mayer, who was present, nudged him and said something like, 'Why worry? You can still fuck her.' At which Gilbert flew into a rage and attacked him. Mayer had long had a personal dislike of Gilbert, and this now turned to bitter enmity. His parts got fewer, and his scripts and directors worse (or so he felt), and in 1933 he had made his last film at MGM, *Queen Christina*, in which he co-starred with Garbo.

Marlene met him socially through the actress Dolores del Rio and her art director husband, Cedric Gibbons, and Gilbert's helpless addiction to drink aroused all Marlene's maternal instincts. As his daughter Leatrice (named after her mother, the film star Leatrice Joy) recalled, 'He was killing himself, and she would not have it. Marlene simply took over.'

She passionately involved herself with him (although they were lovers only intermittently), and got him to seek medical advice about his drink problem, and spent many hours with him, seeing that he took care of himself and giving him encouragement. She kept asking him to be her escort around town – to concerts, restaurants, art galleries, parties and premières. She also involved herself in his home life, helping him trim the Christmas tree and to wrap presents for Leatrice, then aged eleven.

During the time she knew and mothered him he did make one film, *The Captain Hates The Sea*, directed by Lewis Milestone for Columbia Pictures, but it was not a great success. She and he discussed the possibility of trying to set up a film in which they could co-star, and attempted to get hold of the rights to the old story *The Garden Of Allah*, which had been filmed by MGM in 1927. But the ownership of the rights turned out to be mired in confusion, and their idea came to nothing.

Discussing his career together, they came to the conclusion that maybe the best thing for him would be a change of direction. He would change his image from being one of the silent screen's great lovers to playing suave supporting roles in romantic comedy. This was where the role in *The Pearl Necklace* came in. He would play her partner in crime, who passes himself off as a Russian prince.

At Paramount, a team of writers continued to work on the script, under the domineering eye of Ernst Lubitsch. But by now Lubitsch realised that there was no way he could function as the studio's head of production, overseeing every film made there, and at the same time direct a film himself. So he assigned the film to director Frank Borzage.

Borzage had been a director for years. Born in Salt Lake City of Swedish parents, he directed his first film in 1916, when he was twenty-three, and went on to become one of the most highly regarded directors of the Twenties and Thirties – he won the first-ever Oscar for Direction for his 1927 film *Seventh Heaven*, and won the same award five years later for *Bad Girls*. Nowadays rather forgotten, his best films portray the subtleties of love affairs carried on in times of social or political upheaval.

The name of the film also changed – Lubitsch gave it the even snappier title, *Desire*. Its eventual story-line was squarely aimed at Depression America. Everyone in it lived a life of opulence in grand hotels, wearing the finest clothes, even the crooked Marlene and her cronies. The hero, Tom Bradley, a square-cut American automobile engineer from Detroit finishes an assignment for his firm in Paris and has time for a two-week vacation before returning home. He elects to spend it in Spain, a country he has always wanted to see.

While driving there, he becomes entangled with Marlene (playing another Madeleine), who has just pulled off an imaginative theft, swindling a Paris jeweller out of an extremely expensive pearl necklace, which she is now rushing out of the country to give to her companion in crime, Carlos (posing as a Russian prince, while she poses as his niece, a countess).

To get the necklace through customs she drops it into Tom's jacket pocket, and then has a hard time getting her hands on it again. Eventually Carlos manages to get it back by pretending to do a conjuring trick (using a fake necklace), during which the real one mysteriously appears in his pocket.

By this time Tom and Madeleine have fallen in love, and after an agony of indecision she steels herself to admit to him the truth about her theft and her false identity as a countess. She realises that life with a sterling good-hearted American is worth more than all the fripperies of high-class European life, and that she will be happier with him among the smoky factory chimneys of Detroit (one part of the film that is perhaps less believable than the rest).

John Gilbert tested for the role of Carlos, and to his and Marlene's delight, won the part. And the major male role, the Detroit motor-engineer Tom Bradley, went to her old co-star and lover, Gary Cooper. This was unfortunate for Gilbert. When she met Cooper again, Marlene found her old desire for him rekindled. It was true that he had recently married a society lady, and that Lupe Velez was rumoured to still have her eye on him, but nonetheless he and Marlene resumed their affair.

Gilbert found this devastating. Marlene had become his confidante and support (and occasional lover), and with her off cavorting with Gary Cooper he quickly drifted back to the bottle for consolation. Which caused him to have a series of small heart attacks. Which in turn caused Paramount to remove him from the role of Carlos, citing 'medical reasons'. He was replaced by John Halliday, which was a shame because although Halliday was a good actor, he did not have much sexual charisma, and a theme in the plot of *Desire* was to have been his jealousy as Madeleine's love for Tom became more apparent. This theme now disappeared.

Desire began shooting in September 1935. It was eventually decided to film it in black-and-white, rather than Technicolor, but this did nothing to detract from Marlene's beauty. She appears in an endless succession of glamorous outfits – in suits, gowns and dresses – and looks ravishing in all of them (she directed much of her own lighting in the film, as well as some of Gary Cooper's).

But compared to her appearance in her von Sternberg films there is something smoothed-out about her. Although 'the most elegantly amusing jewel thief ever' (in the words of *New Yorker* critic Pauline Kael), she is simply a highly glamourised version of the girl next door. She has lost all her Berlin disillusion, so her mockery is lighter and more conventional. A dozen Hollywood actresses of the time could have played the role as well, and the film is in effect an early specimen of Thirties screwball comedy, with a rich irresponsible beauty finally finding married happiness.

That being said, the film is good entertainment, helped by an excellent lively score by Frederick Hollander (Marlene's old friend Freidrich

Holländer, now in Hollywood and with a new Americanised name). He wrote four songs for Marlene to sing (with lyrics by Leo Robin), although as things turned out she sang only one of them – 'Awake In A Dream', which she performs at the piano to a lovestruck Gary Cooper.

Lovestruck though the real Marlene and the real Gary Cooper might have been, as soon as shooting finished on *Desire* (on 21 December 1935), shocked by continuing reports of John Gilbert's failing health, she ended their renewed affair and turned her attention back to the ailing star.

It was too late. By now his heart attacks were both bigger and more frequent (he even had a severe and terrifying one in her swimming pool), and on the morning of 10 January 1936, at only forty years of age, he was found dead in his bed.

Marlene was completely devastated. She feared that her behaviour had been a major factor in causing his heart attacks. He was given a private funeral (the near-riots at the funeral of heart-throb Rudolph Valentino almost ten years earlier were still remembered). Marlene attended, accompanied by Dolores del Rio and her husband, Cedric Gibbons, and she collapsed in grief in the aisle of the church.

She took to decorating her bedroom with pictures of him, and lighting candles in front of them as if it was a shrine.

In an attempt to make amends, she immersed herself in doing everything that she could to help his daughter, Leatrice, beginning by sending her a lavish bouquet of flowers a week after the funeral. The attached note read, 'I adored your father. Let me adore you.' For a while she took Leatrice out to plays and films (sometimes taking Maria as well), bought her small trinkets and sent her notes addressed to 'Tinker', which had been John Gilbert's pet name for her.

Above all, she did what she could for the child's financial welfare, swearing to lawyers that she had seen John Gilbert's last will, which seemed to have disappeared and claiming that it left all he had to Leatrice, not to the actress Virginia Bruce, who had been his last wife. Leatrice won, but Marlene's almost-undivided attention could not last indefinitely. Even her own daughter did not receive that.

Lubitsch, in his attempts to further 'humanise' Marlene, decided that the second film called for in her current contract would be *Hotel Imperial*, another remake of a 1927 silent picture. In it a simple chambermaid falls in love with a German army office, during the Great War, and, when her love is returned, blooms into unimaginable beauty. It was a picture dogged with ill omens from the start. Its title changed from *Hotel Imperial* to *Invitation To Happiness* and then back again, and ended up as *I Loved A Soldier*. It was originally slated to be directed by Lewis Milestone, who had directed John Gilbert's last film, but before shooting began he was replaced by Henry Hathaway, a competent, professional (and often angrily dictatorial) director whose long and not especially distinguished career lasted from 1932 to 1973.

His idea was that the film should begin 'with a shot of a long, wide hallway, and a woman scrubbing and mopping the floor. She has dirty hair and dirty clothes; she is wearing old carpet slippers. She's a slob. As she gets [the officer] and…falls in love with him, she gets progressively prettier. Then you see Dietrich in all her beauty coming out of the cathedral married, with the Uhlan swordsmen framing her on either side. She has become completely transformed.'

In order to fulfil Dietrich's contract of two films within a year, *I Loved A Soldier* was rushed into production without a properly planned budget, or a proper schedule, and with an uncompleted script (Marlene accepted this, but only on condition that Lubitsch be on hand on the set to oversee Henry Hathaway and improve the material as they went).

Shooting started on 3 January 1936, so it was a week into shooting that John Gilbert died, which did not much help Marlene's concentration. She also caused problems by resisting looking like a slob for so far into the picture, and turning up on the set looking too ravishing too soon. 'You're not supposed to be beautiful until next Thursday,' Hathaway recalled telling her. To which she pleaded, 'Please – can't it at least be *Wednesday*?'

Charles Boyer, whose career, after fifteen years in films, was just beginning to take off, had been cast as the officer. He had been placed on salary in the middle of the previous November, and such were the delays that by the end of January he had worked for only three days. Production was further hampered at the end of the first week in February, when Lubitsch took Marlene off for two days to reshoot the ending of *Desire*.

The Hays Office had objected that she did not seem to show enough moral redemption at the end, so scenes were added (directed by Lubitsch) in which she returns the pearl necklace that she stole to the Paris jeweller, and turns herself into the police, but fortunately is freed on parole in time to marry Gary Cooper before they must set off across the Atlantic to Detroit.

Then it was back to *I Loved A Soldier*. But only for another day. On 9 February it dawned on the powers that be at Paramount that it had already cost them $900,000. They were already blaming Lubitsch for their recent failure, *The Big Broadcast of 1936* (a ragbag of a film starring such popular stars of the day as Burns and Allen, Bing Crosby, Amos 'n' Andy, Ethel Merman, the Nicholas Brothers and the Vienna Boys' Choir), so they seized their opportunity and fired him on the spot.

Marlene, uncertain enough about working without von Sternberg, was not prepared to work without Lubitsch as well, so when he was fired she quit the picture. Her lawyers pointed out to the studio that by firing Lubitsch they could no longer honour the terms of her contract. The film was abandoned.

Legally she was still obliged to make another film for Paramount within the year, but for the moment they were unable to come up with a story for her, so she found herself available for work elsewhere. Being as businesslike as she was, she had investigated other possibilities of work, and had in hand several interesting offers. One came from Alexander Korda, for whom Rudi had worked as a production assistant back in the Twenties in Berlin, and in whose films there she had played small roles several times. After making films in Hollywood and Paris, he had moved to England in 1931, where he would base himself for the rest of his life, becoming a producer rather than a director.

He had also left his actress wife Maria Corda and become involved with another actress, the Australian-born Merle Oberon, who had appeared in a number of his films, most recently in *The Private Life Of Henry VIII*, the first British film to be a world-wide hit, and in its sequel, *The Private Life Of Don Juan*. He had expressed interest in casting Marlene in a romantic adventure film, to be based on the novel *Knight Without Armour*, written by James Hilton (author of *Lost Horizon* and *Goodbye Mr Chips*). A deal was soon struck for her to appear in it, starring opposite Robert Donat.

Her fee for the film (negotiated with Harry Edington) was to be $450,000 – more than any woman had ever been paid before for a single film, and making her for the moment the highest-paid woman in the world. The contract signed, Korda assembled a team of screenwriters and began work.

Meanwhile, there was another project nearer home. The ambitious David O Selznick had left Paramount in 1931 to become head of the newly formed RKO Studios. From there he had moved to MGM, where he headed his own production unit, and in 1935 he had left to form his own independent production company (a rare thing in those days of the big studios). It was called Selznick International Pictures, and his chief partner in the enterprise was the wealthy John Hay Whitney (at whose shipboard dinner-party Marlene had met Hemingway).

The property that Selznick had in mind to film was, as it happened, *The Garden Of Allah*, which he had managed to clear the rights to, and which he had been developing as a script for some time when Marlene became available.

It was based on a 1904 novel by the English author Robert Hitchens, who had sprung to fame when his book *The Green Carnation* was published in 1894. This was a skit on Oscar Wilde's world of the aesthetic movement, and it became a *succès de scandale* when Wilde was jailed in 1895.

The Garden Of Allah was a rather different matter. It told of a rich but devout young woman, who is finding the social life of big cities soul-destroying and is advised by the mother superior of the convent where she was educated that the solitude of the Moroccan desert might help her find peace. In a town on the edge of the desert she meets a timid, uncertain Frenchman, who, unknown to her, has recently absconded from a Trappist monastery, where he was the sole person who knew the secret of the magnificent liqueur distilled there.

He has absconded because he has a craving for a warm, loving relationship with a woman. She senses an inner goodness in him, they fall deeply in love, and marry, setting off on a honeymoon trip into the desert, taking with them a caravan of camels and attendants. But he remains guiltily unsettled and, when eventually the story of his past emerges, it becomes clear to them both that his guilt can only be assuaged by returning to his true calling.

She nobly and lovingly agrees, in a scene of moving renunciation, and we end on a long-shot of his back as he trudges up the long tree-lined avenue leading into the monastery.

Although this story was already regarded as dated tosh as early as 1927, when the silent-film version of it was made by MGM, Selznick realised that at least it could be colourful – and by that he meant Technicolorful. His partner, Jock Whitney, had substantial shares in the firm of Technicolor, and both were anxious to make a film exploiting the company's new process.

Selznick had always admired Marlene as a performer, although he hated von Sternberg's pictures, writing in one of his memos (he was an obsessional memo-writer) that she was 'one of the most magnificent personalities that the screen has had in many years and I think it a crying shame that she has been dragged down as she has been.'

Marlene had got in touch with him at the time von Sternberg left Paramount, when she was looking for someone else congenial to work for, and he had made notes of several roles that he felt might suit her personality – among them Jezebel and Camille. But still he was cautious, saying in another memo that she had been 'hurt to such a terrible extent that she is no longer even a fairly important box-office star. There is no personality so important that he or she can survive the perfectly dreadful line-up of pictures that Marlene has had.'

He had written that before he attended a pre-release showing of *Desire*, and seeing the film somewhat encouraged him. He had continued developing *The Garden Of Allah*, and tested a number of stars, both male and female, for the leading roles. For his female lead he had in fact contracted Alexander Korda's star, Merle Oberon, who had been in Hollywood since 1935 on loan to Samuel Goldwyn. But he continued to keep his ear to the ground, and heard about the troubles attending *I Loved A Soldier* on an almost daily basis.

When Marlene became available, Selznick immediately got in touch with her, conducted secret make-up tests with the help of Dottie Ponedell (Technicolor was tricky to handle in those early days) and, finding them satisfactory, hired her, buying off Merle Oberon with $25,000 and a promise (never realised) to star her in another Technicolor film, *Dark Victory*.

Marlene was to be paid $20,000 a week for ten weeks' work – less than half of what she would be getting from Korda, but still a considerable sum.

He tested many actors to play the monk, including Robert Donat, Vincent Price, Brian Aherne, Noël Coward, John Gielgud, and even the young French star Jean Gabin, but found none to be satisfactory. But now Charles Boyer was free, as well as Marlene, and Selznick decided he would fit the part perfectly.

A small army of writers were involved in the screenplay. Selznick discussed it with writers such as Vicki Baum and S N Berhrman, and considered hiring Dr Karl Vollmöller, who before working on *The Blue Angel* had written *The Miracle* (which contained nuns) for Max Reinhardt. Marlene, through her agent, tried to get Mercedes de Acosta assigned to the task, but to no avail.

A version of the script was prepared by one of Selznick's assistants, Willis Goldbeck, who had worked on the silent film version of the story. Much of what he wrote was used, and he was on hand during the shooting as a script adviser, but eventually the screenwriting credit went to W P Lipscomb and Lynn Riggs, who had written the novel *Green Grow The Lilacs*, on which the show *Oklahoma!* would come to be based.

Desire had its première, again at New York's Paramount Theater, on 11 April 1936, and was widely praised by the critics, almost all of them agreeing with Frank S Nugent of the *New York Times*, who thought Lubitsch had 'freed Marlene Dietrich from Josef von Sternberg's artistic bondage, and…brought her vibrantly alive.' And it would go on to do well, though not spectacularly well, at the box office.

Three days later, on 14 April, Marlene travelled south to Yuma, Arizona. It was in Arizona that the desert scenes for *The Garden Of Allah* were to be shot. Her daughter Maria went with her and again had a role in one of her mother's films, as a schoolgirl in the convent scene that opens it.

Her relationship with Maria was hardly ideal, alternating periods of absence with periods of almost suffocating over-attention. Since the kidnapping scare of a few years before, the child had been educated at home by private tutors, thus robbing her of companions of her own age. Now eleven, she had become shy and uncertain, with a tendency to overeat as compensation. Marlene's lovingly baked cakes didn't help, and Maria was definitely beginning to become plump.

Selznick had built an encampment of tents in the desert to house the cast and crew during the day, in what would not turn out to be the most comfortable of locations. Midday temperatures could rise to as high as 54°C (130°F) and, in order to allow the unit as much comfort as possible, it was arranged that shooting would begin each day at 3am, finishing somewhere around noon.

The cast was truly international – besides Marlene herself, there were Charles Boyer (French), C Aubrey Smith and Basil Rathbone (English), John Carradine (American), and Joseph Schildkraut and the dancer Tilly Losch (Austrian).

The director too was foreign. His name was Richard Boleslawski, and he was born in Warsaw. Now in his forties, he had come to Hollywood via the Moscow Arts Theater (he wrote books on the teachings of Stanislavsky), the German cinema (where he acted) and Broadway (where he directed). Most of his film work shows little evidence of Stanislavsky's 'Method' and is, in the main, rather stilted costume melodrama.

Marlene mistrusted him from the first, mainly because he wasn't von Sternberg, whom she had pleaded in vain with Selznick to have as director. Selznick had insisted on Boleslawski, but with such a mélange of accents among the cast, and Boleslawski a foreigner himself, he had also engaged young Princeton-educated Joshua Logan as dialogue director. Logan was then just beginning a long and successful career on Broadway – his credits as director included *Annie Get Your Gun*, *Mister Roberts* and *South Pacific*.

Marlene set to work on him from the moment they met in the Selznick offices, telling him how much she loved people from New York because they were bright and had taste, and asking didn't he agree with her that the script for *The Garden Of Allah* was rubbish? As Logan recalled, she fluttered her eyelashes at him and said, 'It's trash, isn't it? Garbo wouldn't play this part. They offered it to Garbo and she said she didn't believe the girl would send the boy back to the monastery. She is a *very clever* woman, Garbo! She has the primitive instincts – those peasants have, you know.'

This was all part of a change in her behaviour that established itself quickly at this time and would stay with her for the rest of her life. Now that she had lost von Sternberg, she started to make use of the vast amount she had learned from him about the craft of film-making – about lighting, camera angles, scripting and editing, as well as fanatical attention to detail – and to apply it during the making of every film she was involved in, often to the despair of directors. And all of her effort was aimed not so much at making a good film as at projecting the now-established Dietrich image.

Expressing dissatisfaction with the script was all part of her deeper campaign to have Boleslawski replaced, and once, after the unit reached Yuma, she invited Joshua to her hotel room (not for an assignation – her date for that evening was with the Viennese actor Joseph Schildkraut). To Joshua's surprise the room had pictures of John Gilbert everywhere, each with a lit candle burning in front of it.

Plying Joshua with Scotch, Marlene told him of her mistrust of her director, saying, 'He's a terrible man. He's Russian. No sensitivity. He can't direct women. Wouldn't you like to see him resign?'

Joshua at once said that he thought that would be a terrible idea, putting the whole film in danger, but Marlene persisted. 'Call up Selznick right now,' she said. 'There's the phone. Tell him Boleslawski is not the right man… If he left we could get a good director – like Josef von Sternberg, who just happens to be available. He's exactly right for this, and for me.'

Her barrage continued and she got closer and closer and apparently more and more affectionate, until in desperation Joshua, who was not that sort of boy, bolted. Boleslawski remained on the picture, and Marlene, although somewhat resigned to the fact, kept on pressuring her fellow-players to back her in asking for script improvements (and possibly a new director as well).

As well as Joseph Schildkraut, Marlene was also having a casual affair with the writer and Selznick's assistant Willis Goldbeck, who did his best to calm her dissatisfactions, at the same time keeping Selznick in touch with the tense situation.

Selznick, as was his custom, kept close control of his film from back at his office, firing off a constant stream of memos. He was well aware of Marlene's complaints, and on 28 April sent Boleslawski an irritated cable: 'I AM GETTING TO THE END OF THE ROPE OF PATIENCE WITH CRITICISM BASED ON ASSUMPTION THAT ACTORS KNOW MORE ABOUT SCRIPTS THAN I DO. WOULD APPRECIATE YOU HAVING A FRANK HEART TO HEART TALK WITH MARLENE AND WITH BOYER... I AM NOT GOING TO FACE SIX OR SEVEN WEEKS OF THIS NONSENSE... IT IS HIGH TIME FOR A SHOWDOWN AND I AM PERFECTLY PREPARED FOR IT... I WILL HAVE A LOT MORE RESPECT FOR YOU IF YOU TURN INTO A VON STERNBERG WHO TOLERATES NO INTERFERENCE'.

There was good cause for Selznick to be edgy. The film was budgetted at a whopping $1.2 million, which was stretching his company's resources to their limits, and any delays in what was in any case a difficult shoot could prove catastrophic.

There was a minor delay on 2 May, when Marlene collapsed unconscious in the desert heat and shooting had to be suspended for two days while she recovered. This was just one of four occasions when she passed out from the heat and others fell ill as well.

Boleslawski came down with dysentery, allegedly from contaminated desert water. Sandstorms damaged sets and silted up artificially built lagoons. Expenses continued to mount and early in June the exasperated Selznick ordered the unit back to Hollywood to complete filming there. This would turn out to involve transporting truckloads of sand from the Arizona desert to Hollywood, after they found that sand from elsewhere failed to match in colour.

At around this time Marlene was delighted to hear from Paramount that they had still failed to find a story for her. Thus she would be unable to make the second picture called for in her contract within a year, and so, according to the terms of the contract, they would have to pay her fee of $250,000 for doing nothing.

She also encountered yet another exile from Berlin, the Viennese-born director Fritz Lang. She had never actually met him in Berlin, in the years when he was making films like *Metropolis* and *Dr Mabuse, The Gambler*, but they had met in 1934 when he had left Germany and was working in Paris.

The circumstances of his leaving Germany are slightly mysterious. He frequently told the story of how the Minister for Propaganda, Goebbels, had summoned him to a meeting and offered him the job of running the German film industry for the Nazis, and how he was given till next day to think about it. He claimed to have taken the midnight train to Paris and left for good, realizing that if he refused he would be a marked man.

This seems to be not quite true. Most probably he had several short informal chats with Goebbels (as Marlene was Goebbels' favourite German actor, so Lang was his favourite director), and the possibility of Lang taking over the running of the film industry was doubtless suggested, but more likely than his feeling that he would be a marked man if he refused is that, as the Nazis took ever-firmer hold of the country, he became uneasily aware of the danger he was in from having had a Jewish mother. He was also already viewed with some suspicion by Goebbels in his official capacity, as his latest film *Das Testament Des Dr Mabuse (The Testament Of Dr Mabuse)* was banned in Germany as 'a threat to law and order and public safety'. (Dr Mabuse was a mad arch-criminal, who, although locked up in a padded cell, masterminded a gang bombing and burning railways, factories and banks – he was suspected by some to be a veiled portrait of Hitler).

Although he did go to Paris, Lang did not leave Berlin for good. He made at least one trip back there to collect belongings.

In Paris he directed one film, *Liliom*, from the book by Ferenc Molnár on which the musical *Carousel* was later based, and in which the title role was played by Charles Boyer. Then he moved to America and was taken up eagerly by MGM on the basis of his fine film-making record. In 1936 he had just completed his first American film, *Fury*, starring Spencer Tracy.

The young Marlene in early-'20s Berlin

Marlene and her husband, Rudi Seiber

Marlene and her director, Josef von Sternberg, in 1933

Marlene singing 'Naughty Lola' in *The Blue Angel* (1929)

Gary Cooper and Marlene in *Morocco* (1930)

Publicity still of Marlene on the set of *The Scarlet Empress* (1934)

Daughter Maria with Marlene by her Hollywood swimming pool (1931)

Lionel Atwill and Marlene in *The Devil Is A Woman* (1935)

James Stewart and Marlene at Universal Studios during the filming of *Destry Rides Again* (1939)

Marlene selling war bonds (1941)

Marlene playing her saw in one of her shows for the US forces (1944)

Marlene with servicemen at the Hollywood Canteen (1943)

Jean Gabin and Marlene (1943)

Marlene meeting her mother at Tempelhof Airfield, Berlin (1945)

Marlene in her ringmaster costume at the 1953 circus charity show

Marlene in costume for Orson Welles' *Touch Of Evil* (1957)

Marlene in one of the Jean Louis dresses she wore for her first one-woman show at the Sahara Hotel, Las Vegas (1953)

Publicity still of Marlene with her accordion on the set of Billy Wilder's *Witness For The Prosecution* (1957)

Edith Piaf and Marlene (1959)

Marlene with Burt Bacharach in Paris (1962)

Marlene in the top hat and tails she wore for her one-woman shows

Marlene in Las Vegas (1958)

Marlene, who always went out of her way to help and encourage exiled Germans, went with him to its première. A tall, handsome, courteous man (although another martinet on the set), Lang took to courting her with bunches of roses, and in time they would briefly become lovers.

In June she was asked to recreate her first American film, *Morocco*, for radio as the inaugural production of the new *Lux Radio Theater Of The Air*. At the time she was still occasionally seeing her co-star in the film, Gary Cooper, but their relationship ended abruptly when she chose Clark Gable to broadcast with her instead of him. Gable was then the second-greatest male box-office attraction in America (Will Rogers was the first) and Cooper felt betrayed.

The Garden Of Allah finished shooting on 8 July 1936. It would turn out to be a spectacular piece of photography, with subtle colours and strong compositions, and would deservedly win the Oscar for Best Colour Photography. The plot line, however, remained as dated and unbelievable as Marlene feared, although she gave a good performance and Charles Boyer gave an excellent one – very intense and private, portraying a very private man – and probably better than the film deserves.

One appearance in the film that did displease Marlene was Maria's. She observed that her daughter was looking too plump, and did her best to get her hands on all stills showing her and destroy them. (Maria later remembered that her whole experience on *The Garden Of Allah* had been 'purgatory'. One of her mortifications occurred when Marlene announced to the crew that they should ignore Maria's moods because she was eleven and had started having periods.)

It was a good job shooting finished when it did, because Marlene had not much time in which to organise herself and set off for England and Alexander Korda. She sailed early in July, on the magnificent French liner *Normandie*, taking with her (it was reported) twenty trunks, thirty handbags, two maids and Maria.

There was no Hemingway on board this time, but she did make the acquaintance of a celebrity in another field – Ham Fisher, creator of *Mutt And Jeff* and *Joe Palooka*, and at one time the wealthiest and most famous cartoonist in America. Learning that Marlene would be on the same voyage as him, he bet his friends at New York's fashionable 21 Club that he could wangle a private invitation to have cocktails with her. He won, and on his return got free drinks there for five months.

The *Normandie* docked at Le Havre, and Marlene at once took Maria to Paris and handed her back to Rudi. It was agreed that for the time being she would be sent to a private boarding school in Switzerland – the Brillamont girls' school in Lausanne.

Marlene then set off for London and arrived, wearing mink and red velvet, to be greeted off the boat train at Victoria Station by an enthusiastic mob. When she spoke to reporters she flattered them by saying that when she went back to Hollywood she was going to leave her daughter in an English school, announcing airily that Maria was 'used to being left'.

She was driven to Claridge's Hotel, where she was to stay (and where Korda had rented for himself an entire floor), and at a press conference there met Korda, her co-star Robert Donat, and the Belgian Jacques Feyder, who was to direct *Knight Without Armour*.

The script was co-written by Hollywood veteran Frances Marion and by Lajos Biro. A Hungarian (like Korda), he had, at one time, been a diplomat, but became a screenwriter, and was connected with a couple of films that Marlene had already appeared in – he wrote *A Modern Du Barry*, which she had filmed back in 1926, and the original version of *Hotel Imperial*. He also wrote *The Last Command*, which von Sternberg directed and for which Emil Jannings won his Oscar. (And yes, he was the man who as a sideline invented the ballpoint pen).

Unfortunately, in spite of the writing talents of Marion and Biro, the script for *Knight Without Armour* was pretty rubbishy. Donat was to play an English journalist who is imprisoned in Siberia during the Great War but released during the Russian Revolution of 1917. Attempting to escape home to England, he is forced to pretend to be a Bolshevik, and while doing so encounters the beautiful widowed countess Alexandra (Marlene), and together they make their way across Russia to freedom. They have many adventures and fall in love in the process.

Filming was scheduled to start towards the end of July, but Robert Donat was prey to asthma and, shortly after Marlene arrived in London, he came down with a severe attack of it. So severe in fact that shooting had to be postponed till he recovered.

After six weeks of delay, with crew and cast standing by on salary, and sets built at Denham Studios, Alexander Korda started to consider replacing Donat with some other actor, and maybe drastically reducing the journalist's role. Marlene objected strenuously, saying that if Donat went, she went.

This, of course, was because his illness brought out all her protective qualities. She started working with him to develop a breathing technique that would make things easier for him – it involved inhaling deeply and delivering his dialogue in a single controlled breath.

During the weeks of delay, at a dinner-party given by Alexander Korda, she met an old Hollywood acquaintance, the twenty-seven-year-old Douglas Fairbanks Jr, who had come to Britain in 1934 to play the tsar in Elisabeth Bergner's *Catherine The Great*, and stayed on to make several more films. When she had met him a couple of years previously he had been married to Joan Crawford, but now he was divorced and enjoying the single life. Thanks to his famous name and polished good manners, he was able to socialise with the social elite, even royalty, such as George, Duke of Kent, a younger brother of the future kings Edward VIII and George VI.

As a friend of Robert Donat's, he had heard of Marlene and admired the way she was standing by him. He invited her to go with him to the première of his latest film, *Applause*, and she accepted – to his surprise bringing along Rudi and Tamara, who were then briefly visiting London. Fairbanks found the way in which Marlene and Rudi behaved 'like old friends, or siblings' fairly unsettling, and told himself he was lucky not to be in love with her. Not in love he may have been, but very soon their relationship would grow into one of what he called 'sophisticated intensity'. Within a week he and she were spending almost every night together, either at her suite in Claridge's or in his recently rented penthouse flat, conveniently close by at 20 Grosvenor Square. In a way he preferred being at his flat because he also found unsettling the picture of John Gilbert she kept in her bedroom, with a candle burning in front of it.

As it happened, she was being courted at the time by William S Paley, the young head of CBS, who was visiting London. He, of course, knew Fairbanks, and what was going on between him and Marlene, and didn't like it. Once, when he was on his way to Marlene's suite in the early hours, he ran into Fairbanks coming the other way, and said accusingly, 'I know where *you've* been!'

Fairbanks, enjoying the situation, raised a warning finger to his lips and said, 'Yes...*but don't tell Marlene!*'

Taking further advantage of the delay in filming, Marlene crossed the Channel to Paris, buying clothes there, and collecting Rudi and Tamara (and Maria) to go with her on a visit to Vienna. It turned out to be a short visit, because it quickly became apparent to her that anti-Semitism was now rapidly growing there as well as in Germany, and she and her family left after only a few days.

One of her old Viennese acquaintances had already left the city and emigrated to America – the Jewish stage and film director Otto Preminger. In America he had succeeded in getting work on Broadway, and it was while producing the Clare Booth Luce play *Margin For Error* that he gave a role in it to another refugee – Rudi's old friend and Maria's godfather, Rudolf Forster, who had been helped to get into America by the efforts of both Marlene and Ernst Lubitsch.

Rudolf had become well-established as an actor in Germany, and for him, as for so many in the same situation, it was hard to realise that in America they were almost unknown. Through the efforts of Lubitsch, he was cast as a king in a film for Warner Brothers. But he objected to the throne that was given him and lost the part.

In Preminger's play he was cast as a Nazi diplomat, but became unhappy about the size of his billing and suddenly quit the production, leaving a note for Preminger that simply said, 'I'm going home to rejoin Adolf.' Preminger took the part himself (the first of a number of times he would play Nazis), and Marlene, learning of the incident later, would never forgive Rudolf. For the rest of her life, he would be beyond the pale.

On her return to London from Vienna, she found that a flat had become available in the building where Douglas Fairbanks Jr lived. She rented it and moved out of Claridge's.

Robert Donat was finally recovered enough to begin filming. During shooting, Marlene hovered over him on the set, sometimes wrapping her fur coat around him if the weather was too chilly, and she took to referring to him cheerfully as 'Knight Without Asthma'.

At the same time she continued to look after her own interests, and director Jacques Feyder had to cope with her new self-directing attitude, saying rather resentfully:

She only makes 'Marlene Dietrich films', and accordingly she is concerned with one thing only: that this will be a Marlene Dietrich picture. Her image, her face, her costumes – in her estimation, only these count. Her technical experience enables her to verify if the light on her face is positioned as she wishes. You can usually hear her ordering the electricians around: 'Put two more lamps on the right...reposition the key light higher behind me...'

He also resented her attitude to her costumes, which as far as she was concerned need pay little or no attention to the story or setting. 'It all has to serve Dietrich,' he said. 'That's the sole reality – and if she does or wears something anachronistic, well, then, you just have to change the script to conform to her wishes.' At the same time he marvelled at her charm, observing that she contrived to get her own way in just about everything, while managing to keep alive an impression of being totally co-operative.

In one scene she dispensed with costume altogether. It was to be a bathtub scene, and telling nobody but her dresser that she was going to perform without wearing a flesh-coloured bathing-suit (customary in those days), she arrived on set and threw off her robe, revealing herself stark naked to the astonished (and possibly delighted) crew.

Also present to witness the scene (by some Marlene-induced miracle) was a correspondent from *Time* magazine, with the result that on 30 November 1936 she found herself on its cover (decently clad, of course).

Time magazine was especially interested in Marlene at that particular time because on 19 November *The Garden Of Allah* had opened in New York, at the prestigious Radio City Music Hall. On that occasion, it had been well received by both press and public, although the general opinion was that, while it looked stunning, the story itself was somewhat old-fashioned. Selznick sent Marlene a cable: 'I CAN NOW TELL YOU WITH COMPLETE SAFETY THAT PICTURE IS OBVIOUSLY A GREAT SUCCESS AND...EVERYONE UNANIMOUS THAT IN HISTORY OF SCREEN NO ONE HAS LOOKED MORE BEAUTIFUL THAN YOU DO IN THIS PICTURE AND THAT IT IS YOUR BEST PERFORMANCE TO DATE.'

Towards the end of the filming of *Knight Without Armour* Marlene received a visit in her dressing-room from an old Berlin acquaintance, the beautiful golden-haired actress Mady Soyka, who was the wife of Marlene's old agent, Jonny Soyka. She was accompanied by a journalist, Willi Frischauer, and she had a message from Goebbels. He was offering Marlene the sum of £50,000 (or the equivalent amount in any currency that she cared to choose) if she would come back for just one month to Germany and make a film.

Marlene coolly digested this. 'You can have anything you want,' urged Mady. 'Anything. There will be an immediate reversal of the press campaign against you. The German public will be suitably prepared for your return.'

'Darling,' Willi Frischauer remembered Marlene cooing. 'How nice of you to bring me this generous offer. What a pity I cannot accept it at the moment. You see, I am under contract for the next two years, which takes us to the end of 1938. Then I am committed to do a play on Broadway in 1939. Shall we not return to the idea perhaps in 1940 or 1941?'

Mady knew enough to leave, but the encounter gave Marlene a little more to think about. Not only would she continue to work in America, when she got back there she would apply for American citizenship. (Happy in London, she did for a moment consider applying for British citizenship, but she remembered uneasily that her father's brother, her uncle Max, who had been killed in the Great War, had commanded the first Zeppelin raid on London, and she feared public reaction if this fact became known.)

In November shooting finished on *Knight Without Armour*, and Marlene decided she would stay on in London over Christmas and the New Year, and that Maria, on holiday from her Swiss school, would come to London so that they could spend the festive season (and their birthdays) together.

There was one small financial hiccup. At the time shooting finished, Korda, operating on a financial precipice as usual, still owed Marlene $100,000 of her salary, and found himself unable to pay it.

This did not prevent him from planning further productions, however, and, hunting round for a property that could showcase his two regular stars (Merle Oberon and Charles Laughton) he decided on the Robert Graves book *I, Claudius*. He chose as director William Cameron Menzies, who had recently directed his prestigious but loss-making film *Things To Come*, but Marlene knew that von Sternberg was in London and out of work. He had several times dined with her and Douglas Fairbanks Jr, although, at the moment, he was in hospital recovering from appendicitis. She told Korda that if he would employ von Sternberg as director of *I, Claudius* she would forget the $100,000 – a generous gesture that rather took Fairbanks' breath away.

Korda agreed. He replaced William Cameron Menzies, and for a while it looked as if von Sternberg's failing career might be back on track (since leaving Paramount he had made only two poor films, produced by his old colleague B P Schulberg at Columbia, and it seemed that since ceasing to work with Marlene he was drained of inspiration).

At this time there was great agitation in Britain about the possible abdication of Edward VIII, who had come to the throne on the death of his father at the beginning of the year. The situation aroused all Marlene's Prussian instincts – her respect for royalty and her sense of duty and honour. She decided that the king must be dissuaded from taking this drastic step (especially for Mrs Simpson, whom she thought 'terrifyingly vulgar'), and that she was the woman to dissuade him.

One day in early December she summoned her chauffeur, Briggs, and had him drive her in her enormous cadillac to Fort Belvedere, the king's country residence. Alas, like the Poet McGonagall trying to present his poems to Queen Victoria at Balmoral, she was turned away by the guards at the gate. The king abdicated a few days later, on 10 December 1936, and Marlene, listening with Douglas Fairbanks Jr to the broadcast of his speech, wept.

Maria arrived, as eventually did Rudi and Tamara, and all had an enjoyable holiday season. Marlene was especially happy because Douglas Fairbanks Jr had been offered a strong supporting role in a Hollywood film. He had been asked by David Selznick to play Rupert of Hentzau in a remake of *The Prisoner Of Zenda* (the sort of role for which his father was famous) and urged by Marlene (and his father), had accepted. So later in 1937 he would be joining her in America.

When Marlene set off back there early that year, it was not without work to go to. Even though she had been in Europe for half a year, she was still Paramount's most prestigious star, and had a new contract with them.

Things had changed again at Paramount, now working its way out of financial difficulties as the Depression lifted. There were new names in head office, and as well as giving her a new contract, by the terms of which she was to receive $250,000 per picture for two pictures, they decided a mistake had been made in firing Ernst Lubitsch, and hired him back – as a director in charge of producing only his own pictures, however, and not as the studio's head of production.

They even had in mind the two films she would make. One was to be based on Terence Rattigan's first big success as a playwright, *French Without Tears*. She and Douglas Fairbanks Jr had seen it on stage in London, and at her suggestion Paramount had bought the rights.

The other, which would be made first, had the title *Angel*. It was based on a Hungarian play, *Angyal*, written by Melchior Lengyel, which told of a married couple who are keeping their marriage alive and exciting by each having affairs. This practice runs into problems when the wife's latest lover falls besottedly in love with her (and she to some extent with him), and the eventual outcome, after all the problems are resolved, is that husband and wife decide fidelity is more important, and ultimately more exciting.

Naturally this would have to be toned down somewhat in the new moral Hollywood – especially any suggestion of infidelity on the part of either partner. Lubitsch had already been working on a revised screenplay, in collaboration with his favourite screenwriter, Samson Raphaelson, who had worked with him on half-a-dozen pictures, including *Trouble In Paradise* and *The Merry Widow*. They were also helped out by the English playwright Frederick Lonsdale, author of *The Last Of Mrs Cheyney* and *The Maid Of The Mountains*, although he would receive no credit on the screen.

They replaced the basic premise of the story with the hoary old situation of a wife who loves her husband but, becoming bored when he pays more attention to his career than to her, strays. In their script they made him a high-up English minister, Sir Frederick Barker, who spends all his time flying to international peace conferences to great public acclaim. While he is off at one of these, his wife, Maria (who would of course be Marlene, using her own real first name), flies off in a chartered plane for a few days in Paris. There she calls in at what is quite clearly a high-class house of assignation, run by an exiled Russian countess, where it is obvious that she has, six years before, been one of the countess's young ladies.

She is only making a social call, but is mistaken for one of the girls by a well-born Englishman, Anthony Halton, who is making his first visit to the countess (on the recommendation of a friend). Maria is intrigued and amused by him, and agrees to meet him for a private dinner for two that evening, refusing to tell him her name.

They have a pleasant dinner, but by the end of it, it is clear he has fallen deeply in love with her, calling her (in lieu of her real name) Angel. Beginning to fall for him herself, she flees.

Back in England, her husband runs into him at a luncheon. They take to each other, and it turns out that when both were young officers in the Great War they each enjoyed the company of the same young Parisian sempstress (without meeting each other at the time). Sir Frederick invites Anthony to his palatial home for a meal. Anthony and Maria meet again, but in spite of his protestations of love (while Sir Frederick is out of the room receiving ministerial phone calls), she declares her devotion to her husband.

But his ministerial work continues to come between them. He has to cancel a planned second honeymoon in Vienna at the last minute. Feeling hurt, she thinks that perhaps she might be better off with Anthony after all, and asks to fly with Sir Frederick as far as Paris (where she intends to meet Anthony at the countess's, as he has begged her to). But Sir Frederick, who has become a little suspicious, has his suspicions confirmed when he accidentally learns of her previous flight to Paris.

All three make their separate ways to the countess's house. There is a well-bred stiff-upper-lip confrontation between Sir Frederick and Anthony. Maria is asked to choose between them and, after a slight hesitation, opts for her husband. They set off together to go, as originally planned, to Vienna, and he promises to be more attentive in future.

When Marlene arrived back in Hollywood, she renewed her affair with Fritz Lang, but this soon came to a rather abrupt end when, while still in his bed one day she picked up the phone and called another man to make a date with him. This was too much for even Fritz Lang's casual Berlin sensibility. It hurt his pride and he ended the affair, although, as so often with Marlene, they remained friends.

While preparations for filming *Angel* went on, Marlene took a firm and determined step. Although there were a few things she didn't much like about America – mainly that she found Americans on the whole uncultured and prudish – on 6 March 1937 she went by appointment to the new Federal Building in downtown Los Angeles and formally applied to become an American citizen, giving her height as the somewhat increased measure of 1.7m (5ft 8in), and her age as the somewhat reduced figure of thirty-two (she was in fact thirty-five).

By the rules of immigration, American citizenship would not be fully granted to her for two full years, but when news of it reached Germany the Nazi press were noisily outraged. She had, they said, betrayed the Fatherland, and the journal *Der Stürmer* commented, 'The German-born Dietrich has spent so many years among the film Jews of Hollywood [that] her frequent contacts with Jews render her wholly un-German.' (All this official diatribe did not totally discourage the privately adoring Goebbels – he would continue to keep track of what she was up to, hoping she might see the error of her ways and return home.)

In April, filming began on *Angel*. The role of Sir Frederick Barker was given to Herbert Marshall, who had played the part of Marlene's husband before, in *Blonde Venus*, and the role of her would-be lover Anthony was given to Melvyn Douglas. Again the music for the film would be written by Frederick Hollander, and again she would be costumed by Travis Banton, although rather more restrainedly than before, for the most part wearing clothes that the women in her audience might on a good day aspire to copy.

Somehow it didn't turn out all that well. Intended as a romantic comedy, with such Lubitsch touches as the servants acting as an observant and knowing chorus to the main action, it always threatens to become light and witty without ever getting there. The sets are vast, often giving actors considerable distances to cross before delivering their lines. This slows things down. Even in a fairly static scene, where Melvyn Douglas meets Herbert Marshall after the lunch that they both attend, the quite witty dialogue is played at a snail's pace, making those two talented actors appear leaden.

Marlene is of course elegant and lovely, but she seems somewhat at a loss. During shooting she complained that she had no real idea of what any of the characters were about, and had increasingly frequent disagreements with Lubitsch. Given longer and darker false eyelashes than ever before, she spends (as many reviewers would note) too much time batting them up and down. Such gestures are always a problem for film actors working from take to take – you may think you're only making them occasionally, but when all the takes are cut together it can look ridiculous.

When the film was shot there were the expected problems with the Hays Office. They objected that the countess's house looked too much like a high-class bordello. Which it was. Paramount managed to take the curse off this by reshooting its doorway and adding a large Russian coat-of-arms to it. This seemed to add an air of sufficient respectability.

The Hays Office also objected to the scene of Maria and Anthony (Marlene and Melvyn Douglas) dining *à deux*, and the scene was reshot with them dining together in a small but populated dining-room. Altogether the film was showing all the signs of turning out to be an expensive failure.

As soon as shooting finished, towards the end of June 1937, Marlene began making plans for a European holiday. She knew that her career might be in trouble and needed time to think. Her agent, Harry Edington, had warned her that word in the business was that her English picture, *Knight Without Armour,* was going to be a disastrous flop (there was little on-screen magic between herself and Robert Donat). What with that, and with *Angel* looking like a disaster as well, there was a strong possibility that Paramount would drop her option for another picture.

Early in July, *Knight Without Armour* had its American première at New York's vast Radio City Music Hall. As predicted, it flopped.

Marlene, reaching Europe, headed for Switzerland and collected Maria from her school for the summer holidays. Together they travelled to Austria, to Salzburg, where Marlene had rented a half-timbered chalet on the edge of a lake. Rudi and Tamara would join them there.

So would Douglas Fairbanks Jr. Then still in London, he got a telegram from Marlene asking him to join her at the chalet. Fairbanks arrived, expecting a romantic interlude (with possibly Maria) but was disconcerted to find Rudi and Tamara there as well. Not only were they there, but Marlene had a habit of from time to time hopping out of her bed with Fairbanks and trotting along the corridor to join Rudi and Tamara in theirs.

Tamara was, of course, another product of the freewheeling Berlin of the Twenties, and Marlene was fond of her, partly because of how helpful she was as a sort of substitute mother in Europe for Maria, but the situation was not to Fairbanks' taste. As he recalled later, it 'was not really within my experience, much less my desire, and I made known my displeasure – to no avail, of course. Why did I sustain it? I was completely carried away with Marlene.'

When not hopping from bed to bed, Fairbanks observed, she spent much of her time mothering Maria. 'Her devotion to Maria was very touching,' he remembered, 'although she was so extremely maternal one wasn't sure whether this, too, was a part she was playing. But I remember thinking the child had not much sense of who or where she was. It seemed to me an odd way of bringing her up, but of course no one criticised. That summer Marlene was the doting mother – until she decided to go with her public image again, and then she was the distant, remote and cool Venus.'

This would be an unusually long time for Marlene and her daughter to spend together, and for all five at the chalet it would be an enjoyable time. They attended the Salzburg Theater Festival, which had been founded by Professor Max Reinhardt – now too an exile because he was Jewish. They sat on benches drinking steins of beer in the sunshine, dined at local inns, and listened to Tyrolean music in the summer evenings.

When summer ended, Maria was taken back to school in Lausanne, and the rest of the party returned to Paris. There Marlene, still technically a German citizen, needed to renew her passport to return to America.

Goebbels, keeping an eye on her every move, had realised she would need to do this, and when she turned up at the German embassy she found herself confronted by the ambassador himself and by four German princes for moral effect. They demanded to know why she had applied for American citizenship, and what she meant by various statements she was alleged to have made to the press, which in their eyes sounded un-German. She replied with words to the effect that you couldn't believe everything you read in the press, and instanced several slanderous comments about her that had been published in Germany. She swore that she was 'thoroughly German' and threatened to sue anyone who suggested otherwise.

These indignant protestations had the desired effect, and her passport was renewed, as, at the same time, were Rudi's and Maria's.

A report of her visit to the embassy was at once transmitted to Goebbels, who made a note of it in his personal diary and at once sent someone else to Paris to make her an offer. It was Heinz Hilpert, who had directed her in the play *Parents And Children*, translated from Shaw's *Misalliance*, back in 1928.

He was now in charge of what had been the Reinhardt organization. Reinhardt himself, exiled, had gone to Hollywood and co-directed with William Dieterle (formerly Wilhelm) the 1935 film *A Midsummer Night's Dream*, based on his own famous stage presentation of the piece. It had been enough of a financial disaster for Jack Warner, of Warner Brothers, to abandon any idea of letting him make any further films (a series of five had originally been planned). To Hollywood he was immediately a pariah, although admired, and the best he could do was make use of his reputation and open a drama school on Sunset Boulevard. His career would remain a shadow of its former self until he died in 1943.

Hilpert, however, was not Jewish and so had been able to stay in Berlin. His offer now to Marlene was that if she would return to Berlin he would see that she was presented in plays at the famous Deutsches Theater. Marlene sweetly assured him that that sounded like a wonderful idea, and she would be delighted to accept, as soon as she was free of film commitments. What else could she say? She was not about to rock the boat and have her new passport revoked.

Goebbels, however, took her acceptance at face value. When Hilpert brought the news back to him, he noted in his diary. 'Now I will take her under my personal protection.' And immediately the attitude of the German press towards Marlene changed. It was reported that rumours of her 'un-Germanness' were wholly without foundation. Once again in the German press she was *'unsere Marlene'*.

Marlene and Douglas Fairbanks Jr sailed back to America together. When she landed in New York, she phoned her agent Harry Edington and learned from him that Paramount had decided they would do better without her. *Angel*, which opened on 3 November 1937 at New York's Paramount Theater, had flopped. Intended as Paramount's great prestige film of the year, it was beaten out of sight at the box office by their *Waikiki Wedding*, starring Bing Crosby, who that year would come fourth in the list of box-office earners.

Quite apart from the failure of her English film, *Knight Without Armour*, her previous American picture, *The Garden Of Allah*, hadn't done nearly as well as David Selznick hoped. So Marlene would not get to make *French Without Tears* (which would be made in Britain a year or so later, starring Ray Milland and Ellen Drew).

Paramount would have to pay her the $250,000 she would have received, by the terms of her contract, for making it, but, even so, she was now without a studio, and without any immediate prospect of work. For someone who had earned so much money for seven years now, and who had acquired a taste for the lifestyle that went with it, this might have been disconcerting. But not for Marlene. Although she must have had some inner misgivings, outwardly she behaved with calm insouciance, and after a long-distance phone conference with Rudi, set about reorganizing her life.

When she arrived back in Hollywood, she dismissed her maids and her chauffeur, Briggs (also selling her enormous car). She ceased renting her expensive house and, politely refusing an offer from Mercedes de Acosta to move in with her, sweet-talked the manager of the Beverly Hills Hotel into granting her a long-term account, and moved herself and all her clothes into one of the private bungalows it offered for rent.

Although well aware of how fickle the public could be, and how stars of previous times, such as Pola Negri, had fallen from fame, she had confidence in her own star status, and every reason to believe that any hiatus in her career would be only a temporary one.

8 Comeback

Marlene's situation towards the end of 1937 was by no means hopeless. Other studios were immediately alert to the fact that a potentially valuable property was suddenly available. At Columbia, the director Frank Capra, working on a script about Chopin (to star Spencer Tracy), decided she would make a good George Sand – a role that would allow her to wear trousers. And Warner Brothers thought that a remake of the 1932 film *One Way Passage* (a classic weepie starring Kay Francis and William Powell in a doomed shipboard romance) might suit her style. Through Harry Edington she signed provisional contracts for both projects.

There were other possible avenues to be explored as well. One was a hope she had to perhaps make a film in France, with such a director as maybe Jean Renoir (if Rudi could organise it).

There was also von Sternberg, who was still in England. *I, Claudius*, the film that Marlene had sacrificed $100,000 of her fee from Alexander Korda to get him to direct, had collapsed after several weeks of expensive shooting.

The whole project was blighted by the impossibility of von Sternberg working successfully with his male star, Charles Laughton – a finicky and uncertain actor who needed patient reassurance to help him build up the sort of subtly created role he was capable of, and who hated the domineering one-shot-at-a-time approach of von Sternberg. The whole production was going wildly over budget when the female star, Merle Oberon, suffered a convenient car accident, which seemed to leave her only superficially injured, but which gave Korda the excuse to cancel the production and claim insurance. As a result of this *débâcle*, von Sternberg had suffered a nervous breakdown and been hospitalised, but surely he would soon be recovered and available to work with her again.

There was not much hope for the moment of working with Ernst Lubitsch. The two of them had managed to become friendly again after the tensions of working on *Angel*, and indeed she was lending her support to an organization he had set up to provide advice, aid and money to the growing horde of German exiles flooding into Hollywood. But he was still working at Paramount (directing Gary Cooper and Claudette Colbert in *Bluebeard's Eighth Wife*), and there she was not welcome.

Harry Edington, doing what he could to keep her name at the forefront of public consciousness, asked the influential press agent Eddie Jaffe for advice. Jaffe, knowing it was relatively easy to get items into the sports sections of the papers, came up with the idea of a 'Marlene Dietrich Award' for the racehorse with the best legs, and found a racetrack willing to present it.

It was difficult for her at this time to know what was best for her to do. She could keep trying to find good scripts which would suit and display the Dietrich image, provided a studio agreed to make them, and she could carry on keeping her face and name in the public eye, but that was about all. No record company was interested in recording her, except singing songs from her current films (if there were any), and to return to the stage at that time in America would be seen as a definite sign that her star was waning.

The one medium open to her was radio, so as 1938 began, she started taking radio work. This was not seen as a comedown. By the end of the Thirties, radio was almost as influential a medium in America as movies. It kept actors in the public eye, and there was hardly a major star of the time who did not appear in the occasional radio drama. Marlene performed in several, playing opposite such actors as Don Ameche.

Don Ameche also acted as announcer on the show topping the radio ratings at the time, *The Chase And Sanborn Hour*, whose star was the ventriloquist Edgar Bergen. Marlene appeared on this too, swapping backchat with Bergen's impudent dummy, Charlie McCarthy. As Marlene was so good at impudence, these shows worked well, gently mocking her established image. (Curiously, she and Charlie were also both famous for wearing top hat and tails.)

Marlene and Douglas Fairbanks Jr continued to spend a lot of time together, attending restaurants and clubs, and spending their nights either at his home or in her bungalow in the Beverly Hills Hotel. She also continued to rent her beach house at Santa Monica, and often she would give parties around her pool. At these she sometimes swam naked, which made Fairbanks angry. He would protest – but as usual to no avail.

Sometimes Fritz Lang would visit her at her bungalow or beach house when Fairbanks was there, and Fairbanks, who was still finding Marlene hard to get used to, not only in her behaviour but also in her swiftly changing moods, sometimes asked the older man for advice. This Lang would courteously give him.

One of the things Lang told him was not to appear over-eager – not to call her up quite so often. He also reassured Fairbanks about Marlene's habit of swimming naked, explaining to him that nude bathing was quite common and respectable in Germany.

One thing he never mentioned to Fairbanks, however, was that he too had recently been her lover.

To add to her difficulties at this time, Marlene was being sued by the Internal Revenue Service for two years' back taxes (which she was not only unwilling, but also unable, to pay). Harry Edington helped her out with a shrewd and subtle suggestion. He proposed that she counter-claim, on the grounds that, as her husband Rudi could not speak English, he had been unable to work in America since she had arrived there in 1931, and she wished to have her tax liability reassessed since that year. The authorities accepted that this might be a viable claim, and agreed to consider it, which at least gave her breathing space.

Then, early in May 1938, a worse blow fell. Harry Brandt, president of the Independent Theater Owners of America (an association of theatre-owners not controlled by the studios), published a full-page ad in such trade journals as *Variety* and *The Hollywood Reporter*. Red-bordered to catch the eye, it listed a number of stars whose films Brandt felt consistently failed to make money, labelling them 'box-office poison'.

This list included (among others) Joan Crawford, Mae West, Fred Astaire, Greta Garbo, Kay Francis, Edward Arnold, Katharine Hepburn and Marlene, all of whose last pictures had done poorly. Hepburn, for instance, had recently made the Howard Hawks comedy *Bringing Up Baby*, which had lost RKO $365,000.

Newspapers across America of course copied it, and both Columbia and Warner Brothers lost interest in having Marlene appear in their films. At around the same time she parted company with Harry Edington, although it remains unclear whether he too lost interest in her or whether she fired him for not getting her work.

What is clear is that in the summer of 1938 she again sailed for Europe, and for the reassurance of Rudi. In Paris he had managed to line up three prospective films for her. In one she was to co-star with the famous and much-loved French actor Raimu. Another, called *L'Image*, was to be directed by the veteran Julien Duvivier. The third, *Dédé D'Anvers*, was to co-star Jean Gabin, now with a string of successful films to his name, including *La Bête Humaine* and *La Grande Illusion*, both directed by Jean Renoir. Goebbels had of course heard of these possible productions, and had let it be known that UFA would be perfectly happy to distribute in Germany any film Marlene made in France, whose film industry he felt was free from Jewish influence.

Marlene was anxious to make sure that all was well with her relations in Berlin, but not at all anxious to go there herself. So she went to Switzerland with Rudi to collect Maria from school for the holidays and asked her family to come to Lausanne and discuss things, including the possibility of their leaving Germany.

They came – her mother, her sister Elisabeth, Elisabeth's husband (Georg Will), and her young cousin Hasso. Georg Will was by now out of the cabaret world, and operating a couple of small Berlin cinemas, but he was of course known to the Nazis as an in-law of Marlene's. So when he applied for a tourist visa to visit Switzerland, Goebbels insisted he carry her a message (as the man of the party). He was to tell her that the Führer desired earnestly that she please come home and make films.

Georg Will may have been the man who gave Marlene her first opportunity to appear on stage, but that did not stop her erupting in fury when he delivered his message. That one of her own family would behave as an errand-boy for the 'poisonous dwarf'! Such weakness of character! More than ever she felt the sooner her relatives got out of Germany the better. If they didn't want to settle in America, then perhaps France would be better for them.

They refused. Josephine would not leave her native land, and besides was now responsible for the firm of Felsing & Co, as well as for its major stockholder, Hasso, who at sixteen was still legally her ward.

Marlene bid her family a reluctant farewell and returned with Rudi and Maria to Paris. There she was introduced to her prospective co-star Jean Gabin, and acquaintance with him would be about all she would ever get out of Rudi's proposed films – none of them ever came to be, as their prospective backers shuffled their feet and hesitated until it was too late.

Mercedes de Acosta was then also in Paris, and she and Marlene made contact, meeting and discussing the European situation rather gloomily. Marlene also went to see her old friend Maurice Chevalier, performing at the famous French music-hall, The Casino de Paris. He blew her a kiss from the stage, ignoring the fact that his discoverer, long-time lover and fellow-performer Mistinguett was also in the audience. She had been adored for long years by many Parisians, and the Casino echoed with booing at this tribute to an outsider. Chevalier hastily acknowledged Mistinguett's presence as well.

If Marlene couldn't get her Berlin relatives to leave Germany, at least she could keep Maria as far away from harm as possible. The two would sail for America together, and Maria would continue her education there (with private tutors, because there was still some apprehension about kidnapping).

In November 1938 they sailed on the *Normandie*, and Marlene had a pleasantly sociable crossing, spending time with fellow-passengers Cary Grant, Jack Warner (of Warner Brothers) and his wife, and, as luck would have it, her old pal Ernest Hemingway.

Back in Hollywood, things had not improved. While the gossip-columns avidly continued to report on all her comings and goings – she was by now firmly famous as a personality – in the film world she was widely regarded as unbankable.

She continued energetically to pursue the social round – partly because she enjoyed socializing and partly to keep in touch – but it did her no good. She met Walter Wanger, who had now moved from Paramount and was producing films at United Artists and suggested reviving the aborted *I Loved A Soldier*, this time casting Gary Cooper as the male lead, with the film directed by von Sternberg. Wanger listened to her pitch uneasily, wondering how to tell her that this sounded like a bad idea.

He did, however, realise that the idea of reteaming her with Gary Cooper might have box-office potential, and as it happened one of his directors, John Ford, was then preparing a film that he thought they might be right for. Unfortunately for Marlene, John Ford disagreed. His film was a western, and he felt that her sophisticated image would be all wrong. So Marlene failed to land the female lead (another woman with a past) in *Stagecoach*.

She had found herself a new agent, Charles K Feldman, and he thought Ford was wrong. He realised that Marlene must in some way change her image, and thought that putting her in the less-sophisticated setting of a western might well be the way to do it. He kept the thought in mind.

Now that Marlene was no longer a Paramount star, Paramount had decided there was no longer any need for them to retain the services of Rudi. So suddenly he too was out of work.

He came to America to talk to Marlene and, at the start of June 1939, they went out one night to the 21 Club in New York. There Marlene met another German exile, the writer Erich Maria Remarque. They had an acquaintance in common, Stephan Lorant, who had filmed her disastrous early screen test, and who was now in London editing the magazine *Lilliput*.

Remarque had not fallen foul of the Nazis because he was Jewish, or because he was a Communist (he was neither of those), but because his internationally famous book *Im Westen Nichts Neues (All Quiet On The Western Front)* had given offence to the brave soldiers of the Fatherland because of its realistic portrait of trench life in the Great War. In 1938 they had deprived him of German citizenship.

Fortunately made wealthy for life by his famous book (and by the American film based on it), he was able to make his way to America, with his wife, Ilsa Jeanne Zamboui. She was, however, only his wife in name. They had been married, and had divorced in 1932, and although they had remarried in 1938 it was really only as a noble gesture on his part, enabling her to obtain, with him, American citizenship. By the time Marlene met him, Ilsa was off in Mexico trying to arrange a second divorce.

Remarque, only a couple of years older than Marlene, was a good-looking, intelligent, softly spoken man, much given to melancholy and heavy drinking. (Quite apart from his sadness at having been barred from his native country, never again being able to repeat the success of *All Quiet On The Western Front* was a considerable burden to him.)

The two of them took to each other at once. He, who was no great womaniser, was flattered by the attentions of such an attractive female. She, for her part, was impressed by his intelligence and culture, and moved by his sensitive brooding sadness, which made him seem vulnerable and in need of her care. They shared many tastes, such as that for good food and wine, and for late nineteenth-century art (which she admired and he was knowledgeable about, with a collection that already included works by van Gogh, Cézanne, Renoir and Degas). By the end of the evening they first met she had given him the nickname 'Boni', which was sort of Latin for 'good man', and they went back to spend the night in his room at the Sherry Netherland Hotel (where, by chance, she and Rudi were also staying).

In only a few days' time she and Rudi were booked to sail back to Europe for a holiday on the Côte d'Azur, and impulsively she asked Remarque to join them, which he agreed to do.

Before she set off, however, she had an appointment on the other coast of America. Her waiting period to be accepted as a US citizen had now elapsed, and, leaving Rudi in New York, she set off for LA. There, on 9 June 1939, as one of two hundred successful applicants, she took her oath before Federal Judge Harry Hollzer, stating that she was born in 1905 (thus lopping another year off her age), and received her certificate of citizenship.

She collected Maria, set off back to New York, and on 14 June, they and Rudi and Remarque boarded the *Normandie*. Also in their party was Josef von Sternberg. Now back in America and on the road to recovery from his breakdown, he had been invited by Marlene at the last minute. But before their ship could sail, it was boarded by agents of the Internal Revenue Service, who presented her with a tax bill for $142,193, due (they said) from the money she had earned making *Knight Without Armour*.

That she had earned that money in England, and not in the United States, they claimed was irrelevant. There were naturally pressmen on hand to record Marlene's departure, and the revenue agent in charge, enjoying his moment of glory, explained to them that he had no arrest warrant, but only because he hadn't had time to find a judge to issue one. Marlene confronted the situation with a calmness that astonished many reporters, who on occasion had seen her throw temperamental outbursts on far less provocation (the more established she became as a star, the more she felt entitled to throw tantrums – a not unusual situation).

The agents removed Marlene's luggage from the ship (all thirty-four pieces of it), kept it for an hour, returned it, and then removed it again. By this time she had sent for her New York lawyer, William B Jaffe, and when the question arose of whether she should be allowed to leave the country with so many possessions while owing such a large sum, he argued her case with US attorney John T Cahill, who had also arrived on the scene.

When her luggage was returned a second time, the IRS men had removed from various suitcases a haul of gem-encrusted jewellery of a total value estimated at anywhere from $100,000 to $400,000. It was agreed that this would be placed in escrow pending Marlene's return, and she obligingly posed for the press cameras, sitting atop her largest trunk and pretending to produce the jewels from a large handbag. Delayed by over an hour, the *Normandie* was at last able to sail.

Reaching Paris, they collected Tamara and the lyricist Max Colpet, and the entire entourage headed south to the Cap d'Antibes.

They were booked into the Hôtel du Cap, and Marlene settled down to an enjoyable summer. Remarque spent much of his time drinking Calvados and frequently had to be sought out and brought back to the hotel (usually by Max Colpet) from whatever cove or inlet he had passed out in. But on other occasions he and she would slip away from the rest of the party for picnics in the hills, or for meals at a various little inns, where they would sometimes spend the night.

Frequently she told him that she could not live without him, although he was prone to reflect gloomily that their affair was bound to end. And although he accepted her freewheeling sexual life, rather admiring it as a contrast to his own conventionality, he did find it something of a strain. She, for her part, sometimes found his intellectual cast of mind wearing. She admired him for his articulateness and intelligence, but sometimes wearied of endless discussions between him and the rest of the party about history and the arts and the international situation. She took to fetching her portable record-player and playing them her own songs, explaining the difficulties of making them, either on record or in the films they mostly came from. More than ever, she now craved to be the centre of attention.

She also socialised. As well as the members of her party, she met or made other friends. The Kennedy clan were holidaying at the Eden Roc – Joe Kennedy, then the US Ambassador to Britain, and his family, among them the twenty-two-year-old John F. Marlene invited the family to a cocktail party, at which she danced with both John and his father, and tried to dissuade Joe from his notorious policy of appeasing the Nazis. She also attempted to interest him in becoming a new backer for her hoped-for film with Raimu. Joe, who (for once in his life) had lost money heavily by backing and producing films in Hollywood during the Twenties, declined.

Noël Coward was there, also with an entourage, and Marlene was delighted to meet him. She had always admired his wit and style, and when he had appeared in his first film, in 1935, she had phoned him (although she had never actually met him) to congratulate him. (Although the film, *The Scoundrel* involved many major talents, including scriptwriters Ben Hecht and Charles MacArthur, it was a deserved failure.)

A Canadian whisky-millionairess, Jo Carstairs, moored her yacht a little way along the coast, at Villefranche-sur-Mer, and Marlene went aboard it several times. Carstairs, who had a tendency to wear a crew-cut and slacks, had a plan. She owned an island in the Bahamas, and offered to build a palace on it if Marlene would join her there so that the pair of them could queen it over a court consisting entirely of young ladies. Marlene declined. As she frequently observed, 'Women are better, but you can't *live* with a woman.'

It so happened that Jean Gabin had a home nearby, and naturally Marlene sought him out and they frequently went on drives round the surrounding countryside.

Most of all this holidaymaking she paid for herself, with a cheerful disregard for her current scarcity of employment, and a firm (maybe desperate) belief that something would turn up.

Then, at the Hôtel du Cap, she got the phone call. It was from the Hungarian Joe Pasternak, who had been Universal's man in Berlin while she was making *The Blue Angel*, and had offered her a contract with his studio. Still with Universal, he was now the studio's top producer in Hollywood, having made a series of successful films starring the young singer Deanna Durbin.

There was a connection between Marlene, Pasternak and Deanna Durbin. His name was Felix Jackson. He had written several of Deanna's films, and had indeed married her, but back in Berlin in the Twenties his name used to be Felix Joachimssohn, and he had been an assistant to Viktor Barnowsky when he had produced the Berlin version of *Broadway*.

Jackson remembered Marlene in it. He had directed some of the rehearsals, and at one of them she had proudly shown him a picture of her baby daughter Heidede, and had also told him 'I'm going to be a big star one of these days.' He had smiled then, but of course knew different now, and while working on the script for a western for Pasternak had come up with the idea that Marlene would be excellent as the leading lady. The role was that of a saloon singer, and while the studio had already announced that Paulette Goddard would play it, Jackson felt Marlene would be even better.

Charles K Feldman, Marlene's agent, also urged that she would be good casting, and quite soon Pasternak agreed. That was why he was phoning Marlene. He offered her a fee of $75,000 (and Rudi a job in Universal's foreign department), and was prepared to hire Frederick Hollander to write the songs that she would sing.

Marlene hesitated for various reasons. The fee would be a considerable drop in salary for her, Universal as a studio had considerably less prestige than Paramount, and she wasn't sure she could see herself in the unsophisticated setting of a horse-opera. However, Pasternak had said that he would send her an outline of the plot and some sample pages of script.

The film, to be called *Destry Rides Again*, was loosely based on a 1932 film of the same name, the first talkie ever made by the popular and prolific cowboy star Tom Mix. That film had been based on a run-of-the-mill novel, called simply *Destry*, by western writer Max Brand. The title character, Tom Destry, who is handy with a six-shooter, is framed for murder and sent to jail. On his release, he returns to the town where he was framed. At first he pretends to be suffering from ill health, so as to mislead the villains. But soon he 'recovers' and mows them down.

The original had no such character in it as Frenchy, the saloon singer that Pasternak wanted Marlene to play. Nor was Destry now to be framed and jailed – in fact he wasn't the original Destry at all, but his son, sent for by the drunken but respectable new sheriff of a lawless town (which has given him the post as a joke). The sheriff feels that Tom Destry Jr will be just as effective a gunslinger as his father was, but when he arrives it turns out that, though handy with a gun, he has pacifist and law-abiding principles. Although at first this makes him a laughing-stock, his calm insistence on abiding by the law soon earns him respect without any gunplay, and it is only at the end of the film, when the likeable sheriff is shot, that the young Destry buckles on his guns and cleans up the town, making it law-abiding but somewhat dull.

Frenchy entertains in the saloon where the villains hang out, and indeed is very much on their side. Between singing her songs in the saloon, she helps them cheat an honest rancher out of his ranch in a dishonest poker game, and generally is seen to be a gal on the make, and not averse to the occasional brawl. But gradually she comes to respect and even fancy Destry, and at the end hurls herself between him and a fatal bullet, dying in his arms.

When the outline and script pages arrived, both Marlene and several members of the party read them. Remarque urged her to accept the part. He felt that the low salary was unimportant – this film might revitalise her career, and even give her a new image. But Remarque was only a book-writer, and she turned to the man who knew more about her image than anyone – von Sternberg.

The perceptive Von Sternberg said he thought it would be a good film for her to be part of. 'I put you on a pedestal,' he advised her, 'the untouchable goddess. [Pasternak] wants to drag you down in the mud, very touchable – a bona fide goddess with feet of clay – very good salesmanship.'

Marlene still hesitated, but what with both she and Rudi needing work, and with the IRS hounding her (the matter of her two years' back taxes was still also pending), sitting in the sun on the Côte d'Azur began to seem pointless. Also Maria needed to continue her education.

So she accepted the job. She and Remarque immediately headed for Cherbourg. On 16 August they managed to book the last available pair of connecting staterooms aboard the *Queen Mary*, and soon were sailing back to New York. Rudi, Tamara, Maria, and von Sternberg, moving in a more leisurely fashion, caught another ship ten days later. They were still crossing the Atlantic on 1 September, when Germany invaded Poland, and World War II began.

On around the same day Marlene reported for costume fittings at Universal, and on Monday 4 September filming began, with Felix Jackson (assisted by Henry Myers and Gertrude Purcell) still hard at work on the half-completed script.

Her co-star was James Stewart, on loan from MGM Studios, who had recently had his first big success in *Mr Smith Goes To Washington*, for Columbia Pictures (for which he was also on loan – MGM were at the time having difficulty working out what sort of story he would be best in). In it he played an idealistic young senator fighting against corruption in politics, radio and the press, and the fuss it caused among people aghast at this cynical view of American society was still going on when he started work on *Destry Rides Again*.

Once James Stewart became available to Universal, and was cast by Joe Pasternak as the hero, it was obvious to Felix Jackson that he would not really be credible as the gunslinging avenger of the original story. It was for this reason that the character was changed to something resembling his role in *Mr Smith Goes To Washington*. In that his character name had been Jefferson Smith, and in *Destry Rides Again*, to drive the similarity home, he was given the full name of Thomas Jefferson Destry. And instead of enforcing law and order by gunplay, he would do it by arguing for justice.

The director of the film was the experienced and untemperamental George Marshall, who was particularly at home with comedy (over his long career he would direct Laurel and Hardy, W C Fields, Bob Hope, and Martin and Lewis). His easy-going and efficient manner made for a pleasant atmosphere on the set, far removed from the tension of most of Marlene's previous talkies.

A big difference was that, although made in America (apart from *The Blue Angel*), Marlene's talkies basically had a European sensibility, a striving for 'art'. Both von Sternberg and Lubitsch were European, and had been much influenced by German cinema. Marshall, however, was a Chicagoan, American born and bred, and even when not making a film set in the old West, his sensibility was American – laid-back and unpretentious. By 1939 Hollywood had very much found its own style, and a confidence in it, and *Destry Rides Again* is the first of Marlene's films that feels truly American.

Marlene enjoyed the atmosphere on the set, and everyone found her a joy to work with. This included the cameraman, Hal Mohr, although it helped that he had the sense to learn her preferred setting for the lights, and made sure that they were set as he knew she would wish before every shot.

The only slight friction during shooting came from Remarque, who was often present on set and, as a writer himself, was eager to help Felix Jackson with suggestions as he laboured to complete the script. He became such a nuisance that George Marshall at one point asked Marlene to keep him away, but she simply shrugged her shoulders as if he was no concern of hers.

But Remarque's strongest reason for being on the set wasn't to make script suggestions. In spite of his civilised European acceptance of sexual freedom, he was finding Marlene's promiscuity difficult to cope with. It was bad enough that once back in Hollywood she had resumed her relationship with Douglas Fairbanks Jr. That he had expected (Marlene, while discreet about the details, was always open about her liaisons). What he hadn't expected was that from the instant she met James Stewart on the set, she wanted him. Remarque was sufficiently upset when he realised this to unload his unhappiness onto fellow-writer Clifford Odets, advising him 'Never fall in love with an actress.'

Her passion for James Stewart also disappointed Joe Pasternak, who later admitted that part of his reason for casting her was the hope that he himself might earn her favours. He didn't have a chance – when he suggested such a quid pro quo to Marlene she told him that she would never make love to him as long as Hitler was still living (in 1945, after the war in Europe was over, he tried again, but again she rejected him, on the grounds that Hitler was still alive and living in South America).

It was James Stewart's gentle simplicity that appealed to Marlene. Still a bachelor, he was then thirty-one (seven years younger than her), and her technique for landing him was unusual and ingenious. As Joe Pasternak later recalled: 'He was just a nice simple guy who liked Flash Gordon comics. That was all he seemed to read on the set... [One day] when he was in his dressing room, she locked the door and wouldn't let him out. But she promised that she would come back with a surprise. The surprise was a doll – a life-sized doll of Flash Gordon. She had persuaded the art department to come in over the weekend and make it up for him. It was correct in every detail.'

Although their affair took off immediately, James Stewart never admitted all his life that it was anything but a romantic friendship, saying things like, 'I liked taking Marlene out to dinner and to dance back in the days of *Destry*... And so we dated quite a few times, which was fairly romantic.' The nearest he ever came to painting a different picture was when he once told an interviewer he had been taken off guard by her 'adult concept of life'.

Marlene in her autobiography, published in 1989, barely mentions him, even as a dinner-and-dancing partner. The fact was, they were lovers through most of the filming of *Destry Rides Again* and for months afterwards (she even built a little shrine to him in her apartment, assembled from photos of him and flowers he had given her). Their affair, long a subject of Hollywood rumour, became known as solid fact when, in 1995, extracts were published from the diaries of the increasingly jealous Remarque, to whom Marlene had eventually admitted everything. In part he wrote:

> She slept with him from day one. It was a dream: It had been magical. For him, too. Suddenly, she was able to speak about it. It had all been poetic and romantic, hour by hour. That had held her bound to him, making her happy and unhappy. She never knew from one week to the next. He had never talked about love, but told her he was not in love, couldn't afford it. It had bothered him to be responsible for anybody. She had become pregnant by him the first time they'd slept together. Didn't want to abort the child, in order to continue sleeping with him. But she gave in to his wishes.

Another person who was aware of this new relationship, and jealous of it, was Marlene's daughter, by now fifteen. She even knew about her mother becoming pregnant and getting rid of the resulting child. Which did nothing to help her, by now, deep insecurity. She had been unsettled by the constant changes of school and country, and by her mother's absences, and by the fact that she was taught in America by private tutors, which prevented her from making friends of her own age.

Jo Carstairs, the Canadian millionairess, used to have a secretary called Violla Rubber. Now she had become Marlene's secretary, and in an odd arrangement Maria lived with her – part of Violla's duties were to act as her chaperone and house-mother, leaving Marlene free to live her own life.

She seemed to love half the world with more passion and involvement than she loved Maria, and Maria began to doubt whether she was lovable at all. Not having a hope of ever being as gorgeous and glamorous as her mother didn't help.

There had been a time when Marlene dressed her in replicas of her own outfits, which simply invited unflattering comparison between them, but Maria had effectively put a stop to that during her early teens by overeating to such an extent that by sixteen she would be 32kg (5 stones) overweight. Marlene did all she could to keep photographs of her from being taken and published, but with only limited success.

She had always taken it for granted that Maria would become an actress and she did everything she could to smooth the way for her, by enrolling her in Max Reinhardt's drama school on Sunset Boulevard. In order to minimise comparisons between them, and to avoid charges that Maria was trying to capitalise on her mother's reputation, they agreed that she should adopt the stage name of 'Maria Manton'.

The filming of *Destry Rides Again* was completed on Friday 11 November 1939, after a long last day that finished at five-forty in the morning. The script had continued to be written right up to the end, with the last pages handed to George Marshall and his cast only on the morning of 10 November. Shooting had lasted an efficient eight weeks, and the editing, scoring and previewing would be completed in the amazingly short time of only one week.

The film opened at New York's Rivoli Theater on 29 November 1939, and was immediately a colossal hit. At a stroke Marlene was a bigger star than ever, having made one of the most sensational comebacks in the history of the cinema.

Destry Rides Again truly achieved what Joe Pasternak had hoped. It removed the veil of remote and unattainable glamour from her image, making her seem more human and approachable, and it gave her back some of the cheeky liveliness that she had not been able to show since her days in

Berlin – a liveliness that was truer to her own natural personality. Audiences found her vigorous on-screen scrap with Una Mae Merkel both thrilling and amusing (Universal's publicity department tried to make out that there had been ill-feeling between the two of them, leading to a genuine fight, but in fact the whole thing is carefully choreographed.)

Marlene's lively (almost rowdy) and knowing performance as Frenchy played well against James Stewart's laid-back, honest characterization, although there is little sign on screen of their off-screen sexual chemistry – which is as it should be, because in the film Frenchy and Tom Destry never actually become lovers.

In her on-screen appearances as a performer she also reached new heights. She totally commands her audience in the saloon, with an assured self-belief that makes her irresistible. And Frederick Hollander gave her three fine songs, with lyrics written by the young Frank Loesser, who would go on to write (and compose) songs for such great musicals as *Guys And Dolls* and *How To Succeed In Business Without Really Trying*.

They were 'Little Joe, The Wrangler', 'You've Got That Look (That Leaves Me Weak)' and 'The Boys In The Backroom', which was immediately such a favourite with audiences that it would remain an essential part of her repertoire for the rest of her life.

Late in 1939 Marlene began consulting the professional Hollywood astrologer Carroll Righter. A cultured homosexual with a flourishing clientele, he explicitly approved of her freewheeling sex life (a good astrologer knows better than to antagonise clients), and would consult his charts of the heavens to give her advice on when to see which of her lovers – Fairbanks or Stewart or Remarque or de Acosta. Advice which she not only took, but cheerfully relayed to each of them – after all, you can't be jealous of a person who is acting on astrologer's orders.

One evening things almost got out of hand. Acting on Righter's advice she had planned an evening with Fairbanks, in her bungalow at the Beverly Hills Hotel. But while she was preparing for his arrival Mercedes dropped in and asked for a drink. Marlene carried on getting herself ready, and got into her bath. Mercedes, sipping her drink, sat by her bath chatting. Then the phone rang. Mercedes answered it. Recognizing Remarque's voice, she informed him that Marlene had gone out. Impossible, said Remarque. He'd had an appointment to come to her bungalow an hour ago, and was now ringing to apologise for being late and to say he was on his way. Mercedes insisted that

Marlene had already gone out, but Remarque said he was on his way to check on that with his own eyes.

When told that that had been Remarque on the phone, Marlene suddenly remembered that she'd promised he could come round and read her some of the new novel he was working on, and had forgotten all about it. Mercedes, now becoming somewhat jealous of all these men around the place, said that in that case she'd be off, and left, omitting to inform Marlene that Remarque would be there in a few minutes.

Fairbanks arrived, and Marlene invited him to come into her bedroom and chat to her while she dressed. She was still doing this when Remarque rang the doorbell. To his surprise, Fairbanks answered it. He invited Remarque in and graciously offered him a drink. The two men were standing round somewhat awkwardly when Marlene entered from the bedroom. Surveying the scene with aplomb, she announced, 'I have so looked forward to introducing you two gentlemen. Now, where shall we dine?'

They were still taking in this somewhat breathtaking question when the doorbell rang again. Marlene herself answered it, and Josef von Sternberg swept her up in a passionate embrace.

Soon afterwards Fairbanks became tired of having so many rivals for her attention, 'not only from the more assured and intellectual Erich Maria Remarque, but [also when I discovered] some intense love letters from someone I'd never heard of.' The someone was in fact Mercedes, and when he confronted Marlene with the letters, she was as indignant about his reading her private correspondence as he was about her freewheeling sex life. Words were spoken, and their affair ended.

In December 1939 she twice went into the Decca recording studios, recording three songs at each session, accompanied by Victor Young and his Orchestra. Three were from *Destry Rides Again* – 'You've Got That Look', 'The Boys In The Backroom', and a song written for the film but not used – 'I've Been In Love Before'. The other three were 'Falling In Love Again', and two popular songs of the Thirties – 'You Go To My Head' and 'You Do Something To Me'.

Her career was now firmly back on track. Columbia and Warner Brothers remembered the provisional contracts she had with them, and approached her agent, Charles K Feldman, but for the moment they would have to wait – through Feldman she had already signed with Joe Pasternak to make two more pictures for him at Universal.

She had good news from the Internal Revenue Service as well. Whether or not her renewed and enormous popularity with the public had anything to do with it, they decided that she didn't owe them all those back taxes at all. Accepting her argument about Rudi's inability to work in America (although he was now safely ensconced at Universal), they returned the jewels they had confiscated and even repaid her $23,000 they calculated she had overpaid.

Her next film for Joe Pasternak would be, like *Destry Rides Again*, a comedy-drama. In fact it would be uncannily like *Destry Rides Again* (although, in the light of its success, she would now get twice the salary). Called *Seven Sinners*, it would again have songs by Hollander and Loesser. It would again have Mischa Auer and Billy Gilbert to add comedy, and again Marlene would be a chanteuse in various low joints – mostly in a night-club called 'The Seven Sinners', on the South Sea island of 'Boni-Komba'.

The chanteuse is called Bijou Blanche, and she is an ex-convent-girl who when young had her heart broken by a young naval officer from Saigon. Ever since, she has been wandering from island to island making her living as a singer and befriending lonely sailors, and frequently getting deported by the authorities. She only manages to get ashore on Boni-Komba because the governor there is unaware of her reputation (shades of Shanghai Lily). She becomes involved with another young naval office, Lieutenant Bruce Whitney, but at last nobly gives him up so that he can remain respectable.

What the picture did not have was James Stewart. He had only been on loan to Universal from MGM, and now that he was proving so successful they had decided that after all they could find scripts for him. He was co-starring with his old friend from his Harvard days, Margaret Sullavan, in *The Shop Around The Corner*, which was directed by Ernst Lubitsch.

In any case, he would not be ideal casting for a naval officer. Lieutenant Bruce Whitney would have to be, as Pasternak told the film's assigned director, Tay Garnett, 'a big, rugged he-guy type with competent fists, plus sex appeal'. Here Charles K Feldman came into play. A shrewd man, he was pioneering a new approach to agenting, which was 'packaging' – selling several of his clients to studios at the same time, as parts of one package.

One of his clients was Tyrone Power, and he at first suggested him for the role. But Power was then the hottest star at Twentieth-Century Fox, and Fox demurred at the idea of him getting second billing (as he inevitably would) to Marlene. So Feldman suggested another of his clients, John Wayne.

Wayne, after years of churning out routine westerns for the low-budget studio, Republic, had in 1939 made a major step towards stardom by playing the Ringo Kid in John Ford's *Stagecoach*. He had made a couple more films since – *Dark Command* (at Republic) and *The Long Voyage Home* (again by John Ford, and in which, coincidentally, he had played a seaman). Republic would be happy to loan him out to Universal for *Seven Sinners*. The question was, would Marlene approve of him as her leading man?

Tay Garnett came up with a cunning plan. He arranged to have lunch with Marlene at the studio commissary, and for John Wayne to be hanging around in the doorway as they entered. As he recalled, 'Dietrich, with that wonderful floating walk, passed Wayne as if he were invisible, then paused, made a half-turn and cased him from cowlick to cowboots. As she moved on, she said in her characteristic basso whisper, "Daddy, buy me *that*."' (Which was a line from Somerset Maugham's play *The Circle*, the play she'd appeared in with Elisabeth Bergner in 1923).

She got him, both for the film and personally. He found her mesmerizing. Not only was she gorgeous, she was also willing and able to share in his own extremely masculine world – she would, and did, go to prize-fights and football games with him, and they went on weekend fishing trips to Lake Arrowhead. Basically they became buddies who also made passionate love, with very little deep emotional involvement.

She, for her part, tried to interest him in her passion for reading, but that didn't work at all. Her assessment, late in her life, was that 'Wayne was not a bright or exciting type. He confessed to me that he never read books. But that didn't prevent him from accumulating a nice pile of money over the years. It proves that you don't have to be terribly brilliant to become a great film star.'

His not being terribly brilliant was another reason he appealed to her. She always liked big strong men that she was mentally stronger than. In John Wayne's case, she was able to reassure and encourage him in his acting career. His later wife, Pilar, recalled that 'She was the first person in the film industry, excepting John Ford, to tell [him] that she believed in him.' (With her usual enormous talent for becoming the sort of person that people she liked wanted her to be.)

Now it was John Wayne that she was photographed with everywhere – at the beach, or at night-spots like the Mocambo, the Trocadero and the Brown Derby, often, in order to confuse the gossip-columnists, accompanied by Remarque, or his friend Stephan Lorant, or Rudi (to show how secure her marriage was), or even Mercedes de Acosta.

By the time filming started on *Seven Sinners*, in August 1940, her affair with James Stewart had ended. He was now seriously dating Olivia de Havilland, whom he had originally taken up with partly as a buffer against Marlene's emotional demands, which he had begun to find wearing.

The filming of *Seven Sinners* proved as pleasant and congenial to all concerned as *Destry Rides Again* had been. Tay Garnett was, like George Marshall, efficient and untemperamental, and at ease with films involving ships (he himself had once been a navy pilot, and it was he who had directed the 1932 shipboard romance *One Way Passage* – the film Warner Brothers had considered remaking with Marlene).

Although the off-screen chemistry between her and John Wayne never quite transferred itself into the picture, as Bijou Blanche she gave one of the most likeable and entertaining performances of her life – possibly even better than Frenchy. She was realistic, seductive and humorous, wryly observing her own established image.

She was given several songs to sing. As well as Dorothy Fields and Jimmy McHugh's famous number, 'I Can't Give You Anything But Love, Baby', there were three by Hollander and Loesser – 'The Man's In The Navy' (which she sang wearing white naval uniform), 'I Fall Overboard' (which was eventually included only in an instrumental version) and 'I've Been In Love Before' (salvaged from *Destry Rides Again*, and which she sang wearing a feathered head-dress and a gown that appeared to be composed only of shimmering sequins, sewn onto an almost-invisible figure-hugging lining. This would be the first of a long line of what she referred to as her 'nude dresses', which would form such a feature of her later performing life.)

The film was released in November 1940, and widely acclaimed in the press. Reviewers described her as 'alluring', 'delightfully subtle', 'devastatingly stunning and amusing'.

Joe Pasternak made haste to set up her next. In doing so he took advantage of events in Europe. The Nazis had invaded France in May 1940, and in mid-June, after the occupation of Paris, the country surrendered. This led to a new wave of exiles arriving in Hollywood – French film-makers unhappily following the earlier wave of anti-Nazi Germans.

Among them was the director René Clair, then *fêted* as maybe France's greatest director, having made such artistic and popular successes as *Sous Les*

Toits De Paris, *Le Million* and, for Alexander Korda and starring Robert Donat, *The Ghost Goes West*.

Joe Pasternak snapped him up for Universal, and Marlene was delighted. Not only had she a lifelong love of France, she had recently had a disappointment when the famous theatre company, the Comedie Française, had approached her to appear in their proposed first-ever film. This project had of course collapsed when France did, but the prospect of working with René Clair promised her considerable compensation.

As a story, Pasternak decided on a script by Norman Krasna, a talented and adaptable playwright and screenwriter whose film credits already included *Fury* (Fritz Lang's first American movie), and would go on later to include *The Devil And Miss Jones*, *Indiscreet*, *White Christmas* and *Let's Make Love*.

The script was called *The Flame Of New Orleans* (a choice of setting perhaps suggested by the fact that Frenchy had come to the wild west from that city), and it was set in the mid-nineteenth century.

Marlene was to play the penniless Claire Ledeux, who comes to New Orleans with the intention of passing herself off as a countess, lands a wealthy husband and enters society. She sets her cap at, and succeeds in enchanting, the rich but elderly Charles Giraud, but is diverted from her purpose by the attractions of the rough-mannered Robert Latour, the hard-up owner of a small Mississippi cargo-boat.

Her attempt to enter society is imperilled when another inhabitant of the city, a Russian called Zolotov, believes he recognises her from a previous dissipated life, and no matter how she protests that he must have run across a disreputable cousin, who resembles her, he remains unconvinced. Eventually, of course, she winds up with the poor but handsome sailor.

Nothing about the film turned out as hoped for. Marlene, when given the completed script, found it 'a flop', and on meeting René Clair was disconcerted to find that 'he wasn't exactly the friendliest of men'. Possibly Clair was disorientated by finding himself working in a foreign land. His forte was making carefully constructed, slightly whimsical films satirizing the behaviour and attitudes of the French *bourgeoisie*.

From the moment shooting began, in January 1941, Marlene was unhappy. She did her best to create a good on-set atmosphere – hunting all over Los Angeles for French bread and French coffee to bring to René Clair, in the hope this might make him feel at home and relax him. But he remained cold and autocratic (although she managed to insist on directing her own lighting). And quite apart from the script and the director, she felt unhappy with her leading man, Bruce Cabot, who was playing the sailor. 'An awfully stupid actor' was how she described him, and even René Clair later admitted that he might have made a mistake in casting him, saying 'he lacked subtlety'.

In an interview years later, Norman Krasna recalled, 'I said to Clair, "Since you've got one frozen face [Marlene], try to get someone like Cary Grant for the other part. Otherwise it won't even be talking heads; it'll be *looking* heads." They got Bruce Cabot – as far away from Cary Grant as you can get… He stands still; she stands still. But there's only one person in the world who stands more still than both of them. For the third part [the rich old man] I said, "Get Menjou." And they went and got Roland Young. You couldn't tell if his lips were moving. Between him, Cabot and Dietrich – three people who didn't move!'

It's hard to believe that Krasna was watching the same film. Marlene isn't immobile at all (and neither are Cabot nor Young). She plays her dual role well (Claire briefly pretends to be her non-existent disreputable cousin), playing one charmingly and one brassily. She has just one song, 'Sweet Is The Blush Of May', written by Charles Previn (no relation to André) and Sammy Lerner (no relation to Alan Jay), although there is some doubt as to whether it is actually her voice we hear singing. The song requires a light girlish soprano, and while it has been claimed that the pitch of Marlene's voice was artificially raised by speeding up the recording during the editing process, the singing we actually hear sounds nothing like the unmistakable Marlene.

The editing was again carried out at lightning speed. The film, shot during January and February of 1941, managed to have its première on 24 April – appropriately, at the Orpheum Cinema in New Orleans. But neither there, nor anywhere else, did anyone much like it. Part of the reason why the critics didn't like it was that it seemed out of touch with the spirit of the time. In the light of events in France, they were expecting something a little more meaningful from the distinguished expatriate director, not this light-hearted confection.

All of which is a pity, because the film is a charming and fast-moving piece of elegant fun. Marlene looks gorgeous in her frothy exaggerated gowns, and Bruce Cabot, in spite of her rude remarks about him, is a handsome actor with a good sense of fun, appearing to be only as stupid as his role in the film requires.

All the same, *The Flame Of New Orleans* was obviously going to lose money for Universal. As had *Seven Sinners*, surprisingly, in spite of the glowing reviews that it received. So Joe Pasternak showed no interest in using Marlene for another film.

Her agent, Charles K Feldman, immediately sold her to Warner Brothers, who had been considering using her since late in 1937. The film they had for her was no longer *One Way Passage*, but an original script called *Manpower*, which told of the rivalry between two electrical linemen, who, in the intervals between stringing high-tension cable across the countryside, battle for the favours of a clip-joint singer with a prison record. One in fact is already her husband, but she lives with him mainly for the security of his salary (having quit singing), and it is the other she fancies. Eventually the two men have a terrible fight, up among the high-tension lines during a storm. During it, the husband is struck by lightning and, dying, nobly gives his blessing to the union of his workmate and his widow.

The singer, called Fay Duval, would of course be Marlene, and Warners, while happy to be employing her, were naturally aware of how poorly her last two films had done. So, as insurance at the box office, they cast well-known names as the two leading men – Edward G Robinson (as the husband) would get top billing, and George Raft would get third, with Marlene's name coming between them. She would, however, get top salary, receiving $100,000 to Edward G's $85,000.

George Raft, who adored Marlene, and would have turned down his role if she hadn't been cast, was miffed at having third billing, and even more miffed when shooting started and Marlene and Edward G turned out to have a common interest in fine art – in spite of his thuggish appearance he was a gentle, cultured man with a fine collection of paintings.

Although it was he, not Edward G, who was granted Marlene's off-screen favours (for the duration of shooting only), this made Raft jealous, and he took to abusing Edward G on set, and became so violent in their staged punch-ups that the delays in shooting while tempers were calmed eventually added $200,000 to the budget.

Even the director, Raoul Walsh, something of a tough guy himself, was unable to control Raft's outbursts. But he did turn out a good competent picture. His forte was action sequences, and he liked filming wide open spaces, so with *Manpower* he was completely at home. He was also competent at observing subtleties of character and performance, and he worked well with Marlene, seizing this chance, as he said, to try and broaden his reputation from being simply a 'man's director'.

He also cheerfully allowed Marlene to direct her own lighting – placing a large mirror alongside the camera so that she could check on her appearance, as was her habit. As Edward G recalled, she did all this 'so subtly and sexily that no one was offended and she got precisely what she wanted.' He also noted that she had 'arrogant self-assurance and was sexy, temperamental, demanding…and rough and tough.'

Her performance was also rough and tough, and something of a departure for her – a sort of coarser version of 'Lola Lola', and the coarsest characterisation she would ever deliver. This was the remote and sophisticated von Sternberg 'Marlene' brought down to earth with a vengeance, and she managed it. When the film, shot between March and May 1941 (with a few retakes in June) was premièred in New York in July, and then released, it did reasonably well.

She hardly sang in the film, however, in spite of being cast as a singer, and in spite of the fact that Warners had hired Hollander and Loesser to write her a couple of songs. They wrote 'I'm In No Mood For Music' and 'He Lied And I Listened', but the first ended up as only an instrumental, and her performance of the second was cut to a single verse.

Charles K Feldman, pleased with her success, but aware that playing such a hard-boiled moll was hardly building up the Dietrich image, made haste to get her into another picture – this time with Columbia, who had also been interested in using her since late 1937.

The package he sold Columbia had a new wrinkle – he sold himself to the studio as part of the deal, to be the film's producer. The film would no longer be the Frank Capra project about Chopin, but an attempt to try Marlene in the fashionable genre of screwball comedy. This genre was by 1941 pretty much running out of steam (it had been highly popular all through the late Thirties), but Feldman thought the idea was worth a go. As director he installed another of his clients, Mitchell Leisen, and as Marlene's co-star yet another, the actor Fred MacMurray (not yet the major star he would become in Billy Wilder's *Double Indemnity* a couple of years later).

The film was to be called *The Lady Is Willing*, and in it Marlene, throwing off her *Manpower* sluttishness, would be cast (and why did nobody think of it before?) as 'A Star'. Not a film star, to be sure, but a musical-comedy star named Elizabeth Madden.

Elizabeth starts out cold and self-absorbed, but when she finds herself in possession of an abandoned baby (as happens in screwball comedies), her maternal instincts surface and she resolves to adopt it. Unfortunately, she is single, and in order to do that she must be married. So she starts trying to talk a young pediatrician (Fred MacMurray) into becoming her husband (in name only).

He is another of screwball's stock characters – the scientist who is unworldly and too wrapped up in his own research – but he is fascinated by Marlene in spite of himself, and he likes the baby, and the time comes when he has to perform an emergency mastoidectomy on it to save its life. Marlene has become so depressed by the baby's illness that the show she is appearing in is in grave danger of flopping because of her lack of oomph, but the news of the operation's success reaches her just in time for the show's big finish. She is a wow, the show is a wow, and she and the doctor take an on-stage curtain call together.

Filming began in August 1941, and as so often Marlene started casting thoughtful eyes at her co-star. But somehow Fred MacMurray didn't seem to be responding, which disconcerted her (it was always useful if one's co-star was one's lover – it helped a woman gain a certain control of what was happening on screen as well as off). As Mitchell Leisen recalled, 'She couldn't understand why Fred MacMurray wouldn't fall madly in love with her. I said, "Listen, Marlene, Fred's so happily in love with his wife, he couldn't care less about any other woman, so you lay off. Just make the picture."'

In her private life, things were more interesting. Remarque continued to observe morosely her ongoing liaison with John Wayne, telling her that he hoped it would soon come to an end. As things turned out the affair did gradually taper off, but not in the way Remarque hoped. What happened was that she found another and even more enticing lover – Jean Gabin, by now France's biggest film star.

Gabin had joined the flood of refugees in Hollywood, coming there in the middle of 1941. French to the backbone, he didn't enjoy being there. He felt out of place and homesick, and guilty at doing nothing to fight the Nazis – Hollywood to him was simply a place where he could earn enough money to get back across the Atlantic and enlist with the Free French, the army of expatriate Frenchmen who were assembled and directed by the young General de Gaulle (who was at this time residing in England) in close collaboration with the British government.

Meanwhile he got himself a contract with Darryl Zanuck at Twentieth-Century Fox. Marlene did what she could to make him feel at home in Hollywood (as she did for many refugees), and almost inevitably they became lovers. She helped him to find a house (in Brentwood) and they spent their nights either there or at her bungalow. She invited other French emigrés to meet him, including René Clair and Jean Renoir. Among the few things Gabin had managed to bring with him out of France were three treasured paintings – one by Vlaminck, one by Sisley, and one by Renoir's father, Auguste. These hung on the walls of his house. (He had also brought with him a prized racing-bicycle and accordion, causing some amusement at immigration).

Jean Renoir knew Gabin well (they had already made three fine films together – *Les Bas-Fonds*, *La Bête Humaine* and *La Grande Illusion*), and in his memoirs he recalled the time, writing:

> In the evening, we [he and his wife, Dido] used to meet Marlene Dietrich and Jean Gabin, who were living together. Marlene was singing French patriotic songs in cabarets for the pleasure of doing so, and she always ended with 'The Marseillaise. Gabin thought this ridiculous. He and Marlene had heated arguments. He called her 'my Prussian', and she would reply to this by tapping his forehead and saying in a languishing voice, 'That's what I like about you – it's quite empty. You haven't a single idea in your head, not one, and that's what I like.' The insult left this most subtle of actors quite unmoved.
>
> Marlene was truly a super-star, not only on the stage but in life. At home she was the perfect housewife and an excellent cook, her best dish being *chou farci*. But outside this domesticity she adored the admiring tributes that were paid to her. One night, in a cabaret, she several times asked Dido to accompany her to the ladies' room. Dido was at first taken aback by the frequent request but soon realised that it was simply because Marlene wanted to show off her legs, and took Dido with her on the pretext that she needed to be protected against the women who assailed her. It was simply the enactment of a ritual. But it must be added that the worship of Marlene's legs was amply justified.

In a way, for Marlene, Gabin had it all. He was a fine actor, ruggedly handsome, and French. Not only was he tall and strong, his lostness made him helpless, and made him dependent on her. As she recalled, he would '[cling] to me like an orphan to his foster mother, and I loved to mother him day and night.'

She helped him with his English. She advised him about working in Hollywood and about how to handle his finances (although he admitted later she wasn't too good at handling finances herself). She shopped for him and cleaned for him and cooked French meals for him. No man in her life ever needed her mothering more, and several times in the Fifties and Sixties she would tell people that he was the man she loved more than anyone else.

This was a happy time for Marlene, in spite of her growing concern about the war in Europe. She adored Jean Gabin, and she enjoyed making *The Lady Is Willing*, getting on well with the director, Mitchell Leisen. Leisen, who had come to directing via costume and set design, was a witty courteous homosexual, and he thought that Marlene was 'the most fascinating woman who ever lived'. His forte was directing witty romantic comedies, and although some felt he was more concerned with the stylish look of his sets and actors than with performance or story, this is underrating him. He made many films worth watching.

Filming on *The Lady Is Willing*, which began in August 1941, went well until the 25th of that month. On that day, while filming a scene in which she was holding the baby in her arms, Marlene tripped over a toy fire engine lying on the floor and, doing all she could to keep the child from harm, fell heavily, breaking her ankle.

Later she would claim that Carroll Righter, her astrologer, had warned her not to go to work that day, and that her disregarding his advice and having such an accident had confirmed and deepened her belief in astrology. But this is a little dubious. Professional film actors do not screw up the schedule by saying they are not coming to work today because their astrologer advises against it, and professional astrologers are adept at saying after such an accident, 'Don't you remember I said that on such-and-such a day there might be the possibility of misfortune.' Which can convince the unwary.

This broken ankle would be the first of a succession of fractures that Marlene would sustain, as her bones were brittle from childhood malnourishment. She was rushed to Cedars of Lebanon Hospital, where her leg was encased in plaster-of-paris from toe to thigh. The whole incident made national news (*Life* magazine even printed a succession of frames from the camera filming her when she fell, showing the whole incident). This helped to publicise the film, but it still suffered from the fact that for the rest of the shooting she could only be filmed from the waist up.

By 29 October, when the unit transferred to New York to finish off the film with a few location shots, she was almost healed – her leg by then was out of plaster and simply taped up. And she was still in good spirits. As she was about to get off her train at Grand Central Station, where of course a troop of reporters and press photographers were assembled, she borrowed a decorated walking-stick from Mitchell Leisen, whispered to a publicity man, 'Watch Mama make the front pages of every paper in New York,' and stepped down to pose for pictures and describe dramatically the way her accident had happened.

But her time of cheerfulness was soon to end. Only five weeks after shooting finished, on Sunday 7 December 1941, the Japanese bombed Pearl Harbor, and the next day America too was at war.

9 The War Effort

America's entry into World War II sent Marlene into an uncharacteristic bout of depression. Everything in her life suddenly seemed imperilled. She had lived before in a country that was at war, and she remembered the hunger, the hardship, and the hundreds of thousands of men going into battle, many of them to return maimed, many never to return at all.

She hated the Third Reich for what it had done to so many of her colleagues, and what it had done to destroy the two countries she loved best – France and Germany. And it was disconcerting for her to know that at least two members of her family were enlisted and fighting for the Nazis. These were her Aunt Jolly's two sons – Hasso, now nearly twenty, who was the son of Uncle Willi, and Rudolf, born of her previous marriage, who had been called up even though by birth he was American.

Wartime America brought other pressures. Germans in California, unless, like Marlene, they had taken out American citizenship, were subjected to an 8pm curfew. This applied, for instance, to both Rudi and Remarque. (Rudi would quite shortly move to New York, where he got a job with Twentieth-Century Fox, supervising the dubbing of their films into foreign languages. This was to avoid the further threat of possibly being interned – New York was less paranoid than California.)

She was further depressed by the state of her career. On 27 December she turned forty (although not many people knew that), and she was uneasily aware that, although she was still being offered work, good scripts for her were becoming increasingly thin on the ground. Her near-contemporary, Garbo, had just had a failure with the substandard comedy *Two Faced Woman*, which made her even more unsure of herself than usual. Garbo became increasingly choosy about scripts presented to her and, as things turned out, would never complete another film.

Marlene was also aware that during the late Thirties a whole new generation of glamour girls had arrived on the screen. Ingrid Bergman, like herself, was seen by the studios as being in the Garbo mould – a cool, beautiful, sophisticated European. But there were others as well – stars like Rita Hayworth, Lana Turner and Maureen O'Hara – who represented a new type of goddess. They were more approachable, sexier, more American. Stars were no longer seen, as they had been when she arrived in Hollywood, as remote, unattainable and magical. This was a legacy from the days of silent movies, when stars could not be heard, which helped give them a dream-like remoteness.

Marlene feared, as all stars are prone to, that soon she would be a back number (it would not be many months before the most famous legs in Hollywood would not be hers but Betty Grable's, and Marlene would never get her image painted on the nose of a Flying Fortress). Even before the outbreak of war she had been concerned about her situation, telling a reporter, 'Of course, I'm going to quit working. I want a chance really to see a bit of life before I die… A film star's career…can last only as long as one's youth lasts, and one's youth fades far quicker on screen than on the stage – I'm going to quit while I'm still at the top.'

People did occasionally come to her with proposals for stage roles. One recently had been Kurt Weill, still uncomfortable about the fact that the two songs he had written for her in Paris had turned out unsuited to her voice – that voice whose timbre he so admired. He very much wanted to hear her sing his songs, and suggested to her that she might star in a musical he had just co-written with Ira Gershwin (lyrics) and Moss Hart (book).

It was called *Lady In The Dark*, and it was essentially a rather downbeat skit on the American addiction to psychoanalysis. Originally it had been written for the great star of the American stage, Katherine Cornell, but had turned out to need a star more at home with music and glamour, so how about Marlene? She hadn't been interested, possibly because she had enough musical sense to know that her voice wasn't really up to these new Weill songs either. (The part eventually went to Gertrude Lawrence, who made the show a considerable hit.)

So Marlene's performing career wasn't all that it might be, and nor was her private life. She had fallen out with Douglas Fairbanks Jr, who in any case was back in London. Mercedes de Acosta was also in Europe, and Remarque was deeply involved in finishing *Arch Of Triumph*, the novel he had been working on for some time. This was set among German refugees in Paris and had a central female character (a woman of easy virtue) who was based on Marlene as he had known her. When the film was made in 1948, starring Charles Boyer, Remarque pleaded for Marlene to be cast in the role, but it went (unsuitably) to Ingrid Bergman.

Of course she was devotedly happy with Jean Gabin, but aware that the instant the Free French accepted him into their ranks he would rush off back across the Atlantic, and into active service. Furthermore, at the moment he was heavily involved in making his first American film, which had begun shooting on 24 November.

Based on a novel by Willard Robertson, and with a screenplay by John O'Hara (with some additional work by an uncredited Nunnally Johnson), it was called *Moontide*.

In it, Gabin was to play a longshoreman, Bobo, who mistakenly believes he has killed a man and hides out by getting a job on a barge. From the barge he rescues a waif, Anna, who has attempted to drown herself, and begins to fall in love with her. But he has a parasitic sidekick, Tiny, who becomes jealous of his love for Anna and uses the alleged murder to try and drive them apart.

Acting on Marlene's advice, Gabin had insisted that the film's director should be Fritz Lang, then under contract to Twentieth-Century Fox. But the film became fraught with difficulties. Lang disliked having to film the waterfront scenes on an artificially built indoor set on the lot, and protested to Darryl Zanuck, whom he detested (and who detested him). He also didn't like the script. Nor did Gabin, continually protesting as shooting proceeded that it was far too wordy (his English, almost non-existent when he arrived in America, was still not good).

Eventually, after three weeks of enduring the indoor waterfront and Gabin's protests, Lang had had enough. He needed a way to get off the picture, and at around the end of the first week in December he had an inspiration. Leading Gabin off into a corner of the set, and adopting a man-to-man tone, he admitted that he too had had an affair with Marlene.

Gabin was furious. Coming home that evening he indignantly confronted Marlene with this accusation. She reacted with amazement. 'With that ugly Jew?' she said, giving him a big hug. 'You must be joking, mon amour.'

Whether or not Gabin believed her, 12 December was Lang's last day as director. Zanuck released him from his contract, provided he would owe Fox an additional film, and he was replaced by the competent but uninspired Archie Mayo.

Marlene, in her depressed mood at that time, spent New Year's Eve alone in her bungalow and, according to her daughter Maria, would often during the following months break down in tears for no immediate reason.

There was, however, hope on the horizon. Even in this time of unhappiness she had already begun to involve herself in what would be, to her, the most important and valuable time of her life – that would dissolve her despair and allow her to feel that her life had some meaning. This was war work.

Immediately after Pearl Harbor, the Germans and Italians formally declared war on the USA, and that same day several members of the film industry hastily formed a body to 'help in entertaining the armed forces and in supporting the war effort'. They named it the Hollywood Victory Committee. Clark Gable was declared head of its Screen Actors' Division, and Marlene attended its inaugural meeting, held in the Beverly-Wilshire Hotel on 22 December. She was given the job of organizing the selling of war bonds (which were to raise funds for the War Department), and the next day was heard plugging them on radio, on the same programme as several other stars, including Judy Garland.

Before long she was travelling America coast-to-coast to sell bonds – at rallies, on street corners, in bars and night-clubs. It was the night-clubs that got her into a spot of bother. It had been arranged across the country that banks could be phoned at all hours of the day or night, so that people wishing to pay for bonds by cheque could have the validity of their cheques vouched for. This phoning would be done by agents of the US Treasury Department, who were always present at bond-selling exercises. In night-clubs Marlene had taken to sitting in the laps of payers by cheque, flirting with them and refusing to get up until a Treasury man signalled that everything was in order.

One night, when she was selling bonds in Washington, she and the Treasury officials she was with were summoned to the White House by President Roosevelt. When their car arrived there, at two in the morning, it turned out it was only Marlene he wanted to see. She was ushered into his office, and he sternly told her (as she remembered), 'I've heard all about what you are doing to sell bonds. We are very grateful to you for all this. But I expressly forbid you to confuse acquisition with prostitution. From now on, you will no longer give any performances in these night-spots. That's an order!'

Given a direct order by her country's commander-in-chief, of course Marlene obeyed.

Even as she began her bond-selling efforts, there was a film for her to make. Charles K Feldman had sold one of his packages to Universal. A two-picture deal, it included his clients Marlene, Randolph Scott and John Wayne, who would be credited in that order, and himself as producer. The first of the two films was to be the fourth remake of an old Rex Beach story, originally written in 1905, called *The Spoilers*.

Set in Alaska during the Gold Rush of the 1890's, the film told (again) of the rivalry between two tough prospectors (Randolph Scott was the slightly crooked one) for the favours of saloon proprietress Cherry Malotte (of course Marlene).

The picture, directed by the unassuming journeyman director Ray Enright, looked well enough (it was Oscar-nominated for both Best Art Direction and Best Set Decoration), but it turned out to be as routine as it sounds. It was spiced up a little by peppering Marlene's dialogue with double-entendres, but nobody's heart really seemed to be in it. Marlene didn't even sing.

During the filming, which took place during January and February 1942, she was pleased to be working again with her old buddy John Wayne, but felt the film ill-omened from the start. Her mood deteriorated when, on 16 January, just after shooting began, Carole Lombard, whom Marlene knew and liked, was killed returning from a bond-selling tour when her plane crashed near Las Vegas.

She was exhausting herself. Not only was she energetically selling bonds, she had also begun visiting military bases to entertain the troops. These visits, organised by the Hollywood Victory Committee, usually included other entertainers as well, such as comedians Groucho Marx or the Ritz Brothers. Marlene of course sang. She often gave them one of her songs from *Seven Sinners* – 'The Man's In The Navy' – changing the title when appropriate to 'The Man's In The Army' or 'The Man's In The Air Force'.

Only a few days after shooting was completed, during the last days of February, she entered the La Quinta Hotel, a desert spa southeast of Palm Springs, where she stayed recuperating for over three weeks. The papers reported she had been ill and was convalescing, and it is possible that she had simply overworked herself, but her daughter Maria told friends that she had become pregnant by Jean Gabin, and had had an abortion, without consulting him, an act that drove him to fury. Gabin was given to rages with her, occasionally violent and mostly from jealousy, so there was enough turbulence in their affair to have added considerably to any exhaustion she was feeling.

While recuperating, Marlene gave the occasional interview. Again she announced to the press that she was going to abandon Hollywood and return to the stage – that she had been asked by a New York producer to appear in a revival of Wilde's *An Ideal Husband*. This was true enough, but when the producer withdrew his offer she abruptly reversed field, saying in another interview, 'I'm not thinking of the stage now. Time for that later, when you get older and harder to photograph.'

When she recovered, she did go to New York, but for a brief holiday with Jean Gabin, whose filming of *Moontide* had finished back on 7 February. They went to plays, and to visit old friends, and Marlene attempted to lift herself out of her depressed mood by spending three afternoons shopping at the establishment of the famous couturier, Lily Daché. She bought ninety-eight items. They included a scarf, a white turban, fur gloves and a fur possum muff, handbags, accessories, and a Persian lamb jacket.

When she got the bill, it was for almost $5,000, which at the time she was unable to come up with. By the end of the summer the store felt it had to sue her for non-payment, and it took her nearly a year to pay off the full amount.

Continuing her war work, in the summer of 1942 she was invited by Bette Davis to put in appearances at the Hollywood Canteen. This was a project that Miss Davis had helped to organise – a place where servicemen could come to eat and dance and be entertained. Its special feature was that not only would the entertainment be provided by Hollywood stars, but so would the cooking and the table service, and you might even get to dance with a star. Marlene joined in and was in her element. She sang songs and danced with the enlisted men, she cooked meals and she made cakes. In Miss Davis's words, 'Marlene not only contributed glamour out front, but backbreaking labour in the kitchen.'

She also embarked on a further nationwide bond tour, accompanied by other stars, including Linda Darnell and Dorothy Lamour. And she began appearing in another entertainment, Orson Welles's *Mercury Wonder Show*, that he was presenting in a tent on Cahuenga Boulevard.

Welles was a showman to his backbone, loving vaudeville and circuses and magic, and he had intended to include in his show a mind-reading act, to be performed by himself and the woman he was soon to marry, Rita Hayworth. But Rita Hayworth was the top star of Columbia Pictures, and Columbia head of production Harry Cohn wasn't having the studio's valuable property mixed up in any public performance over which he had no control. So he vetoed Welles's proposal, and Welles turned for help instead to Marlene. She was delighted, and happily played Welles's on-stage assistant, wearing one of her near-nude, sequins-and-nothing gowns. This bothered Jean Gabin, who took to coming to the shows with her and acting as a stage-hand, simply to keep an eye on her.

Although she was glad enough to be entertaining and encouraging servicemen at home in America, Marlene had felt, from the time America entered the war, that the real theatre of operations was in Europe, and that was where she should be.

During her bond tours and elsewhere she learned from other performers of the existence of an organization called USO (United Services Organization). This had been founded back in 1941, before America entered the war, by a consortium of social services, mostly with religious backgrounds, that included the YMCA, the YWCA, the National Catholic Community Service, the National Jewish Welfare Board, the Salvation Army, and the National Travelers Aid Association. Its aim was to provide recreational, social, welfare and spiritual facilities for off-duty service personnel at home and abroad – the Hollywood Canteen itself, as well as its sister organization, the New York Canteen, were branches of USO.

When America entered the war, USO became more allied to the military organizational structure, and among other things sent performers abroad to entertain troops near the front line. Marlene got in touch with them and begged to be sent overseas. They duly noted her request and said they would do what they could, and for the moment she had to be content with that.

In August 1942 she began filming the second of the Dietrich-Scott-Wayne pictures that Charles K Feldman had lined up (and was producing) for Universal. It was called *Pittsburgh*, its story took place over decades, and it had an explicit message for wartime. Marlene played Josie 'Hunky' Winters (known as 'Countess') in a coal-and-steel community, and it told of two husky miners (Wayne was the slightly crooked one this time), who climb to the top of their industry, brawling over Dietrich the while. They also fight over labour principles, but eventually both agree with Hunky that, in wartime, men and management must pull together for the patriotic good.

The film was routinely directed by routine director Lewis Seiler, and Marlene in it looked adequately glamorous, whether in evening gowns or covered in coal dust, but this was a far cry from having been the queen of Paramount ten years earlier, when every aspect of her appearance – make-up, lighting, costume – was the subject of detailed preparation. Now she was just another stunning woman to add glamour to a picture, and in a role that a dozen other actresses could have played.

But at this time in her life Marlene didn't much care what films she made, provided she looked reasonably good in them. The important thing was her war work, and the only important thing about film-making was that it brought in money to enable her to carry on with it.

During the filming of *Pittsburgh*, another aspect of her life altered as well. Her affair with John Wayne finally ended. They had continued, as usual, to be lovers off screen, but eventually Wayne had tired of hearing how wonderful Jean Gabin was.

Gabin, meanwhile, was himself filming again. *Moontide* had turned out poorly, but Zanuck had lined up another project for him. This was called *The Imposter*, and it was to be directed by an old Paris colleague, Julien Duvivier, with whom he had made two films back in the mid-Thirties. But Duvivier, in spite of his long and efficient career (he made films for almost fifty years), was at best merely a stylish director.

The Imposter was a war film, set in Algeria, and in spite of having a writer as good as Marc Connolly (as well as a couple of others) work on Julien Duvivier's original story, it again turned out poorly, even when retitled *Bayonet Charge*, or when reissued as *Strange Confession*.

During the period while Gabin was making it, a strange thing began to occur at his rented house. During such afternoons as he was there, if he happened to be sitting in the garden, a woman took to appearing in the garden next door, at around four o'clock, wearing a floppy hat and sunglasses, and discreetly peering at him through the shrub hedge separating them. It took him a little while to realise that it was Greta Garbo. This rather disturbed him, but Marlene simply shrugged. It was rather flattering to her to have her heroine, Garbo, stalking the man who was now her lover.

In the late summer of 1942, at around the time she began filming *Pittsburgh*, Kurt Weill reappeared in Marlene's life. Still anxious to have her sing his songs, he was collaborating on another Broadway musical, and wanted her to star in it. The musical was going to be based on a comic novel called *The Tinted Venus*, which had been written by the English novelist F Anstey back in 1885.

The script, as it would eventually develop, tells of how Rodney Hatch, a humble American barber, sees a statue of Venus, owned by a wealthy art dealer, and impulsively slips onto its finger the engagement ring he has just bought for his fiancée. The spirit of the real Venus enters the statue and she, obeying the decrees of the Fates, knows she must marry the man who has brought her back to life. In the course of the plot she banishes the barber's fiancée (a shrew) to the moon, even though he loves her, but eventually, when she comes to understand what life as a provincial housewife entails, she opts to return to Mount Olympus.

Weill had had the idea of retitling the piece *Love In A Mist*, but the husband-and-wife team of librettists, Sam and Bella Spewack, who had been brought in by producer Cheryl Crawford, thought that was over-romantic for a somewhat tart story, and suggested *One Touch Of Venus*. Which would remain its title.

Marlene did like Weill's music, and she agreed to see him and Cheryl Crawford, and listen to the score. They had several such meetings, at which Marlene would politely listen to Weill's music, as well as Crawford's plans for costumes and staging, but none of these meetings were somehow entirely satisfactory. At that time Marlene apparently used her musical saw (which she was then frequently playing in troop entertainments) as a sort of social weapon. As Cheryl Crawford wrote in 1977, 'I was accustomed to many varieties of eccentric behaviour from stars, but I must confess that when Marlene placed that huge saw securely between her elegant legs and began to play, I was more than a little startled. It was an ordinary saw about five feet [1.5m] high and was played with a violin bow. We would talk about the show for a while, then Marlene would take up the musical saw and begin to play; that, we soon found out, was the cue that talk was finished for the evening.'

Often the tune she played was Weill's 'Surabaya Jonny', which was at least a little encouraging, but in spite of Marlene offering suggestions about both music and staging, there was still no sign that she was willing to commit herself to starring in the show.

In an attempt to get a clearer idea of her feelings about the show, Cheryl Crawford invited Marlene (and Jean Gabin) to join her and Weill for dinner at a popular steak house on Sunset Boulevard, the Cock and Bull. The dinner didn't much help. As Crawford would write, 'There was very little talk about our project, but Marlene and Gabin were delightful to watch, two such beautiful people in love with each other.' But she did get one encouraging remark from Marlene, who airily told her not to worry, she would soon be in New York for further discussions.

Meanwhile, relations between Marlene and her daughter were becoming increasingly strained. Maria was still a student at the Reinhardt school on Sunset Boulevard, studying not with Reinhardt himself, but with his second wife, actress Helen Thimig, and sometimes with Natasha Lytess, who would famously go on to become Marilyn Monroe's dramatic coach. Maria was desperate to build a life of her own, away from her mother's influence, and the instant she turned eighteen, on 12 December 1942, thus attaining majority, she announced that she was getting married.

The man she had in mind was the British character-actor Richard Haydn, then aged thirty-seven, and Marlene was having none of him. She made a statement to the press, who had got wind of the matter, that no marriage would take place 'for the duration'. Presumably Richard Haydn's desire to marry Maria was not deep – he may have been swept off his feet by her desperate desire for independence, and by the strength of her character, which was proving almost as formidable as her mother's – because almost at once the engagement was called off, and Maria for the moment was stymied.

In February 1943, Jean Gabin, who was by now thirty-nine, at last got his call-up papers from the Free French (things involving the Free French generally took some time, mainly due to the difficult circumstances they were working under, with De Gaulle in England and pockets of would-be fighters all over Britain, Portugal, North Africa and other places). He was to embark from the port of Newport News, and Marlene agreed she would accompany him to the nearby town of Norfolk, Virginia, to see him off. As an earnest sign of how seriously she was taking their relationship, she agreed to look after his prized possessions till they could be together again – his three paintings, his racing-bicycle and his accordion.

With a few weeks in hand, they headed first for New York, where it had been suggested that Marlene might appear on stage in a play based on a popular novel of the day. The book was *Laura*, by Vera Caspary, and Marlene had declared herself anxious to be involved, which suggests that her foot-dragging about signing a contract for *One Touch Of Venus* arose mainly from her uncertainty about singing Weill. In New York, however, she learned that the production had been indefinitely postponed as the author had sold the rights of her book to Twentieth-Century Fox.

Her procrastination about *One Touch Of Venus* had not, as it happened, caused Cheryl Crawford any more problems than she had already. The book by Sam and Bella Spewack had, she felt, not been good enough, and she had realised she would have to find another writer. Weill's lyricist, the comic poet Ogden Nash, suggested humourist S J Perelman, and Cheryl liked the idea. As she said, 'Ogden and Sid had known each other for some time and were friends. But we agreed that the only fair thing to do was to tell Bella our decision before we involved anyone else.' (When told, Bella fainted twice and, when she recovered, remained so furious that she never spoke to Cheryl Crawford ever again.)

At another meeting with Weill and Cheryl Crawford, Marlene reaffirmed her interest in being Venus (especially in gowns, as planned, by Mainbocher). From her suite in the St Regis Hotel, she made a number of visits to the Metropolitan Museum of Art to study all the representations of the goddess she could find. She purchased vast quantities of grey chiffon and summoned Weill and Crawford several times to her suite, where she stripped off all her clothes (at least once in front of them), swathed herself in chiffon, and posed.

Cheryl Crawford recalled, 'she struck poses, and she asked our opinions. She looked divine, of course, but we couldn't work out what this had to do with her commitment to our show. I remember she was very keen on one Venus [she had seen] in particular – one with gorgeous buttocks.'

After several posing sessions the pair prevailed on Marlene to come to the Forty-sixth Street Theater so that they could hear how her voice sounded in the auditorium. Those were the days before singers in musicals used microphones, and when she arrived, with Gabin for moral support, it was obvious to everyone present that she was very nervous indeed. It was fifteen years since she had sung live in an auditorium so large, and she was afraid she had lost her ability to project (as well as to sing the rather challenging songs of Weill). It turned out she had. She sang Frederick Hollander's 'Jonny', and her voice, probably constricted further by nervousness, was barely audible to those in the fourth row of the stalls.

Nonetheless, her pride prevented her from withdrawing from the show then and there, and Cheryl Crawford, knowing how good she would look as Venus, convinced herself that with enough rehearsal Marlene would be able to carry off the role.

But still there was no contract, and Cheryl decided it was time for drastic action. She arrived at the St Regis next day, bringing with her the papers for signing. To her surprise, Marlene was packing to go back to California.

'You're leaving?' asked Cheryl. Marlene said, yes, she was. And not only that, but she had the most terrible headache (which translated as 'Please don't be cross with me, I'm only a poor weak creature').

Cheryl immediately said she had just the thing for that, and produced a small amount of a white powdered stimulant. Marlene took it and, unaccustomed to such stimulants, was in a moment full of joy and excitement. Cheryl seized the moment to put the contract in front of her, and Marlene cheerfully signed it. The next day she and Gabin headed south to Norfolk, then he went off to embark, and she returned to Hollywood.

There she shortly received the script for *One Touch Of Venus*, now newly revised by Perelman, Nash and Weill, who were somewhat disconcerted when for several days they heard nothing. Eventually, on 16 March, they phoned her, and to Weill she explained, 'I cannot play this – it is too sexy and profane,' going on to say, 'You know, Kurt, I have a daughter who is now eighteen, and for me to get up on the stage and exhibit my legs is now impossible.'

Weill attempted to explain that, on the contrary, the piece was witty, sophisticated and intriguing. But she would have none of it. Even though in his disappointment he became angry, she continued to maintain firmly that she would not exhibit herself in such a sexy and profane show.

Resigning herself to the situation, Cheryl Crawford obligingly tore up the contract, and was fortunate enough to find a replacement in Mary Martin. *One Touch Of Venus*, directed by Elia Kazan and choreographed by Agnes de Mille, became a huge success.

There were others in Hollywood besides Marlene who wanted to help the war effort. At the house of studio head Jack Warner, Charles K Feldman had seen a Paramount short in which Vice President Henry Wallace spoke of the war against fascism being a 'people's war', and stressed the importance in it of the 'common man'.

Impressed by this idea, he conceived the notion of a film featuring a string of war stories from all over the world, to be made on a non-commercial charity basis by all those involved. He assembled an amazing string of famous writers who were prepared to involve themselves – it included Clifford Odets, Lillian Hellman, Dalton Trumbo, Ben Hecht, Pearl Buck,

Edna Ferber, Maxwell Anderson, Lion Feuchtwanger, George S Kaufman and Moss Hart. Jerome Kern agreed to provide the music, and several directors expressed a willingness to be involved, including Alexander Korda and Lewis Milestone.

In the same way, he assembled a string of actors. Some were his clients, some simply friends – they included Irene Dunne, Randolph Scott, Merle Oberon, Jean Arthur, Margaret Sullavan, and Marlene. The agreement he made with them was that none would work more than twelve days, and all the profits would go to a charitable war fund.

Unfortunately, various organizations within the American film business balked. The Screen Actors Guild prohibited any of its members from taking part in charity pictures, and the Motion Picture Producers and Distributors of America deliberately refused help. But fortunately, several of the big studios were willing to take on the project. Universal would have, but did not have enough capital. MGM and Fox put in bids, but eventually, at the beginning of 1943, it was Jack Warner's enthusiasm for the picture that won it for Warner Brothers.

The picture, now called *Battle Cry*, was to be directed by Feldman's friend and colleague Howard Hawks, and it was announced that among the many stars who would appear in it, besides Marlene, were Ingrid Bergman, Charles Boyer, Claudette Colbert and Leslie Howard. Work on the script proceeded, the writers involved now including William Faulkner, but suddenly, at the beginning of August 1943, Warners pulled the plug. Costs had climbed to $232,348 before shooting even began, and they simply couldn't afford to make it.

Marlene, increasingly anxious to get overseas, continued to pester USO, and in March 1943 was at last told that her request would be granted, although there would undoubtedly be some delay while they sorted out schedules, itineraries and the composition of shows. They would also, of course, have to tie in with any commitments she might have herself.

For the moment there were few. With no play or film to appear in, except possibly *Battle Cry*, and with Jean Gabin gone, she continued to involve herself in war work in America – and she also started devoting a large amount of time and attention to Maria.

Maria, still chafing to be free, was not entirely happy with this sudden flood of maternal affection. But hope was close at hand. A talented young actor had appeared at the Reinhardt school, and she liked him. He was twenty-three, his name was Dean Goodman, and after enlisting in the military he had been given a medical discharge. Now he was assisting the legendary acting teacher Maria Ouspenskaya, as well as appearing himself in local productions.

At first his relationship with Maria was quite casual. They met socially, and occasionally dated, and that was all. But Maria wanted more. She was pretty (if a little plump), bright and talented, and had her mother's determination to make people like her. She took advantage of Marlene's absence (in New York and taking Jean Gabin to Virginia) to see as much of Dean Goodman as she could, and in June 1943 he suddenly found himself engaged. As he would remember, 'Maria was the aggressor in our relationship, and only later did it become clear to me that she wanted most desperately to get away from home and mother. She was also very adamant that I not meet Marlene, and she admitted why: she said she was afraid that every man she brought home would eventually be found in her mother's bed.'

Goodman found himself being rushed to the altar, even though his friends warned him to be cautious. 'Maria was convinced she was in love with me,' he recalled, 'and I thought I was in love with her. Right up to the wedding – because I didn't want to seem like an opportunist or a starstruck fan – I didn't insist on meeting Marlene, she had no desire to meet me. Rudi simply wasn't around, and Maria wasn't eager for me to meet either one! It was a very strange and swift courtship.'

Marlene, while having no desire to meet Maria's intended, moved as fast as her daughter did, spurred by the fearful realization that perhaps she would no longer be needed. She had Dean Goodman's credit rating and character investigated, but found nothing he could be faulted on (he had even taken a part-time job as a clerk in a warehouse to earn a little more money for himself and his future wife). When that failed, she confronted Maria with the question of how she would feel having Jewish children, and followed that up by having her lawyer summon Dean to his chambers and raise the same question. To which Dean replied that he would have been proud to be Jewish, but as it happened he wasn't. The somewhat embarrassed lawyer also asked him, as instructed by Marlene, whether he was a homosexual and whether he was not in fact romantically involved with the aged Maria Ouspenskaya (both rumours that she had heard). He said he wasn't either, and took a small pleasure in pointing out that they seemed to be mutually exclusive. He added that in any case he would be a more suitable companion for Maria than her current domestic companion, Jo Carstairs' ex-secretary, Violla Rubber.

The lawyer apologised for having had to ask such questions, and suggested that perhaps it would be a good idea for Dean to phone Marlene himself and try to set her mind at ease. Which he bravely did. Over the phone, Marlene told him that being a gentile didn't make him any better, because she knew, even if Maria couldn't see it, that all he was was a fortune-hunter, and that if he thought that she (Marlene) was going to support both him and her daughter he'd got another think coming. When he replied that perhaps Maria was worth loving for some other reason than her mother or her mother's money, Marlene seemed taken aback for a moment, but still remained resolutely opposed to the wedding.

It took place at the Hollywood Congregational Church on 23 August 1943, and neither Marlene nor Rudi attended. But Marlene wasn't finished yet. The newlyweds moved into a small apartment, and were surprised, returning home one day, to find that Marlene, desperate to prove she was still necessary in her daughter's life, had moved several pieces of furniture into it from the collection she had in storage. They were further surprised a little later to arrive home one evening and find that the place had been scrubbed from top to bottom, with the windows washed, new curtains hung, and flowers everywhere. 'Marlene had done it all herself,' Dean recalled. 'The building manager and our neighbours had thought the woman in bandanna and work clothes was a hired domestic.' (Cleaning would increasingly become an obsession with Marlene. She had always been houseproud, but eventually it would almost become an illness – a desperate attempt to impose order and control on her whole environment.)

During this period she was hired by Universal to do a single day's filming. They were making a morale-boosting entertainment film, as all the studios did during the war, partly to cheer up both servicemen and civilians, and partly to emphasise what a parade of magnificent stars they had on the payroll.

This one was to be called *Follow The Boys*. It was held together by a sketchy plot in which two show dancers (George Raft and Vera Zorina) meet, fight, make up and marry. Then he volunteers for the war, but is turned down on medical grounds and instead becomes a hard-working organiser of the Hollywood Victory Committee. Through a misunderstanding, his wife leaves him, but he keeps sending entertainers overseas, eventually setting off with a group of them himself, bound for Australia, and is torpedoed by the Japanese in the Pacific. His wife, having borne him a child, becomes a symbol of motherhood and hope for the USO.

Among the galaxy of stars in the film were W C Fields, Jeannette MacDonald, Sophie Tucker, the Andrews Sisters, Dinah Shore, the Delta Rhythm Boys, Artur Rubinstein, Donald O'Connor, and a whole host of bands, among them those of Ted Lewis, Charlie Spivak and Louis Jordan.

The whole thing was produced by Charles K Feldman, but even so Marlene got into the picture only by default. One of the items presented was to be Orson Welles, as 'the Great Orsino', performing part of his magic act (as he was accustomed to do in his *Mercury Wonder Show*), in front of an audience of servicemen and women. He planned to saw a woman in half, and again had tried to get Rita Hayworth. But again he was thwarted by Harry Cohn, so as an excellent substitute he chose his mind-reading partner, Marlene.

In the film, with the aid of a certain amount of rather clumsy special-effects work, he installs her (wearing harem costume) in an upright cabinet, then supervises as two GI's from his audience saw it across the middle. When the two halves of the cabinet are opened, Marlene's famous legs dance off in one direction, while her upper half stays on stage long enough to hypnotise him, so that he falls like a log.

The act is one of the most enjoyable episodes in what is necessarily a hodge-podge of a movie. Marlene admired Welles deeply, and very much enjoyed working with him. As with Ernest Hemingway, he and she became buddies, she deeming him 'a genius', and he once describing her as 'the good soldier of all time'.

As well as producing *Follow The Boys* for Universal, Charles K Feldman had by this time also managed to set up a deal to produce two films for MGM, both to star Marlene. For these she would be paid (in advance) the sum of $100,000.

Fifty thousand dollars a picture was not as much as she had been used to getting, but she was glad to have it, because her mind was now totally focussed on making overseas tours for USO. She decided to devote her whole time to them, once they happened, and if that meant that for the duration she would be unable to earn, so be it. Her plan became to gather into her bank account every scrap of money she could lay her hands on before being sent overseas.

Her first MGM film began shooting in October 1943. It was *Kismet* – the same *Kismet* that would in not too many years become a famous musical, but which then was simply an Arabian Nights fantasy with the odd song here and there. The play had been around for years and its central role of Hafiz, the King of Thieves, had been created by the famous actor Otis Skinner, who had played it on stage for years, and on film twice – in 1920 as a silent, and in 1930 as a talkie.

Coincidentally, a version of it had also been made in Germany in 1930, directed by Marlene's old friend William Dieterle, who had directed her in her first important film role, in *Der Mensch Am Wege (The Man By The Wayside)*. And it was he who would now be directing the MGM version, which was ironic in a way, because as a young man, beginning his career as a director, he had wanted films to be shot more realistically, in real locations, whereas *Kismet* would be about as unrealistic and stagy as any film ever shot.

Marlene's role was almost a new addition to the story – almost, because it was based on a very minor character in all the previous versions. She would play Jarmilla, an exotic Macedonian queen living in a private apartment in the palace of the wicked Vizier, who intends to marry her after he has taken control of the whole Arab empire.

Hafiz was to be played by Ronald Colman, and the main love story in the film is between his beautiful sixteen-year-old daughter, Marsinah (Joy Ann Page) and the handsome prince (James Craig) who has recently inherited the Arab empire from his late father. Hafiz, a lovable rascal, is eventually banished to a far-off minor princedom (but made its prince), and takes with him Jarmilla, who has fallen for his devious good-looking charm.

The whole thing was carefully designed to be a piece of high-class escapist fantasy, aimed squarely at wartime audiences. It would be filmed in Technicolor and have a budget (enormous in its day) of three million dollars.

Marlene, although given second billing (to Ronald Colman) would in fact have little screen-time. She would appear in only half-a-dozen scenes, and have one big set-piece – an exotic pseudo-Arabian dance, choreographed by Jack Cole and substantially danced by a veiled stand-in in long-shot. (Years later she claimed she was also to have had two songs, specially written, like the rest of the film's score, by Harold Arlen and Yip Harburg, but refused to sing them on the grounds they were wrong for her.)

Her costumes were designed by MGM's executive designer, Irene. Working together, she and Marlene came up with the idea of encasing her legs in strands of real gold chain, and Marlene stood patiently with her legs apart for hours while men with pliers laboured between them to twist gold wire into links. Unfortunately, once she got onto the set and attempted to run though her dance (or her close-ups to be fitted into the dance), the chains kept breaking.

Another solution had to be found and, clinging to the idea of gold, Marlene came up with the concept of having her legs gilded. They turned out to require four coats of gold paint, but the result was spectacular – so much so that *Life* magazine devoted many pages to showing exactly how the effect was achieved.

Pictures of her gilded legs would dominate the posters for the film all over America, but the effect, while spectacular, was unflattering to her. As were Irene's pseudo-Arabian costumes. And her make-up, with a mouth so plastered with dark red lipstick that all its shape was lost. And her hair, piled up six inches high on her hair in lacquered blonde waves and ringlets that seem made of wood-shavings. All in all, it would be fair to say that Marlene never looked worse in a film in all her life – garish and inelegant.

Much she cared. She had quite a good time making the film, finding the other members of the cast and crew congenial, and in any case her mind was on other things. Most evenings, after filming, she would go off to her stint at the Hollywood Canteen. And here the gilded legs gave her a problem. It turned out that the four layers of gold paint could only be removed with a great deal of effort and wood alcohol, and the alcohol, reacting with the paint, left her legs a pale greenish colour. So she took to leaving the gold paint on till after the Canteen, which made her a bigger hit there than ever.

The actor Roddy McDowall, then in his teens and working there as a busboy, remembered her making an entrance, saying she was 'nuclear, before there was a Bomb. She levelled the place and popped the eyes of every serviceman there; and not just theirs. I thought later that nobody in the history of show business had ever done so much with so little. I don't know if she was a real blonde, but she was real *gold*.'

Filming on *Kismet* finished on the last day of the year, by which time Maria's marriage to Dean Goodman had ended. He had gone on a short tour as a member of John Carradine's Shakespeare company, and when he came home at around Christmas Maria announced to him that their marriage had been a mistake, and that she was leaving.

He was taken aback, but on the whole soon came to agree. He had never wildly fancied her, and the whole marriage had been entered into in too much haste. So amiably he agreed that she was right, and suggested perhaps they should get a divorce, but was taken aback again when she flatly refused, saying, 'But my parents never divorced, and like them we can have our freedom and the respectability of the contract.' Good mother or not, Marlene had influenced her deeply.

As soon as she finished *Kismet*, Marlene set about getting more money into her bank account. She gathered up almost every possession she had acquired since coming to America, and put them up for auction. Furniture, clothing, tableware, silverware, and a collection of a hundred and fifty pieces of European porcelain – all were sold. (Hearing about the sale, Remarque worried that she might auction a number of rather passionate letters he had sent her, but she didn't.)

Even much of her jewellery went, although she did retain quite a few expensive pieces, eventually hiding them in a strongbox in a Geneva bank, where they would remain as security for the rest of her life. But of course she did not sell Jean Gabin's paintings, or his racing-bicycle, or accordion. Those she had safely stored, before setting off to New York to await the pleasure of USO.

10 Into The Field

Waiting around for USO to give her an assignment was a little like being in the army, or indeed like film-making. Endless hours of hanging around waiting for something to happen, interspersed with sudden bursts of activity.

In Marlene's case, much of the hanging around was done in a waiting-room at 1 Park Avenue, where Abe Lastfogel of the William Morris Agency vetted acts hoping to perform for USO, either at home or overseas. In a way it was worse even than trying to get a peacetime booking, because the scripts for USO acts had to be passed by the army censors as well, not so much for military reasons, but to make sure that the material was suitable for the ears of young innocent service personnel.

She chafed at the inactivity, declaring to anyone who would listen, 'I will not sit here working at my little job and let the war pass me by.'

In time, she was made a member of a company of five. The other members were a hillbilly comedienne from Texas, Lin Mayberry; a Jewish crooner, Milton Frome, who could also play straight man; a hard-drinking western swing musician from Oklahoma, Jack Snyder, who could play piano or, if one was not available, accordion; and most important to Marlene, a thirty-year-old night-club comic from Chicago, Danny Thomas, fresh from appearing at the Roxy in New York.

Danny Thomas, who was to MC the shows, became Marlene's mentor. It was a long time since she had been coached in cabaret techniques by Rosa Valetti in Berlin, and she was somewhat out of practice at appearing before live audiences, in spite of the performances she had given at the Hollywood Canteen and on bond tours. Not only that, but techniques in 1940's America were a lot faster and slicker than they had been in 1920's Berlin. Danny gave her tips on how to handle audiences – how to slow them down, how to hot them up, tricks for handling hecklers, how to use silence. He coached her in timing and delivery – both for singing her songs and for exchanging repartee. 'Above all,' she said later, 'he taught me how to *talk* to them.'

The company rehearsed in a shabby room above the famous Lindy's restaurant, just off Broadway, and before the end of February 1944 were sufficiently prepared to give tryout concerts at various military camps and at bond rallies. These were assessed by USO officials, and to the performers had exactly the feel of auditions.

Eventually they were deemed good enough to be granted a booking at one of the army's major venues – a camp at Fort Meade, Maryland – and they performed there on 20 March, accompanied by the 128th army band. The company performed well, and Marlene herself was a stunning success. She wore, as reported, 'a long-sleeved gown of flesh-colored net peppered with dazzling golden sequins'. Interspersing everything with wry comments, she sang 'The Boys In The Backroom' and 'Falling In Love Again', she played 'Pagan Love Song' on her saw, and she performed the simple mind-reading act she had learned from Orson Welles, using Danny Thomas as her partner. Without apparent effort she moved from being merely a member of the company to being its headliner.

The audience of twelve hundred GI's loved her, and glowing reports were returned to 1 Park Avenue. Within two weeks, the company was told to report for a ten-week tour overseas. The final paperwork was prepared and, while that was being done, Marlene made a last-minute trip to buy clothes. From John-Frederics she bought a tan hat, and from Franklin Simon an olive gabardine suit and beige scarf. Deliberately she chose military colours, but at the same time made sure to be extremely chic.

Like all USO performers, each member of the company was officially given officer status, the idea being that if any were captured they might stand some chance of being treated like officers. Marlene was to be a major, Danny Thomas a captain, and the others lower ranks.

Early in April, along with a detachment of soldiers, they boarded an elderly army transport plane, a C-54, and set off from New York. Not until they were airborne were they allowed to open the sealed envelope that would tell them their destination. It turned out to be Morocco's chief port – Casablanca.

This was the first time in her life that Marlene had made a proper flight (in those days Hollywood studios like Paramount forbade their major stars from travelling by air – they were too valuable as properties), and it was a rough baptism. The unheated plane became bitterly cold when flying at altitude, and steaming mugs of coffee helped only a little. Then they flew into a fierce electrical storm, which raged round them for several hours.

Everyone aboard except Marlene became airsick, and she rose to the occasion, covering the ailing soldiers with blankets, and pouring slugs of whisky from a bottle she had smuggled aboard for herself and Danny Thomas (who promptly threw his up). Then she set about distracting everyone from their discomfort by relating intriguing stories about life in Berlin in the Twenties.

The storm passed, but the flight went on and on. What with a refuelling stop in Greenland and another in the Azores, it took them twenty-two hours to reach Casablanca. It was night when they arrived, and because of blackout regulations there were no runway lights, but somehow the pilot got them down. By this time Marlene, having managed only three hours' fitful sleep, had caught a chill.

On disembarking, they found out that, due to an administration blunder, the officers at the American base supposed to house them for the night had been given the wrong date for their arrival. As they had not been expected, there were no quarters available.

There was the usual running around and panicking, they were bundled into a hastily requisitioned Red Cross convoy truck, and eventually a building was found for them near some soldiers' barracks (normally USO performers were kept separate from GI's). It was optimistically described as a bungalow, but in fact was a damp, cold one-room hut, smelling strongly of decay.

Marlene shrugged, telling Danny Thomas she hadn't come expecting much comfort. She sought out the hut's primitive latrine, then returned to the room where they were all to sleep, tucked her hair inside her cap, and, still wearing her uniform, plus a regulation bomber jacket, climbed in under the blankets provided and settled down for the night. As a pillow she used a knapsack into which she had packed four sequinned evening dresses – her costumes for their shows, tailored for her by Irene. (These costumes were practical as well as glamorous – as they were mostly sequins, they would need no ironing.)

From Casablanca the company made its way along the northern coast of Morocco, and then Algeria, passing through such towns as Rabat and Tangier, travelling in open jeeps and giving two shows a day, on improvised stages, to such large troop concentrations as they found along the way. They reached Oran, and gave performances there, then travelled on to Algiers, arriving at the camp where they were to be billeted on 11 April. To Marlene's stunned delight, Jean Gabin was there to greet her, wearing the uniform of a Free French tank commander. As Danny Thomas recalled, they 'attached themselves to each other so amorously that the GI's cheered for at least five minutes while they clutched and kissed in full view of everyone.'

Their meeting had been a stroke of luck. Gabin had found out she was coming to Algiers only by accident, by running into an American army officer called John Lodge, who in his brief career as an actor had played Count Alexei in *The Scarlet Empress*. Not only that, Gabin was to be there for only a day-and-a-half more – if she had arrived two days later they would have missed each other.

That night the company were to give their performance in a major venue – the Algiers Opera House, which seated two thousand. It was a treat to be performing in such a place, but they soon heard that troops in Algiers were very hard to please. Previous performers there, such as Joséphine Baker, the famous French chanteuse Damia, and the opera singer Tino Rossi, had all been given a cold or even hostile reception.

The trouble was that Algiers was throbbing with Allied personnel, mostly from Britain, America and Canada, who were all on stand-by for the invasion of Italy, which lay away to the northeast across the Mediterranean. The invasion had originally been planned for January, but it had been delayed for months by strong German resistance, and as a result all the troops were hyped up and on edge.

This did not make them into easy audiences, and when Marlene and the company began their show at the Algiers Opera House, the atmosphere in the auditorium was tense and unwelcoming.

The tuxedoed Danny Thomas bounced onto the stage to open the show, and was greeted by two thousand voices demanding to know why he was not in uniform. 'Are you crazy?' he said. 'Don't you guys know there's a war on? A fellow could get *hurt*!'

That broke the ice. At once the house was, if not warm, at least interested. He went on, in a beautifully planned opening, 'Tonight Marlene Dietrich was to have been with us…'

This was news to his audience, who had no idea she was anywhere but in America, but as Danny went on to explain that the reason why she would not appear was that 'an American officer had pulled rank for her … *services*', disappointment began to dawn. There were boos and catcalls. Then, from somewhere in the stalls a voice called loudly, 'No, no! I'm here!' and Marlene her very self fought her way towards the stage, dressed in what appeared to be chic military uniform and carrying a small overnight case.

When she got on stage, she at once opened the case, and took out a pair of evening slippers and one of Irene's sequinned gowns. Apparently oblivious of the audience, she began to undress, changing out of her uniform and into the gown. As Danny Thomas recalled, 'The guys *screamed*.' Hastily he pulled her behind a screen, from which she appeared seconds later, wearing the sequinned gown and looking like 'every woman in the world they were hungry for rolled into one'. Jack Snyder played a brief piano intro, and she sailed into 'The Boys In The Backroom'.

From that stunning opening on, the show was a smash. The audience was so riotous in their enjoyment that Marlene's mind-reading act, dependent on subtle signals between Danny Thomas and herself, was a disaster. As she threaded her way through the audience, she was besieged with requests for her autograph, for a kiss, for a look at her famous legs, for a dance. The routine was ruined, but somehow nobody seemed to care.

It didn't even seem to hurt the atmosphere when three times the show was interrupted by the wail of air raid sirens. Each time Marlene was hauled off the stage, and pushed to the floor by Danny Thomas and Lin Mayberry, on which her comment later was, 'I was more afraid about my teeth than my legs.'

The British press baron, Lord Beaverbrook, who was then Churchill's wartime minister of supply, was in Algiers at the time on official business. As it happened, he was a devoted fan of Marlene's, alleged to own personal copies of all her films. Hearing she was in the city, he invited her to come to the house where he was staying, after her show. She went, accompanied by Jean Gabin, and they all later stood on the balcony together, watching distant flashes out over the sea and hearing the rattle of gunfire as Coastal Air Force Beaufighters engaged in a dogfight with German aircraft (it turned out they were successful, shooting down three Junkers 88s and one Dornier 217, for no Allied losses).

The excitement of it all, and the chance reunion with Jean Gabin, gave Marlene the feeling of a good omen for the rest of her tour.

This feeling of elation rapidly dissipated the next morning when she made a tour of a makeshift hospital, intending to cheer up the injured. This was the first time she had encountered the results of real warfare, and she was deeply moved by the sight of so many young men so grievously wounded, some with limbs missing and some blinded.

Determinedly, she visited every bedside, and in one ward, when those who could cheer would not stop cheering her, she sent someone to collect her saw from the jeep, and played them sentimental old favourites like 'Swanee River', 'Oh, Susanna' and 'My Darling Clementine'. A reporter named Louis Berg, who was there, remembered that there was hardly a dry eye in the place.

Later that day she bade a reluctant farewell to Jean Gabin, and soon afterwards the little company continued on its way.

Touring was not comfortable. Performing twice a day, and occasionally as many as four times, they travelled from place to place in open jeeps, often through rain and through sandstorms. There were shortages of such basic things as soap, and even water. Their food was mostly standard issue, out of tins, although at camps where they were to perform they got a change – frankfurters and sauerkraut. That was always what it was – frankfurters and sauerkraut. And always eaten out of doors. As Marlene recalled, 'Even when there was indoors, we ate outdoors, with rain on the food and cold grease running down. We didn't mind. It was food, and millions were perishing of starvation in Russia.'

Marlene's performances on the tour never varied much. They didn't need to. She sang her songs, and played her saw, and did her mind-reading act, and the troops lapped it up. Also in North Africa at the time was an old colleague of hers, Joshua Logan, who had been dialogue director on *The Garden Of Allah*. Now a successful stage producer in civilian life, he too was organizing touring shows for the troops, and he saw one of her shows when their paths happened to cross. He recalled:

Someone said, you must see the performance tonight at this opera house. It was packed with GIs in full equipment...their guns, their canteens, their everything. And there was a sound from the orchestra and Dietrich walked on the stage in what she calls her nude dress. It had spangles, but there was a sort of pink space in between the spangles that looked as though the spangles were sewn on a nude body. And she held her arms out and there was an animal sound from these men that lasted five or six minutes. They just roared and *ahr-r-r-r-r-ed*, and it was a thrilling thing to see, because they really cared, you know. And she was just wrapped up in it. She just stood there and it held her up.

Which was very perceptive of Joshua Logan, because the war was changing Marlene in an unexpected way that was quite separate from the effect of the war itself. Since she became a huge international star, she had never played to live audiences. Now she was, and the reception she was getting was something quite magnificent – vast torrents of admiration quite different in scale from the sort of applause she had received, even on her best days, in revue in Berlin. Different, too, from the applause a film star gets, when the performance has been shot weeks or even months before and in another place.

She was beginning to discover that she liked this feeling of audiences adoring her – audiences that she was now experienced enough to control and dominate. And eventually, after the war, this new discovery about performing would alter her whole career.

Although her performances on tour didn't alter much, they did, quite early in the tour, acquire one significant addition. She heard the song 'Lili Marlene', which with its wistful melody and lyric, speaking of a soldier's sense of loss, would have suited her even if it hadn't happened to contain her adopted name.

The lyric to the song had been written simply as a poem, way back in 1915, by a German soldier of the Great War. His name was Hans Liep, he was young and in love with two local girls, one named Lili and one named Marlene, and one night while on duty outside a barracks in Berlin, he composed the poem.

Years later, early in World War II, a German composer (and Nazi-sympathiser) called Norbert Schultze set it to music and gave it to his girlfriend – the Swedish singer Lale Anderson – who in 1941 made the first recording of it. It was played often on German radio, and the soldiers of the Third Reich took to it enthusiastically.

Then, after the disastrous German defeat at Stalingrad in January 1943, Minister for Propaganda Goebbels banned the song. He felt it was too melancholy to be good for military morale. But by that time it had been overheard by Allied troops, first of all by those fighting the desert war in North Africa. It became so popular in Britain that it was recorded by both of the top female pop singers of the day – Anne Shelton and Vera Lynn.

Once Marlene heard it, it became part of her repertoire for life. There was something about it that moved her deeply, with her sense of the waste of young lives in war, and one night, while still in North Africa, she was about to sing it on a broadcast for the Armed Forces Network when her feelings became too much for her, and she shouted into the microphone, in German, '*Jungs! Opfert euch night! Der Krieg ist doch Scheisse! Hitler ist ein Idiot!*' ('Boys! Don't sacrifice yourselves! The war is shit! Hitler is an idiot!'). Then she went into 'Lili Marlene', also in German, until an army announcer seized the microphone from her, reminding her that this was supposed to be an English-language broadcast, for American troops.

She had an enormous respect and affection for soldiers – of any country (after all, she was the daughter of one). As she toured, she continued to visit American army hospitals, often in tents close to the front line, and in a *Vogue* interview she recalled such visits, saying, 'I remember all the big things and all sorts of little things – how those angel-hearted wounded boys in the hospitals would say, "There are some Nazis over there. They're sick. Please go over and talk to them. You can speak German." And I'd go over to those blank-faced, very young Nazis. They'd look me over and ask, "Are you the real Marlene Dietrich?" All was forgotten, and I'd sing "Lili Marlene" to everyone in that hospital. There was no greater moment in my life.'

In late May the long-planned invasion of Italy began and, as it pushed forward, Marlene and her troupe were not far behind. They performed in Sardinia, in Corsica, in Naples. Sometimes they were not sufficiently far behind to find things entirely comfortable. About 80km (50 miles) north of Naples, at Cassino, a Nazi force was doggedly resisting.

Cassino was a historic town, set around a steep hill, on whose slopes were an ancient abbey, and a monastery believed to date back to the sixth century. British and Polish troops, backed up by Americans, had been besieging it for weeks. The Germans had been sheltering in the abbey, but the Americans brought up a huge mobile gun, a 240mm howitzer, which eventually levelled it (and most of the town). At this point the Germans took refuge in the monastery.

The Allies were still shelling that on the evening of 15 May when Marlene and company got lost nearby. While they were driving round unknown country roads, hunting for the division they were attached to at the time, their jeep broke down and they were forced to spend a cold night huddled in a grove, listening all the time to artillery fire that seemed dangerously close.

It was still dark when a truck drove up and those in it obviously spotted them. Men got out and approached the party, and to their relief they heard them speaking French. Hearing this, Marlene said, '*Je suis Marlene Dietrich*', to which she got the sarcastic reply (in French), 'If you are Marlene Dietrich, I am General Eisenhower.'

She produced a flashlight and lit up her famous features. She proved her identity, but received a shock herself on realizing that the speaker was the well-known French actor, Jean-Pierre Aumont, who had already appeared in a dozen films.

He was leading a group of Free French soldiers, who were also slightly lost, and now realised he was in an extremely ticklish situation. Reflecting on it later, he said: 'Being made prisoner wasn't a very agreeable prospect for me. But to be responsible for Marlene's capture! In the eyes of the Germans she was a renegade serving on behalf of the American army and against her own people... Under the veneer of her legendary image, however, I saw a strong and courageous woman. There were no tears, no panic.'

Fortunately, he quite soon managed to find the French camp he was looking for, and, although it took a few hours, eventually Marlene's Americans too.

But her situation continued to be perilous. On 23 May the Allies began to make a push to capture the beachhead of the coastal town of Anzio, and on 25 May it was taken by the American Fifth Army.

Marlene and her company were only a short while behind it, arriving the same day. That night, as the first Allied entertainers there, they performed on a beach still littered with shell-cases and other battle debris. Fighting in the area had not yet ceased, but Marlene had insisted that their show must go on. The area where they performed was surrounded by a protective ring of tanks, and as Marlene launched into 'I Can't Give You Anything But Love, Baby' she was lit by hundreds of soldiers aiming their flashlights at her.

The effect was eerie, shimmering, and spectacular, but her own thought, as she began her song, was more down-to-earth. 'Well,' she thought, 'if they don't like my act, all they have to do is turn off their flashlights.' They didn't, and later she said she felt as if she'd passed the toughest test of her career.

It was not long after this, on 6 June, while performing before another large audience of soldiers, that she was handed a piece of paper. It contained news that everybody had been waiting months to hear, and she at once read it aloud. Allied troops had at last invaded occupied France, landing in Normandy. It was D-Day, and Marlene wept on stage.

Rome was only 50km (30 miles) north of Anzio, but resistance there was fierce, and it was 4 June before the Allies gained a foothold in the city. But getting total control of it was another matter, and when Marlene and company arrived there a week later, there were still fierce street battles in progress. Fighting was going on at the Forum, and around Trajan's column, and the little troupe of performers took on the role of stretcher-bearers, ferrying dozens of injured into a large hall.

There Marlene sang and joked and generally held up morale until nightfall, afterwards joking, 'It gave me the opportunity of kissing more soldiers than any woman in the world. No woman can please one man; this way, you can please many men.' When the city was finally liberated, the scene, she wrote, was 'like an Easter parade...the boys threw cigarettes and chocolate.' Driven in her jeep through the city, she was almost buried in thrown flowers, and her military escort at the time, Lieutenant-Colonel Robert Armstrong, later described her as, 'an incredibly brave lady, just like one of the boys in her Eisenhower jacket, boots and helmet.'

By this time the planned ten weeks of the tour were over, and the company were due to be flown home to America. But Marlene herself would be delayed. She had never entirely recovered from the chill she had caught during the flight out. It had gradually developed into a persistent sore throat, she was exhausted, and while in Rome came down with a serious case of pneumonia.

This might easily have proved fatal, but army doctors ordered that she be taken at once to a hospital in the coastal town of Bari, down near the heel of Italy. There they had a small supply of penicillin, which had first come into use in 1941, but was restricted to the military until after the war. With the aid of it, Marlene quickly recovered, and went out of her way to find out as much as she could about this new miracle drug, which had saved the lives of so many servicemen. She learned that it had been discovered by the not-yet-knighted Alexander Fleming, and stored his name away in her mind.

She was flown back to New York at the end of June. It was another world. When she phoned to check in with her agent, Charles K Feldman, she discovered that he had been unable to arrange any film work for her. There had been some talk of her co-starring for Warner Brothers in a film version of the stage play *Dark Eyes*, which had three strong female roles in it. The plan was that she would co-star with Garbo and Fanny Brice as sophisticated continental 'artistes', but the studio finally decided instead to cast it with all-

American girls – some combination of Alexis Smith, Faye Emerson, Ann Sheridan and Jane Wyman. So that was out.

MGM did want her to appear at the première of *Kismet*, which would be at New York's Astor Theater on 22 August, but they had been unable to find a suitable story for the second film she was contracted to make for them.

This was not disastrous news. If MGM continued to fail to come up with a second film, she would still be able to keep the $50,000 they had paid her for it, for doing nothing. And she was by now more heavily involved emotionally in the war than ever. She began to describe it as *her* war. Having seen fighting, and the results of fighting, she became increasingly irritated that civilian Americans seemed to have no appreciation of the harsh reality of warfare. Her feeling that Americans were basically naïve grew stronger.

While in New York, although still somewhat weak from her illness, she attended a war-bond rally on Wall Street. A few days later she returned to Hollywood, and worked for a while at the Hollywood Canteen.

She duly returned to New York to appear at the première of *Kismet*, and a few days later was overjoyed to learn that, on 25 August, Paris had been liberated. Towards the end of that month she flew off to Europe on another USO tour. Her company was the same, except that her MC, Danny Thomas, had been replaced by comedian Freddie Lightner.

This time they were heading for newly liberated Paris, but not directly. They gave performances at various places along their route – in Labrador, Greenland and Iceland (giving two shows in each) – and once they arrived in England would stay there for a little while.

After her arrival in London in early September, Marlene ran into Douglas Fairbanks Jr, who had by then become an officer in the US navy. Their old quarrels forgotten, they again became friends (although not lovers).

By coincidence, their old residence, 20 Grosvenor Square, had been taken over by the US military as part of Allied Command. She made herself known there and became a regular visitor, taking delight in showing Commanding General Jacob Devers and his officers round her old apartment, showing them how to make best use of the cupboard space, and telling them the best way to furnish it.

This led to a change in her manner of touring. It gave her access to the top brass of SHAEF (Supreme Headquarters, Allied Expeditionary Forces), and the camps she visited in future would often be at the explicit request of high-ranking officers. This was better than hanging round the William

Morris Agency in Park Avenue waiting for an engagement, and USO would largely cease to be involved in her arrangements.

At 20 Grosvenor Square she met Colonel Barney Oldfield, who before the war had been a journalist and publicist (although he had also been an officer during the Great War). His job when she met him was managing military press and public relations during the European campaign, and for the next year he helped her arrange tours and generally kept an eye on her.

Recalling his impressions of her, he said, 'Dietrich was a very strong-minded lady. She could be glamorous and she could be earthy. I saw her gnaw on a German sausage like a hungry terrier, but of course she could make a grand entrance that would upstage a reigning queen. She could be as authoritarian as Caesar, and she could pout as prettily as a six-year-old whose lollipop was stolen after only one lick.'

While in London, she made several broadcasts over the radio station ABSIE (the American Broadcasting Station in England). These broadcasts were aimed directly at Germany, and the programmes she made were called, *Marlene Sings To Her Homeland*. She sang songs from her films and familiar old German melodies, dedicating them to the Allied soldiers who were 'about to meet up with you boys and destroy the Reich'.

Also while in London, she made records for broadcasting to Germany. She was approached by an organization known as MO (Morale Operations), which was set up by the American OSS (Office of Strategic Services), the forerunner of the CIA. Its job was the production and dissemination of propaganda, and among its operations was the Musac project, run jointly by MO London and by the British Political Warfare Executive.

The main production of the Musac project was a radio programme, *Soldatensender West*, which was broadcast from southern England every day, from 8pm to 8am, on a dozen medium-wave and short-wave frequencies, and beamed at Germany and German-occupied countries in Western Europe. It broadcast news and entertainment – the news provided by the British, the entertainment by the Americans.

Most of the entertainment consisted of songs – American popular songs by such famous songwriters as Cole Porter, Vincent Youmans, Vernon Duke, and Rodgers and Hammerstein, all given German words by OSS agent Lothar Metzl, who before emigrating to America had written songs for the Viennese theatre. The music was also specially arranged to appeal to the German ear by none other than Kurt Weill.

Many of the songs were recorded for broadcast by Weill's wife, Lotte Lenya, among a number of other singers, including Greta Keller, Jarmilla Novotna, and Greta Steuckgold of the New York Metropolitan Opera. And a few by Marlene's daughter, Maria.

When she was contacted by Lothar Metzl, Marlene agreed to participate, and it indicates the high regard in which she was held that only she, among all the singers, was told of the involvement in the project of the OSS. She made her recordings in London, and among the songs she sang were 'I'll Get By', 'My Heart Stood Still', 'I Couldn't Sleep A Wink Last Night' and, naturally, 'Lili Marlene'. All of these, like all the other songs in the project, were broadcast over *Soldatensender West* some eight times a day. But however much these songs, and her other broadcasts, may have helped the Allied cause, they earned her the undying hostility of many Germans.

While involved in broadcasting in London in 1944, she was disturbed to learn that the BBC's Dance Music Committee had a confidential list of seven European performers whose work was not to be played over the air – all seven were under some suspicion of being Nazi collaborators. The list was called 'Collaboration Artistes And Their Material', and the seven names were Charles Trenet, Mistinguett, Maurice Chevalier, Alfred Cortot, Lucienne Boyer, Sacha Guitry and Doctor Mengelberg.

The only name on the list that really meant anything to Marlene was Maurice Chevalier, and she was very upset by his inclusion, feeling that he could not possibly be a traitor. As she said, late in life, to her friend and biographer David Bret, 'Chevalier was a decent man. I mean, he might have done things out of stupidity, but never because he was a traitor.' Which is true. He was a performer, his whole living was performing and making himself likeable, and if his audiences in occupied Paris were mostly German soldiers, well then, they must be wooed like any audiences.

London had a version of the Hollywood Canteen, called the Stage Door Canteen, and one night Marlene put in an appearance. But that was about all it was – she simply appeared on the stage, said something like, 'Hello, boys. Glad to see you,' and was off again, leaving that particular audience feeling somewhat cheated.

One of the high-ranking officers she met in London was General George S Patton. Patton was an extraordinary man. Of wealthy family, his whole character was arrogant and aristocratic, in an almost eighteenth-century way, far removed from the democratic turn of mind that is generally felt to permeate American society. He was a disciplinarian, a showman, an aggressive and ruthless leader, and a maverick. He only obeyed orders when they suited him, and was disliked by almost every senior officer he ever served under and by those who served under him, who nicknamed him 'Old Blood And Guts'. Yet he took care of his men, and in fast-moving attacking battle was magnificent – bold, direct and with little finesse.

Almost as soon as Marlene met him, they became lovers. After all, she had known autocratic military men since her infancy, so he was a type she felt at home with, and, as he was sixteen years older than she was, she might even have felt something paternal about him. He had command of the US Third Army, and it was often his men that she would entertain once she got to mainland Europe.

She crossed to France (as did Patton) at around the beginning of October, and by the time she arrived in Paris had decided on a plan of campaign. Using her high-up connections in the armed forces, she would arrange tours as close to the front lines as possible, and between tours return to Paris for rest and recreation.

When she booked herself into the Ritz Hotel, she soon learned that Ernest Hemingway was living there, and met him in the hotel's rue Cambon bar, accompanied by his lady friend, *Time* correspondent, Mary Welsh. He was still married to the much-respected journalist Martha Gellhorn, but she was not in Paris at the time, and in any case their marriage was nearing its end.

Mary Welsh was short-haired and petite (Hemingway called her his 'pocket Venus'), but Marlene was not impressed by her, describing her as 'stiff, formal, and not very desirable'. Mary, for her part, was more detached, describing Marlene as being 'as sinuously beautiful in her khaki uniform and the knitted khaki helmet liner...as in the see-through sequin dresses.' She also noted that Marlene 'was a business woman concerned with every detail of her program from transport to accommodations, to sizes of stages and halls, to lighting and microphones. Business seemed to be her religion.'

Although in love with Mary Welsh, Hemingway retained (as he always would) a deep affection for Marlene. During her interludes in Paris he would proudly squire both women to official meetings and receptions, boasting of the help they gave him in his hotel suite, which was, he would proclaim, 'the Paris command post for all veterans of the 22nd Infantry Regiment'.

He had genuine connections with the 22nd Infantry. Having flown several missions with the RAF in his capacity as a war correspondent, he also crossed the Channel when D-Day came, among the invading US troops, attaching himself to what was known in full as the 22nd Regiment of the Fourth Infantry Division. With them he fought in Normandy, earning respect among them for his abilities at gathering intelligence and at guerrilla warfare. And with them he participated in the liberation of Paris.

Happy to be in Marlene's company, he told her of his exploits, and she in turn shared hers, sitting on the edge of his bath while he shaved and telling him items of war news she had gathered in London, and about her affair with General Patton, both there and now in Paris.

Not all was harmony between Hemingway and Mary Welsh. One night in his room they had a huge row, and Hemingway, who was drunk and annoyed, hit her. Whereupon she called him 'a poor, fat, feather-headed coward,' and walked out.

Hemingway asked Marlene to go and talk to her – to tell her he was deeply sorry, and he loved her, and ask if she would marry him. Marlene did, and when the three had dinner together that evening, Mary Welsh accepted the proposal. Eventually, after Hemingway's divorce from Martha Gellhorn, they would marry. 'I didn't render him any special good service,' Marlene remarked later.

Nonetheless, she continued to be helpful. As December 1944 approached, she decided to give the pair of them, as an early Christmas present, the double bed from her own room, in exchange for the twin beds in Mary's room. In high spirits, the two women made the swap, heaving mattresses and bedsteads through the corridors of the hotel, ignoring the protests of the staff. Hemingway was delighted with the gift, calling it 'useful as well as beautiful'.

Soon both he and Marlene would be off to various battle fronts, he to file reports, she to give shows. Mary would be left to sleep in the double bed alone, and she caught a bad case of scabies from it.

Most of Marlene's shows during the winter of 1944–45 were given for troops of the Third and Ninth Armies, at bases in whatever parts of eastern France, Belgium and Holland were liberated.

Frequently, when with the Third Army, she would travel and dine with Patton. Often he would summon her to whatever temporary office he had on some pretext, such as to receive a report on her shows, or to ask whether she would come with him on a hospital tour. On at least one occasion she fell asleep in his office. He picked her up, still asleep, carried her to his car, drove her to her barracks and put her into bed, and next morning, when she awoke, he was still there by her side.

For her part, she helped keep up his morale, just as she did for his men. He appreciated this, and on one occasion chose an official password in her honour. It was 'Cheesecake'.

For a while he based himself in the town of Nancy, in eastern France. Among the showmanlike additions to regulation uniform that he was famous for were a pair of pearl-handled wild-west-style six-shooters. It was while they were in Nancy that he gave Marlene, as a present, a smaller (but effective) replica of one. This, as they both knew, had a hidden message. It was for use on herself if she had the misfortune to be captured.

This was the time of what Winston Churchill tagged 'The Battle of the Bulge', and what has also been described as 'Hitler's Last Gamble', in which he tried to make a fast armoured attack from German lines to the port of Antwerp, cutting the Allied armies in two and seizing their main supply port.

It would be Patton's finest hour as, starting on 22 December, his Third Army raced from Nancy through the hills of the snow-covered Ardennes, fighting all the way, and liberated the Belgian town of Bastogne, thus linking up with General MacAuliffe's 101st Airborne Division, which had been besieged there. (It was General MacAuliffe, in Bastogne at this time, who, when called on by the Germans to surrender, famously replied simply 'Nuts!' – or some such word.) This advance of Patton's, in one of the worst winters on record, helped to fatally weaken the Nazi advance.

In the freezing winter, Marlene took to drinking Calvados, the apple brandy that her friend Remarque was so addicted to, to keep out the cold. Often the smells of petrol fumes and smoke, and of war in general, would make her throw it up again, in which case she would simply slug some more to keep herself going.

Frequently the only place she could find to lay her sleeping-bag was a corner of a frozen field, or maybe a ruin, infested by rats that would run over your face with their icy feet. Like any soldier, she washed her face and hair and underclothes in snow melted inside her helmet. And somewhat to her surprise, she caught crabs, which she'd thought could only be passed on from another person.

While Marlene was not in the spearhead of the Third Army advance, she and her company were not far behind. Indeed, she was with Patton in his jeep as he rode in triumph into Bastogne on 26 December.

In spite of Patton's triumph, this was was a low time for her. As she wrote years later: 'That Christmas of 1944 was a lousy one. I kept asking myself how Christian men could adopt their term "turn the other cheek", when we were at war. The Jews were more convincing, for the Old Testament said, "An eye for an eye, and a tooth for a tooth." Since that time I have renounced the existence of a God, or of any guiding light. Goethe said, "If God did make this world, then he should take another look at his formula."'

While in Bastogne, she was somewhat unnerved to learn from one of the Germans taken prisoner that a high-ranking German officer had put a price on her head. Ironically, his surname too was Dietrich – Sepp Dietrich. It was no real surprise to discover that there was a price on her head (it was war, and to Germans she was aiding and abetting the enemy) but it put even more of a chill into the already chilly air to have it formally confirmed.

Now it wasn't only the cold that was affecting her. She also found herself becoming afraid. She knew that the Allied front line she was part of was gradually advancing towards and into Germany, and although she desperately wanted her country to be liberated, and to be part of that liberation, she knew now that she was a wanted woman. 'I'm not afraid of dying,' she told senior officers at the time, 'but I am afraid of being taken prisoner.'

In January 1945 she and her company arrived at the town of Maastricht, in the south of Holland and close to the borders of both Belgium and Germany. Colonel Barney Oldfield, who was there at the time with a press corps, regarded her with admiration, saying, 'Like the rest of us that winter, she had to wear long, woolly, drop-seat underwear, heavy trousers and gloves. But she ignored the weather and changed into nylon stockings and a sequinned evening gown – and in this glamorous outfit she stuck the musical saw between her legs and played for her cheering audience.'

Thirty-two kilometres (twenty miles) from Maastricht, just over the German border, was Aachen, which, on 20 October 1944, had been the first major German city to be taken by the Allies. At the end of January, Marlene and company arrived there, and for the first time since well before the war she set foot on German soil.

The army asked her to act for them as an interpreter, to tell the (naturally rather nervous) inhabitants to clear the streets so that Allied tanks could pass through. To her surprise and relief the inhabitants received her warmly, giving her a perhaps misleading impression of the reception she might get from Germans in the future.

A less welcome surprise from Aachen was that she and all her company became infested with lice.

Going on a little further, to perform in the town of Stolberg, she ran into a reporter from the International News Service, Frank Conniff. Questioned by him about her future film plans, she said, 'I am through with Hollywood. It was a very difficult place to live in anyway.' This was a somewhat offhand remark, because her mind was considerably elsewhere. Looking at the ruins round them, she added, 'I hate to see all these ruined buildings, but I guess Germany deserves everything that's coming to her.'

During February she was ordered back to Paris – to the Ritz – to recover from mild frostbite and from an attack of influenza.

While she was still there, in March, a version of the Stage Door Canteen opened, on the Champs-Elysées. It kicked off with three special gala nights, and Marlene appeared at all three, as did her friends Noël Coward and Maurice Chevalier. Noël sang 'Mad Dogs And Englishmen' and 'Let's Not Be Beastly To The Germans', and Maurice sang 'Mimi'. Marlene, wearing an Eisenhower jacket over a silver lamé skirt, and thus mixing male and female, sang 'The Boys In The Backroom' and 'Lili Marlene', and somewhat surprised Noël Coward with her ability (by now well-practised) to hold an audience.

Hemingway also returned to the Ritz (and to Mary Welsh), and Marlene was saddened to learn that his son Jack had been reported wounded in action during the previous October, and taken prisoner by the Germans. To cheer herself (and Hemingway) up, she began to improvise on the grandiose funeral she was planning for herself.

Notre Dame would be the setting and the time late afternoon, so that flickering candles would embellish the scene. Rudi would be travel agent, major-domo, usher, maître d', and undertaker, welcoming friends, lovers and admirers. The guests would include Douglas Fairbanks Jr, in a full-dress naval uniform, carrying a wreath from the English monarch. Gary Cooper, James Stewart and John Wayne would be admitted in cowboy boots, while Jean Gabin would lean sulkily against the cathedral doors, wearing a trench coat, with a cigarette dangling from his mouth. Remarque, melancholy and vague, would be at the wrong church at the wrong time for the wrong funeral.

The list went on, as it would over the years, as Marlene built it into a sort of set piece to amuse friends, those to be present altering as people fell out of her favour or died, and as new friends and lovers appeared on her scene. 'There'll never be such a show,' Hemingway told her at this first recital. 'You're immortal, my Kraut.'

One night he invited an officer there for drinks, and introduced him to Marlene. The officer was General James M Gavin, and Marlene was immediately attracted to him (rather to the disappointment of Mary Welsh). And as so often with her lovers, from her first violin teacher on, he was not only attractive, but also potentially useful.

General Gavin, although extremely senior, was a lot younger than Patton. He was thirty-seven, looked ten years younger, and had become the youngest general in the history of the army, having lied about his age in order to enlist. Tall, slim and with a gentle, courtly manner, he was, as Colonel Oldfield recalled, 'a very glamorous figure'. He was also known to be very brave, having once fought for a month with a broken back, a feat that earned him both the Silver Cross and the Purple Heart.

He was now the commander of the 82nd Airborne Division, and this was of great interest to Marlene, because with her inside knowledge (gathered from Patton and Hemingway and others) she knew that the 82nd Airborne Division was to play a central role in 'Operation Eclipse' – the Allied plan to storm Berlin. It was entirely possible that General Gavin would be the first commanding officer to set foot in that city.

She had long been concerned about her mother, seizing every chance to question officers or newspaper correspondents who might have information. Was Josephine still alive, and if so, where was she? Marlene had not seen or heard from her, or from any of her Berlin family, since their meeting in Lausanne in 1938. Becoming friendly with Gavin would be a smart thing to do.

Her affair with him began the night she met him, in his suite at his hotel, and when, shortly afterwards, he returned to the 82nd Airborne Division, now in Germany, she went with him. She became the Division's mascot, and Gavin decreed, with the wholehearted approval of his men, that 'Lili Marlene' should become their unofficial anthem.

The whereabouts of her mother was only one of two questions that were increasingly preoccupying Marlene. The other was, where was Jean Gabin?

Early in May, she learned from senior American officers who had met senior French officers that his tank unit was then in Bavaria, and managed to make her way there.

'She charmed her way onto more planes than Bob Hope,' recalled Colonel Oldfield. 'With an entire troupe. She could commandeer a jeep and driver and all sorts of privileges, and these were accorded to her as if she were a queen in the eyes of those she dealt with.'

In Bavaria, she did more charming, and got permission to 'fraternise' with French troops. This led to the situation where General De Gaulle, conducting a review of the 2nd French Tank Division, in the town of Landsberg-am-Lech (a little way west of Munich), was somewhat taken aback to see a woman in American army uniform (and loafers) running alongside the lines of tanks and calling out, 'Jean! Jean!'

Gabin emerged from his tank, and greeted her with an affectionate, 'Damn it to hell, what are you doing here?'

'I want to kiss you,' she explained. Which she did.

A few days later, on 7 May, Germany surrendered and the war in Europe was over. Hitler was dead, and Goebbels was dead, both by their own hands.

A couple of days after that, on 9 May, an item of intelligence reached the US army headquarters in Munich. As the Allied armies had pushed eastwards, they had begun to come across, and liberate, the infamous concentration camps, which, with their deliberate extermination programmes, had turned out to be much more horrifying places than anyone outside Nazi Germany had ever imagined.

One of the first camps to be liberated (in mid-April, by British troops) was Bergen-Belsen, near Hannover. And in the camp, the intelligence reported, with her husband, was a woman who was claiming to be the sister of Marlene Dietrich.

Marlene was informed, and found the news both terrifying and mysterious. General Omar Bradley, overall commander of US land forces, and who of course had frequently encountered Marlene, ordered his own army plane to fly her at once from Munich to a small airfield called Fassberg. This was about 80km (50 miles) from Bergen-Belsen, and she was driven there in a jeep, through a countryside of ruins.

The assistant commandant of the liberated camp was, as it happened, another ex-Berlin Jewish exile. Now a Captain in the British army, his name had been Horwitz, but on adopting British nationality he had changed it to 'Horwell'. He was busy puzzling over paperwork to do with the repatriation of camp inmates, when he was interrupted by an orderly with the surprising news that General Omar Bradley's driver was asking to see him.

He was even more surprised when the driver turned out to be Marlene, who entered and saluted smartly. She explained that she believed her sister and her brother-in-law were in the camp, and wanted to know what she could do to help them.

This made Captain Horwell rather uneasy. He was well aware that, although they were inside the camp, Elisabeth and Georg Will had not exactly been prisoners. Georg had been a *Truppenbetreuungsoffizier* (Special Services Officer) for the German army. His Berlin cinemas had been closed down by Goebbels and he had taken the job of running the camp canteen and cinema for the Germans at Bergen-Belsen (as well as a small cinema in Fallingbostel, a nearby town, for the benefit of German troops). He and Elisabeth, and their son, had lived, and were still living, in a comfortable private flat within the camp, with their own furniture and a private store of food.

Horwell hadn't really taken to Georg Will, who, knowing the British definitely regarded him as one of the enemy, had gone to considerable lengths to let him know in no uncertain terms that he had an important American army 'connection', although without saying exactly who it was.

Marlene was stunned by all this. Georg and Elisabeth were fetched to Horwell's office. Elisabeth was not in the best of health, and looked it, but did her best to behave with Prussian correctness. When Horwell offered her a cigarette, she took it, but then refused a light. When Marlene asked her why, she explained that she didn't smoke, but it would be impolite to refuse a cigarette from an Englishman.

Marlene learned from her sister that their mother was still alive, although the apartment in the Kaiserallee that she had lived in since the Twenties had been destroyed by bombing. Elisabeth did, however, have an address in Berlin where she was last known to be, and this she gave to Marlene.

The British would soon take away Elisabeth and Georg's flat, and their stores of food, in spite of Georg's vociferous protests about 'unjust treatment', and in spite of Captain Horwell's pleas to his commanding officer on their behalf – pleas that he knew inside he was really making on behalf of Marlene. Like so many half-guilty Germans of the war years, they would eventually be freed to go their way.

After she left Bergen-Belsen, Marlene couldn't have cared less about them. She remained bitter about the Third Reich for the rest of her life, and on the odd occasions she mentioned Georg Will, she would refer to him as 'that Nazi'. Elisabeth she never ever mentioned at all – even on occasion denying that she had ever had a sister.

Although the war was over, USO continued to function for a few weeks more, and Marlene, still technically on duty in Bavaria, had pleasanter news of her family when she was asked if she knew one Hasso Conrad Felsing, as there was a German soldier of that name, who had been captured by the Russians and was currently in a prisoner-of-war camp in Salzburg. He was claiming to be her cousin. Marlene, pleased to hear Hasso had survived, confirmed that indeed he was.

She had no time to search Berlin for her mother. She passed the address Elisabeth had given her on to General Gavin, and continued touring, until suddenly she had to be flown back to New York for treatment for a badly infected jaw. Lin Mayberry travelled with her, as did a number of returning GI's.

When they landed at La Guardia, on a rainy 13 July, nobody was there to meet Marlene but Rudi, who had to stand helplessly by while customs confiscated the pearl-handled revolver that General Patton had given her.

He stayed with her while they took a taxi (with Lin Mayberry) to the St Regis Hotel, then left. Marlene, who had no cash, persuaded the hotel to pay for the taxi and put it on her bill. She then borrowed some spending money from the reception desk, and checked into a suite. There she held a small party for the GI's she had flown home with, allowing those who wanted to to use her en suite bath, and ordering food and drinks on room service.

When they eventually left, she phoned Charles K Feldman in Hollywood. He didn't mince words. No money had come in from previous work, and she had no immediate prospect of more. This was depressing enough, but worse was that she found Americans in general almost totally unaware of the real nature of war. America seemed a country wrapped up in itself, in which the only thing to be taken seriously was success in business, and where the attitude to anything not business was light-hearted, flip and offhand.

Marlene became desolate. 'I was utterly confused,' she said later. 'I had already accustomed myself to being a resident alien and then becoming an American citizen... I came back to America, a country that had not suffered in the war, a country that really didn't know what its soldiers had gone through over there on foreign soil. My hatred of "carefree" America dates from this time.'

She stayed in America only a short while, posing dutifully for the press as a returned heroine, and kissing returning servicemen for the cameras. She wrote replies to letters from women who told her that their sons or boyfriends had met her in Italy, and gave an interview, along with Lin Mayberry, to the army magazine *Yank*, saying that she had 'been so close to the army for so damn long that [she] didn't feel normal talking to civilians.'

By August, with her jaw healed, and technically still a member of USO, she was back in Paris. This time she checked into the Hotel Magellan, near the Trocadero, and soon was giving a version of her show at the Olympia Music Hall.

She didn't stay long at the Magellan. Jean Gabin had been demobbed, and was staying at the Ritz, and she moved in there with him. She also re-met Margo Lion, who had spent the war in Marseilles, in the far south of France, in a region never completely occupied by the Nazis.

She returned to Bavaria, and visited army camps east and south of Munich. There she learned that her cousin Hasso, who had been involved in the siege of Stalingrad, had been captured by the Russians and interned, but was now in Allied hands.

In September she was contacted at the Ritz by General Gavin, who had good news. Although 'Operation Eclipse' had eventually been abandoned, he, together with Colonel Barney Oldfield and another officer, Lieutenant-Colonel Albert McCleery, had been in the first American column to enter Berlin. The date had been 1 July.

On Gavin's orders, McLeery managed to track down Josephine. She was living in desperate poverty in the Berlin district of Friedenau, in a furnished room on the Fregestrasse. It was the address Marlene had been given by her sister.

Colonel McCleery called on Josephine, who was at first alarmed by his visit, and then confused by his news. She had believed that Marlene was dead – partly because Goebbels had announced that London had been totally destroyed by German bombs and rockets, and, when she had heard some of Marlene's broadcasts for ABSIE, she had assumed her daughter must have been killed.

Marlene got onto a military shuttle flight from Paris to Berlin – to Tempelhof airfield. At the same time Colonel Oldfield, accompanied by an interpreter and two photographers (he was a skilled publicist), arrived at Josephine's home and gently persuaded her to come with them to the airfield.

There mother and daughter met, the mother, now sixty-eight, grown frail and shrunken but still with a face full of strength of character. She wore a grey tweed suit, which was now hanging a little loose on her; Marlene wore female army uniform for a change – a battledress blouse and skirt. The two greeted each other with tearful affection.

Their reunion, while published all over the world, was hardly mentioned at all in the Berlin press, and US army intelligence began to register that Marlene was regarded as considerably unpopular – indeed, actively hated – by many Germans.

Not yet fully aware of this herself, Marlene seized the opportunity to spend a few days exploring the city she had loved. She moved into a corner of her mother's room, and General Gavin arranged for Josephine to be sent lavish extra rations. She arranged to give a few performances at the Titania-Palast, for members of the forces of occupation. She learned that the main premises of the firm of Conrad Felsing had been reduced to a ruin and that Aunt Jolly's American son, Rudolf, had also been in the siege of Stalingrad, and had been killed.

She sent a note backstage to Hubsie von Meyerinck, who had appeared with her so long ago in *It's In The Air*, and who was starring as Mack the Knife in a revival of *The Threepenny Opera*, which it was now possible to stage again after it had been banned by the Nazis in 1933. She gave him a list of people she used to know, whom she had heard were still in Berlin, and whom she wanted to invite to a reunion in her mother's room. They included Alexa von Porembsky, who used to be a showgirl with her in her early days, and Heinz Rühmann, who had acted with her in Bernard Shaw's *Misalliance*.

Hubsie invited them, and they all duly turned up at Josephine's room at the appointed hour, only to discover that Marlene would not be there. She had heard that Rudi's parents were alive in an internment camp in Czechoslovakia, and dashed off there to visit them. On her return to Berlin, she arranged a meeting with the formidable Marshal Zhukov, commander-in-chief of Russian forces of occupation in Berlin. It turned out to be a long meeting, but by the end of it Zhukov had agreed to have the Siebers relocated to Berlin, where they would be housed and allotted ration-cards in a manner appropriate for the in-laws of an international star.

Another meeting with her old Berlin associates was arranged. Again they came, and this time Marlene was there. She bombarded them with questions about other old acquaintances, and what they thought about their behaviour under the Nazis. Many reputations came under scrutiny, and she heard that many friends had sadly been killed or had simply disappeared.

She handed round American cigarettes, and proffered advice. She urged Rühmann to latch onto the new Broadway stage success, *Harvey* (which he would do, and have a considerable Berlin success in it). Carried away by memories of the old days, she suggested they all get together and revive *It's In The Air*. Why, she could probably even prevail on Margo Lion to come back from Paris, so that the pair of them could again join Hubsie in singing 'Kleptomaniacs'.

The room fell silent. Suddenly she began to realise that even to these people she was now an outsider, sitting there in her American army uniform – a conqueror of their country who had once been a member of it.

On her return to Paris, she was sent by USO on a new sort of assignment – to go to the famous coastal resort of Biarritz, down in the southwest corner of France, and there to lecture on the films she had made.

She was still there when she received a telegram telling her that on 6 November her mother had died – peacefully in her sleep, of heart failure. In distress, she at once telephoned General Gavin, who was at the time in London attending an important press conference.

As there were strict regulations limiting fraternization between Americans and Germans, and as he was so senior, he undertook to organise the funeral himself, and set off at once to Berlin with Colonel Oldfield. The trip was not without incident. Their plane flew into a severe storm and was diverted from Tempelhof airfield to Schweinfurt, hundreds of kilometres south of Berlin. There, General Gavin learned of an organizational emergency involving his 82nd Airborne Division, and was obliged to involve himself in a morass of phone calls, interviews and inter-departmental memoranda.

Colonel Oldfield had to carry on to Berlin alone. 'Do everything you can for her,' were General Gavin's last instructions.

At Friedenau, Oldfield arranged a burial plot and a coffin was hastily constructed by GI's out of old German school desks. Eventually Marlene arrived from Biarritz, and at night her mother was buried. The church adjoining the burial ground had been bombed out, so the short funeral service had to be held in the churchyard, where it rained.

Marlene wept bitterly. It was the end of an era. She had lost, she said later, 'the last bond that tied me to my homeland.'

11 Après La Guerre

After the war, Marlene, like many who had served in it, found peacetime difficult. It was impossible to explain to anybody who hadn't been near the action how terrible the reality of battle was. Civilians, no matter how sympathetic, seemed foolish and remote, and Americans in particular she found annoying. In statements to the press she insisted that her USO tours had taught her so much about 'real life', about courage and commitment, about life and death, about basic values, that she could never return to Hollywood and the false glamour of film-making.

So although, in November 1945, USO flew her back to America, she had no real intention of staying there. She crossed the country to Los Angeles, but, instead of renting a house, lodged for a while with Orson Welles and his wife, Rita Hayworth, who then lived on Carmelina Drive, in Brentwood. (Her daughter Maria, following in her mother's footsteps, was by then herself overseas touring for USO.)

She stayed for several weeks, helping around the house and badgering Welles to arrange for her an introduction to Garbo. There were a number of possible reasons why she did this. She may have wanted to see how Garbo (four years younger than herself) now looked, after several years away from the cameras. She may have been curious to meet the woman who had been the lover of Mercedes de Acosta (and John Gilbert) before she was.

Welles claimed he thought she still adored Garbo – an adoration undiminished over all the years since Marlene had first seen her in silent films in Berlin. Whatever the reason, a small party was arranged at the home of the actor Clifton Webb. Welles escorted Marlene there, and introduced her to Garbo.

Marlene immediately went into full fan mode. She gushed, saying she was thrilled to meet her heroine, and telling Garbo she was divine, a goddess, an immortal muse, an inspiration. The shy and reclusive Garbo became acutely embarrassed. She smiled with tight politeness, and muttered something dismissive about Marlene being too kind, but Marlene pressed on, rising to heights of adulation interspersed with the recipient's muttered thanks, until at last, mercifully, she ran out of steam.

After the party she remarked to Welles that it was all nonsense that people believed Garbo wore no make-up, saying, 'She has beaded eyelashes! Do you know how long it takes to have your eyelashes beaded?' She also observed that 'Her feet aren't as big as they say.' The two would never meet again.

In some ways the feeling of war lingered on. On 21 December 1945, Marlene's old comrade General Patton died, after his neck had been broken twelve days earlier in a jeep collision in the German town of Mannheim.

By Christmas 1945 she was back in Paris with Jean Gabin, whom she not only loved but who she felt understood what the real things in life were. He too felt out of place. He was entering what he would later call his 'grey period', and very much needed Marlene's mothering. What he liked best of all, she recalled, was 'to curl up in his mother's lap and be loved, cradled and pampered'. Which was pleasant for both of them, but they also knew they needed to find work.

Old friends Max Colpet and Margo Lion were in Paris as well, and were asked by Marlene to try and find suitable projects. She insisted Gabin go out with her to plays and films and smart cafés, so as to keep in touch with people who were making things happen. They were often accompanied by old friends of hers like Noël Coward, and they made new friends like the poet and film-maker Jean Cocteau, and his star Jean Marais. Cocteau thought that Marlene was 'the most exciting and terrifying woman I have ever known' (he would in time ask her to portray the poet's muse, Death, in his 1950 film, *Orphée*, but Marlene, not a poet herself, found the idea morbid).

They met the film director Marcel Carné and his frequent collaborator, writer Jacques Prévert. During the war they had made the famous film *Les Enfants Du Paradis* (an attempt to make a large expensive movie that would give no offence to the occupying Germans but provide work for as many actors and film technicians as possible, for as long as possible). Before the war they had made two films that starred Gabin – *Quai Des Brumes* and *Le Jour Se Lève* – and when Gabin and Marlene attended a performance of the Roland Petit ballet, *Le Rendez-vous*, all four decided that it could easily be made into a Gabin-Dietrich film.

Prévert got to work on a script, and press releases about 'Marlène Et Jean' fuelled public expectation. The score for the ballet was written by Joseph Kosma, and Prévert wrote a lyric to a melody from it, calling it 'Les Feuilles Mortes'. This translates rather leadenly into English as 'Dead Leaves', but the haunting melody was well suited to Marlene's voice, and Gabin liked it so much when it was played to him in a Paris bar that he asked to hear it over and over again.

That was all well and good, but there were problems with the script – or rather, Marlene had problems with the script. The story was set in occupied France, then still an extremely touchy subject in France, and it had elements in it of both collaboration and racketeering. But what bothered Marlene was that she was to play a simple housewife trying to cope as best as she could with the wartime situation, and this made her unhappy. As Carné recalled, 'She was, shall we say, less than enthusiastic, and began to make a thousand suggestions – each one of which seemed, to Jacques and me, utterly absurd. One example: she wanted to play a night scene completely out of character, descending from a cab and paying the driver by taking the money from the top of her stocking!'

The film was to be made by Pathé, and Marlene's contract with them stipulated that she was to have script approval. Which she exercised to the full. While discussing points in the script with Prévert, Gabin would continually ask, 'What will La Grande say?', 'What will La Grande think?', until eventually Prévert said angrily that the next time he heard anything about La Grande's wishes he'd throw up.

Eventually it became clear to all concerned that Marlene was never going to make Les Portes De La Nuit. Gabin definitely didn't want to make it without her, but he was in something of a hole – his contract with Pathé did not give him script approval and, furthermore, he had been paid his salary in advance. But fortunately for him, the wording of his contract did give him approval of the schedule, and if he could prove he had other work commitments he could remain unavailable until Pathé got tired of waiting for him. So he found another project to be involved in, hanging onto the salary he had been advanced, and Pathé sued him (having no grounds for suing Marlene).

Les Portes De La Nuit did get made, starring Edith Piaf's young lover, Yves Montand, and it turned out boring (around Paris it was known as 'Les Portes D'Ennui'/'The Gates Of Boredom'). Only one good thing came out of it – the song written for Marlene, 'Les Feuilles Mortes', given the English title 'Autumn Leaves', became an international hit.

The other project that Gabin involved himself in was one he had had on his mind for some time. It was a novel called *Martin Roumagnac*, by Pierre-René Wolf, and he had owned the rights to it for about ten years. His judgement was not good. It was a rather stilted piece about a *crime passionel* in the French provinces, and nobody he had offered it to, including Carné and Prévert back in 1937, had been the slightest bit interested. But Gabin persisted. Now he talked the competent but uninspired Georges Lacombe into directing it, and Marlene agreed she would be in it.

Although she would get top billing in the film, her role would in fact be smaller than Gabin's – or rather, shorter, because two-thirds of the way through it he kills her. She plays Blanche Ferrand, a Parisian woman who has come to live in a provincial town where she makes a living selling birds and (it is whispered) by entertaining gentlemen callers in her room upstairs. Which she does. The townspeople shun her, except for a shy local schoolmaster (Daniel Gélin), who loves her from afar and realises that what the townspeople do not understand is that she is simply a true believer in freedom.

The local bridge-builder, Martin Roumagnac (Jean Gabin), falls for her, and she, liking his noble simplicity, falls for him. She takes him on a trip to Paris, where he becomes gloomily aware he is a fish out of water, not knowing how to order a meal in a restaurant, or which fork to use, or how to dance. Back in his home town, things go from bad to worse as he becomes increasingly aware of the wagging tongues talking about her 'room upstairs'. What he has not realised is that her trip to Paris has made her disillusioned with her life of mindless gratification, and it is unfortunate that it is just as she is burning souvenirs of her past in her grate that he enters and knocks her senseless. After he leaves, the house burns down with her inside.

He has a spiteful elder sister (Margo Lion) who never liked Blanche, and who gives him an alibi. At his trial, the feeling is that it is Blanche who is on trial for her loose and unconventional ways, and he is acquitted. The town holds a fête in celebration, and during it he is shot dead by the schoolmaster, and dies nobly in expiation of his sin.

The film, as completed, is not as bad as it might sound, but it is very much a potboiler. When released in America it was dismissed as containing little of interest but shots of Marlene's legs, but it does have some well-observed vignettes of provincial life, and many of her scenes with Gabin do give some feel of the real-life electricity that sparked between them.

Not that their affair was running completely smoothly. Early in 1946 General Gavin had returned to Paris and Marlene had also resumed her affair with him. In January they were flown to New York by the army to attend a Victory March, and were clearly so close that gossip-writer Walter Winchell stated in his column that Marlene and 'a certain very young general' would shortly marry. Gavin had been made aware of this item by Colonel Oldfield and chose coolly to ignore it, but such whisperings did not help his marriage. Within two years, his wife, who had known of the affair for some time, would sue him for divorce, saying to friends, 'I could compete with ordinary women, but when the competition is Marlene Dietrich, what's the use?' (She had wanted to cite Marlene formally as co-respondent, but Marlene's lawyers succeeded in getting her name dropped from the suit; her affair with him had petered out at around the end of 1947.)

Jean Gabin was no happier about the affair. When he and Marlene had dinner with Noël Coward one evening in March 1946, Coward reported that they argued continuously throughout the meal. Marlene insisted she must have her independence. Gabin said that in that case he'd begin an affair with an actress he'd recently met. Marlene at once became furiously jealous, insisting that the prerogative of having many lovers was the privilege of great actresses, like Sarah Bernhardt.

Max Colpet, who witnessed their increasingly turbulent relationship, felt that 'she had protracted her affair with General Gavin so as to demonstrate her independence from Gabin, who was very possessive.' In his rage, he took to knocking her about. If she dressed smartly, he took it she was dressing for some lover. If she dressed down, it was to allay his suspicions. If she said nothing about someone he feared she fancied, she was hiding her feelings from him. If she admired someone openly, she was using some subtle trick.

Among those she met and admired at this time were the stunningly handsome but vulnerable-looking actor, Gérard Philipe (who did not become her lover, although she filled his dressing-room with admiring flowers), and the singer Edith Piaf (who did, although their friends took care that Gabin never knew).

When his forty-second birthday was coming up, in May 1946, Marlene asked him what he would like for a present. He asked for the three paintings he had left in her care when he sailed from America. With wide-eyed innocence she claimed she thought that he had given them her as a gift. Hastily he agreed, yes, yes, he had. But couldn't they perhaps come to Paris so he could hang them on his apartment wall and look at them?

Marlene sent a telegram to America, and soon the pictures arrived. Gabin was moved to tears to have them on his wall again.

Still contemptuous of America, both for the films it made and for its mindless self-absorption, Marlene still hoped to build her future film career in Europe. But no new projects presented themselves and her money was running low, so when she received an offer from director Mitchell Leisen, who had directed her in *The Lady Is Willing* in 1942, she accepted. She would go to Hollywood to star in his film *Golden Earrings*.

Gabin was unhappy about this. He wanted her to divorce Rudi and marry him, and had been pressing her to do so for months. This was rather a mistake on his part because, as she told Robert F Kennedy during a dinner conversation in 1963, when discussing Gabin's wish to marry her, 'I hate marriage. It is an immoral institution. I told him that if I stayed with him it was because I loved him, and that is all that mattered.' (She was doubly shocked at around the same time when von Sternberg remarried – once because she despised marriage, and again because she felt it as a betrayal of their close friendship.)

Her decision to go and film in America caused Gabin to at last see the light. Romantic hope died, and he finally saw clearly that she would never marry him. If he was to satisfy his desperate desire to have a wife and family, he would have to find somebody else.

After reaching this conclusion, he shut her resolutely out of his life, not even coming to see her off when she left. His resolution was made easier to keep by his knowledge that when she packed up her things for the trip Marlene had made sure to include the Sisley, the Renoir and the Vlaminck. It would, however, take her quite some while to understand that not only was their love-affair over, but also Gabin had no intention of joining her crew of ex-lovers who were now dear friends. Within a year she would feel shocked and betrayed when he married French actress Maria Mauban.

Mitchell Leisen met her off the plane in Los Angeles. He had had to work hard to convince Paramount that she was the right female star for *Golden Earrings*. After all, she had been away from Hollywood for over three years, which in the film world was a lifetime. But with the help of Charles K Feldman, who happened to be both his agent and Marlene's, he had at last won his case. She was to play his gypsy heroine, Lydia, and her co-star was to be Ray Milland, who had recently won the Best Actor Oscar for his role as an alcoholic writer in Billy Wilder's *Lost Weekend*.

The film, set before and during World War II, is told in flashback by Major-General Ralph Denistoun (Ray Milland), explaining to war correspondent Quentin Reynolds (played by himself), how he came to have pierced ears. It seems that before the war, working for British intelligence in Germany, he was trying to make contact with a certain Professor Krosigk, a good German who had invented a new poison gas and wanted the Allies to have the formula (Krosigk was played by Reinhold Schünzel, who twenty years before had appeared with Marlene in *The Bogus Baron*).

Denistoun had been captured by the Gestapo, but managed to escape, wearing a stolen Gestapo uniform, and soon found himself in the Black Forest, where he met a beautiful Hungarian gypsy (Marlene), stewing a pan of fish. When she learned of his situation, she disguised him as a gypsy, staining his face with walnut juice and piercing his ears for golden earrings. After becoming accepted by the rest of her gypsy band (and becoming her lover), he set off with her to find the Professor's house. When they found it (after he wiped out several Nazis), they discovered that several other Nazis were there, attending a cocktail party. They managed to get into the party as fortune-tellers, and eventually, with some difficulty he succeeded in making the Professor understand that he was not really a gypsy, but the Allied contact he was expecting. The Professor paid them for their fortune-telling act with a five-mark note on which he had written the secret formula, Lydia guided him through rugged countryside to the border, and he successfully got it back to London, although heartbroken at having to leave her.

Now, he explains to Quentin Reynolds, she has managed to find the name of his London club, and has sent him a package containing his golden earrings, as a signal for him to come and find her now the war is over. He finds his way back to the place where they parted. She is there, they are reunited, and they ride off together in her gypsy caravan.

Although this was nothing more than a romp, it turned out to be a high-spirited romp, mixing suspense, comedy and romance. Marlene especially was in fine form, with her face darkened (she designed her own make-up), wearing a wig of black ringlets, the same gypsy costume and headscarf throughout the film, and barefoot – she insisted on being barefoot for authenticity, having, with her usual professional thoroughness, gone out of her way to visit real gypsy encampments before leaving France. Her performance was lively, witty and sensuous. She was more energetic than she had been since *Destry Rides Again*, and she looked beautiful.

Unfortunately the shooting of the film, which took place from August to October 1946, was not without its troubles. A union dispute caused the studio to be picketed, with the result that many members of the cast and crew, including Marlene, Ray Milland and Mitchell Leisen, had to live permanently in the studio for some time to avoid crossing picket-lines.

Worse was that Marlene and Ray Milland took a strong dislike to each other. This dislike originally came from him. It was rumoured around the studios that when he had learned she was to be his co-star, he had threatened to walk off the picture rather than play love scenes with such an 'old bag' (she was four years older than he was). It was also possible he was afraid that she would walk off with the picture (which to a large extent she did). His confidence was not great. He had been acting leading roles successfully in Hollywood since 1931, but it was only in 1945, with *Lost Weekend* that he had achieved a major triumph.

Whatever the reason for his dislike of Marlene, she swiftly reciprocated it. As Mitchell Leisen famously recalled: 'When we were shooting the scene where he first meets her as she's stirring the stew, Marlene stuck a fishhead into her mouth, sucked the eye out, and then pulled out the rest of the head. Then, after I yelled cut, she stuck her finger down her throat to make herself throw up. The whole performance made Ray violently ill.'

None of their animosity shows on the screen, however (nor does the scene with the fishhead, which must have been lost in the editing). The film was quite liked by the critics and popular enough with audiences to make Paramount three million dollars at the box office over the first two years of its release – a popularity aided to a considerable extent by the fact that it was condemned by the Legion of Decency, who disliked the almost non-existent suggestion of unmarried lovemaking.

After filming finished, in mid-October, Marlene went for a holiday in New York, staying there through Christmas and the New Year (and her forty-fifth birthday). It was very much a family time. She saw a lot of Rudi (and Tamara), and of Maria, who at the time was teaching acting at Fordham.

Maria also had her birthday in December, becoming twenty-two, and she had a new man in her life. He was a scenic designer called William Riva, and she was so much in love with him that she had seriously set about losing weight to make herself as attractive to him as possible. It had worked, and when he asked her to marry him she broke away from her mother's philosophy of life by at last agreeing to give her first husband, Dean Goodman, a divorce. She and William Riva were planning to marry on the following 4 July – Independence Day.

On 4 January Marlene set off back to Paris to attend the première of *Martin Roumagnac*. She sailed on the *Queen Elizabeth*, and with her went Rudi (leaving Tamara behind). Rudi, at fifty, still had ambitions to become a film producer, and he had the idea of making a film about Europe before the war, using German actors who had lived through the Nazi years, whether in Germany or in exile, and starring Marlene.

This announced idea may simply have been a pretext to help him get a visa to enter Berlin and see his family, but if that was his real plan, it failed. His request for a visa, referred from the US embassy in Paris to the War Department in Washington, was refused. It was gradually dawning on the world that post-war Europe was very different from the pre-war one. Hard boundaries were being drawn between the capitalist world of the west and the communist world of the east. Germany was now divided in two, and Berlin, itself divided internally, was behind the Iron Curtain.

In spite of having appeared in *Golden Earrings*, and as yet unaware of the popular success it would be, Marlene still believed that her film career would now lie in Europe. During a press conference when the *Queen Elizabeth* docked, she seized the moment to belittle the American industry, describing *Golden Earrings* as silly, escapist fantasy. 'You must bear in mind,' she said, 'the American film public is seventy-five percent children, and you have to meet their standards.'

Martin Roumagnac can have done little to boost her confidence in a European film career. After the première, it was panned by the critics. 'Oh lord, oh lord, take it away!' one of them wrote, and that remark was typical. Marlene later commented that maybe three people saw it, and all three hated it. Jean Gabin was rumoured to have tried to have all copies of it destroyed, but that may have been less because he thought it a poor film than from a desire to destroy anything that reminded him of his liaison with Marlene.

Marlene, for her part, was surprised and distressed that on her return to Paris Gabin cold-shouldered her. He was present at the première, of course, which she attended with Rudi, but he was only as polite as was necessary. For years she would hope desperately to become close to him again, but to no avail. And people noticed. Rumour said that when she heard of his impending marriage she rushed to Paris to dissuade him, but he refused to see her. It was said that when he bought a burial plot in Normandy, she bought one alongside. On learning of this, he sold his. It was said that the apartment she eventually bought on the Avenue Montaigne, the one where she spent her last years, was chosen because it was near to his. But it was all too late. When a reporter asked Gabin, in 1949, whatever had happened to a once-projected sequel to *Martin Roumagnac*, to be called *Première Mondiale*, he simply said, 'The old woman is too unstable.' Nobody was better than Jean Gabin at being laconic.

Momentarily at a loose end, Marlene did find interest and excitement in the Paris of 1947. There was Dior's New Look, for instance, which she adored at first sight. She adopted it enthusiastically, and its feminine, small-waisted style with its full skirts suited her. There was also a new style of film-making, originating from Italy, and called neo-realism. This was an attempt to use a detached, documentary style of film-making, often using non-professional actors, to depict the disrupted society of post-war Europe through small human incidents, using them to reflect and illuminate the society around them. Marlene had seen one of the earliest of these films, Roberto Rossellini's *Roma, Città Aperta (Rome, Open City)*, and became an enthusiastic convert to the style.

Shortly after she had seen the film, Rossellini brought Anna Magnani to Paris to perform Jean Cocteau's one-woman play *La Voix Humaine*, and Marlene insisted on taking as many of her friends as she could to pay him homage, among them Edith Piaf, Jean Marais and Max Colpet.

Rome, Open City had been the first film in a planned trilogy. The second had been *Paisàn*, and Rossellini was now preparing the third, to be called *Germania, Anno Zero (Germany, Year Zero)*. For this he needed a German writer, and Marlene suggested Max Colpet. Rossellini hired him, and as Colpet worked on the script Marlene, having nothing else to do, became his typist, pecking away with two fingers on a portable machine, with results that were usable without being anywhere near immaculate.

There came a time when Rossellini wanted Colpet to come to Berlin, but Colpet refused. His family had died in German concentration camps, and he had sworn he would never set foot in Germany again. Marlene urged him to go, saying she would go with him, and eventually he capitulated and they went.

She had another reason for wanting to go to Berlin besides helping Rossellini's film and Colpet's career: she knew Billy Wilder was at present filming in Berlin. Although she and Billy had never known each other in Twenties Berlin, they had often met since, first in Paris in the Thirties, and later in Hollywood, and had become good friends. In fact, while she had been filming *Golden Earrings*, he had frequently dropped in to watch from the neighbouring set where he was directing Bing Crosby in a successful and underrated film, *The Emperor Concerto*.

That had been an amiable semi-musical fantasy, set in pre-Great-War Austria. The film he was working on, originally called *Operation Candybar*, but now with its final title, *A Foreign Affair*, was considerably different. While also humorous in tone, its humour would have a bitter edge, and its depiction of life in ruined and poverty-stricken Berlin during the post-war American occupation would even have a slight neo-realist quality, at least when compared to other films of Billy Wilder, whose natural style was artificial and stylised.

To Wilder it would be a hard film to make – while Marlene had loved Berlin as the city of her childhood and youth, Wilder, a Viennese, had loved it as an incomer, which in some ways can bite deeper. It was where, in the Twenties, he had found his own voice, his true road, his first true friends. To film it as it was in 1946, devastated by a combination of the Nazi regime and Allied bombing, was heartbreaking. Hence the bitterness of his humour.

The film was not fully in production yet – Billy was in Berlin with a camera crew and a few key actors to pick up shots of the ruined shell of the city, impossible to recreate in a studio with anything like the intensity of the real thing. The bulk of the filming, mainly the interiors, would be shot back at Paramount at the end of the year.

There was a role yet to be cast – a Berlin night-club singer who has been there all through the war, and is obviously not averse to having high-ranking Nazis as lovers, but who, being totally apolitical, is now quite capable of enthralling occupying American officers. This was a role that Marlene was almost born to play, but when Wilder suggested it she at first hesitated, unsure about portraying a woman who, while not exactly a Nazi-sympathiser, was sympathetic to some influential Nazis.

The songs the singer was to sing had already been written, by Frederick Hollander. He hadn't originally written them for *A Foreign Affair*, but for his Tingeltangel Club, a night-club he'd attempted to establish in Hollywood, recreating the disenchanted Berlin cabaret atmosphere of the Twenties. When that failed, Paramount had bought them for the film. Wilder had already screen tested the actress June Havoc performing them, and he showed this test to Marlene.

June Havoc was the sister of Gypsy Rose Lee, and as a child had been the original of the character 'Baby June' in *Gypsy*. Although Hollander's songs were excellent, they were not even remotely in her style, and when she saw the test Marlene realised that no American could possibly perform them adequately. She must take the role herself.

Studio filming was not to begin until the end of the year, so she had plenty of time to make her way back to Hollywood, and she and Rudi did not leave Paris until the end of October. By this time Maria had duly married William Riva. That was in July, and in August *Golden Earrings* had had its première and was on its way to becoming a box-office success, which was reassuring to Paramount, who were about to hire her again.

En route to Paramount, Marlene stopped off in New York to visit Maria and her new husband, who were now living in a tiny cold-water apartment at 1118 Third Avenue. Although she had already sent them a refrigerator as a wedding present, she was still uncertain about the possibility of Maria being happily married. But on seeing her and William Riva in their new home, she felt that both seemed both happy and settled, and gave the marriage her blessing by scrubbing and waxing the apartment from top to bottom.

Before leaving New York she also had a function to attend. On 18 November she was to go to West Point, the top military academy in America, to be formally awarded the country's highest civilian honour, the Medal of Freedom. It was given for valour, and she would be the first woman ever to receive it.

For the ceremony she wore a chic black Dior suit, onto which (after reading her citation) Major-General Maxwell D Taylor pinned her medal. She was so proud of it that, after she had been in Hollywood only a little time, various old friends, such as Ernst Lubitsch, refused to attend parties if she was going to wear it again.

Unfortunately for Lubitsch, that was a threat he never got a chance to carry out. On Sunday 30 November, while showering after making love, he dropped dead of a heart attack. The blonde he had just made love to was paid her fifty dollars by his chauffeur, Otto.

Lubitsch's death cast something of a pall over the set of *A Foreign Affair* when filming started a few days later. Lubitsch had been a hero to Billy Wilder, who had co-written the script for his film *Ninotchka*, and had much admired his craftsmanship, especially the subtle way he used props as an economical way to illuminate changes in character and carry forward the story. They also shared an amused and cynical attitude to human weakness. In both their cases this had underneath it a strong layer of sentimentality, but in the middle of the twentieth century there was so little cynicism in American films that even a touch of it was instantly noticeable and, to many, shocking.

In *A Foreign Affair*, a team of congressmen is sent on a five-day visit to Berlin to investigate the effect that European decadence might be having on the morals of decent American servicemen. Among them is a congresswoman, Phoebe Frost, played by the film's top-billed star, Jean Arthur. She is a young, strait-laced woman with a no-nonsense attitude. As a favour, she has brought with her a chocolate cake sent to a certain Captain John Pringle (played by John Lund) from his childhood sweetheart back home in Iowa.

John Pringle, although likeable and handsome, is something of a cad, and already sufficiently involved in the seamier side of Berlin to have dealings with the black market. He soon swaps the chocolate cake for a mattress, which he takes as a present to his mistress, Erika von Schlütow (Marlene), who is living in an upstairs room in a half-bombed ruin of a house and scraping a living by singing in a dive called the Lorelei Club.

As the script develops, Phoebe falls in love with Captain Pringle, gradually becoming more relaxed and girlish. In the course of his work for army intelligence, he has to investigate Erika's past to discover whether she must he sent to a de-nazification camp. It turns out she must be as she not only hobnobbed with the highest in the Nazi party, but was the mistress of one of its senior officers, who is forced out of hiding by his jealousy and is killed attempting to shoot up the Lorelei Club. Erika goes off to her camp, undaunted and vamping the military police escorting her away, and Congresswoman Phoebe advances on Captain Pringle in such a way that it is clear he will have no option but to give up being a rolling stone and end up with her back in Iowa.

Although she got only second billing, the film turned out to be triumphantly Marlene's. Jean Arthur is good, making her transition from strait-laced to lovestruck with deftness and wit, but she was notoriously a nervous actor (although it doesn't much show on the screen), indecisive about how to play her roles, and loathing the publicity and loss of privacy that went with stardom.

During the making of *A Foreign Affair*, her nervousness made her finicky and difficult about how well she was being filmed, which caused Marlene to detest her, and her natural timidity wasn't helped by the fact that Marlene was in her element. She had a great role in a good script, and she was among friends. During spare moments she entertained John Lund and the rest of the crew with war stories, often chatting in German to Billy Wilder and Frederick Hollander. Often she would cook German or Viennese dishes for Billy, which they would consume in her dressing-room during lunch breaks, while poor Jean Arthur retreated to her dressing-room in tears.

One night during shooting, Billy's front door bell rang, after midnight. It was Jean Arthur, escorted by her husband. Tearfully, she accused Billy of burning one of her close-ups (the one where she looked so beautiful). He asked what she meant. 'You burned it, Billy,' she said. 'Marlene made you burn that close-up. She doesn't want me to look good.'

Billy had to take her into a projection room the next day and show her her close-up, still intact. It cured him of talking to Marlene in German and of lunching in her dressing-room.

But Marlene didn't spend all her spare time preparing lunch. She made love to more men during the shooting of *A Foreign Affair* than ever before. As Lund recalled: 'Marlene was always sitting outside her dressing-room watching the parade go by like it was a sidewalk café. Rumour had it she was having an affair with just about everybody who walked past. I remember a couple of muscle-men stunt guys that she just *devoured*.'

Good as her performance in the film was, with a Berlin disillusion that was deeper and richer than she had been capable of earlier, her best moments were her three songs, 'Black Market', 'Illusions' and 'The Ruins Of Berlin', all performed in the Lorelei Club and accompanied simply by a solo piano. The role of the pianist was taken by composer Frederick Hollander himself.

What is so unusual about her performance of these songs is that it is less mannered than she ever was before or after in her life. Especially in her latter-day live performances she tended to make everything just that bit too perfect, too calculated. In *A Foreign Affair*, when she sings of disillusion, she gives the impression of being deeply disillusioned, not simply adopting a pose for effect.

The film as a whole was far too disillusioned for many, especially those in the US government with some involvement in the occupation of Berlin. The Department of Defense, for instance, issued a statement complaining that it gave a false picture of American servicemen, who were of course honest and upright and sexually pure. They had the film banned from showing in Germany, describing it as 'crude, superficial, and insensible to certain responsibilities which the world situation, like it or not, has thrust upon…the movies.'

Civilian reviews were mixed. *Life* magazine featured a close-up of Marlene on its cover, saying, 'Dietrich steals the show in an uproarious Hollywood view of low life in Berlin.' Others, such as *Cue*, felt that the war and its aftermath were too recent and tragic to be treated with humour. They called the film 'a messy conglomeration of bumbling humor, pointless vulgarity and occasionally comic caricature.'

Paramount Pictures, aware of the hostile criticism, and no less jumpy than any other major studio, discreetly withdrew the picture from release.

When shooting on it had finished, in February 1948, Marlene at once hurried back to New York. Maria was expecting her first child, and Marlene felt there was nobody as capable as herself at running a household. 'I'm doing the chores while Maria's pregnant,' she announced to reporters at the time. 'The daily woman's no good – American women have no idea of how to keep house.'

She was aware that the arrival of Maria's child would make her a grandmother (indeed, the newspapers were already marvelling at the coming-into-existence of a glamorous granny) and it was possibly this intimation of ageing that caused her at around this time to have a face-lift.

The child, a son, duly arrived on 28 June 1948, and was named John Michael Riva. His godfather was Marlene's current lover and escort-around-town, I V A Patchevich – then the publisher of *Vogue*, which accounted for her frequent appearance in fashion magazines at that time.

As so often in the past, Marlene rose to her new role, and for a while proudly took to wheeling the child round Central Park in his pram, while wearing a nurse's uniform bought in Bloomingdale's, in order to pass herself off as a nanny.

For the moment totally reconciled to her daughter's marriage, she took $40,000 of the money she had made from *A Foreign Affair*, and bought the Rivas a brownstone house on East 95th Street (such a gesture might not of course have been pure generosity – it could also have been her staking a claim of ownership). To be near to them, she moved into the Plaza Hotel.

Grandfather Rudi was occasionally on hand as well. He was still in New York, living in a small apartment with Tamara, who suffered from a slowly deteriorating nervous condition – a condition that had not been helped by Rudi's insistence, each time she became pregnant, that she have an abortion. He liked his life kept simple.

To enable her to remain in New York near her grandchild, and to continue living in the style to which she was accustomed, Marlene increasingly took radio work. She had broadcast fairly regularly since the Thirties, doing radio adaptations of her films, as well as other dramas, and had frequently appeared as a guest on the shows of such as Bing Crosby, Perry Como and Tallulah Bankhead.

Towards the end of 1948 she appeared as the heroine in an adaptation of *Madame Bovary*. Claude Rains and Van Heflin were also in the cast, and the piece was directed by Fletcher Markle. Markle, a protégé of Orson Welles's and the second husband of actress Mercedes McCambridge (who had then not yet appeared in any movies), had done some writing (uncredited) on Welles's *The Lady From Shanghai*. He had ambitions to become a film director himself, and earlier in the year had managed to get backing for a low-budget independent production he had co-written, called *Jigsaw*. Most of the backing had come from the film's star, Franchot Tone, cast as a New York Assistant District Attorney who, in the course of solving a series of murders, uncovers an anti-religious racist hate group.

Because the film had this worthy aspect, Markle had no difficulty in getting a number of famous actors to make uncredited brief guest appearances. Among them were Henry Fonda, Everett Sloane, Marsha Hunt, Burgess Meredith and Marlene. Her appearance is extremely brief, a matter of a few seconds only, when she is seen emerging from a night-club (called, oddly enough, 'The Blue Angel') and saying to the man she is with (played by Markle himself), 'No, no, no – I'm not interested. Some time later, perhaps.'

That appearance was too short to qualify as a proper appearance at all, but a more substantial role was soon on its way to her. At the beginning of 1949 she received an offer from Alfred Hitchcock, then working at Warner Brothers, to appear in his next production, together with a few pages outlining its plot. He wanted her to play a glamorous star of the London theatre, currently appearing in a West End musical.

She accepted the role, but not without stipulating that her off-stage costumes in the film were to be by Dior. Dior agreed to provide them, but only if he were given a credit on the screen. To which Warner Brothers said, fine, but only if they got a twenty per cent discount off his price. They agreed, and all was settled.

Based on a Selwyn Jepson novel called *Man Running*, the film was to be called *Stage Fright*. It was a fairly straight English whodunnit, which was not a type of story that much appealed to Hitchcock, but he had taken it on for three reasons. One was that several reviewers of the novel had commented that it read like a Hitchcock picture, and he, as he said 'like an idiot, believed them!' A second reason was that he was fascinated by the idea that the heroine of the film, a student actress, has to play the role of somebody she isn't in order to try and unmask the villain. The third was that some of the action was set around a London school of acting, and as at the time his daughter Pat was still a student at RADA, what could be more pleasant than to film there, and to spend time with her during the filming?

The plot of the film is that RADA student Eve Gill (Jane Wyman) picks up the young man she is in love with, Jonathan Cooper (Richard Todd) in her car, when the police are chasing him. They escape the police, and as they drive along she asks him what this is all about. Jonathan, who is also an actor, is a friend of the West End star Charlotte Greenwood (Marlene). He tells Eve (in a long flashback) that Charlotte came to his flat in a blood-stained dress and told him that she had killed her husband during a quarrel. She asked him to go to her house and collect a clean dress for her, and while leaving the house with it he was spotted by her maid, and thus became suspected of the murder.

Eve takes him to the remote seaside cottage of her father (Alistair Sim), who, enjoying the drama, agrees to let him hide there, and Eve returns to town to work at exposing Charlotte as the murderer. In the course of her efforts, she bribes Charlotte's predatory maid to let her take over her job for a few days, pretending to be the maid's cousin. Gradually she discovers that Jonathan is more than just a friend to Charlotte, but is able to get over her disappointment as she finds herself falling for the young Scotland Yard detective in charge of the case (Michael Wilding).

In the end it turns out that Jonathan lied to her about Charlotte and the blood-stained dress, and that he himself was the murderer. In a good climactic scene under the stage in Charlotte's theatre, Eve is trapped there with him (while trying to help him escape). She hears the detective yelling that Jonathan is a killer and, suddenly understanding this is true, talks him into giving himself up.

Playing the part of a star performer, it was of course necessary that from time to time Marlene should be seen performing. Naturally this meant she should sing, and finding songs for her proved a considerable headache for Hitchcock, who was not notably musical.

For one song, to be sung (twice) as a background to other action, she borrowed her friend Edith Piaf's signature tune – 'La Vie En Rose'. But still there was the problem of finding her a big number.

Hitchcock suggested that a Cole Porter number from back in 1926, 'The Laziest Gal in Town', would suit her style, but Marlene felt the song was too old. He suggested Fannie Brice's famous number 'Second Hand Rose', which was even older, and another Porter song, 'Great The First Time'. Both these she also rejected, and prevailed on Hitchcock to commission a song from her old colleague Mischa Spolianski, now in London, who had composed songs for *It's In The Air* and *Two Bow Ties*. He wrote one, called 'When You Whisper Sweet Nothings To Me', and while that too was suitable as a song to be sung behind action, it wasn't good enough to be her star piece. Hitchcock suggested a song with a lyric by Ogden Nash, who had written for *One Touch Of Venus*, but she didn't like that either.

Eventually, for want of anything better, Marlene agreed to sing 'The Laziest Gal In Town'. Which led at once to the problem that the censors felt that one of Porter's verses was far too suggestive. He was approached, and helpfully agreed to write a toned-down replacement. She sang it in the film with such success that it would remain in her repertoire for the rest of her performing career.

Marlene didn't have top billing on *Stage Fright*. That went to Jane Wyman, who had just received the Best Actress Oscar for her performance in *Johnny Belinda*. But Wyman, like Jean Arthur in *A Foreign Affair*, felt plain next to Marlene. 'I ran into great difficulties with Jane,' Hitchcock remembered: 'In her disguise as a lady's maid, she should have been rather unglamorous… But every time she saw the rushes, and how she looked alongside Marlene Dietrich, she would burst into tears. She couldn't accept the idea of her face being in character, while Dietrich looked so great. She kept improving her appearance every day and that's how she failed to maintain the character.'

During the filming, which ran from mid-June to mid-September 1949, mostly at Elstree Studios, Marlene's relationship with Hitchcock was formal and slightly distant. Other directors she had worked with had tended to be martinets, like von Sternberg, or sociable professionals like George Marshall. Hitchcock, while totally in control of the entire process of film-making, was quietly spoken and reticent. Basically a shy man, he was never totally at ease with actors, and tended, when directing, to talk more with his camera crew and technicians. Marlene found this disturbing. 'I never got to know him,' she told Hitchcock's 1978 biographer, John Russell Taylor. 'He frightened the daylights out of me. He knew exactly what he wanted, a fact that I adore, but I was never quite sure if I did right. After work he would take us to the Caprice restaurant, and feed us with steaks he had flown in from New York, because he thought they were better than the British meat [these were still the times of post-war austerity], and I always thought he did that to show that he was not really disgusted with our work.'

Unusually for Hitchcock, who liked to design every aspect of his films, he let Marlene take her usual course of designing her own lighting and make-up, and even her own camera angles. She would discuss her scenes with cameraman Wilkie Cooper, and tell him where she would stand, how she should be framed, and how she and the camera should move. But Hitchcock was canny. He knew that she was playing the role of a glamorous star, and who better to light and frame Marlene for glamour than Marlene herself. Commenting on her activities on his set, he said, 'Marlene was a professional star. She was also a professional cameraman, art director, editor, costume designer, hairdresser, make-up woman, composer, producer and director.' Even allowing for a certain amount of Hitchcockian irony, that is considerable praise.

She and the reticent Hitchcock eventually acquired a long-lasting affection for each other, but there was another man on the film to whom she became much closer. This was the tall and handsome Michael Wilding. He was vulnerable, where Hitchcock, for all his reserve, was strong and confident. Early in the schedule, when they had only recently been introduced, she approached Wilding with a speculative look in her eye and announced, 'I am too old for you.' Wilding, who was eleven years younger than she was, tried gallantly to think of something appropriate to say, and as he fumbled for words she interrupted him with, 'Why not settle for just kissing me?'

'From that moment on,' Wilding recalled, 'we became inseparable. In fact she would not move a step without me. She insisted that I accompany her everywhere, and she took as much interest in my appearance as she did in her own.' Members of the crew, including Hitchcock himself, remembered in later years that their love-making was not of the discreet kind, often taking place in their dressing-rooms on the sound stage.

Their closeness survived after the film was over, but would end abruptly a few years later when it was announced that Wilding had become engaged to Elizabeth Taylor. Marlene was outraged, asking a friend, 'What's Liz Taylor got that I haven't got?' The engagement made her 'very sad'.

When *Stage Fright* was released, it was not much of a success, although it is a better film than its reputation as a minor work suggests. It suffers from various defects. Hitchcock himself felt that it suffered from a lack of tension caused by the fact that nobody, including the murderer, is in any immediate danger for most of the time. And this lack of tension is made worse by the fact that the film tends to rather amble along, its pace slowed by the large number of much-loved eccentric British bit-part players (Miles Malleson, Joyce Grenfell, Alastair Sim), all doing their well-known party-pieces.

The rather muddled plot is also confused by Hitchcock's mistake in allowing Richard Todd's long flashback at the front to be a lie. Why a lying flashback does not work is because film is too real. If we see a thing happening, it happened. The impression is quite different from hearing a character tell a lie. An image on the screen is simply too strong. Hitchcock never made the same mistake again.

After shooting finished, Marlene stayed on in London for a month or so, socializing with friends like Noël Coward, before heading back to New York. There Maria was expecting a second child.

12 Films, Family And Fleming

In New York, in spite of the fact that she had no immediate work in prospect, Marlene continued to live like a star, residing at the Plaza Hotel and giving cash subsidies and lavish gifts to Rudi (and Tamara), and to friends such as Max Colpet, who by now had also moved to the USA and adopted the name of Max Colby. In spite of her enormous practicality in so many areas, she was never good at handling money.

One of her friends who was in New York at the time was Ernest Hemingway. He was staying at the Sherry-Netherland Hotel, and on the evening of 16 November 1949 she visited him there for what turned out to be a somewhat boozy evening, as one of a group that included his publisher Charles Scribner Sr, athlete George Brown, and Hemingway's friend and future biographer, A E Hotchner.

Hotchner recalled that Marlene dominated the conversation, talking about her continuing work for USO, about her astrologer Carroll Righter, about herself and her plans for the future, and passing round photographs of her grandchild.

'During the war,' she proclaimed at one point, 'everybody was the way people should be all the time. Not mean and afraid but good to each other. It was different in the war. People were not so selfish and they helped each other.' To some present this seemed to be over-glamourizing a rather unpleasant recent past.

What she did not take on board was that another member of the group was journalist Lillian Ross, who was there because she was working on one of the *New Yorker*'s famous profiles, the subject of course being Ernest Hemingway himself.

When the profile appeared, on 13 May 1950, Hemingway appeared in it as something of an old soak, and Marlene was quoted at length about her life around Maria. Talking of a typical day at the Rivas' Third Avenue apartment, she said:

'I'm the baby-sitter. As soon as they leave the house, I go around and look in all the corners and straighten the drawers and clean up. I can't stand a house that isn't neat and clean. I go around in all the corners with towels I bring with me from the Plaza, and I clean up the whole house. Then they come home at one or two in the morning, and I take the dirty towels and some of the baby's things that need washing, and, with my bundle over my shoulder, I go out and get a taxi, and the driver, he thinks I am this old washerwoman from Third Avenue, and he takes me in the taxi and talks to me with sympathy, so I am afraid to let him take me to the Plaza. I get out a block away from the Plaza and I walk home with my bundle and I wash the baby's things, and then I go to sleep.'

Marlene was livid when she read this. She blamed Hemingway for having allowed her privacy to be invaded by not explaining what Lillian Ross was doing at the Sherry-Netherland. She'd taken her to be some sort of secretary.

But journalism was changing. Celebrities were no longer being handled with kid gloves as people whose mystery it was in the media's interest to preserve. The public, it was now felt, was eager for more realistic details. After she realised this, Marlene became more astute in handling her own publicity. She wrote an article for the *Ladies' Home Journal* on 'How to be Loved', which gave advice to wives about welcoming their husbands home after a long day with a well-cooked meal, and always looking ravishing. This prompted one wife to comment, 'Marlene Dietrich is, no doubt, a splendid example of how any woman can look at fifty, if she looked like Marlene Dietrich at twenty-five.'

She was asked by the publishers Doubleday to write an autobiography, provisionally titled *Beauty Is An Illusion*, and she accepted, although it would be many long years before such a book (with a different title) would see the light of day.

By this time her attitude to America was changing. Although she still felt Americans and the American film industry were naïve and self-absorbed, she realised that, for the moment at least, there was where her career lay, and not in Europe. After all, since the war she had had major roles in three American films (even if one was shot in England).

But suitable new roles for her were thin on the ground. Several were suggested, which she either rejected herself or were lost to others. Elia Kazan offered her a role in *Man On A Tightrope*, written by Robert E Sherwood and set behind the Iron Curtain. She was to play a travelling carnival performer, but the role eventually went to Gloria Grahame. Orson Welles offered her the part of a shady aristocrat in his planned film *Confidential Report* (also known as *Mr Arkadin*), but delays meant it would not eventually get made until 1955, and without her. Another old friend, Clifton Webb, who had recently regained box-office success with his series of *Mr Belvedere* comedies, in which he played a waspish but likeable pedant, suggested she appear opposite him in *Dreamboat*, playing a silent-movie star, but that role went to Ginger Rogers.

There were theatre offers as well. Orson Welles wanted her to appear with a repertory stage company he was trying to set up, playing Lady Brett-Ashley in an adaptation of Ernest Hemingway's *The Sun Also Rises*. But the company never did get set up in the end. She was also offered roles in two Broadway musicals, one called *Carnival In Flanders*, the other, with songs by Frank Loesser, called *After My Fashion*. These she declined because, after her *débâcle* with *One Touch Of Venus*, she feared her voice was not strong enough.

Maria in her own small way was doing better. After her second child, another son, was born in the spring of 1950 (and named John Peter Riva – all four of her sons would have the first name John), she resumed her acting career, now under her married name of Maria Riva. Aided and advised by Marlene, she soon became fairly well-established in television drama. Her first appearances, beginning on 4 July 1950, were as a regular performer in a series of half-hour pieces, which had the overall title *Sure As Fate*. The director of the show was a strikingly handsome Russian-born Swiss-Mongolian (and graduate of the Sorbonne), with dark wavy hair, which he would shortly shave off to become a huge success on both stage and screen in the musical *The King And I*. He was of course Yul Brynner.

Shortly after Maria had returned to acting, Marlene at last received a solid offer herself. She was again to appear in an American film made in England, this time by Twentieth-Century Fox. Its title was *No Highway* (in America, *No Highway In The Sky*), and it was to be directed by ex-Berliner Henry Koster. Marlene had known him slightly since their Berlin days, when his name used to be Hermann Kosterlitz, but had never worked with him in Hollywood. Nonetheless, the film had a character in it who was a movie star, and Koster insisted to executive producer Darryl Zanuck that there was nobody in the world who could play a movie star as well as Marlene could. Zanuck agreed.

Although Koster had never worked with Marlene, he had recently had a huge success directing her proposed co-star in the smash-hit comedy *Harvey*; the star in question was of course her old lover, James Stewart. There would, however, be no off-screen liaison between them this time. James Stewart had by now been married for over a year to the only wife he would ever have, or need, Gloria. She was a wealthy and witty socialite, who had briefly dabbled in the worlds of modelling and fashion design, and the two were devoted to each other. In fact, they had come to London together, so as not to be separated.

Marlene set off for London in September 1950, but en route stopped off in Paris, this time having succeeded in getting the film company to buy her outfits from a different fashion-house, that of Pierre Balmain.

The *directrice* of Pierre Balmain, the aggressive but charming Ginette Spanier, remembered her arrival there well, Marlene that morning being *très grande dame*. When she was shown a mink cape, priced at the equivalent of £4,000, Ginette recalled, 'She looked at me and, still without a smile or a "Good morning," said, "I find it rather poor." On which the longest and most expensive mink stole in the establishment was produced, to which, still without a smile, Marlene said, "I'll have that."'

Ginette was more impressed than abashed. Later she described how Marlene knew exactly which outfit would 'feed the legend... She thinks out a whole wardrobe in terms of her various appearances. She even sees her social life in terms of star appearances. She goes straight for her needs, bearing in mind what background she will appear against, what other performers she will "top". Marlene is intelligent, ruthless, and...knows exactly what she wants.'

Then came the fittings, and Ginette soon learned that Marlene could easily demand half-a-dozen fittings if even a seam in a lining appeared to be wrong. At one point, finding her staff run ragged, Ginette burst out in exasperation: 'First they'll look at your face. Then they'll look at your legs. Then maybe they'll take an interest in the story. If they have time to concentrate on the shadow of a seam in the lining of your dress, the picture must be a flop.'

Marlene explained to her patiently, as if to a child. 'You do not understand. Everything on the screen is enlarged twenty times. If, in twenty-five years' time, my daughter Maria sees the picture and notices the seam all puckered she will say, "How could Mother have stood such a thing?"'

Ginette's staff became so harassed as the morning wore on that she thought it diplomatic to call a lunch-break at their usual time. Marlene announced that, as she had nowhere to dine herself, she would simply wander around until everybody returned. Ginette, intrigued by her as well as not wanting to lose a new customer, invited her to dine at her home on the Avenue Marceau.

Marlene accepted. By chance that day was the birthday of Ginette's husband, a physician by the name of Paul-Emile Seidmann, and Ginette had bought him a pot of caviare as a present. Marlene ate the lot, and he was furious, which, in Ginette's opinion, 'reflected no credit on either of them.' Nonetheless, after that first occasion Marlene became a frequent visitor to the Seidmanns, and she and Ginette became enthusiatic lovers wherever they met, in Paris, London or New York.

The film Marlene was to make, based on a novel by Nevil Shute, dealt with the then-topical subject of metal fatigue in aircraft (Shute himself was an aeronautical engineer). James Stewart plays Theodore Honey, an American aviation scientist who for eleven years has been working in England for a British airline. His wife was killed in the blitz, and he lives with his ten-year-old daughter, Elspeth (Janette Scott). Although he loves her dearly, he is an egghead, and has brought her up in a totally intellectual atmosphere. This has caused her to be regarded at school as a swot, making her unpopular and sapping her self-confidence.

He has been trying for some time to convince the British airline he works for that a certain model of aircraft they fly becomes unsafe after about 1,400 hours in the air. They are just convinced enough to send him on a flight to Labrador to inspect the wreckage of one such plane that has recently crashed there.

During his flight, he is alarmed to discover that the plane he is on, which is of the same model he has been concerned about, has entered the danger zone. He attempts to warn the pilot, but as he is a bumbling and absent-minded type of professor, his warnings are dismissed. He has more success trying to convince a fellow-passenger, the movie star Monica Teasdale (Marlene), who is beginning to feel that film-making is a bore, and that a life making films is trivial and pointless. She listens to him, and so does a sympathetic air-hostess, Marjorie Corder (played by Glynis Johns). But they can do little to help.

During a refuelling stop at Gander, in Newfoundland, he seizes his opportunity to wreck the undercarriage of the plane and thus prevent it from flying on. The star and the stewardess, impressed by the strength of his conviction, by now totally believe in him, but his action leads to him being brought before a board of enquiry back in England, where he must justify what he has done, or lose his job and face court proceedings.

The star and the stewardess, who have both come to love him for his manly (although bumbling) honesty, do their best to help. They visit him at his house, meet Elspeth, and give him advice about bringing her up. 'Keep on telling her she's pretty,' says the star.

But eventually the star, after briefly deluding herself that maybe becoming a conventional housewife might rescue her from the pointlessness she finds in her career, bows out, and it is implied that he will live happily ever after with the air-stewardess. After further metal-fatigue tests and an examination of the Labrador wreckage, the enquiry completely exonerates him.

Filming began in October 1950, and almost at once ran into difficulties when James Stewart came down with appendicitis and needed an emergency operation, which kept him off the set for ten days. Nor were his troubles over after that. In November, his wife Gloria discovered she was pregnant, and the doctor she was seeing advised her to fly back to America as soon as possible, as he was dubious about a woman flying once pregnancy was advanced. She flew back at once, leaving James Stewart to suffer what he later described as the loneliest Christmas of his life. It would have been all right in his long years as a bachelor, but a happy marriage made all the difference.

Nonetheless, he gave a good performance in the film, his character's naïvety about the world coming across strongly in a long conversation with the disillusioned film star, during which he explains to her how much her films had meant to his late wife. It is true that Henry Koster, who could be heavy handed, somewhat undermines his performance by giving him too many hoary absent-minded professor gags, like continually forgetting his hat or umbrella, but on the whole these don't do too much harm.

Marlene's characterization too is excellent and, whether by accident or design, many of her lines vaguely reflect her own life and character. Lines such as 'I would have stopped working a long time ago if I could have figured out what to do with myself,' and that her career is just 'a few cans of celluloid on a junk heap someday.' Neither of which is exactly Marlene. Although she came to adopt something of the second attitude later in her life, she was never likely to stop working until she physically had to, if that meant stopping being seen and admired by multitudes.

During the film she was at first a little wary of the younger and pretty Glynis Johns (as Glynis was of her), but she was kind to the ten-year-old Janette Scott. Although Janette was a third generation actor, who had been on the stage for years, she was ignorant of film work, and Marlene coached her, telling her such things as, 'Find the lights. Tilt your head back so the light can hit your cheekbones... Rock back on your heels so the light shines in your eyes and they don't go dead... No, no, rock *forward* on your toes – you've lost the light! No one will see your eyes if you don't find it.'

As Janette recalled: 'She got cameraman Georges Périnal to let me look through the viewfinder and taught me to ask about lenses so I'd know how large I was in the frame and could adjust my gestures to the size of the image. She took me to the editing room and explained cutting to me... And stressed the importance of dressing well off the screen as well as on... She didn't teach me about glamour; she taught me to be serious about my craft.'

Not only that, on Janette's eleventh birthday, which happened to be 12 December, the day before Maria's, Marlene went into maternal mode and organised an on-set birthday party for her.

Her off-screen life during the filming brought her a number of pleasures. Shortly after shooting had started, on 3 November, the French government made her a Chevalier of the Légion d'Honneur in recognition of her war work. She would formally receive the award in Washington almost a year later, when the decoration was pinned on her by the French Ambassador, Henri Bonnet.

Three days after hearing she was to get the award she attended a dinner-party with Noël Coward. At the party were Tyrone Power, Montgomery Clift, Gloria Swanson and her old friend Clifton Webb. Also, unfortunately, her old friend Michael Wilding was there, and she did her best to ignore him, now that he was actively involved with the nineteen-year-old Elizabeth Taylor. She covered up her embarrassment by talking a lot, mostly about her Légion d'Honneur, and it was ironic that the next day, in a newspaper interview, she would give the opinion that: 'Women talk when they have nothing to say. They chatter about a lot of nonsense that interests no one but themselves. They should keep quiet and not open their mouths just because they like the sound of their voices.' (This may give some clue as to why she felt women were impossible to live with.)

Another dinner-party, later during the production, was a different matter. She had never forgotten the name of Alexander Fleming, whose penicillin might well have saved her life. Since 1944 he had been 'Sir Alexander Fleming' and it turned out that Mischa Spolianski and his wife could arrange an introduction to him through a relative of theirs, a Dr Hindle, who was himself a researcher into the yellow fever virus.

In her autobiography Marlene claims that all she really wanted to do was look at 'almost the greatest of my "heroes"' from a distance, but the Spolianskis assured her it would be no problem to arrange a meeting. They would invite Fleming to their house one evening, if she would prepare the menu. As she wrote:

> I trembled with anxiety, wired Erich Maria Remarque in New York and asked him which wine I should serve with the dinner, and he answered me promptly, why all this excitement? Because Alexander Fleming had the reputation of being an excellent connoisseur of wine and London's greatest gourmet to boot.
>
> What a challenge! I got permission to leave the studio early, and I was at my friends' at the right time for the banquet I had thought up and believed I could prepare. At eight on the dot Alexander Fleming was at the door, accompanied by Dr Hindle.
>
> I took his coat, a simple gesture that almost moved me to tears because the little loop on the collar (which was supposed to serve as a hanger) was torn. I knew Fleming was a widower. My friends and I had decided in advance that penicillin was never to be mentioned in our table-talk since I was convinced he never wanted to hear anything about it.
>
> We sat down at the table. I observed Fleming, who ate as though there was nothing and nobody around him. I was quiet. But my table companion, Dr Hindle, heartily helped himself, praised the dishes, the wine, the tastiness of each course. [The main dish was goulasch.] I thought he was doing that just to reassure me. I uncorked one bottle of wine after the other (those Remarque had recommended), and finally the dinner was over... I felt uneasy because Fleming had not uttered a word. I wondered if it was due to a suspicion of admirers, male and female, something I have understood only too well. Finally, we rose from the table and made our way to the living room.

Again silence, again embarrassment on my part. Would my friends keep their promise?

They did. We spoke about the great success of Mischa Spolianski's *Tell Me Tonight (Be Mine Tonight)*, about all the songs he had written. Fleming hummed some bars from 'Tonight Or Never' and, here and there, proudly sang a few words.

Suddenly Fleming placed a hand in the pocket of his jacket [and] produced a tiny object, which he handed me across the table. 'I've brought you something.' I touched his hand and took the object. It was a small round glass jar. 'That's the only thing I thought I could give you,' he said. 'It's the first penicillin culture.'

We were on the verge of tears (except Dr Hindle, of course), and the evening ended with kisses and the vow never to lose sight of each other. Upon my return to America I regularly sent Fleming eggs and other groceries which at that time were lacking in England.

This is a good and perceptive picture of Sir Alexander. A small, blue-eyed, broad-shouldered man, who had been raised on a remote Scottish farm, he remained shy all his life, feelings making him uncomfortable. Although those who came to know him well understood that he was in truth sensitive and affectionate, his shyness tended to make him brusque.

One thing Marlene omits to mention is that as well as the eggs and groceries, at least once she sent him his horoscope, specially drawn up by Carroll Righter. What this dyed-in-the-wool materialist, who even thought psychiatry 'a load of rot' made of it is hard to say. Certainly he seems to have accepted it with politeness and generosity of spirit, never uttering a word of disbelief. But then, Marlene was so far outside the only world in which he felt truly at ease – the medical world – that the forthrightness he was famous for there never came into play. One thing is certain: he was so fascinated by the opening she gave him into a new society that through her he made several other friends in it. On the day he died of a sudden coronary thrombosis, 11 February 1955, he was to have dined with Douglas Fairbanks Jr and Eleanor Roosevelt.

When she returned to New York, Marlene found a new interest. It was Yul Brynner, who in her absence had shaved his head and opened on Broadway in *The King And I*, to great acclaim. Marlene visited him backstage, and almost at once they became lovers. Although he was married to the actress Virginia Gilmore, he was as casual about marriage ties as she was. As Yul's son, Rock, who remembered meeting Marlene often in his father's dressing-room, recalled, 'She was the most determined, passionate, and possessive lover [my father] had ever known, not in the least concerned about discretion... It was up to Yul to enforce discretion, [so he] rented a studio flat secretly, just for his romantic trysts, and especially for the nights he spent with Marlene.'

But their relationship wasn't only physical. She admired Yul for his intelligence and culture as well. Together they haunted antiquarian bookshops and art galleries, often conversing in French (Yul spoke several languages fluently). They spoke about painters, mostly post-Impressionists, and about great works of literature, often, at her apartment or his, reading them aloud to each other.

At around this time she rented a four-room apartment at 993 Park Avenue. Through most of 1951 she would gradually furnish it. In time there would be bookshelves containing works by writers such as Tolstoy, Dostoevsky, William Faulkner and Ernest Hemingway. She lined the walls with mirrors 'to make it look bigger', and with paintings by Cézanne, Delacroix, Utrillo and Corot, as well as the three paintings that had been Jean Gabin's. There were autographed photographs of friends, among them Cocteau, Callas, Coward, Hemingway, General Patton and Sir Alexander Fleming (whose small glass dish of penicillin culture she also proudly displayed).

Although in the early months of 1951 she had no film offers, Hollywood did present her with one golden opportunity. She was asked to appear at the 1950 Academy Awards ceremony, which was to take place on 29 March 1951 at the Pantages Theater. She was to present the Oscar to whoever won the award for Best Foreign Film.

Given plenty of warning of this event, she used the time well. First she found out what colour the set would be: red, white and blue. Then she phoned every contact she could think of, making dozens of calls to find out what every other woman on the stage that night, either prizewinners or presenters, would be wearing. It turned out that most of them would be dressed in formal evening gowns, mostly in white or pastel shades, some with bouffant skirts, and some decorated with beads and sequins.

She would dress differently. She decided to wear plain make-up, no jewellery, and a simple black Dior sheath dress, figure-hugging from neck to foot, but slit dangerously high up one side. To make sure it was slit up the most effective side, she made more phone calls to find out from which side of the stage she would be making her entrance. While she was about it, she also checked on the Pantages Theater's intended lighting set-up.

When she made her entrance and slowly crossed to centre stage, she stole the show. All the papers and periodicals reporting on Oscar night (which was not then televised) agreed that the night was hers. (The award for Best Foreign Film, incidentally, went to *The Walls Of Malapaga*, a René Clément film starring Jean Gabin.)

Yul Brynner kept urging her to return to the stage, possibly to co-star with him, and at one time in 1951 it was even announced that they would appear together in the play *Samarkand*, translated from the French of Jacques Deval. But again, as with the Broadway musicals she had been offered, she quite soon withdrew from the project, unsure of her own ability to sustain regular nightly performances.

In spite of her scarcity of work, she was by now adept at keeping her name before the public. She had become her own publicity machine, working in a much more professional and wide-ranging manner than she had been capable of in her twenties, when the best she could do was get herself talked about around Berlin.

She announced a press luncheon to celebrate the twenty-first anniversary of her arrival in America. It was held on 4 May 1951, in the Colonial Room of New York's Ambassador Hotel, and the place was jammed with reporters. She entered escorted by her daughter Maria. Highlights from her films were projected, and after the meal she was photographed cutting into a gigantic cake.

At around the same time, she also got a considerable amount of publicity mileage out of her fury with the Paris weekly *France-Dimanche*, which had ill-advisedly published a series of articles, claiming to be written by her and telling inaccurate stories of her life. She sued them and, as well as getting a lot of publicity, eventually won her case (it was settled out of court four years later).

In the middle of 1951 she did at last get a film to make – one specially written for her by her old friend Fritz Lang. Although she had fallen out with him for a time after he attempted to cause friction between herself and Jean Gabin during the filming of *Moontide*, they had remained in kindly communication. In 1946, while in Paris, she had taken the trouble to let him know that a letter in a Paris newspaper had named him as a closet Nazi. After sending Marlene a letter of grateful thanks, Lang had sued the paper and won.

The film was to be made on a small budget for a small production company called Fidelity Pictures (releasing through RKO), which was a considerable comedown for a man who in his early years as a director had been granted enormously long schedules and almost endless backing, but he had wanted to make a picture with Marlene for years.

The story he had come up with for her was a western. This may sound odd in a very German director, whose most famous films were dark urban dramas with a jaundiced view of modern society – such as *Metropolis*, *M*, *The Testament Of Dr Mabuse* and *Fury* – but Lang had loved stories of the wild west since boyhood. His bookshelves contained dozens of well-thumbed paperbacks by such famous names in the genre as Max Brand, Eugene Cunningham and Zane Grey.

The film he had written to star Marlene was a Lang original, one he had been working on for several years, and had eventually licked into shape with the help of the writer Daniel Taradash. Originally entitled *Chuck-a-Luck*, from a sort of saloon roulette played using a vertical wheel, it was eventually called *Rancho Notorious*. (In fact chuck-a-luck is a game played by spinning an hourglass-shaped cage containing three dice, but for the purposes of the film it's a vertical wheel with numbers round it.) The central male character, Vern Haskell, was played by Arthur Kennedy, who appeared in dozens of films during the Forties and Fifties, many of them westerns, and mostly as an excellent supporting actor. Only rarely did he get to play the lead.

At the beginning of the film, in a small town, Vern's pretty fiancée is raped and killed during a robbery. This turns him into a bitter and vengeful man who feels martyred by fate (very much Fritz Lang's own view of himself at the time). When he follows the two men who carried out the robbery, he finds one of them dying, having been shot by the other, who actually carried out the rape and murder.

All he can get out of the robber as he dies is the mysterious word, 'Chuck-a-Luck', in answer to his question about where the murderer is headed. Riding on from place to place, he at first finds no-one to whom the word means anything (beyond simply the saloon game). But gradually, piece by piece, he finds that the word has something to do with a woman called Altar Keene (Marlene).

It is obvious from the men who remember her that Altar Keene, although a saloon girl, is someone of enormous beauty and charisma. In a series of three flashbacks, told by three different men, we see her indulging in cheerful horseplay in a saloon full of drunken men, posing elegantly in a carriage drawn by two white horses, and finally singing in a crooked gambling-saloon. She then gets fired, but before leaving, wins a fortune on its crooked chuck-a-luck wheel. She gets away with winning her fortune with the help of a handsome gun-slinging outlaw who has just showed up there, and who prevents the saloon-owner from seizing her winnings back. His name is Frenchy Fairmont (played by Mel Ferrer).

Vern learns that Frenchy is currently in jail in a nearby town, awaiting hanging. Going there, he gets himself jailed as well, and helps Frenchy to escape. In gratitude, Frenchy takes him to the remote ranch, in the hills of the Western desert, that Altar has built with her winnings and given the name of 'Chuck-a-Luck'. It is a hideout for those on the run, which Vern pretends to be, and there he at last meets Altar Keene.

As well as Frenchy, there are about nine other outlaws there, and soon Vern realises that as well as running a hideout, Altar is making a fortune by taking a ten per cent cut of the proceeds of any robbery that anyone staying at Chuck-a-Luck commits. He is sure one of the outlaws must be the man he is after, but has no clue to help him know which, until Altar, celebrating her birthday with a party, wears on her expensive gown a diamond brooch that he had given his fiancée as an engagement present.

Vern contrives to spend time with Altar in order to find out which one of them gave her the brooch, and finds himself becoming strongly attracted to her, as she is to him, in spite of the fact that to all the world she is known as Frenchy's woman.

He joins the outlaws in a robbery, which is bungled. A couple of outlaws are killed, Frenchy is shot in the shoulder, and Vern's real mission is revealed. It turns out that the man he is after is the one called Kinch. He manages to arrest Kinch and turn him over to the local sheriff, then returns alone to Chuck-a-Luck and confronts Altar, telling her the truth about who he is and what he wants, and berating her for her selfish and immoral life.

Altar decides to give up her wicked life, and Frenchy. She will give him Chuck-a-Luck and go away with Vern. But Kinch has escaped from the sheriff, and makes his way to Chuck-a-Luck, where all the surviving outlaws are now assembled. There is a shoot-out in which Kinch is killed and Altar is mortally wounded, having deliberately stepped in front of a bullet meant for Frenchy. She dies, cradled by both him and Vern.

Filming began in October 1951, shortly after Marlene went to Washington to be formally awarded her Légion d'Honneur, and from the start there was trouble. Lang wanted her to play an older woman in the film (except in the flashbacks), hoping that this would help her sustain her film career by allowing her to move into more mature roles, as he was sure that even she would have to do sooner or later. As he recollected, 'I had the foolish idea, foolish because it led to a lot of unpleasant fights with her, of wanting to give Marlene a new screen image.' Even his choice of character-name for her – 'Altar' – had overtones of the German word for an ageing man – 'alter'. But Marlene would not go along with his idea. As Lang said, 'She became younger and younger until finally it was hopeless.'

Lang didn't help things with his martinet-like behaviour on the set. Overbearing and often abusive, he dictated to his actors every move, every gesture, obsessively marking out where they were to move and stop with industrial masking tape on the floor. This caused trouble for Marlene because he was a tall man with long strides, while she was a little below average height. Arthur Kennedy (who admired Lang for his work, and who had returned to films from Broadway, where he had been in Arthur Miller's *All My Sons* and *Death Of A Salesman*, simply to work for him) thought he behaved on the set like a 'depraved aristocrat'. He gave, said Kennedy, the impression of 'an ageing, jealous man who had the air of a lost lover'.

Marlene took to telling him all the time how von Sternberg would have done it, which of course made the on-set atmosphere even worse. All in all the filming was a miserable experience for everyone involved, and by the time it ended, during December 1951, Lang and Marlene were not even on speaking terms with each other. When speaking of him for the rest of her life she would revile him, saying that of all the directors she ever had, he was the one she hated most of all.

In spite of this, the film is well worth watching, even though it does not quite succeed in being, as Lang hoped, a 'western for adults'. It works well, even though the low budget meant using unconvincing painted backdrops for many of the scenes in the desert, and despite the fact that it was ruthlessly cut down to eighty-nine minutes by its producer, Howard Welsch, who wanted it short so that exhibitors could squeeze in extra performances on Sundays and holidays.

Arthur Kennedy makes an excellent hero, confident and efficient, with a tense embittered smile. Marlene, who never looked quite as good in colour films as in black-and-white, looks good. Her costumes suit her – both the frilly romantic saloon-girl dresses she wears in the flashbacks, and the more severe, almost masculine, outfits she wears in the main part of the film. She sings two songs – or rather, one-and-a-half, the half being 'Gypsy Davey', which she breaks off from in the gambling-saloon flashback, and 'Get Away, Young Man', which she sings at her birthday party. Both music and lyrics were credited to Ken Darby.

The film would get fairly good reviews, and Marlene would get even better ones, *Variety* calling her 'as sultry and alluring as ever', and *Time* saying, 'Marlene sings throatily, lazily crosses her beautiful legs, and looks sultry'. As it came out, both *Look* and *Life* would feature her on their covers.

The month after shooting on *Rancho Notorious* finished, in January 1952, she began a thirteen-week radio drama series of her own. Called *Café Istanbul*, its setting bore a strong resemblance to the film *Casablanca*, which was hardly surprising as the director of the series, Murray Burnett, had co-written the (unproduced) play *Everyone Comes To Rick's* on which *Casablanca* was based. Each episode ran for half an hour, and it went out every Sunday night on the ABC network, with Marlene playing Mademoiselle Madou (a name borrowed from the character based on her in Remarque's book *Arch Of Triumph*). Every week she would be involved in another exotic wartime adventure, frequently warbling a few bars of some romantic continental song.

Most of the original story-lines came from Murray Burnett, and Marlene played a large part in developing them, usually with the help of Max Colpet (now Colby), who wrote under a variety of pseudonyms so that ABC wouldn't catch on that one writer was producing so many scripts.

In February 1952 she embarked on a brief tour to publicise *Rancho Notorious*, accompanied by Mel Ferrer. They had got on well together during the filming, backing each other up in arguments with Fritz Lang, so having him along was pleasant for her. But another aspect of it would prove to be more important.

Their first stop was at a cinema in Chicago, where she was simply expected to appear on stage and utter a few polite words in praise of the film. But she had decided to do things differently. Without telling the house manager, she arranged accompaniment for herself and, after making her entrance in a full-skirted strapless gown, she launched into 'Falling In Love Again'. The audience clapped and cheered and stamped their feet and whistled, while she disappeared briefly into the wings and re-emerged wearing a black bodice, with long bare legs. In this costume she sang three more songs, to continuing applause.

This was by way of an experiment. Bearing in mind her success with live audiences during her wartime tours, she was beginning to consider the possibility of doing solo stage performances.

The publicity tour eventually wended its way back to Los Angeles, where a typically 'Marlene' event occurred. She learned that Kirk Douglas (whom she had met through Billy Wilder, but only once), was stricken with pneumonia, which he'd contracted while getting soaked making Howard Hawks's *The Big Sky*, a film about early nineteenth-century trappers exploring the Missouri River.

Immediately she descended on him, offering (as he recalled) 'soup [and] affectionate sex. But that was less than the mothering, the closeness. Marlene is an unusual person. She seemed to love you much more if you were not well. When you became strong and healthy, she loved you less.' He was bedridden for a few weeks. She ministered to him for a few weeks. Then he was well, she was gone, and for the rest of her life their meetings were infrequent and much less intimate.

With her voice being heard weekly on radios across the nation, and thus becoming a stronger element in her public image, her mind turned to the possibility of making records. She had made recordings for Decca in 1939, when she recorded for them her songs from *Destry Rides Again*, and a few more for them in 1941, but for the past ten years she had recorded almost nothing.

One exception was the songs she had recorded in German for the OSS during the war. She had been given copies of these, and had the bright idea of taking them to Columbia's head of artists and repertoire, Mitch Miller, to see whether Columbia thought they might be worth reissuing on one of the new long-playing records, introduced by Columbia in 1948 and now well on the way to driving the old shellac 78rpms out of existence.

Marlene thought they might be worth reissuing simply for historic interest, but Miller felt that these German versions of well-known American songs, with Kurt Weill arrangements, deserved to be remade with the much-improved recording techniques of the Fifties. Marlene at first hesitated, telling him, 'Oh, *never*. I will never feel that way again.' But quite soon she agreed. The recordings were made in July 1952, on a rainy night recommended as propitious by her astrologer, and the resulting ten-inch LP (there were such things in the early days of LP's), became a considerable hit, still regarded by many as her best-ever album. The songs are (with German lyrics) 'Lili Marlene', 'Mean To Me', 'Alice Doesn't Live Here Any More', 'The Surrey With The Fringe On Top', 'Time On My Hands', 'Taking A Chance On Love', 'Miss Otis Regrets' and 'I Couldn't Sleep A Wink Last Night'.

Pictures of her were taken during the recording session by photographer Eve Arnold, who remembered her wearing, 'a short cocktail dress on which there was a large, gaudy diamond clip, and there were those wonderful legs.' Eve, who at that time had never photographed a major film star, was impressed by Marlene's thoroughness, saying, 'When she went through the pictures, she wrote instructions on each (in eyebrow pencil) for retouching: narrow down the chin, cut down the waist, remove the dimple from the knee, the ankle should be slimmer, etc.'

The success of Marlene's LP led Mitch Miller to try teaming her almost immediately with the ex-big-band singer Rosemary Clooney, then riding high in the charts. Their voices worked well together, with Marlene playing the sophisticated older woman advising the younger Rosemary, and they recorded two tracks – 'Good For Nuthin' and 'Too Old To Cut The Mustard', against a sort of barrelhouse arrangement in which harpsichordist Stan Freeman was heavily featured. The songs did well, with 'Too Old To Cut The Mustard' even making it into the Top 40, and over the next year the pair would record together again twice, although Marlene disapproved of Rosemary's casualness about her off-stage appearance, telling her, 'I know you're working, Rosie, but you really *should* comb your hair!' (All the same, they were friendly enough for Marlene to coach Rosemary in how to roll a cigarette when she was to play a saloon singer in her 1952 cod-western film *Red Garters*.)

At the beginning of 1953 she recorded (with the Percy Faith orchestra) the song 'Time For Love' – the theme-song (and title) of her new radio drama series. This was actually her old series under another name. She, producer Murray Burnett, and writer Max Colby, had moved from the ABC network to CBS. There *Café Istanbul* became *Time For Love*, and Marlene, instead of being Mademoiselle Madou, became Diane La Volta. But otherwise it was the same mixture as before, and again the series would run for thirteen weeks.

In April 1953 there was to be a charity benefit in New York, in aid of sufferers from cerebral palsy. It was to be held at the opening night of a season that the Ringling Brothers-Barnum & Bailey Circus was to have at Madison Square Garden. Many celebrities were to appear, either playing clowns or riding round the ring on elephants.

Marlene's daughter Maria was active in cerebral palsy causes, and so had been invited to be a clown. Through her Marlene was invited to become involved. She would, she said, but not as a clown or on an elephant. She would consent to appear only if circus-owner John Ringling North would allow her to be ringmaster of the whole affair.

He would, and she set about designing a suitable costume. It turned out to be a ringmaster's shiny black top hat and bright red tail-coat, with black shorts ('I invented the short pants later known as "hot pants",' she would claim), long black nylon tights, shining black boots and a whip. 'Hel-loooo,' she cooed into her microphone. 'Are you having any fun?'

Again she was a sensation, attracting press attention from almost every newspaper and periodical in America. And she received an offer that would gradually set her whole life off in a different direction. Bill Miller, of the Sahara Hotel in Las Vegas, asked her if she would accept a booking to appear in its night-club as a solo performer. Yes, she would.

Before she could devote her full attention to this project, however, Rudi was stricken with severe gastric ulcers. This was in May 1953, and his condition was so serious that he required surgery. Half of his stomach had to be removed, and for a while his life was feared to be in danger.

It was clear that he could no longer cope with life in New York, or on the fringes of the film business, especially as Tamara's highly neurotic (though undefined) state had continued to deteriorate. Friends hunted about and located what seemed a suitable and peaceful place for them to live. It was a run-down farm in California, in the San Fernando Valley. One of Rudi's friends, a banker named Hans Kohn, lent him $10,000 to make a down payment, a mortgage was taken out, and he and Tamara moved to the country to become chicken-farmers (an idea that was very much Rudi's own). Marlene would stand by to pay the bills and the mortgage installments in case the project failed to make money.

Meanwhile, there was the Sahara Hotel for her to consider.

13 From Screen To Stage

The idea of Marlene taking up a cabaret engagement in Las Vegas was discouraged by several of her friends. Both Noël Coward (who had by 1953 acquired two dots over his first name) and Maurice Chevalier advised her against it.

They felt it was a long time since she had performed in cabaret, and that what was known in Fifties America as 'cabaret' was in any case not the same thing. It was simply saloon singing in the posher surrounding of a night-club, with audiences that were likely to be inattentive, especially in Las Vegas, where most of them were there for the gambling in any case, and any entertainment was simply to give them a breather from the tables.

Marlene was not deterred. In the middle of 1953 she went to the Sahara Hotel, both to finalise the fee and contractual details of her engagement, which was scheduled for December, and to have a look at the venue, and at other performers there, to make sure exactly what would be involved.

When she went to the Congo Room, where she would be appearing, she checked the sound and lighting set-ups, the sight-lines, and the condition and situation of the dressing-rooms. Visiting the recently opened Sands Hotel, accompanied by Montgomery Clift, she observed with satisfaction the performance of Tallulah Bankhead. Bankhead, for all her energy, personality and abrasive wit, had no singing voice, and if she, using simply monologue, could manage a twenty-minute spot, so could Marlene.

Another performer whose act she caught, again with Montgomery Clift, was Eddie Fisher. Then twenty-five, he was a likeable and unthreatening young singer, popular with both the very young and the increasingly old, having risen to fame on the Coca-Cola-sponsored TV show *Coke Time*. Liking the look of him, Marlene invited him to her table one night after watching his show and, during their conversation, asked him to come to her apartment in New York when he finished his engagement. He came, she greeted him in a revealingly low-cut beige gown and, after a candle-lit dinner, things took their usual course. 'I was both excited and little scared,' remembered Fisher. 'But Marlene knew how to make me feel like a man. The ceiling of her bedroom was mirrored.' (So much for a woman who had had come to resent being repeatedly cast as a hooker.) Their affair would last through the summer and autumn of 1953.

Now that she was at last her own director and producer, Marlene set about planning her show. She hired a musical director, Peter Matz, both to oversee her musical arrangements and to conduct her band. And she decided that the man to design the gowns she would wear was the film costumier Jean Louis. Jean Louis was currently under contract to Columbia Pictures (it was he who had designed Rita Hayworth's costumes for her film *Gilda* – in particular the black off-the-shoulder evening dress in which she sang 'Put The Blame On Mame').

To hire Jean Louis she needed the approval of Columbia's head of production, the abrasive Harry Cohn. As it turned out, Cohn was happy to be co-operative, because he was after Marlene to appear in his forthcoming film *Pal Joey*. It wasn't long, however, before she fell out with Cohn by insisting that the star of the film should be Frank Sinatra, whom she knew slightly and admired. Cohn, not especially interested in using Sinatra, whose career at the time was somewhat in the doldrums, suggested instead a new Columbia contract player, Jack Lemmon. Marlene considered Lemmon a 'nothing', and said that if he was to play Pal Joey she wanted no part of the picture. At which point Cohn said, in that case forget about Jean Louis. (The film of *Pal Joey*, as it happened, would not get shot and released until 1957, and it would star Frank Sinatra.)

On hearing the news, Jean Louis was distraught. He wanted to design Marlene's costumes. 'Don't worry,' Marlene told him. 'I'll find a way.' Which she did. After a string of phone calls she managed to get in touch with Frank Costello, a man so powerful in the mob that later in the Fifties he was able to put the wind up the ambitious John F Kennedy. Costello phoned Cohn, reminding him that he had growing children, and Cohn soon agreed that Marlene could certainly have the services of Jean Louis, for a fee of $7,500, provided she did not enter the Columbia studios through the front gate, but sneaked in through the prop department to his workrooms.

She was to have three gowns, made of beads sewn onto net, one black, one white, one flesh-coloured, each over flesh-coloured silk that made her look naked – a technique that Jean Louis had already used for Rita

Hayworth in her 1953 film *Salome*, a film Marlene had seen (although notably terrible, it was directed by her old friend William Dieterle).

Marlene started commuting from New York every other weekend in order to attend fittings. Sempstresses would be on hand, being paid double and triple time. 'We could work with very sheer material,' Jean Louis recalled, 'because Dietrich didn't need any foundation. It was all Dietrich in those days, *everything*. She would come directly from the plane through the prop room and stand motionless for eight or nine hours a day in front of mirrors while we made the dresses *on* her. It takes energy and discipline to stand like that, and she's *so* disciplined. She would say, "I don't like symmetry. Move that sequin," and we would, but that might make a symmetry with a rhinestone, so we would move *that*, and this went on all day, all weekend. I was terrified these spiderweb fabrics would go up in flames from her cigarettes. Two weeks later she would fly back to go through it all again, never impatient, because she was a perfectionist who knew exactly what she wanted. She could have been a designer herself – she knew how to sew, how to use a needle and thread, and she repaired her own costumes on the road.'

These weekend fittings were complicated by the fact that, during her brief visits to California, Marlene often wanted to fly off and visit Rudi in the San Fernando Valley (whenever Tamara was feeling stable enough to stand her presence). When time came for her to head off and appear at Las Vegas it got worse. 'We must finish by five so I can make my plane,' she would say. Five o'clock would come and go and, as Jean Louis further recalled, 'we would still be sewing sequins and rhinestones by hand. Marlene would then announce that she had a reservation at six, then another at seven, then another at eight. Finally we knew that the last plane left for the desert at nine and it would be over – she *had* to leave. She studied every sequin, every rhinestone, then just dropped these exquisite, fragile dresses from her shoulders to the floor, *boom!*, wadded them up in tissue paper, threw them, in a box like they were her grandchildren's diapers, and got on her broom to Las Vegas. It was a nightmare and a joy because Dietrich knew what she wanted and when you were finished it *looked* like something!'

It all paid off. On 16 December 1953, opening at the Congo Room, she was a smash. The fee she had agreed, $90,000 for three weeks, had made her the highest-paid entertainer in the world (probably in the universe), and she was worth every cent.

She was introduced by comedian Dick Shawn, and preceded by a couple of acts involving ponies and jugglers, then on she came wearing the black net gown that made her look almost naked, over which she wore a long black chiffon cape trimmed with black fox – which she soon let fall.

The audience gasped, the press photographers popped their flashbulbs, and after a dramatic pause Marlene uttered the longest-drawn-out 'Hell-oooooo' you ever heard. She sang half a dozen songs, and the house was hers.

At her performance on the second night, she did much the same, except that this time she wore the gown of white net (over flesh-coloured silk). The photographs of this made the papers all over again.

After her shows, Marlene would go each night and pose for photographer John Engstead, sitting for him from one to four, then staying up to wait while he processed the films and presented them for her approval at around seven, when she would give him instructions about retouching and printing before at last going to bed.

Her whole three weeks at the Sahara Hotel were a happy time for her. During her engagement, dozens of her friends came to see her, to applaud her, socialise with her, and share her triumph. And the hotel offered her a contract to appear there in a year's time and perform her act again.

Noël Coward admitted he had been wrong. Not only that, he set about planning a Las Vegas appearance of his own. When she heard about this, Marlene offered him the services of her musical director, Peter Matz. Which was a mistake, because Coward's performance there would also be a considerable success, and Peter Matz would stay with him, forcing Marlene to find a replacement for herself.

Unfortunately, there was an unsettling occurrence just after her last appearance. Her friend Clifton Webb had come and see her, accompanied by a socialite friend, the Countess di Frasso (a rich American who had married into Italian aristocracy, and whom Marlene knew slightly). During their return journey by train to New York, Clifton Webb was shocked to find the Countess dead in her roomette, still clad in her mink coat and wearing a diamond necklace worth around $200,000. She had died of a heart attack, aged sixty-six.

This disturbed Marlene greatly. While she herself was still only in her early fifties, it made her feel uneasy that so elegant and vivacious a woman as the Countess di Frasso could be prey to death. It seemed unfair. Getting old had no place in her plans and, in order to counteract it, that spring she had her second face-lift.

The early months of 1954 were, for Marlene, otherwise uneventful. She lived at her apartment in New York, and saw friends. She went to the theatre with Noël Coward and with Orson Welles, and dined with Hemingway (having by now forgiven him for not explaining to her who Lillian Ross was). And she spent much time with her two grandsons, cleaning their home and buying suitable clothes for them and for their mother, Maria – all of which made Maria feel somewhat inadequate.

In April she reprised her role as circus ringmaster for the cerebral palsy benefit show, and at around the same time began making a string of transatlantic phone calls, setting up a booking in London to perform her night-club show. It was to be at the Café de Paris, in Leicester Square, and although she would get only about half the fee she had received in Las Vegas, she knew that London was a prestigious place to appear.

There her act would have a few small changes. Her 'nude' dresses would be more obviously lined. Her patter between songs would contain small pieces of autobiography. She had added to her retinue a lighting expert, Joe Davis. And Peter Matz, having abandoned her to work with Noël Coward, had given her a friend of his as a replacement, a 25-year-old pianist and arranger called Burt Bacharach.

Marlene landed at Heathrow airport on 16 June, and was met off her plane by Noël Coward, bearing a bouquet of carnations and sweet peas for her. She was wearing a grey beret and a grey suit, its skirt slightly shorter than was then the fashion at the time. Together they were driven to the Dorchester Hotel, where she was booked into the elegant Oliver Messel Suite, with its grand piano, gold-plated bed and gilded decor. There she would both sleep and rehearse.

Five days later, on 21 June, came her opening night. It was a crowded and glittering occasion. Celebrities came to see her, and crowds thronged the streets to see both Marlene and the celebrities. Many of her audience had been at their tables for three hours when, at quarter past midnight, Noël Coward introduced her with some verses he had written, and as he finished them with the words 'legendary, lovely Marlene', a white spotlight picked her out at the top of a staircase, wearing a floor-length white fox coat over one of her 'nude' dresses. To welcoming applause she slowly descended to the stage.

Her show was now longer that it had been in Las Vegas, lasting thirty-five minutes. She began by announcing 'a few songs I have sung in pictures, on records, and during the war'. Then she sang them, holding the audience spellbound. She ended with 'Falling In Love Again' and, having announced it as her final number, she rebuked her audience after it for asking for an encore, saying, 'I told you that was the last one.'

That opening night was recorded for Columbia records, and the resulting album would be the first of a number preserving her performances.

Her run at the Café de Paris lasted for six weeks, and during the course of it she was introduced by a succession of celebrities, among them David Niven, Alec Guinness, Jack Hawkins and Robert Morley (whose introduction rambled on for so long that she was heard muttering loudly from her dressing-room, 'Who this Morley and why he not shut up and let me get on?')

It was not long after this that she was asked by the actor and drama teacher David Craig if she ever suffered from stagefright. Looking puzzled, she asked him why on earth she should. He explained that, 'having taught actors all my life, most of them were terrified of clubs because the audience was not captive.' He gave various other reasons, and at last she said, quite dispassionately, 'Oh, I know why! They are paying to see the most glamorous woman in the world, and I am she!' But that was only part of it. There was no reason why she should feel stagefright any more than a soldier going on parade. Everything about her shows was planned and rehearsed, down to the last flick and intonation. They were as precise as military manoeuvres.

As well as her shows, she frequently performed for charities. While in London, she and Noël Coward attended a 'Night Of A Hundred Stars' at the Palladium, where they did a dance duet to 'Knocked 'Em In The Old Kent Road' (a number Coward didn't know well and she didn't know at all). The evening raised £10,000 for the Actors' Orphanage.

After her London run finished, in August, she went to Monte Carlo to appear in its Bal de Mer, an annual benefit in aid of polio sufferers. She was dressed in a costume of scales and plumes designed by Jean Cocteau, and introduced by a Cocteau prose poem read by his lover, Jean Marais. It went, 'Marlene Dietrich!... Your name, at first the sound of a caress, becomes the crack of a whip... The secret of your beauty lies in the care of your loving kindness of the heart [which] holds you higher than elegance, fashion or style; higher even than your fame, your courage, your bearing, your films, your songs… [You approach us like] a frigate with a figurehead on the prow, a flying-fish, a bird of paradise, a legend, a wonder…!'

When she returned to Paris with Jean Marais, she spoke to him at length of her great love for Jean Gabin, and over the next few weeks he frequently had to escort her to various Gabin films that were being revived, during which she laughed, cried and reminisced. When not at the films, she insisted he take her to a small bistro from which she could observe Gabin's home on the rue François. There she would sit for hours, longing for a sight of him.

Also while in Paris, she put on a trench coat and army cap to take part in a march of former Resistance Workers and members of the American Legion, to celebrate the tenth anniversary of the liberation of Paris (25 August 1944). On her coat she wore her American Medal of Freedom and her French medal of the Légion d'Honneur.

By September she was back in New York. She visited Maria and her family, and sympathised with Maria over the failure of her recent Broadway play, *The Burning Glass* – a failure even though Sir Cedric Hardwicke and Walter Matthau were in the cast. Fortunately, for the moment Maria was still regularly acting on TV, and thus making some money – which did not stop Marlene from smothering the Riva family with her usual help and generosity.

Then Marlene hastened back to California, to prepare new costumes with Jean Louis for her second Las Vegas booking, and to visit Rudi (and Tamara) at their run-down farm. While there she shopped for groceries, cooked, looked after the ailing Rudi, and handed on some of her no-longer-wanted clothes to Tamara, whose mental condition was by now showing signs of increasing instability.

In October 1954 she opened again at the Sahara Hotel. Her new Jean Louis gowns were a slight variation on the previous ones, tending to make her lower half look nude, rather than her upper half. And she experimented with a wind-machine in the wings, having it blow on her during her final number, sending the chiffon of her gown billowing round her. Half way through her four-week run she was offered a contract to return for two more years, each time again for four weeks, and at a salary each time of $100,000.

During one show, she spotted John Wayne in the audience and, as she took her bow, beckoned to him to come backstage. He did, but made the mistake of taking with him his fiancée, Pilar Palette, who would shortly become his third and last wife, and who had come to the show with him. In her dressing-room, Marlene greeted him with a big kiss. He introduced Pilar, and Marlene immediately turned her back and began to talk to somebody else. Yet another man was being unfaithful to her.

At around the time her 1954 Las Vegas show closed, Harold Arlen, whom she had known since he composed what music there was for her film *Kismet*, was readying a new musical for Broadway. Called *House Of Flowers*, and written by Truman Capote, it was trying out in Philadelphia, and Marlene, knowing that Arlen was at the time suffering badly from ulcers, went there to mother him. She made sure he drank plenty of milk, and between times busied herself as a sort of unpaid maid-of-all-work for the production. She made coffee for the cast, and mended their costumes, and she advised Pearl Bailey on stage jewellery, telling her that as rhinestones were bigger they had more glitter for the money than real diamonds. She even sent for some of her own to lend to Pearl. Unfortunately, by the time the production was ready to move to Broadway she had begun offering so much advice to cast and crew that she had to be asked to stop.

This was all part of her feeling that her talents were underemployed. Back in New York, as Christmas approached, she complained bitterly to her friends (Coward and Hemingway among them) that apart from her night-club act there was little for her to do. She complained by letter to Charles K Feldman, who was still her agent, that she was eager to try new kinds of film, so why was nobody taking advantage of the publicity she had gained by appearing in Las Vegas and London? Having no idea how she might possibly be used in a film at that time, he had no option but to become evasive.

So 1955 had another slow beginning for her, the first big event being her return to London's Café de Paris in June. This time she was introduced on opening night by Douglas Fairbanks Jr, and again her audiences contained many celebrities. An unusual one, who came (by bus) to see her show on 5 July, was the formidable Labour MP, Bessie Braddock – formidable both in size and in determination. Bessie invited her to visit the House of Commons, and on 13 July she did, astounding many MP's who were under the impression she was Greta Garbo.

At around this time, Noël Coward – perhaps stimulated by her plaints of having no work, and perhaps because he was a little short of work himself, having by 1955 fallen somewhat out of fashion – wrote a musical for her and himself to star in. It was called *Later Than Spring*, and as he wrote in his diary, 'it was about a fascinating *femme du monde* (Marlene) and an equally fascinating *homme du monde* (me) ... [with] an articulate pair of companion secretaries (Graham [Payn] and Marti Stevens).'

Graham Payn was Coward's long-standing boyfriend and the actress Marti Stevens was a new enthusiasm of Marlene's. She was the daughter of the powerful film mogul Nick Schenk, president of Loew's International, which was the parent company of MGM.

As it happened, the musical was never staged with the originally planned cast, but it did turn up on Broadway a few years later, retitled *Sail Away* and starring Elaine Stritch. It would be Coward's only successful musical of the Fifties and Sixties.

On 4 October 1955, Marlene opened for a third four-week stint at Las Vegas, wearing a new (but similar) Jean Louis gown. Then, in December, she was back in New York, attending the première of the film *Oklahoma!* in the company of its producer, Avrom Hirsch Goldenbogen, better known to the world as Mike Todd.

Todd, then aged forty-eight, was one of the greatest hustlers of all time. A showman himself, he had long admired Marlene's showmanship, and during his years as a successful Broadway producer had often tried, without success, to get her to appear in his shows. Now he was in movies. With some backing from the powerful firm executive, Joseph M Schenck (elder brother of Nick, and thus, by coincidence, Marti Stevens's uncle), he had developed, with the American Optical Company, the wide-screen process Todd-AO.

The Fifties was the decade when the film industry, alarmed by the swift rise of television, had decided that its great advantage was the size of the cinema screen, and thus the bigger screen they could have, the better. The boldest and biggest screen system there was was Cinerama. Mike Todd had helped develop it, but he was dissatisfied with the fact that it required three cameras (and three projectors). He developed Todd-AO in order to fill a screen as big and wide as the Cinerama screen, but using only one camera and one projector.

Oklahoma! had been the first film shot using his new process, and now he was planning a follow-up. It was to be a vast star-studded extravangaza, called *Around The World In 80 Days*, based on the novel of the same name by Jules Verne, and starring David Niven. Among the hundreds of stars who were to show up in cameo roles, he wanted Marlene.

Later he would claim that of all the stars he hired, Marlene was the hardest to land. Eventually he told her, 'I'll shoot the scene and show it to you and forget the cost. I'll burn the negative if you don't like it.' She agreed, for a short scene he later claimed cost $150,000 to shoot. The film was long enough to need an intermission, and Marlene opened the second half, as the manageress of a saloon in San Francisco's notorious 'Barbary Coast' (the film is set in the 1890's).

Not only did Mike Todd land her for his film – from around the end of 1955 he and she became lovers (as Eddie Fisher found out by mistake when he was at a party at Mike Todd's apartment and recognised some of her clothes hanging in the closet).

Her short scene, lasting only some thirty seconds, was shot during March 1956, and shortly afterwards her affair with Mike Todd faded away when he set off shooting location scenes around the world and Rudi had another heart attack. Marlene went to California to nurse him through most of April, also making sure that Tamara was properly cared for. (It would not be long before there would be nothing for it but to have Tamara admitted to residential care, and she would go to Camarillo, one of California's state mental institutions.)

After looking after Rudi, Marlene returned to London, via New York. She had a third successful run at the Café de Paris, and then crossed the Irish Sea to make four appearances at a Dublin theatre. There her act acquired something new. After opening as usual in a 'nude' Jean Louis gown, and singing several songs, she made an exit into the wings and, while the band played the introduction to her next number, made a quick change, emerging in less than a minute dressed in top hat, white tie and tails, and smoking a cigarette. The astounded audience applauded wildly as she straddled a chair and launched into 'One For My Baby'.

The quick change took immaculate planning and a number of assistants. As she hit the wings, she shucked off her shoes, then her gown. At the same time an assistant removed her jewellery and wiped off her lipstick. Over her body stocking went trousers, shirt and tie in a single piece, then black socks, coat and shoes. Another assistant handed her two hairbrushes loaded with Brilliantine, which she used to plaster down her hair, before tucking it into her top hat. She was handed a lighted cigarette, and on she went, relaxed and detached. (The biggest problem, she once explained, was the socks. She could never find a way to put them on without having to bend down.)

She found this trick so effective that it would stay in her act for years. As she explained to the humour-writer Art Buchwald a few years later, 'The woman's part is for the men, the man's part is for women. It gives tremendous variety to the act and changes the tempo. I have to give them the Marlene they expect in the first part, but I prefer the white tie and tails myself... There are just certain songs that a woman can't sing as a woman, so by dressing in tails I can sing songs written for men.'

Another addition she would try out in her shows, as they got longer, was a line of dancing girls. She would join in a chorus-line with the girls, it being understood that when it came to the high-kicks, Marlene would kick higher than anyone else, even though they were thirty years younger than her.

In August 1956 she went for a holiday in Paris with Noël Coward, staying with Ginette Spanier and her husband, Dr Seidmann. Coward found her rather a trial, noting in his diary that she dominated the conversation, talking endlessly of her past – of John Gilbert, Erich Remarque, Jean Gabin and Michael Wilding. Not only that (he noted), she was 'in a tremendously *hausfrau* mood, and washed everything in sight, including my hairbrush (which was quite clean).'

This sort of obsessive cleanliness was, of course, Marlene's attempt to assert control over the world. It was related to her desperate attempts to stay young, with face-lifts and lighting and anything that would help. Ageing to her was a loss of control over her very self, and control was ultimately the thing she wanted most. As Coward mused in that same diary, 'How foolish [of Marlene] to think that one can ever slam the door in the face of age. Much wiser to be polite and gracious and ask him to lunch in advance.'

Although *Around The World In 80 Days* would not be premièred until October 1956, Marlene's cameo in it was so well-publicised by the astute Mike Todd that before that date she was offered, and played, another (and larger) film role. United Artists, who were to distribute *Around The World In 80 Days*, had also made a deal to distribute in America an Italian-backed film called *The Monte Carlo Story*.

The original story for this had been concocted by its producers, Marcello Girosi and Dino Risi, as a vehicle for the famous Italian actor and director, Vittorio de Sica. Although de Sica had won world-wide fame in the Forties as one of the neo-realist directors that Marlene so admired, with such films as *Sciuscia (Shoeshine)* and *Ladri Di Biciclette (Bicycle Thieves)*, he had begun his career as a charming romantic leading man. He was by now in his fifties, and *The Monte Carlo Story* was to be a light romantic comedy, starring him and Marlene.

In the story, set (naturally) in Monte Carlo, the handsome but broke Count Dino, who is addicted to gambling, decides to seduce into marriage the beautiful Marquise de Crèvecoeur (Marlene), not realizing that she is as broke as he is, and is similarly plotting to get her hands on the money she thinks he has. As they circle round each other, they genuinely fall in love, with the result that when they discover the truth about each other's financial circumstances, they decide to join forces and fleece a rich American father and daughter. They pretend they are brother and sister. The Marquise makes overtures to the father, the Count charms the daughter, but eventually conscience triumphs and they decide that true love is worth more than gold. The film ends with them sailing off to make the best of poverty in a small and ancient motor-yacht owned by the Count – he steering and she manning the galley.

It had originally been planned that de Sica himself would direct the picture, but he was a gambling addict in real life, and managed to lose his acting fee at the Monte Carlo gambling tables before shooting even began. Upset by this, and wishing to spend a lot of time winning back what he had lost, he backed out of the chore of directing. The producers, wanting to save every penny they could, gave the job instead to writer Sam Taylor, who they had brought in to turn their story-line into a screenplay.

Sam Taylor had never directed (and never would again), and it shows in the finished film, which is heavy handed and plodding. And the shooting of it, during the late summer of 1956, was a miserable experience for all concerned. This was partly due to Marlene, who took a vehement dislike to the fifteen-year-old American actress playing the rich daughter. Her name was Natalie Trundy, and she was pretty enough to have got herself onto the cover of *Paris Match*. This made Marlene so furious that one afternoon, after shooting a scene with the girl, she suddenly slapped her. The cast and crew were shocked by the unexpectedness of this, and the naturally courteous de Sica was so appalled that from then on he referred to his co-star as 'that witch'.

Nor was Marlene pleased at being banned from the Monte Carlo Casino because off screen she preferred to wear slacks. She tried phoning Aristotle Onassis, who was in Monte Carlo at the time with Maria Callas, and who Marlene knew to be a major stockholder in the Casino, but Onassis felt unable to change its dress code simply for her. And what made things worse was that Prince Rainier and Princess Grace, who she was sure could have worked things out for her, happened to be away from Monaco at the time.

Needing to take out her temper on someone, she rounded on the manager of her hotel, the Hôtel de Paris, storming that there were only a miserable dozen roses decorating her suite. 'You call these *flowers?*' she raged. 'I want five thousand flowers, not a dozen!' She got them.

Her rage with the hotel manager was witnessed by Bernard Hall, who had helped her with the choreography of her shows, and who by around this time had also became her secretary, companion and general factotum – a situation he would remain in for decades.

It was Bernard Hall who also observed another misery for her during the shooting. Some scenes were filmed aboard a yacht, which, as it happened, belonged to King Farouk. De Sica was given to turning up for work after a heavy night at the Casino, and Marlene had become prone to seasickness. As Bernard recalled, 'De Sica would show up looking green from his hangover, with Marlene already aboard Farouk's yacht looking green from seasickness. The only thing they had in common was colour.'

Nonetheless, there were a few pleasures for her on *The Monte Carlo Story*. For a start, she had managed to arrange for her gowns to be designed by Jean Louis (although there was nothing as outrageous among them as she wore on stage). And as one weekend approached, she asked director Sam Taylor if she might turn up late on the following Monday, as she had been asked to go to Paris to discuss a proposed recording of Kurt Weill's opera *Mahagonny*, in which she was to play the role of Mrs Begbick.

Impressed, Sam Taylor said yes, and slightly rearranged his schedule. On Monday she duly returned at noon, but said nothing about *Mahagonny*. Unable to restrain his curiosity, at the end of the day Sam asked her how the discussions went. Laughing, she said, 'Sam, you didn't *believe* that story?! *Yul* was in Paris, and I wanted to get laid!' (She was also heavily involved during the filming period with a young Frenchwoman, who, as Sam Taylor recalled, 'Had been passed on to Marlene by a Hollywood actress friend.')

After making *The Monte Carlo Story*, Marlene had a third face-lift, and by Christmas was back in New York, spending the festive season with Maria and her family. Sam Taylor, invited to visit, recalled that, 'the sense of family was overwhelming. Marlene was the matriarch, doing a real German

Christmas tree with packages beautifully ribboned and wrapped so they could be opened from the bottom and then rewrapped like little props under the tree for the whole holiday season. It was very beautiful and Marlene *adored* her [two] grandsons. Her self-interest ended when they were around... Family was the steel rod of her life; the thread that stitched it together. She was like a man; she was ambitious and went out to conquer the world and bring it home to her family.'

On 14 February 1957 she opened again at Las Vegas, this time at a new venue, her booking having been switched to the newer and more fashionable Sands Hotel. She of course wore a new, but similar, Jean Louis gown, but this time made her entrance wearing over it a luscious white wrap, measuring 3.7 by 2.4m (12 by 8ft) and composed of (it was said) five million swan feathers. This she would wear in show after show for years.

After her four-week engagement she had to hasten off to Los Angeles, where she was scheduled to appear in a film (she had been asked to be in it at only two days' notice). Although her own screen-time would amount to about four minutes, and although her actual filming took only one night, it would give her one of her best roles, and in the best film she ever appeared in – probably. It was Orson Welles's *Touch Of Evil*.

Welles had become director of *Touch Of Evil* in rather an odd way. It was conceived as a B movie by Universal producer Albert Zugsmith. A dark thriller set either side of the US-Mexico border, its hero is a Mexican narcotics agent, Ramon Miguel Vargas, newly married to a young American, and its anti-hero is a crooked American cop, Hank Quinlan.

Welles, always in need of money for his various projects, had agreed to play the cop. Charlton Heston, approached to play the lead, read the script, heard that Orson Welles was involved, and agreed to do it, assuming Welles was to direct. Learning this was not so, he announced firmly that he would only become involved if Welles did direct. Zugsmith managed to persuade Universal, and Welles agreed to direct, but only on condition he would have a free hand to rewrite the script.

The story, as developed, tells how Vargas (and his wife, played by Janet Leigh), are crossing the border when a car, which has just come over into America, blows up, killing the two people inside. Both Vargas and Quinlan begin their investigations, and Quinlan soon has a suspect, a young Mexican. He plants dynamite in the young Mexican's bathroom so as to secure a conviction, but Vargas is wise to him. Vargas begins to investigate not only the crime but Quinlan's past, meanwhile trying to protect his innocent young wife from various vicious drug-criminals, both Mexican and American.

It is a magnificent dark nightmare of a picture, and with a splendid cast including, as well as Heston, Leigh and Welles himself, Akim Tamiroff, Dennis Weaver and Joseph Calleia. Welles being Welles, he was also able to call on several highly talented old friends to appear in small roles, unpaid (or working for the union minimum) and usually uncredited. Among them were Keenan Wynn and the chilling Mercedes McCambridge. Marlene did better. For her small role she received a credit and union minimum plus $7,500, although she and Welles both insisted diplomatically she had worked for nothing.

Her role had not even been in the screenplay at all until Welles thought of using her. She was to play a Mexican brothel-madam who is also a fortune-teller. Her costume, which she hastily assembled from various Hollywood costume-departments, was gypsy-like. With dark ringlets, she somewhat resembled the way she looked in *Golden Earrings*. In the part, her sophisticated air of having known so much that she is almost beyond experience, allows her to play what is almost the voice of fate with chilling warmth. Her famous line, the last line of the film, referring to Hank Quinlan, she believed was the best-delivered line of her life – 'He was some kind of a man. (Pause). What does it matter what you say about people?' (A line she always enjoyed repeating.)

Universal were baffled by the finished film. It wasn't at all what they'd bargained for, and they were completely unsure how best to market it. It didn't fit into any known category. As a result they sat on it for several months, which meant that Marlene's next picture was finished and released before it.

That next picture was Billy Wilder's *Witness For The Prosecution*. This was an Agatha Christie piece that began as a novel and had been adapted into a play, which had been successful on both sides of the Atlantic. Marlene's approach to getting the title (and leading female) role was new for her. Made more bold by her success in mounting her own shows, she actively campaigned to get the part.

As so often in the setting up of films, nothing was simple. For a start, the director originally scheduled for the picture by independent producers Edwin Small and Arthur Hornblow Jr had been Joshua Logan. But he turned down the job, and instead they offered it to Wilder, who accepted.

Then rose the question of leading actors. Acting on the sensible principle of not backing films one at a time, Small and Hornblow wanted to follow it by making *Solomon And Sheba*. And to cut costs, they wanted to make a deal whereby the leading actors in *Witness For The Prosecution* would go on to star in that. This, as might be expected, wasn't easy.

They approached William Holden to star in both, but he wasn't available. They approached Tyrone Power, and he said no. Meanwhile, Marlene was campaigning for the female lead. Billy Wilder was on her side, but still a male lead had to be found who would agree to co-star with her. Gene Kelly was approached, and he was agreeable to playing in both films, and to partnering Marlene. At the same time Edwin Small, who was not sure about Marlene in *Solomon And Sheba*, was making offers to both Ava Gardner and Rita Hayworth.

Wilder, refusing to accept Hayworth, proposed Kirk Douglas for the lead – not only because he had worked successfully with Douglas in their film *Ace In The Hole*, but because he knew that Marlene and Kirk had had a brief affair (Marlene had no secrets about their 'affectionate sex'), and thus thought they might have on-screen chemistry. As he worked on the script with writer Harry Kurnitz, he started tilting the role more and more towards Marlene.

Kirk Douglas was either not interested or not available. Scripts were sent to Jack Lemmon and to Glenn Ford. At this point Tyrone Power suddenly became interested after all (the fee he was offered of $300,000 per picture for the two pictures may have had something to do with this, although, as things turned out, he would die before *Solomon And Sheba* was half completed and be replaced by Yul Brynner.

So Power and Dietrich it would be, although soon a third star was to be added. The plot, revolving round a big courtroom scene, needed what Wilder described as a 'cement block', to anchor the story. So as the wily defence lawyer he cast Charles Laughton. He would get second billing, Marlene third.

The plot, much simplified, tells of an elegant middle-class woman, Christine Vole, who defends her husband, Leonard (Tyrone Power) against a charge of murder, by convincing the jury that she is an untrustworthy witness against him. In fact, though knowing him guilty, she loves him enough to try and get him acquitted. She wins her case, at which point he admits that he loves another woman; producing a convenient revolver, she shoots him dead.

Marlene, having seen the play, wanted to play Christine Vole for a very definite and practical reason. She was aware that her one-woman shows were publicizing her widely as 'Dietrich' – the glamorous ever-beautiful icon, as unchangeable as the heavens. And while this was all very reassuring and flattering and financially rewarding, she wanted to show the world that there was more to her than just a magnificent image.

She wanted to show she could act, and as Christine Vole she indeed played a part considerably differently from the familiar image. Christine is not a glamour-queen;, she is a cold, chic woman, capable of plotting, lying and even killing for love. And Marlene, costumed elegantly by Edith Head, played her well.

As one concession to her stage career, Billy did give her a probably unnecessary flashback scene in a pre-war Berlin night-club (to explain how she and her husband met). Looking for a number for her to sing (accompanied by her own accordion) she and Billy dug through the archives and found a German song from between the wars, 'Auf Der Reeperbahn Nachts Um Halb Eins', which literally means 'On The Reeperbahn At Half Past Midnight', but which in its English version became 'I May Never Go Home Any More'. Marlene liked it so much that she sang it regularly in her shows.

During the filming, which took place from June to August 1957, Marlene behaved well. She was happy to be working again with her friend Billy (although they took care not to repeat the mistake of eating Marlene-cooked meals together in her dressing-room during the lunch break). She came on to Tyrone Power, but he turned out to be more embarrassed by her advances than intrigued, and she enjoyed a mutual admiration society with Charles Laughton.

Laughton's wife, Elsa Lanchester, who in the film played his nurse (both she and the lawyer loathing each other), had a more baleful eye. 'Marlene,' she recalled, 'would go to bed early, and get up at 3am and go to [Wally] Westmore at Paramount to be made up. It took two hours to apply her face lifts... They are pink flesh-coloured tabs (rectangular). One end of the tab has two long black threads hanging from it. The tabs are glued to the side of the head where the skin is to be lifted. After they have dried, the threads are woven into hair at the back of the head, forcing the tabs to pull the skin very taut. A wig then covers the network of threads... It is ironic that in an effort to be young, she aged, [because] she dared not pull or twist her face for fear of loosening a lift.'

It is true that in the film Marlene is tight – rather than moving her head, she tends to move her whole body. But this is in the character of Christine Vole, a woman in rigid control of her emotions. Marlene was proud of her characterization, even hoping that it might win her an Oscar (at the time she phoned veteran Hollywood reporter Radie Harris, asking her to please hint in her column that she ought to get one – although later she would claim, in her memoirs, that winning an Oscar for *Witness For The Prosecution* meant 'nothing at all to me'). As it turned out, she wasn't even nominated.

After the filming was completed, Marlene returned to New York. Again she attended theatres with Noël Coward, and she spent time with Maria and William and her grandsons. But she was lonely. She spent much time in 1958 making short trips around America, visiting anyone she could think of that she knew even slightly.

It was a quiet year for her. Early in it she made her annual appearance at Las Vegas, now earning $40,000 a week for her four weeks. Her show image was by now sufficiently well-known that Carol Channing could incorporate an imitation of her in her own act. While in Las Vegas, Marlene went to see it. Channing, wearing a diaphanous *négligée*, lay on the floor waving her mesh-clad legs at the ceiling and, in an exaggerated German accent, chattered on about 'herself' – about her songs, her films, her wardrobe, her travels, her war service, and ended by saying, 'But enough about me – let's talk about *you* for while. What do you think of my outfit? Is it too flimsy for a grandmother?'

The management, aware that Marlene was in the audience, swung a spotlight on her to see her reaction, just in time to catch her rising majestically to her feet and sweeping out. She soon transmitted a request to Channing that she drop the impersonation, but Channing, knowing she was onto a good thing, continued to use it for several years.

Maria had spent much of 1957 as part of a touring company performing *Tea And Sympathy*, the then-fashionable play attempting (albeit a little timidly) to deal with the subject of homosexuality, but finally came to the conclusion that acting was not for her. In 1958 she bore a third son, John Paul, and shortly afterwards she and her family decided to emigrate to London.

Marlene began doing weekly five-minute spots on the NBC radio program *Monitor*, dispensing advice to the uncertain. They were not always hugely helpful, including such bromides as 'Know your own limitations and be realistic about them. If you are a good carpenter, take pride in being a good carpenter.' And 'Teenagers must be patient, more tolerant of our failures. We have some love and some wisdom to give, and of course we have to maintain our sense of humour.'

From April to June 1959 a retrospective of her films was held at New York's Museum of Modern Art, who called it *Marlene Dietrich: Image And Legend*. It was the first time any such retrospective had been held celebrating the work of a star, and Marlene co-operated fully in its planning, lending photographs of herself from her own collection, and helping prepare a compilation of clips from her films. At the opening of the retrospective, on 7 April, she wore a Jean Louis gown from *The Monte Carlo Story* (one of silver lamé overprinted with gold) and followed the showing of the compilation with a speech (carefully written by herself), saying to the audience:

Thank you – and I don't ask you who you were applauding – the legend, the performer, or me. I, personally, liked the legend. Not that it was easy to live with – but I liked it. Maybe because I felt privileged to witness its creation at such close quarters. I never had any ambition to become or be a film star, but the fascination this creating process held for me gave me the élan to work and work very hard to please Mr von Sternberg. When I say work very hard I mean it... The legend served me well, and I venture to say it served well all the other directors who took over after he decided I should go on alone... It has been said that I was Trilby to his Svengali. I would rather say I was Eliza to his Henry Higgins.

The event was such a success that it was repeated on a morning ten days later, especially for students of film. Although that too was a success, the whole retrospective did nothing to help her get films to make (although it did revive interest, which has never since died, in the work of Josef von Sternberg).

It was disappointing to Marlene that her retrospective, let alone her performance in *Witness For The Prosecution*, of which she had been proud, led to no more film work. Gradually she realised that her central career from now on must be her shows, which she set about developing with more energy than ever.

14 One-Woman

Marlene began planning a three-city tour of South America, with performances in Rio de Janeiro, São Paulo and Buenos Aires. Her retinue for touring, as well as her line of girl dancers, would typically include a hairdresser and a wardrobe mistress, sometimes her manager (Major Donald Neville-Whiting, who had been the impresario of London's Café de Paris), her secretary and choreographer Bernard Hall, and, most important of all, her musical director, Burt Bacharach.

Bacharach, who had by now embarked on a successful career as a songwriter, was a tower of strength. He helped her to choose and pace her songs, created new and more up-to-date arrangements for her, specially written to support and highlight her voice, and guided her in varying her delivery more – when to croon, when to purr, when to insinuate, when to belt it out. He became to her shows what von Sternberg had been to her films. As she herself said, he was 'my director, my teacher, my maestro'.

He was also her lover, having had the good fortune when they first met to be suffering from a cold, which at once brought out all her tender loving care and vitamin C tablets. 'He was,' she wrote, 'the most important man in my life after I decided to dedicate myself to the stage... I lived only for the performances and for him. On tour, I washed his shirts and socks. In short, I took care of him as if he were my saviour.'

But in spite of all the kind words she said about Bacharach being her teacher and her maestro, he was never her director (except in a musical sense). She was now in total control of her career and of the way she was presented to her audiences. More and more she came to despise the years she had spent in films, subject to the demands of a string of directors ('my dictators', she took to calling them).

Her appearances became orchestrated, both on stage and off. When she arrived at Rio de Janeiro, on an afternoon in July 1959, she was mobbed at the airport by an estimated twenty-five thousand fans, many of them professional extras paid to be there. Her appearance was a huge success, as it would be in São Paolo and in Buenos Aires. There she was mobbed again as she attempted to enter and inspect the theatre where she was to perform, and she appeared to faint. Photos hit the wire services of police carrying her inert body through the crowds, but as she later candidly admitted, 'I didn't really faint, but it was the only way I could get inside. Besides, there were many photographers present, and it was a good chance for publicity.' After this she demanded police protection when she arrived in the evening for her show.

Her performance continued to evolve. Her dresses, while still by Jean Louis, and still in the same style, were no longer quite as see-through. Also, as her figure began to shrink with increasing age, she began to wear under her dresses a padded foundation garment that was the exact shape she had been in her prime. Nor did she any longer open with a drawn-out 'Hellooooo', but briefly inspected the audience with mock-surprise and launched straight into whatever was to be her opening number. Her patter between songs changed subtly too, from more or less straight reminiscence to a heightened, romantic view of her life, more highly coloured and less slavish about the facts.

Towards the end of November 1959 she took her show to Paris. As planned, she was met off her plane at Orly by Maurice Chevalier and by her wartime acquaintance Jean-Pierre Aumont. She was to appear at the Théâtre de l'Etoile, where the Parisian audience was prepared to be *blasé*. Boldly, she made no attempt to woo them. Introduced fulsomely by Maurice Chevalier, she strode the stage like an empress, singing in near-faultless French and almost daring them not to like her. It wasn't long before they did, and their liking grew to enchantment and then noisy adoration. *'Marlene Triomphe!'* read one review headline. *'Une Auguste Simplicité'* read another.

Noël Coward, oddly enough, slightly misunderstood what she was up to, noting in his diary, 'Marlene is a fabulous success. She looks ravishing and tears the place up. Privately I didn't like anything she did except "One for My Baby". She has developed a hard, brassy assurance and she belts out every song harshly and without finesse. All her aloof, almost lazy glamour has been overlaid by a noisy "take-this-and-like-it" method which, to me, is disastrous. However the public loved it.'

She had also added a new song to her repertoire – one that was something of a departure for her. It was a recent popular song, Pete Seeger's 'Where Have All The Flowers Gone?', and it had been brought to her attention by her daughter Maria. At first she was doubtful. After all, this was an anti-war song and, while she understood the tragedy of war, she had never been a pacifist. But both Maria and Bacharach urged her to try it. He made her an arrangement of it, and in Paris she tried it out. Soon she came to love it. She could sympathise with its feeling of regret about young lives lost in battle, and furthermore, she discovered it translated easily into both French and German. It would become a regular part of her repertoire, as, in its wake, would Bob Dylan's 'Blowin' In The Wind'.

Off stage in Paris, she socialised with Noël Coward. Also with Orson Welles, Margo Lion, Jean Cocteau, Jean Marais, Jean-Pierre Aumont (and his wife, Marisa Pavan – twin sister of Pier Angeli), and with the Italian actor Raf Vallone. Vallone, then in his early forties, was extremely good-looking, and Marlene, in spite of her ongoing relationship with Burt Bacharach, began a brief tempestuous affair with him. After finishing her run in Paris, she hastened back to Las Vegas to make her annual appearance there, then, early in 1960, hastened to Rome to spend time with Raf.

Bacharach, meanwhile, was hard at work planning another European tour. This would be a brave step for Marlene – it was to be a tour of Germany, and she needed all Bacharach's support and encouragement to undertake it. How would she be received? Would she even be safe?

The tour, promoted by American jazz impresario Norman Granz and a German colleague, Kurt Collien, would include concerts in Berlin, Hamburg, Oldenburg, Düsseldorf, Essen, Cologne, Hanover, Wiesbaden, Munich, Stuttgart, Frankfurt and Vienna, and for each she would receive the equivalent of almost $4,000. To help publicise the tour, it was arranged that *Destry Rides Again*, never before seen in Germany, would be shown at local cinemas.

Once the news of her forthcoming appearance was announced in the German press, in March 1960, articles, editorials and letters began to appear there, mostly denouncing her. 'Who has invited this person who worked against us during the war to perform as a visiting actress? Marlene, go home!' was a typical reaction. 'Aren't you, a base and filthy traitor, ashamed to set foot on German soil? You should be lynched, since you are the most wretched war criminal,' said a letter. (It should be remembered that most Germans had heard little about her, except filtered through the propaganda of Goebbels, since about 1934. It was his image of her as a money-grabbing traitor that many of them held in their minds.)

While all this was brewing, Marlene, with her chorus-line and supporting staff, fulfilled a three-week engagement at Lake Tahoe, Nevada, after which she and Bacharach set off for Paris, where she had arranged fittings at Dior and Balenciaga. On 14 April they stopped off in London, and there she was taken out to dinner by Noël Coward. To him she admitted her trepidation. As his diary recorded, 'She was in a dim mood, because all is in a state of chaos [and] the German press has come out against her.'

Much of the chaos arose from cancellations. In the face of so much public opposition to her, first her Vienna appearance was cancelled, then the one in Essen. Eventually, out of seventeen towns and cities that had originally accepted her, five withdrew, and the number of concerts she was to give in Berlin dwindled from five to three. But determinedly she pressed on.

When she met Art Buchwald in Paris, she told him, 'I don't understand it. Before the war I was attacked by Goering for becoming an American citizen. After the war I was attacked by the German press because I wouldn't come to Germany, and *now* they're attacking me because I am going. The logic...escapes me.'

She flew into Berlin on 30 April, fifteen years after last being there, and was met at the airport by a reception committee headed by Mayor Willi Brandt, who escorted her to the town hall in Schöneberg, close to where she was born, to sign her name in the Golden Book of honoured visitors.

She was not to give her first performance for a few days, and in between she was taken on a tour of the UFA studios, where she spent quite a while, chatting to staff from the highest to the lowest, and being greeted by two Hollywood Berliners. One was Wilhelm (or William) Dieterle, who had directed her in *The Man By The Wayside* back in 1923 and in *Kismet* in 1944. He had recently returned to Germany, and would shortly retire. The other was Kurt (or Curtis) Bernhardt, who had directed her in 1929 in *The Woman One Longs For*, and who was simply over from California on a visit.

Her opening night took place on 3 May, at the Titania-Palast, where she had sung in 1945 for members of the forces of occupation. Of its 1800 seats, only 1400 were occupied, many of those by people given free tickets to fill out the house. This was only partly because of hostility to her; it was also partly because many Berliners simply couldn't afford the prices.

As in Paris, her approach to her audience was tailored to the occasion. While it was romantic, even nostalgic, there was no note in it of apology for herself or her life. (At a press conference in her hotel room, at which she wore her ribbon of the Légion d'Honneur, she told a reporter, 'I am not particularly glad to be here or there or anywhere. All my former friends here either left Germany or died in concentration camps, and so there are none left for me to see.') Her programme of songs was also specially tailored. Burt Bacharach had worked hard, writing arrangements for almost a dozen German songs she had never before sung in her shows, quite a few of them written by Frederick Hollander back in the good old days.

She opened with the two songs she felt most likely to be remembered – 'Falling In Love Again' (her usual closer) and 'Lola'. She bravely included in her programme the German version of 'Lili Marlene', rightly unashamed of her wartime activities, and she ended (by then wearing a white tuxedo) with a song of soft regret, 'Ich Hab' Noch Einen Koffer In Berlin' ('I Still Have A Suitcase In Berlin').

The audience, Willi Brandt among them, gave her a standing ovation. For once she broke her rule and sang encores, and in all she received eighteen curtain calls.

The reviews were enthusiastic. 'She stood there like a queen – proud and sovereign' said *Der Abend*, and the *Berliner-Zeitung* reported, 'She is not only a great artist, she is a lovable woman – she is one of us. Marlene Dietrich has really come home!'

All the same, the enthusiasm and spare cash of Berliners remained limited. At the second of her three nights at the Titania-Palast only five hundred seats were filled, and the management, desperate to get a more respectable house for the third night, announced they would accept East Berlin marks as if they were on a par with those of West Berlin (which they by no means were). By doing that and by giving away even more free tickets, they did manage to almost fill the place.

The rest of the tour went well. She got good houses, and considerable applause, and nobody in any audience threw rotten fruit or bad eggs, as it had been feared someone might. The nearest to this, and it was bad enough, came near the end of her tour, when she was in Düsseldorf. It was 16 May, and as she set off from her hotel, the Park Hotel, to go to the theatre, there were some two thousand fans waiting outside. An eighteen-year-old girl dashed out of the crowd and reached to touch the sleeve of her mink coat. Marlene turned towards her, and the girl began tugging at the coat, as if trying to pull it off her. Then she yelled out 'Traitor!', spat in Marlene's face, and yelled to the crowd, 'I hate this person who betrayed Germany in the war!'.

Bernard Hall was accompanying Marlene at the time, and the shock of this act of hatred stayed with him. Remembering it, he felt it was a pivotal moment in Marlene's life. As he recalled, 'I personally think Marlene had gone to Germany in the first place to see if she might one day go back to retire there, live out her days in her birthplace... Not bloody likely after that spit in the face! That made it clear she could never go home again, because they didn't want her.'

In Wiesbaden she had a different misfortune. While wearing her white tuxedo and high-kicking with her chorus-line, she became a little too enthusiastic and tumbled off the front of the stage. Quickly she scrambled back, waving to the audience and laughing as she brushed off her trousers and rejoined the line. It wasn't till next day that Burt Bacharach managed to persuade her to let him take her to a clinic. It turned out she had broken her collar bone, but she refused to let it deter her. For all her performances, until it healed, she used the belt of her raincoat to strap her upper arm to her body and allowed no audience to guess she was injured.

There were two possible contributory factors to her fall. One suggestion was that she was momentarily blinded by the spotlight that was on her. But it could have been that she was slightly tipsy. More and more, as the years went on, she was taking to sipping scotch and champagne backstage, both before she went on and between numbers, in order to brace herself to perform, which she found physically more difficult as the years passed.

Her last German booking was in Munich, and there she was an undiluted success. Even standing room was sold out. The roof rang with applause from the moment she appeared, and at the end of her show, after endless encores, she was given an astonishing sixty-two curtain calls.

From Germany she and her show went on to appear in Copenhagen, then to Israel, first to Tel Aviv, where she broke a taboo by singing in German (after asking her audience if anyone would object). Nobody did, and she sang them 'Lili Marlene'. This was quite an achievement in view of the fact that, earlier the same month (June), Sir John Barbirolli had had to conduct the choral parts of Mahler's Second Symphony in an English translation. 'It's bad enough to lose your Fatherland,' she told the audience. 'I couldn't give up the language too.' At the end of the show they applauded her for thirty-five minutes.

She performed in Jerusalem, and in Haifa, and offered to stay on in Israel for an unscheduled extra day to give a benefit concert for Israeli orphans. By eleven o'clock on the morning after she made the offer, the concert was sold out, on word of mouth alone.

During July, taking a break from performing, she attended the Locarno Film Festival, where she and Josef von Sternberg were to be jointly honoured. There was a screening of *The Blue Angel* and *The Devil Is A Woman*, then a formal dinner, after which both director and star were asked for their comments. These comments fell somewhat short of being illuminating. Von Sternberg, now living in cultured semi-retirement in California, although quietly pleased that his films were by now increasingly respected, simply said politely how grateful he was to be so honoured. And Marlene discouraged detailed questioning by simply declaring, 'As an actress, I belong to an album of souvenirs, an album that will remain silent.' She was, of course, off her home ground. This was not an audience for one of her shows, nor a dinner-party of friends, to either of which she might have held forth. And besides, von Sternberg was there. To him, on such an occasion, she would still defer.

Then it was back to a punishing touring schedule. During the remainder of 1960 she performed in Paris, Brussels, Dallas, Los Angeles, Toronto and San Francisco. And in January 1961 she was booked for a fortnight in Boston, where attendance figures were poor on account of continual blizzards during the first week.

Shortly after Boston, she signed a contract to appear in another film. This would give her, even more than *Witness For The Prosecution* had done, a chance to appear as a character completely different from her glamorous stage persona. The film was *Judgment At Nuremberg*, based on the trials of Nazi war criminals, and she would play the supporting role of Frau Bertholt, widow of an executed German general.

It wasn't easy for producer/director Stanley Kramer to get her to play the role. She needed absolute reassurance that his film (scripted by Abby Mann) would be honest and thoughtful. It would be. Stanley Kramer was nothing if not honest and thoughtful. He had honest and thoughtful to burn, turning out in the Fifties and Sixties a series of earnest socially conscious films such as *The Defiant Ones*, *On The Beach* and *Guess Who's Coming To Dinner?*

Which is not to say that they did not on occasion contain excellent performances, and Marlene, once she had accepted her role, gave a good one. The film had a long shooting schedule, from near the end of January right on through May 1961, although Marlene was only on call during April. She had insisted on her costumes being designed by Jean Louis, who fitted her out in simple black elegance, appropriate to an officer's widow. Once on the set, with the approval of director and writer, she worked hard at polishing her dialogue, making sure it was appropriate to the character she was to play and incorporating memories from her own upbringing. As Stanley Kramer observed, 'She understood the implications of the script, the ramifications of German behaviour better than anybody.'

She also, of course, arranged her own lighting. But when she saw the finished film she was displeased. Before starting work on it she had submitted to a fourth face-lift, and it had, for the moment at least, given a tightness to her face, especially around the mouth, that tended to make it look mask-like. This suited the austere and dignified sadness of her character in the film, but was not how she wanted to look.

The filming itself she enjoyed. She had great respect for the star of the film, Spencer Tracy, who played the part of the presiding American judge, and she was proud of the scenes she played with him. They got on well, and she bought strudel and cookies to share with him on the set.

After shooting finished, the next few months were sad ones for her. In May 1961 Gary Cooper died of cancer. He was only just sixty. Marlene attended his funeral in Beverly Hills.

At the beginning of July, her close friend Ernest Hemingway shot himself, the macho front with which he faced the world having at last failed to counteract his inner uncertainties. Marlene later recalled that, on hearing of his death, she felt angry with him (which, she pointed out, is one way of dealing with grief).

And in a way it did not help that Maria, now living in England, gave birth to a fourth son, John David. There was something about the constant procession of generations that was unsettling to anyone attempting to make time stand still.

What did help her morale was that, also in 1961, while visiting Paris, she met the actor Zbigniew Cybulski. Then aged thirty-four, he had leapt to international fame in the Andrzej Wajda film *Popiól I Diament (Ashes And Diamonds)*, set among the wartime Polish resistance. He had a powerful screen presence, handsome and brooding, creating a sense of romantic alienation from the world that, with justice, earned him the description of 'the Polish James Dean'.

He was also bisexual, haunted by anxieties (he was never seen in public without tinted glasses), and over-fond of the odd tipple. Marlene adored him, later telling her friend and biographer David Bret (years after Cybulski's death), 'He was the kindest, the most beautiful man in the whole world. He was so beautiful that every time I see his photograph I cry... [He] was the kind of man any woman would have died for...a god.'

Together they went to see her friend Edith Piaf perform at the Paris Olympia. By this time in her life Marlene had rented an apartment in Paris, on the fourth floor at 12 Avenue Montaigne, and she and Cybulski spent time there. He had a cameo role in the play *Le Thé À La Menthe*, and at the apartment she helped him practise his lines. They became lovers, and would remain so, whenever they met, for the rest of his life.

The publishers Doubleday, who back in 1950 had asked her to write her autobiography for them, had, by the autumn of 1961, rather given up hope of ever receiving it. As a sort of consolation prize, they offered her a contract to compile a book of her opinions on life, interspersed with a few of her favourite recipes. She accepted, and her secretary Bernard Hall helped her to compile it, hunting through the press-clippings albums she had been building up since arriving in America in 1930, for any usable opinions she might ever have expressed.

The book shortly appeared, entitled *Marlene Dietrich's ABC*. It contained (among her recipes) lamb chops, goulash and pot-au-feu, and among her opinions – 'Egocentric: If he is a creative artist, forgive him.' 'Gabin, Jean: A magnificent actor without knowing the tools of the trade. Rough outside – tender inside. Easy to love.' 'Germany: The tears I have shed over Germany have dried. I have washed my face.' 'Nail polish: Dark nail polish is vulgar.'

Apart from working on her *ABC*, the second half of 1961 was a quiet time for Marlene, although in December things perked up a little. She recorded the commentary for an allegorical documentary film about the rise of Hitler and Nazism, based on a fable by Goethe called *Reineke-Fuchs (Reynard The Fox)* and itself called *The Black Fox*. This would win the year's Oscar for the best feature-length documentary.

In the same month, on 14 December, *Judgment At Nuremberg* was premièred. For ill-judged reasons, Stanley Kramer had decided to give it its first showing in Berlin, possibly believing that Germans were ready by 1961 to be told by America exactly how they had gone wrong.

Some of the film's stars went to Berlin to attend the showing – Spencer Tracy went (accompanied by Katharine Hepburn), as did Montgomery Clift (who showed up on the stage drunk). But not Marlene. In discussions with

Stanley Kramer she explained to him that, in the light of her recent reception there, it was possible that her presence might do more harm to the film than good. Which, he had to agree, was true.

As things turned out, nothing could have harmed the film in Berlin. The general feeling among the audience at the première was cold outrage. At a party afterwards, set up to cater for a thousand invited guests, only about a hundred turned up. The run of the film, planned to follow the première, was cancelled.

Five days later, on 19 December, it opened in New York, with a première that Marlene did attend. It was greeted with reverent respect and eventually nominated for eleven Oscars, of which it was awarded two. Abby Mann won one for his screenplay, and the Austrian actor Maximilian Schell, who had played the part of a defence attorney, and who had spent his time on the film reassuring everybody ('every hour, on the hour,' remembered Kramer) that he was not German, won the Oscar for Best Actor.

To close the year, Marlene returned to Las Vegas to present her show at the Sands Hotel, again for four weeks. But performing was getting harder. The circulation in her legs, now that she had turned sixty, was poor (a legacy of years of heavy smoking). Her ankles had a tendency to swell, and the high heels she wore in performance didn't help.

Nor were lifts, such as Elsa Lanchester had described, sufficient any more to pull her face into youthful tautness. By 1961 she was braiding her hair to sterile surgical needles, which were then embedded in her scalp, daubed with antiseptic and concealed under her wig, and from 1962 her Jean Louis gowns were made to fit her so tightly that she could take only the tiniest of steps in them.

The touring continued. Among the American cities she performed in over the next two years would be Washington, Minneapolis, Los Angeles, San Francisco, Dallas, Colorado Springs, and of course Las Vegas, where she now appeared at the Riviera. Outside America she would play Toronto, Vancouver, Tokyo, Johannesburg, Stockholm, Cardiff, Edinburgh, and the resort of Taormino, in Sicily.

Many of her shows were recorded and issued on LP by Columbia, and Marlene kept a careful eye on the production of these LP's. No performance of a song went out that she did not approve, and although her applause at many concerts went on for several minutes, she was not above extending it by mixing in repeated passages. As a gift to her (and maybe with tongue in cheek), Columbia boss Goddard Lieberson pressed a private LP for her consisting of nothing but her ovations.

This was not perhaps the best idea he ever had. Marlene had already enjoyed playing tapes or records of her applause to people. One journalist had had to listen to the ten-minute ovation she got in Rio de Janeiro, and another, in 1960, was made to listen through all sixty-two of her Munich curtain-calls. Now she had the LP. When Judy Garland was interviewed by Jack Paar on NBC Television's *Tonight Show*, she remembered a social evening when Marlene had played the whole thing to captive friends. 'We sat there listening for *hours*,' she remembered, 'and I turned to Noël and whispered, "I hope there isn't another side," and Noël just looked at me. There *was*!!'

Late in 1962, Marlene went to Switzerland and entered the well-known rejuvenation clinic, run by Dr Paul Niehans, at Clarens, near Vevey. There she was injected with chemicals and hormones (derived from the cells of unborn lambs). It was a popular treatment at the time, and she would continue to make regular trips to Dr Niehans for the next dozen years.

After her spell at the clinic, she stayed in Switzerland and spent Christmas with Marti Stevens and Noël Coward, at a chalet he had rented. Then it was back to the touring.

In the autumn of 1963 she went with Zbigniew Cybulski ('Spishek', she called him) to the Edinburgh Festival, where he was appearing in a play. He was a success, and fêted as a celebrity, although his natural shyness meant that when not on public display he mostly stayed quietly out of the limelight, getting drunk with Kenneth Tynan and learning the words to dubious songs. And, of course, sneaking off for private *tête-à-tête*s with Marlene.

At around the same time, she was asked by Noël Coward if she would do a small walk-on role, playing herself, in a Paramount comedy he was making, called *Paris When It Sizzles*. Although written by the talented comedy-writer George Axelrod, and co-produced by him and by the film's director, Richard Quine, it turned out insufficiently lively. Marlene, while happy enough to have a paid-for trip to Paris, had little to do. All she does in the finished film is step out of a white Rolls Royce (herself dressed in white), and silently enter the front door of the House of Dior. As it happened, this was not all that far from her apartment.

Not long after this, she lost two of her Paris friends. On 10 October 1963, Edith Piaf died. Jean Cocteau, on hearing the news, was deeply distressed, and the next day, while he was preparing a eulogy for her, to be read on the radio, he too died.

Marlene soldiered on, appearing that same month at the Albert Hall in London, as a guest singer at the annual reunion for veterans of El Alamein – the Desert Rats. And on 4 November, still in London, she was top of the bill at the Prince of Wales Theatre in a Royal Command Performance, attended by the Queen Mother. Also in the show were pianist Erroll Garner, the cast of the stage musical *Pickwick* (led by Harry Secombe), the cast of the musical *Half A Sixpence* (led by Tommy Steele), and the newest pop sensation, The Beatles. Marlene, ever young, claimed they 'electrified' her.

At the beginning of 1964, Marlene set off, with Burt Bacharach and the other members of her show, to tour behind the Iron Curtain. She would begin in Poland, and on 16 January she flew from Paris to Warsaw, and two hours after landing gave a press conference at the Hôtel Eurpejski. Zbigniew Cybulski was in Warsaw at the time, and she had sent messages asking him to be there, but he did not show up. (Later he would claim to her that he was terrified by the idea of meeting her on his home territory, although possibly what was bothering him was what the effect on his image might be if it was known that he was having a relationship with a woman so much older than himself.)

Marlene wasn't at all sure what kind of reception she might get in Poland. Poles had seen many of her films, albeit in censored versions, this being part of the Soviet Union, but they had no idea of what she might be like as a singer-entertainer. But her press conference went well. Poles were well-disposed towards her because of her record in fighting the Nazis.

She gave six concerts at Warsaw's Palace of Culture. It had been planned that she would give one concert a day for three days, but such was the demand for tickets that she doubled up her schedule and gave two a day. All were sold out. In deference to Polish feelings, of the fifteen or so songs she sang at each show, only one was in German – Max Colpet's song 'Allein In Einer Grossen Stadt' ('Alone In A Big City'). She didn't sing 'Lili Marlene'.

Her audiences were so enthusiastic that here again, as in Germany, she sang encores, eventually having no option but to reprise songs she had already sung. And Cybulski did show up to her concerts – in fact he attended all six of them. Between shows he escorted her on a visit to the old part of the city, where she wished to place a wreath on the Memorial of the Warsaw Uprising, erected to commemorate those who died in the Ghetto.

He did not go with her when the Association of Polish Theatre and Film Artists gave her a formal reception, or when she went to address the Polish University Students' Debating Society on the subject of the war. But he did accompany her when, after her final Warsaw concert, she went to a coffee house, the Café Oczki, to meet members of the Polish Medical Students' Film Club. She answered their questions about her life in Berlin, and her life in Hollywood, using a mixture of French, German and English, and speaking through a translator who had met her back in the Twenties when he was a boy and his father had been Polish military attaché in Berlin.

The evening turned into rather a riotous one. There was vodka available as well as coffee, and everybody got a bit inebriated. The café happened to have a beat-up piano, and by luck there was a student there who knew many of her records, and who was musician enough to be able to play them for her. Marlene sang through the night, and there came a moment late on when she was perched on Cybulski's shoulders wearing his windcheater (it was part of his hip image to wear a windcheater), and singing out through an open window to a group of student fans clustered round it in the icy cold.

She felt so appreciated in Warsaw that, when she was leaving, she broke down in tears at the airport. Eventually collecting herself, she told the fans who had come to see her off (Cybulski not among them), 'I don't want to say goodbye – just let this be au revoir, until the next time.'

Then it was on to Moscow, where she was booked to appear at the Variety Theatre, which seated eleven thousand. Her hotel room was somewhat spartan, as was usual in Russia, and to Marlene this austerity spelt uncleanness, so she made sure to scrub, wax and disinfect it. She also did this to her dressing-room at the theatre.

The theatre was booked solid, in spite of the fact that Russians had seen even fewer of her films than Poles had, and had no idea of her stage act. For them she sang mainly popular ballads and folk songs, and again was a great success. She took eleven curtain calls, and then, as the audience continued to applaud, returned from her dressing-room for a twelfth, barefoot and wearing a blue cotton wrap. 'I cannot speak Russian, which is very sad,' she said in English. 'I can tell you I have always loved you, loved you for your great writers, your poets and your composers, and for the Russian soul. And so I will learn Russian and come back to you again and sing to you in Russian.' She knew how to be what people wanted her to be.

After one concert in Moscow, she went by train to the great city of Leningrad (formerly, and now once again, St Petersburg), where her performance was again a success. The Russian author, Konstantin Paustovsky, came on stage to thank her, and she at once knelt at his feet. A poet was to be honoured.

She went on to Riga, then back to Moscow, making one appearance in each. She seduced and enthralled her audiences, as she could everywhere, but increasingly a new habit of hers was showing itself. She was becoming, and would remain, short-tempered with reporters. When one Russian asked her a question relating to her wardrobe and her good looks, she slapped him down with, 'That's the same kind of stupid, boring old question.'

She was like this everywhere. Back in the States, she lectured a group of pressmen, 'You are the dumbest people in America. I have never heard of such stupid questions.' And in an exchange a few years later, with the fashionable interviewer Rex Reed, she complained, 'That horrible woman from the *New York Times* came to ask me if I like long skirts or short skirts. Fashion bores me. Why don't they ask me about important things, like women's liberation?'

'Okay', said Reed, 'what do you think about women's liberation?'

'Nothing,' she replied. 'It bores me.'

A lot of her problem was that much of the time she was simply exhausted, and as the years passed she would become increasingly irascible with her work colleagues too. And the more often she was irascible, the easier it came to her to be so, as happens with any feeling.

Another reason for her irascibility was that in 1963 she had given up smoking, encouraging herself to do so by making a bet with Noël Coward that she could give up more easily than he could. With the stronger willpower, she won, and the cigarette, which had for so long been a part of the old Marlene image, disappeared from her life for ever.

At least, from her physical life. She continued to crave cigarettes, often even dreaming of them, and she encouraged those around her to smoke like kipper-houses, and if possible blow the smoke in her direction.

In July 1964 she took her show to South Africa, playing a concert in Johannesburg, and it was on her way back from there, while she was giving a performance in a club in Cannes, that a photographer employed by Zsa Zsa Gabor, who was present, took an on-stage picture of her. Startled by the flash, Marlene immediately stopped in mid-show and demanded that the camera be handed to her and the photographer ejected. Zsa Zsa pretended to placate her. 'So he will give you the film, darling,' she said. 'Anyway, he couldn't sell it for a penny.'

By the end of that year, at the beginning of December 1964, she was back in London, this time at the Queen's Theatre on Shaftesbury Avenue. Her act had changed again. Gone was the line of chorus-girls. Gone was her quick change into top hat and tails (which had become increasingly difficult for her). Now her show was simpler, stronger and longer. It was all Marlene.

Harold Hobson, reviewer for the London *Times*, was not alone in finding her illusion spellbinding. Moved by her performance, he wrote:

> Not all the sirens in Homer could sing ['Where Have All The Flowers Gone'] as Miss Dietrich sings it. [She] is grave and thoughtful, and beneath the dusky tones of her low and quiet voice there is a mastered passion, a controlled tempest of emotion. Her pale beauty is quite extraordinary; what makes it unique is that she looks as if she has brought it back from the gates of hell. It is an appalled and a significant beauty... It is the face of someone who has seen unmentionable things, the massacre of children... This of course is only an appearance. It tells us nothing of the real experience of Miss Dietrich. But on the stage it is tremendous, an unforgettable thing... It exalts, it strengthens, and we leave the theatre with hearts uplifted... The world seems a better and braver place, and a happier one.

Off stage, her life continued to bring troubles. Even as she was giving the performance that Hobson so admired, she feared that she had cancer of the cervix. The month after her run at the Queen's, she was in Switzerland attending a gynaecologist, who confirmed to her that, yes, she had. This news was particularly frightening for her because she knew that thirteen years earlier the stage star Gertrude Lawrence had died of just that ailment (while co-starring in the Broadway run of *The King And I*, with Yul Brynner).

It was arranged that she would have radiotherapy, and while still in Switzerland she was given radium implants. Fortunately these would cure her, but the strain of the whole business tended to make her drink more and become even moodier.

1965 was a poor year for her personally. Towards the end of March she learned that Tamara was dead, murdered by a fellow-inmate at Camarillo. She was buried in the Russian Orthodox section of Hollywood Park Cemetery, under her real name, Tamara Nikolaevna. As soon as she could, Marlene flew with Bernard Hall to California to spend two weeks with Rudi, who was still in poor health. There, still undergoing radiotherapy, she cooked and scrubbed and washed and ironed, while Bernard Hall worked around the little farm, doing such chores as feeding chickens and goats, and weeding strawberry beds. Rudi, who Bernard found to be now a gentle, courtly old man, was broken-hearted at losing Tamara. He said such bitter things that Marlene, driving away with Bernard as they left, burst into tears, convinced her husband no longer loved her.

Also in 1965, von Sternberg published his book of memoirs, *Fun In A Chinese Laundry* (the title taken from that of an early silent film made by the Edison studio, and hinting at his amused contempt for the whole business of film-making). It is a witty, intelligent, bitter book, and his chapter on Marlene reveals clearly how deep his feeling for her had been and remained. But his disappointment that their personal relationship had never been all he might have wished shines through in his ironic accurate assessments of her.

When he first met her, he said, 'She was frank and outspoken to a degree that some might have termed tactless. Her personality was one of extreme sophistication and of an almost childish simplicity.' He had obviously continued to follow her career with attention, praising her for breaking Israel's taboo by singing on stage in German, and saying she was, 'no ordinary woman; her ability to enrapture our jury of peers is remarkable.' And of her attitude to himself, he said, 'Her constant praise is rated as one of her admirable virtues – by others, not by me. She has never ceased to proclaim that I taught her everything. Among the many things I did not teach her was to be garrulous about me.'

Marlene, after reading a copy of the book, burnt it. This was not the sort of praise she either asked for or wanted.

More to her taste was that the same year Israel awarded her its Medallion of Valour for her wartime work in fighting fascism. The news of this was announced on American radio, and von Sternberg happened to hear it in his Westwood home. One of his film students who was there asked him, 'Do you ever hear from her?'

'Only when she *needs* something,' he said.

In the autumn of 1965, Burt Bacharach was in London, busy writing and conducting the score (including the title song) for the Peter Sellers film *What's New, Pussycat?*, which was directed by Clive Donner. Marlene, who was to appear in London, joined him there, and so, just before Marlene's show, did film star Angie Dickinson. Clive Donner was present (at Angie's request) when Bacharach explained to Marlene that he and Angie were going to be married, that he now wanted a settled married life (in California), and that he was, after almost twelve years, going to leave the Dietrich entourage.

As the quiet and courteous Donner recalled, 'Marlene went into a fury, more in sorrow than in anger, perhaps, but it looked and sounded a good deal like anger. [She expressed] a certain helplessness without Bacharach that was completely contradicted by the imperiousness of her rage. She told him he was ruining *his* career. Not by leaving her to compose and conduct for films, but by marrying somebody who wasn't a *star*.'

In spite of her outrage, Marlene gave an impressive show, after which she and Bacharach travelled to Scotland, where she was to appear in the Edinburgh Festival. Angie went with them, and Marlene, on arrival in Edinburgh, at once caused considerable upheaval by insisting that the Festival's official programme must be withdrawn from circulation. She did not approve of the photograph of her that adorned its cover, and ordered all the twenty thousand copies printed to be destroyed.

After the Festival, Bacharach ceased to work as her conductor, pianist and musical director. But he did make sure that she had a replacement. In fact, two. The job of conducting for her would in future be shared by an Englishman, William Blezard, and an American, Stan Freeman (who had played harpsichord on her records with Rosemary Clooney). But neither would replace Bacharach as her musical Svengali – after he left, the songs she sang changed little, and her act tended to set into a predictable routine. While she would not exactly be 'helpless' without him, there had been some truth in what she said.

Early in 1966 she began touring again. In February she returned to Warsaw, and this time, to her delight, Zbigniew Cybulski did meet her off the plane. She was so happy to be with him again that she let him attend her rehearsals, a privilege that by now she granted to few. She even sang a couple of songs simply because he liked them.

Within ten days she had given six concerts in Warsaw, five in Gdansk, and two in Wroclaw (known to Germans, who had annexed it for over two hundred years, as Breslau). Her final concert was one of the six in Warsaw, and at the end of it Cybulski came on stage and presented flowers to her. And when she left to fly to Paris, he came with her to the airport.

By the autumn she was broaching a new continent, making her first tour of Australia. In Melbourne, fans were so pleased to see her that the crush round her cracked two of her fragile ribs, and it was reported in *Variety* that her performance received an ovation 'as great, if not greater, than that [recently] accorded Joan Sutherland.' In Sydney, where she was the last great star ever to appear at the soon-to-be-demolished Theatre Royal, her ovation went on for fifty minutes, until even she had to beg the audience, 'Please go home, I'm *tired*!'

While in Sydney she was approached by a twenty-five-year-old journalist, Hugh Curnow, who pestered her to give him an interview, saying he needed the job to buy food for his children (of which he and his wife genuinely did have three). Although her conductor on her Australian tour, William Blezard, didn't take to Curnow at all, calling him 'a dreadful opportunist', something about him appealed to Marlene.

The publishers Doubleday (although she had cobbled together *Marlene Dietrich's ABC* for them) still had an agreement with her that she would someday write her memoirs for them. But fifteen years had gone by and, the publishing world being what it is, the rights to them had somehow passed to the firm of Macmillan, who were gently pressuring her to put pen to paper. She offered the job of ghost-writing them to Curnow. He accepted, and she arranged with the Sunday newspaper he worked for to get him leave of absence while he came to Paris to work with her, burrowing though her scrapbooks.

Curnow came to live with her in her Paris apartment, and naturally they became lovers. But he was not one to keep secrets. In letters to fellow-journalist Charles Higham (who in 1977 would become a Dietrich biographer himself), he revealed, 'She's made of finest steel, [but] totally without shame in her vanity.' Bound by 'bandages' to keep her figure trim, she had to be '*unwound* – like a mummy!' by her maid.

He also revealed in his letters to Higham that he didn't much enjoy their sex life, becoming weary of Marlene's eternal preference for oral sex. Eventually he was rash enough to complain to Marlene herself about this. She threw him out. The memoirs were shelved, and the advance she had been paid for them was eventually returned to Macmillan.

While delighted to have seen so much of Zbigniew Cybulski during her tour of Poland, Marlene had been a little concerned about him. He seemed not to be looking after himself – drinking too much, which had led to him putting on a little weight. Over the months since she had seen him, Polish friends kept her aware of his condition, and she became alarmed at hearing that he was desperate without her, and drinking even more. So alarmed that at the beginning of January 1967 she hastened to Wroclaw, where he was filming, booked herself into the Hôtel Metropol and sent word to him that she would be there.

They spent several healing days together. Then she wanted to visit Warsaw, and a certain amount of dithering went on. In spite of his continuing filming commitments, Cybulski decided he would go with her. He booked them both couchettes on the midnight train, and then reluctantly decided that perhaps it would be better if he stayed. As she recalled: 'We said our farewells, and although his heart was aching he gave me his word that he would catch up with me as soon as he had finished working on his film.'

Then came disaster. Cybulski suddenly decided at the last minute that he could not bear to let her go without him. He dashed to the station in time to see her train pulling out. Trying to jump aboard it while it was accelerating (a stunt he had performed in one of his films), he fell under the wheels and was killed. It was 8 January, 1967.

Nobody told Marlene, even when the train, after an emergency stop, was shunting to and fro as station staff struggled to free his body, and she asked someone what was the matter. As the night was cold, she was given extra blankets and something hot to drink, and told to try and sleep.

In the early morning, as the train pulled into Warsaw, she was eventually told. Naturally distraught, she was allowed to stay on the train till she could pull herself together, and reporters waiting to interview her were requested not to mention the accident. They dutifully didn't, and somehow she got through their questioning.

During the rest of 1967 she would tour Australia, Scandinavia, Canada, South Africa, Japan, Israel, Denmark, England, Scotland and Wales, still playing to packed houses. In Australia she appeared at the Adelaide Festival, and while passing through Sydney was approached by Hugh Curnow. She refused to make space for him in her schedule, and later that same day, while covering an oil rig story, he was decapitated by the whirling blade of a helicopter. Marlene was deeply shaken on hearing the news. She blamed herself, telling William Blezard, 'If I hadn't come to Adelaide, it wouldn't have happened.'

Later in the year, appearing in Liverpool, she had a small family reunion when she was visited backstage by her cousin Hasso, whom she had not seen for thirty years – not since the family had met in Lausanne in 1937 to discuss possibly leaving Germany. By 1967 he had a charming British wife, Shirley, and a British passport. Shirley had naturally met Hasso's mother, Marlene's aunt (or ex-aunt) Jolly, now remarried and living in Switzerland, and on meeting Marlene she was struck by the similarity between the two women. 'The long fingernails, the way [Marlene] wore her jewels, the way she moved, the aura, the glamour, were all the same. They could have been sisters.' Jolly was, after all, only a year or so older than Marlene, and Shirley was not at all surprised when Marlene told her that Jolly was 'the most beautiful woman I ever saw in my life.'

In May, while resting briefly between tours at her Paris apartment, Marlene heard that Rudi had had a near-fatal heart attack, followed by a stroke. He had been rushed into hospital, and she at once cancelled a short holiday she had planned in Switzerland and hurried to his side. When she got there, he was in a coma, and, taking a room in the hospital, she stayed near him for twenty-four hours a day until he recovered consciousness and was pronounced out of danger.

It was clear that, in such poor health and now aged seventy, he would no longer be able to work. With Tamara gone, he had a housekeeper to look after him, but he would be totally dependent on Marlene for his keep.

Maria and her family were not as well off as might be either. Her husband William, after moving to England, had abandoned stage and film design and started up a business designing and making children's toys and games. But it was taking its time establishing itself, even though this was the 'Swinging Sixties', when there seemed to be so much money around in Britain that any new project, especially one involving arts and crafts, could survive. So as he and Maria now had four sons, the younger two at school in England and the older two in Switzerland, they too needed subsidies from grandma.

'Do you think this is glamorous?' she asked an unfortunate reporter who enquired about her life as a performer. 'That this is a great life and I do it for my health? Well, it isn't. It's hard work. And who would work if they didn't have to?' Not only, she claimed, did all the expenses for her shows come out of her own pocket, but she also had to pay the US Internal

Revenue Service eighty-eight cents out of every dollar that she earned. 'So I work. And as long as people want me, and I have them eating out of my hands, I shall continue.'

Although she had by this time performed in major cities all over the world, in every inhabited continent, there was one conspicuous omission. She had never played New York. But Alexander H Cohen had plans to change that. He was one of Broadway's most stylish producers, having put on plays and musicals and one-man shows (including Maurice Chevalier's), as well as mounting the telecasts of the annual Tony awards, and he had been after Marlene for three years. He had had meetings with her on three continents to discuss the matter, but she was afraid of Broadway, fearing its audiences might be too knowing and too hard to please.

He learned that she would be en route from Paris to make a June appearance at Montreal's Expo67, and prevailed on her to stop over in New York and have dinner with him so that they could discuss the matter again. That evening he succeeded in signing her for a six-week run, her one immoveable condition being that he hire (and pay for) Burt Bacharach as her conductor. She also asked for (and got) Joe Davis as her lighting designer, the Lunt-Fontanne Theater to appear in, and she was to receive an enormous forty per cent of the box-office gross, with a guaranteed minimum of $25,000.

She was to open on 9 October 1967. When she arrived at the theatre a few days before, she inspected it and found it to be filthy in spite of its great reputation. She checked every dressing-room, unmolested by security guards because (she pointed out) there weren't any, and set out to scrub out every one. She checked (and mostly also found she had to clean) every phone, light-bulb and air-conditioning filter. She of course checked the condition of the stage – both how clean it was to stand on and how clean it looked from the balcony. She noted that the wallpaper was peeling and that the carpeting, in both public and private areas, was filthy, and declared that the whole place would be a disgrace in the provinces of Romania. Rex Reed learned all this and set it down in a long article in the Sunday *New York Times*, heading it 'Dietrich: I'm Queen of Ajax'.

From her opening night, however, it turned out that she need not have worried about the reception she would get on Broadway. Reviewers adored her, and even if some of them seemed to be adoring her as much as an amazing relic of the past as anything, there was no doubt among them that she was magnificently in command of herself and her audience, and gave a dazzling performance.

Enthusiastic admirers thronged the streets, shouting and cheering, both before and after her performance, and it was the same inside the theatre. After her final number, fans threw flowers onto the stage, from both stalls and balcony. Years later it was admitted by Alex Cohen that many of them were professional extras, hired by Marlene, who also provided the flowers to be thrown. This too, became a regular part of her presentation. In her total professionalism she would even carefully choose which seats the flowers were to be placed on, so that they would shower evenly from all parts of the house.

After the first night there was a celebrity party at the Rainbow Room, for which even Rudi showed up. He was described by Alex Cohen's assistant, Davina Small, as 'shrunken and small and old, but very sweet.'

The six-week run was such a success that Alex organised another similar run for Marlene the next year, in 1968, with the same conditions (Bacharach, Joe Davis, etc), but this time at a different theatre, the Mark Hellinger, which was also not up to Marlene's standards in terms of cleanliness. Alex found her insistence on everything being just right something of a trial. During preparations it was her habit to have hundreds of notes that she typed laboriously herself hand-delivered to him. 'She sits there at her typewriter and bangs away at it,' he complained. 'If she has nothing to complain about, she invents things to keep me on the alert.'

But it all paid off. As well as filling the house every night, in 1968 her show won her a special Tony award (the only professional award she ever received in her life), which she accepted in the annual televised show that Alex produced.

Also on stage in New York in 1968 was Mart Cowley's highly successful play, *The Boys In The Band*. This was the first American play to openly depict the homosexual *milieu* in a hostile and repressive society, and it was bitchy, witty, compassionate and unsparing. Marlene got Alex Cohen to take her to it, and afterwards backstage to meet the all-male cast. She invited all of them to come to her show, and some weeks later, they did (she wasn't at her best that night – several of the 'boys' felt she might even have been slightly intoxicated, and afterwards she apologised to them for a poor performance). She took them to a post-performance meal at Sardi's restaurant, reminiscing to them about her lesbian life in Berlin and claiming,

'I became involved with women when men found me intimidating.' And she took a particular shine to actor Frederick Combs, who in *The Boys In The Band* played a haunted, reluctant homosexual. This motherly interest lasted for only a short while, until it dawned on her that his real-life character was considerably different from his on-stage one. Once she discovered that on the whole he was cheerful, confident and optimistic, she quickly dropped him.

Her friends, depressingly, continued to die. In December 1969, von Sternberg died (she attended his small funeral discreetly, her head shawled, standing in shadow). In September 1970, it was Remarque, and on the first day of 1972, Chevalier. Noël Coward, sympathizing, once said to her, 'All I ask of my friends nowadays is that they live through lunch.'

She herself received increasingly frequent reminders that she was perhaps not immortal. On 7 June 1972, appearing in London, she fell over on stage (from a combination of too-tight gown, too-high heels, and perhaps from herself being a little too high). The rest of the show had to be cancelled.

The Tony awards show in 1968 had been one of her few brief appearances on television, but TV had been on her mind for some time. As long as Maria was successful in the medium, she had rather steered clear of it, but since Maria had retired she had briefly considered several offers. The cosmetics firm, Revlon, for instance, had offered her two million dollars to host a series of specials, and even before that Orson Welles had suggested basing a TV spectacular on the show she had given in Paris in 1959. What had caused her to reject these was a combination of fear of losing control (in TV she would be a technical newcomer), a wish not to tread on Maria's turf, and the fact that the IRS would take eighty-eight per cent of her earnings.

At last, in 1972, Alex Cohen prevailed on her to give television a try. He arranged a deal whereby she would receive a fee of a quarter of a million dollars from the sponsors (Kraft Cheese) – at the time the highest-ever fee for a one-off TV show. Not only that, she would have Stan Freeman as her musical director (things had changed since the days when just after he began to work for her, she had phoned Burt Bacharach in his presence and wailed, 'He's terrible! He's terrible! Come back!'), and she would have Joe Davis as her lighting designer. The show, to be taped in London, would be transmitted in England on the BBC and in America on CBS, and after that the rights in the show would revert to Maria. Part of her reason for doing the show at all was to provide security for her daughter and family, in case she herself

KW NAIL CORP
275 2A BROADWAY
NEW YORK, NY 10025
212 864 9306

C O P Y
05/06/2004 11:41
Sale:

Transaction #   8
Card Type   AMEX
Acct   xxxxxxxxxxx3034
Entry   Swiped
Sale: $6.00
Reference No. 00000008
Auth Code   529912
Response   APPROVED

Alexander Cohen (who
w/his wife Hildy also
produced the World of
Stars") called her
" the Singing (item)!"

became unable to perform. Another part was her desire to create a permanent record of herself in her show.

She also had the right to choose the venue where she would perform, and chose the New London Theatre, Drury Lane, because she liked its acoustics and its lighting set-up. The show, which was to be called *I Wish You Love* (after the song by Charles Trenet), was scheduled to be taped in the autumn of 1972.

It was while she was in London at that time, that her friend and protégée Marti Stevens was appearing there in the Stephen Sondheim musical, *Company*. Marlene went to see her in it, and went backstage afterwards, telling Marti that a woman she had met in the audience had said this had been one of the most wonderful evenings of her life. 'How sweet of you to tell me that!' said Marti. 'It's always gratifying to know when someone has enjoyed the show.'

Marlene looked at her with puzzled solemnity. 'Oh, darling,' she explained. 'It wasn't the show that thrilled her. It was meeting me.'

The taping of *I Wish You Love* turned out to be a disaster. For a start, the New London Theatre, for all its modern acoustics and lighting technology, was so new that it wasn't quite finished. Workmen were still busy bolting down seats and doing other construction work while Marlene and the TV crew were trying to get on with technical run-throughs. There was even the odd cement mixer grinding away. The stage was dusty from all the building work that was going on, and Marlene got down on her hands and knees and scrubbed it.

To design the set, Marlene had requested, and got, Broadway designer Rouben Ter-Arutunian. But his set, which was supposed to be pink, was instead nearer orange. Like 'red sails in the sunset,' Marlene exploded, and demanded it be changed. A pink backcloth was hastily erected. This would come out too pink on transmission, and would prevent the line producer from seeing the subtle signals she used to cue her music.

Worst of all, she was completely unable to control a TV production. In a world where most of the technicians were deeply involved in arcane electronic mysteries, involving VTR and unheard messages over the talkback and little flashing lights, she found herself more or less ignored. Joe Davis rigged up his lights for her with his usual subtlety, then found all his lighting effects completely wiped out when the brighter lights needed for television were slammed on.

Marlene took out her frustration on everybody in sight, especially Alex Cohen. When he asked her to come and be introduced to the sponsors, who after all were paying her enormous fee, she exploded. '*Kraft Cheese*?! He wants me to meet *Kraft Cheese* when I have a show to do!!'

Used to running her own painstaking perfectionist rehearsals, in TV she found out that all she was going to get were 'technical runthroughs'. And to make things worse, when performance time came, in front of an invited freeloading black-tie audience whom she loathed, she found that the speakers bringing her the sound of her music were so far away that they were not only hard to hear, but also gave her a brief time-lag. Any precise interplay between herself and her musicians was impossible.

And although the show was to be taped as far as possible in one continuous run, there were inevitably a few retaken inserts, and she found it hard, when doing them, to maintain the flow and rhythm of a genuine live performance. Looking at the tapes afterwards on video machines installed in her suite at the Savoy Hotel, she took to loathing the show's potential viewers, on the grounds that they would be getting her performance free. 'I never got nothing for nothing in my life,' she complained.

She thought the whole thing a disaster, and even though in many ways it was, all the problems she had can't stop quite a lot of her magic from coming through. She worried that the programme was so bad ('They are all robots, these people in TV') that it might put people off coming to her stage shows. She wished it could be destroyed.

The show was to be aired by the BBC on 1 January 1973, and by CBS in America on 13 January. Interviewed at the Waldorf-Astoria in New York by 150 television reporters, she told them all, in a rage, how terrible it was. Alexander Cohen was forced to sue her in courts in both Britain and the USA to get her to stop talking. He also withheld the final $100,000 of her fee, which she was due to get when the show had been transmitted, on the grounds that she was damaging its chances.

On 14 January 1973, the day after *I Wish You Love* was transmitted in America, a black-tie invitation-only gala was held in New York to celebrate the songs of Noël Coward. It was called *Oh! Coward*, and he chose Marlene to attend it as his companion. By now, he was showing his age, frail and stooped, and Marlene, wearing a chic pantsuit, let him take her arm as they entered, although it was not entirely clear who was propping up whom. It was Noël's last public appearance. He died, aged seventy-three, on 26 March.

Aware of her mortality, Marlene increasingly devoted time to being the custodian of her own legend – and by that she meant the legend that she had built up herself over the past twenty years, not any image she might have presented earlier. More and more she spoke slightingly of her film work, saying 'I hated being a film star,' still referring to her directors as 'my dictators', and deploring 'pansy' film fans who wanted only to talk of *Shanghai Express*.

On tour, suffering from pain and exhaustion, she became more demanding, more intolerant. The foundation garments she wore under her stage gown, to replicate her shape at its best, had become thicker as her body aged into scrawniness. Now made of foam-rubber, they were virtually hollow statues of the Dietrich she had been. In hotels, staff were allowed into her rooms only when she was there, and never ever when her costumes (with or without foundation garments) were laid out.

Her hotel bathrooms had to have extra-strong lighting installed, so that she could check the perfection of the full stage make-up she now never appeared in public without. And her suites had to have two baths – one for her to bathe in, the other for the mountains of floral tributes she received everywhere she went. She came to loathe these, and used the second bath simply to dump them in, their cards unread.

Anything that wasn't the show itself became an irrelevant nuisance – a waste of her dwindling energy – and she snubbed other sponsors as she had snubbed Kraft Cheese. In June 1973, in Paris, she was to play a short run at L'Espace Pierre Cardin, a new venue recently opened by the couturier himself. For her appearance he had new velvet curtains hung in the auditorium, and redecorated two dressing-rooms (with adjoining bath). In these he installed new plumbing fixtures and a refrigerator, as well as a new carpet. He covered their walls with fabric and on them hung antique mirrors from his own Paris flat. When she came to inspect the premises, Marlene simply said, 'Stick to pressing pants. You obviously know nothing about the theatre.'

Her phobia about photographers had grown stronger (no image of her over which she did not have total control must escape into the world), and on her first night at L'Espace Pierre Cardin she noticed there were a number in the auditorium. Fleeing into the wings, she announced over a backstage microphone, 'I will continue singing only if the photographers leave the theatre.' Thinking they had all left, she came back on stage and continued.

But one was still there. His shutter clicked, a fist-fight broke out (which left the photographer bloodied) and Pierre Cardin fainted.

After the show, she told him that she would never appear at his theatre again until he had the stage floor re-covered. He had it re-covered next day. Marlene's only comment, after walking up and down on it experimentally for a while was, 'It still creaks.'

Also she was becoming increasingly accident prone, which was not a good thing for somebody with brittle bones to be. Partly this was caused by failing eyesight, but her next bad accident wasn't caused by this, or by having a drop too much backstage. She was performing for a week at the Shady Grove Music Fair, in suburban Washington, and as Stan Freeman, who was both her musical director and her pianist on that occasion, recalled:

> It was our second night at this place, which had a deep orchestra pit, with the stage quite high above us. At the end of every performance Marlene would acknowledge the orchestra and shake my hand or kiss my cheek if we were all on stage, but here it was difficult for her to bend over to reach me in the pit. The second night I decided to make it easier for her by standing on the piano bench. She grabbed my hand and suddenly I could feel the piano bench giving way and I shouted, 'Marlene, let *go*!' But she couldn't hear me over the applause and music. I went over backwards with Marlene still clutching my hand and over she came, scraping against loose nails and instruments and I don't know what. There she was on the floor of the orchestra pit, a bloody mess, and the orchestra is still sawing away at 'Falling In Love Again', and the audience is applauding and shouting, 'Beautiful show!' and she's screaming, '*Go home! Go home!*' but they don't know what's happened and just kept on applauding. Finally she says, 'What do they *want*? I should do it *again*?!'

She had been dragged across a protruding nail that had ripped open both her gown and and a huge flap of skin half the length of her right thigh. Bleeding profusely, she was taken to her hotel room, where it was proposed to send for a doctor. But the doctor she insisted on was in the middle of an operation, and she refused point-blank to see anyone else.

She wrapped hotel towels round her thigh to try and stop the bleeding, but next morning felt so much worse that she allowed the hotel doctor to come and examine her. Appalled by the extent of her injury, he had her taken by ambulance to George Washington University Hospital, where they carried out emergency repairs. After this she announced, to the horror of doctors and nurses, that she had no intention of staying in bed, she had shows to perform.

She played out her week at Shady Grove and then, against medical advice, took a plane to her next venue, which was to be four nights in Toronto. The wound was still obviously deteriorating, the thigh around it turning black, but still she would fulfil her commitment. She was in so much pain that a wheelchair had to be used to get her to the wings, but once there she had enough guts to step smartly out onto the stage and do her seventy-five minute show. Her audiences never suspected there was anything wrong. Only the other members of her show could spot that the Dietrich strut did not quite have its usual snap.

After Toronto, however, even she could see that something had to be done. She flew to Houston, to be treated by the famous surgeon, Dr Michael De Bakey. He told her she would need skin grafts to repair the wound, and bypass surgery to the veins in her legs, so that sufficient blood would reach the grafts to allow them to heal.

She had to cancel a proposed appearance at Carnegie Hall, scheduled for early January 1974, and at first insisted that after that she would be ready to go back on the road. But she was not to heal as quickly as she thought, and eventually also had to cancel a January concert in Dallas and a February concert in Los Angeles.

By the middle of 1974 she was ready to go back on the road. In July it was announced that in September she would begin a series of six London concerts, at the Grosvenor House Hotel, in Park Lane. Then, in August, while living in her Paris apartment, she fell, breaking her right hip. But the concerts had been announced, posters had been printed, and Richard Burton had agreed to announce her on opening night. There was no way she was going to cancel.

She was flown back to New York, to Columbia-Presbyterian Medical Center, where a steel pin was surgically implanted in her broken hip-bone. A few weeks later she was flown to London, to the Grosvenor House Hotel, where she was also to stay, and there, on 11 September, she opened.

Again she was brought to the wings in a wheelchair (from her room, where until that moment she had remained hidden). There she stood up and, this time just a shade unsteadily, made her entrance in front of an audience that included Princess Margaret. Sheridan Morley, who reviewed her show for the London *Times*, reported, 'At the end, the audience gave her a standing ovation and somehow it didn't seem quite enough; the first of her kind and almost certainly the last of it, [she is] a living statue of liberty [and] offers the greatest solo turn I have ever witnessed.'

After the show, Princess Margaret had organised a party in her honour. Richard Burton was to be there, as was film director Franco Zeffirelli, and Kenneth and Kathleen Tynan. But Marlene refused to attend, claiming, 'I haven't got anything to wear.' That was her public excuse. To Stan Freeman she muttered, 'I'm a *queen*; I should stay up late for a *princess*?'

After London, the tour continued – back to America to play Miami and Dallas, back to London, this time to appear in Wimbledon, then back again to America to play Los Angeles (where Rudi showed up to be with her).

By this time, doing all she could to hide the ravages of time, she was beginning to insist that her stage lighting be dimmer and more diffuse than it had been. Also that curtained runways be constructed backstage, through which she could scuttle from dressing-room to stage and back without being seen. She was also by then refusing to meet the press at all.

In the autumn of 1974, while bravely considering trying another tour of Germany, she was back again in Australia, playing Melbourne and then Sydney, her musical director on this occasion being William Blezard. This was her third Australian tour in ten years, and attendance there was beginning to fall off. Her houses were often half-empty.

On 22 September, she opened in Sydney at Her Majesty's Theatre, for a run of a few weeks. But as her show at the end of the first week opened, the orchestra started playing Burt Bacharach's overture, which began with a lush arrangement of 'Falling In Love Again', Blezard, his back to the stage, was watching his musicians for a sign that she had made her entrance. He recalled, 'I heard a dissonant suspended blues chord and I thought, "God, that's a funny chord, it shouldn't sound like that!" and then the chord started to disintegrate and I realised later it was at that moment they saw her fall.'

What had happened was appallingly simple. For over a year she had been favouring her right leg, torn and grafted and pinned, by placing more weight on her left. And suddenly the femur of that left leg, weak like all her bones, had snapped under her weight. As she grasped for the curtain to hold herself up, the broken femur tore through muscle and skin in a compound fracture.

She fell to the floor and, as Blezard turned to see her struggling there, she yelled, 'Get the curtain down! Get it *down*!'

The curtain came down. She was carried to her dressing-room and then rushed to St Vincent's Hospital, where her leg was encased in plaster from waist to ankle.

One good bit of news was that an insurance policy she had taken out on her famous legs, with Lloyd's of London, was still in force by a mere four days. Bad news was that her future bookings would have to be cancelled indefinitely. Doctors even suggested that her performing days might be over for ever. Also bad, and nothing to do with her leg, was news from California that Rudi had had another stroke and had been admitted to the UCLA Medical Center.

Once her plaster had set, Marlene was taken to the airport and lifted onto a plane, bound for New York for treatment. But she was still Marlene, broken leg or no broken leg, and, when she realised that the plane was to make a touchdown at Los Angles International Airport, insisted on being lifted off there, so that she could be booked into the UCLA Medical Center, where she would be near her ailing husband.

She was, but Maria, who had also rushed to Rudi's side, soon prevailed on her to let herself be moved on to New York, again to the Columbia-Presbyterian Medical Center, where they had already mended her broken hip, and where her leg would probably receive better treatment. Marlene, in her weakened state, agreed, and had herself checked in there as 'Mrs Rudolf Seiber'. She had not even managed to see Rudi, who in any case was drifting in and out of consciousness.

She would be in Columbia-Presbyterian for over seven months, and would not make a good patient. Indeed, the stronger and better she felt the worse she behaved, finding it intolerable to be so helpless and dependant. To prevent anyone seeing her in such a state, she had a sign fixed to the outside of her door, saying, 'No Visitors! No Information!'

Even old friends like Joshua Logan and Katharine Hepburn found themselves turned away. Flowers and other gifts were thrown in the bin as soon as they arrived. She loathed the food, often throwing platefuls of it across the room untasted, and at one point she fired three private nurses in as many weeks.

Eventually, in May 1975, she was recovered enough to be released, to the relief of the much-badgered staff, and, accompanied by Maria, flew to Paris, where she could recover in the peace and privacy of her own apartment, attended by Bernard Hall.

She was depressed to hear that her old colleague Frederick Hollander had died on 18 June, but it wasn't long afterwards that she received the worst news of all. On 24 June 1975, back at home in the San Fernando cottage he had shared with Tamara, Rudi had died of a heart attack, sitting upright in a rocking-chair. Doctors told Marlene firmly she was not well enough to travel to his funeral, but she paid for it, having him buried not far from Tamara in the Hollywood Memorial Park Cemetery.

It was Rudi's death that finally disheartened her. Up to the moment of it, in spite of her age, her weak bones, her poor circulation and her increasingly poor sight, she had been cheerfully discussing by phone, with both Stan Freeman and William Blezard, the possibility of soon going back to work. For all their separateness, Rudi had in a way been the still centre of her life – always there somewhere for her, always on her side.

With Rudi gone, she would never perform in public again. All that remained now was the legend.

15 Legend

After Marlene was brought by Maria to her fourth-floor Paris apartment, in the middle of 1975, she almost never left it. Knowing that she would be unable to perform again, she determinedly rearranged her life.

She who had been so sociable became a near-recluse. Friends passing through Paris and calling at the apartment would be told over the intercom by a maid, or a masseuse, or a cook (all of whose voices, as it happened, bore a marked resemblance to Marlene's), that Miss Dietrich was away. She kept up a fiction that her life was still filled with globetrotting – that she lived out of suitcases and was always trotting off to New York or Sydney. People calling would be told that she was lunching at Versailles, or off motoring to Zurich, or flying to Tokyo. Among the many who called and received such replies were Jean-Pierre Aumont, Douglas Fairbanks Jr, Mr and Mrs James Stewart, Mr and Mrs Billy Wilder.

Most days a cleaning woman would come and, as well as doing the dusting and polishing and hoovering, would cook simple meals, with the instructions to leave them outside the unopened bedroom door. Marlene took to spending a lot of time in bed. Waking at six, she would drink the first of many cups of Earl Grey tea. She would watch television, but rarely films or dramas. Mostly it was news programmes, or tennis (she liked watching the young men's legs). When the papers arrived – *Le Figaro*, the London *Times*, the international *Herald Tribune* – she would read them from cover to cover. And she read a lot of books. Often these were her beloved poets – Goethe, Rilke, Schiller – but she also read many new books, of all kinds. The shelves of her apartment came to be overflowing with books.

Once or twice a week a secretary (often Bernard Hall, who was one of the very few people she did continue to see) would call and help her to deal with the mass of letters that continued to arrive, from fans and friends and people with business propositions. And in between times she would sip at Johnny Walker whisky and make endless phone calls. The phone became her social life. She had a number of friends, old and new, whom she would call regularly – among them Stephan Lorant, Max Colpet and the actor Roddy McDowall. Even on transatlantic calls, she would talk to them for hours.

There were two main reasons for her self-imposed isolation. One was her increasing difficulty in getting around at all. The other was a decision she had made that as few people as possible would see her get old. The memory of her – the image she had taken so much trouble to create – must not be impaired. She would not have herself photographed in the street, as the ageing Garbo was from time to time on the sidewalks of Manhattan.

This could prove inconvenient. As her sight continued to worsen, she often needed to have her eyes tested. But an optometrist could not bring his bulky equipment to her, and there was no way she was going out. So she hit on the solution of sending pairs of her old glasses to friends, often as far away as California, and asking them to choose slightly stronger ones from the racks of spectacles on sale in drugstores and elsewhere.

On the walls of her flat were a few photographs of herself – one from one of her shows, wearing her swansdown coat, one from the film *The Devil Is A Woman*, a film she was fond of, saying 'I was never more beautiful.' She still disliked talk about her films, but more and more there was another reason for her dislike, apart from not having had total control over them, or of her image in them. It was that many times while making them she had been happy, and now that her life was diminished and increasingly sad, she resented memories of happier times, finding them more painful than pleasant.

One wall, which she called her 'dead wall', bore pictures of friends no longer alive – among them Ernest Hemingway, Noël Coward, Maurice Chevalier and Gary Cooper. Another wall was her 'awards wall', where hung awards and citations she had received, including of course her American Medal of Freedom and her Légion d'Honneur.

One table bore a collection she had made of every 'Marlene Dietrich' doorplate off every dressing-room she had ever had since going to America. And hidden away in drawers and cupboards and wardrobes were thousand upon thousand mementoes – photographs, letters, posters and many of her costumes, especially the Jean Louis dresses. Taking up much space in her living-room were two Blüthner grand pianos. These had been given to her as payment by East German companies that had pirated some of her records and whose currency in the West was almost worthless. Although beautifully polished, as one would expect, both were out of tune. No piano-tuner would be permitted to enter her apartment.

Her main concern was how to make some money. Her outgoings were now much less – she no longer travelled, and no longer needed the extensive wardrobe she had once enjoyed, and she no longer had the expense of keeping a show together. But still she did need money, and had never been good at husbanding the vast fees she had so often received. It hurt her that she might no longer be able to give Maria and her family the financial aid she liked to feel made her essential to them (although Maria did still own the house in New York that Marlene had bought for her and William). Also there were friends who might be in need.

Although physically unable to perform, she was still as mentally alert and firm-minded as ever, so what could she find to do?

It was Maria who suggested she might again consider writing her memoirs, and in 1976 Marlene took up the idea. Through her agent, Robert Lantz, she approached publishers, and, as so often in her life, the whole situation soon became chaotic.

First Simon & Schuster announced that she had accepted an advance of $300,000 from them. But it wasn't long before the American firm of G B Putnam announced that she had accepted an advance of $200,000 from them. Which she had, her reason for accepting the lower offer being that Putnam's had agreed she need not make promotional tours (they, like Simon & Schuster, were unaware that she would now be unable to). Simon & Schuster sued Putnam's for three-and-a-half million dollars for loss of projected earnings.

Marlene was at first unsure how to begin writing a book, phoning writer friends to ask them for helpful hints, but soon enough she started pecking away on her portable typewriter, choosing to write in English and dismissing any suggestion that she hire a ghost-writer. She sent pages of what she had typed to writers she knew, including Irwin Shaw and Kenneth Tynan, but their suggestions were unhelpful to her.

It was quickly obvious to all who read sections of her work that it was going to be little more than a selection of shallow anecdotes, interspersed with equally shallow (but forthright) declarations about her philosophy of life. She was going to say nothing very revealing (or very interesting) about the talented men she had known, and she had a cheerful disregard for dates, or even facts. For instance, fwhen it came to family, her father and stepfather were merged into one, her sister Elisabeth did not exist, and Rudi and Maria were barely mentioned.

She was to submit her completed manuscript to the London office of Collins and, when she did so, it was rejected. Eventually she would be forced to return their advance, although that would not turn out to be the end of the matter.

Other events continued while she wrote. In 1977 she learned that the German writer/director/actor Ulli Lommel was about to release a fictional film called *Adolf And Marlene*, which would show her, played by Margit Carstensen, repulsing the advances of a lecherous Führer. This was by no means a piece of catchpenny tripe – among the cast was the outstanding director, Rainer Werner Fassbinder – but Marlene was having none of it. She sued, getting the film's distribution drastically curtailed.

Germany was still very conscious of her. The Berlin Film Festival announced that in 1977 and 1978 it intended to show a two-part retrospective of her films, and the city of Berlin offered her honorary citizenship if she would come there in person to accept it. She refused.

Her old friend Billy Wilder was planning his film *Fedora*, about an 'ageless' movie star whose agelessness eventually proves to be a fraud – she is now confined to a wheelchair and is impersonated by her own daughter. This had similarities to Marlene's own situation, although in fact it was based on a novel by Tom Tryon. In any case, when offered the title role by Billy, she sent the script back at once, scribbling indignantly on the cover, 'How could you possibly think...?!' It would be made in 1978 with Hildegard Knef in the title role.

In 1978 she would – rather unexpectedly, and mostly because she needed the money – make another film appearance. It was in what was then the most expensive German-backed film since World War II, and was shot in Berlin with an international cast and crew. Called *Just A Gigolo*, from the song of the same name, a German song called 'Schöne Gigolo', it was set in the Berlin club world of the Twenties, and starred David Bowie, Sydne Rome, and Kim Novak.

One character in it was to be a pimp, operating from the famous Hotel Eden, and originally the role was to have been played by Trevor Howard. Unfortunately his health was not up to it, and the German producer, Rolf Thiele, had the imaginative idea of casting Marlene. There was no reason why the role could not be a madam, rather than a pimp, and who could embody the Berlin of the period better than Marlene.

Negotiations were entrusted to the film's major screenwriter, Joshua Sinclair, who, after some preliminary discussions with Maria, was permitted to visit Marlene's apartment and talk to her about the project. She agreed to appear, and it was further agreed that she would receive $25,000. Maria would also receive a fee for being the fixer, and through her it was agreed that various conditions would obtain. Marlene would not film for more than two half-days, she would not climb any stairs, she would certainly not sing the film's title song ('That horrible old song'), and she would not leave Paris. This would involve considerable expenses for the production company, as they would not only have to bring the director and a skeleton crew to Paris, they would also have to bring the set they needed and reconstruct it in a hired studio.

Much of the main shooting in Berlin had already been completed by the time Marlene's two half-days were arranged, in February 1978. The director was the British actor/producer David Hemmings, who also had a role in the film, and he recalled her arrival at the Paris studio. Naturally he was somewhat nervous – nobody had seen Marlene in public for nearly three years, and there had been rumours about her health and general condition.

A car arrived, and at first there was a definite feeling of disbelief and shock when a stocky middle-aged woman emerged. This feeling lasted for the short while it took people to realise that this was Maria, but was somewhat renewed when a frail old lady, infirm, leaning on a cane and walking with difficulty, shuffled forward. She wore, Hemmings recalled to Marlene's biographer Steven Bach, 'a jeans pant-suit, a Dutch boy wig and cap, and huge dark glasses.' Worst of all, as they saw her face clearly, the crew observed that she 'had painted on a mask of what Dietrich looked like to her forty or fifty years before, an image and age-fix from which she either didn't know how to retreat or just couldn't *see*.'

It was the not seeing that was the problem. Her eyesight by now was decidedly dim, and although she had worked hard in front of her mirror, in the brightest light she could arrange, all she had managed to achieve was a mask like a self-parody. Fortunately the film's make-up man, Anthony Clavet, was both extremely talented and a devoted Marlene admirer. He and she retreated into a curtained-off dressing-room area that had been prepared in a corner of the stage. There he created for her a more up-to-date version of the famous Dietrich image (the skin of her face was still good and the amazing bone-structure still there underneath it). He also, as he worked, built up her confidence, reassuring her that she would be as splendid as ever.

She came out from behind the curtains a different woman, wearing the costume that she had collaborated in designing – black jacket, black skirt slit to the thigh, shiny black boots, white gloves, and a wide-brimmed black hat with a delicate veil. Part imperious horsewoman and part chic femme du monde, it was the perfect costume for a decadent character called the Baroness von Semering.

Even though she firmly made sure to check her lighting, it was obvious that Marlene was nervous – after all, it was sixteen years since she had last stood in front of a movie camera, and gone were the days when the whole idea of stagefright was a puzzling curiosity to her. Hemmings was surprised at how extremely nervous she was.

> I don't know what intuition drove me (he told Steven Bach), but I suddenly said to my assistant (this was in the morning, mind you), 'You know what I'd really like? A *large* scotch and water!' Suddenly I was being pulled by the hand like a small boy into her dressing room.
>
> Everyone was aware that Maria watered down anything she *knew* her mother had, but there was this innocuous-looking airline bag. Dietrich zipped it open to reveal dozens of little airline bottles, all scotch, I believe. Out they came and Dietrich and I sat there having our little nips. It was – I don't know – *camaraderie* that eased everything immeasurably. It was the kind of thing two actors would do, covering nerves no audience ever suspects. It was 'I know you better now,' and she relaxed and so did I and we did our work.

It was during this interlude that Marlene agreed to sing 'Just A Gigolo', even though she loathed it, realizing that, as the title song, it was essential.

On her first half-day she performed her few lines of dialogue. On her second she came in to sing the song. Hemmings had asked her to make an entrance through an arched doorway, walk (without a cane) to a foreground piano, and sing the song in one continuous take. This was both generous and right of him, because he wanted audiences to see that she could still walk perfectly, and he knew that she wanted the same.

The film was to be released in two languages, German and English – like *The Blue Angel* – and she made two takes of the scene in each language. 'When she finished,' said Hemmings, 'I was supposed to say "Cut!" and I couldn't. The moment was so charged and the spell she cast so total that the beats went by, one-two-three-four, until finally I came to my senses and said, "Cut!" And there was – literally – not a dry eye in the house.'

The film didn't turn out well, so full of laboured and self-conscious decadence that nobody, neither press nor public liked it. It was all unreal – except for Marlene. Ageing, and a shadow of what she had been, she was still an outstanding star and presence. This would be the last time she would ever appear on stage or screen, and the film gave her a fine and fitting final performance.

Also in 1978, her memoirs resurfaced. Somewhere along the line her manuscript had been translated into French, possibly with some idea of getting the book published in France, and this French translation had found its way into the hands of the German publishers, Bertelsmann, possibly through Maria or through Robert Lantz. The firm of Bertelsmann decided that it was to be translated into German (but with the translator uncredited, so as to give the impression that German was the language Marlene had written it in), and they would publish it in 1979 under the title *Nehmt Nur Mein Leben – Reflexionen (Just Take My Life – Reflections)*, which words are from Goethe.

Not only that, but sections of the book, amounting to almost sixty per cent of the whole, would be published in the German periodical *Stern* and in the German edition of the American magazine *Esquire*.

Various editions continued to emerge over the years. The French translation, somewhat modified, got published in France in 1984 as *Marlène D*, and an abridgement of this version, again translated into German, this time by Max Colpet, was published in Germany three years later as *Ich Bin, Gott Sei Dank, Berlinerin (I Am, Thank God, A Berlin Woman)*. And England would finally, in 1989, get an English version. Except it was only a translation into English of *Ich Bin, Gott Sei Dank, Berlinerin*, and thus an abridged version that had been translated from English into French into German and back into English (by an Italian) – which did not do a lot for well-known quotations from such as Noël Coward and Ernest Hemingway.

Back in her apartment, Marlene's life continued much as before. Her eldest grandson, John Michael, who turned thirty in 1978, had married and adopted a son his wife already had. And in 1979 her second grandson, John Peter, then twenty-nine, had a son. Which made Marlene a great-grandmother twice over, and kept alive her concern that she had a flourishing family to provide for. What didn't help in this was that in January 1979 she had a bad fall in her apartment, again breaking her left thigh bone. This time it would never properly heal, and from now on she would be almost totally wheelchair-bound.

She continued to watch much television, and in around 1979 she became aware that from time to time her image would appear. A 1965 feature-length compilation film, *The Love Goddesses*, had used her gorilla-costumed song 'Hot Voodoo' from *Blonde Venus* as its title sequence. The dismally bad 1970 film *Myra Breckenridge* (which would be Mae West's next-to-last movie), reused the footage of Marlene's song from *Seven Sinners*, 'The Man's In The Navy'. This was not to mention all the appearances by impersonators or parodists.

None of these manifestations of her brought in a penny. But why not, she thought, make something for television that did? The one part of her that was still in good working order was her voice, so why not, using that, as well as footage from her films and shows, make a TV documentary for which she would get paid?

But who could she approach to direct it? Her first thought was naturally her friend Orson Welles, but Welles was too chaotically busy trying to set up his own projects. She thought of the bright young American critic-turned-director Peter Bogdanovich, but his career, after successes like *The Last Picture Show* (1971) and *What's Up, Doc?* (1972) had rather faltered with *Daisy Miller* (1974), *At Long Last Love* (1975) and *Nickelodeon* (1976), and besides, she decided, she probably didn't need a name director. She knew every foot of film she'd ever shot, and which she wanted to use, and what she wanted to say, and all she really needed was a competent and obedient person who knew the ropes of film-making and would carry out her wishes. Also, of course, someone who would help her find the necessary backing.

She hit on the idea of asking Maximilian Schell, who had won the Best Actor Oscar for *Judgment At Nuremberg* (his sister Maria, as it happened, had appeared in *Just A Gigolo*, although Marlene, who had not met her, was not impressed by her as an actress). Now in his late forties, as well as acting, Maximilian had done some directing, and he had the great advantage of speaking both German and English fluently.

It all took some time to arrange, but finally a German-American co-production was set up, and in the autumn of 1982 Maximilan arrived at the apartment with a sound-recording crew and with the American Terry Miller, who had been Marlene's booking agent since her earliest Las Vegas days, and who was now semi-retired. He was acting as her agent for the documentary, and was there to protect her interests.

It had been agreed that Marlene would do six sessions, recording sound only, speaking to Maximilian about her career. In no circumstances would she ever be seen – no filming of her would be done, no videotaping, not even a photograph. This documentary was to be about her past career, not about her life now, or about any of her private life.

Once they arrived, she rolled in in her wheelchair, explaining it by saying she had broken her toe the day before by tripping over a piano bench while trying to get to her photocopying machine. As Bernard Hall, who was present, had already explained that she would be in a wheelchair because of tripping over a piano leg on her way to answer the telephone, this imparted a certain air of unreality to the proceedings.

The unreality soon got much worse. Marlene and Maximilian turned out to be at total cross-purposes. Her idea of the film was totally conventional, a series of clips from her films and shows, intercut with stills of herself and maybe some fellow-actors, and with a voice-over by herself telling who was what. She had already sent his producer, some months before, a list of the films she wanted to include, and was by no means pleased that she had recently phoned the copyright-owners of some of them and learned that so far no request to use any clips had been made.

Maximilian explained to her that using clips from old films costs an arm and a leg, and there was no point in him ordering up even a second of film until he was sure he would be using it. This did not please Marlene, who already had in her head a very clear idea of exactly which clips should be used. But Maximilian had different ideas about the whole project. He had great admiration for Marlene, and realised he had been presented with the opportunity of making a film that could be quite some distance out of the ordinary. And a film was what he intended it to be. A ninety-minute film for showing in cinemas – not a TV piece at all (except of course later, like any cinema film).

Marlene had expected a conventional script, almost a pre-written commentary, for her to deliver and which would be laid over preselected images. Maximilian wanted them to converse, and converse freely, in a mixture of German and English, about her life, letting whatever emerged dictate the shape of the film. This, she protested angrily, was amateurish. Didn't he know that true professionals always worked from a script?

He had hoped that, even if he couldn't film her, he could at least film the interior of her apartment. She wasn't having it. That would be totally pointless – the documentary was to be nothing to to with her private life. He wanted to show to her, on videotape, scenes from her famous films, in order to get her reaction while watching them. This, to her, was again pointless. She knew her films inside-out, so why should they waste time projecting them (she did not mention that she found such reminders of her old life painful). She would rather deliver thought-out and considered opinions and memories, rather than ad lib them while watching the footage. And in any case, videotape was amateurish.

The film turned out well. In Maximilian's hands it became as much about the difficulty of making a film with Marlene as about her life, although that is strongly present as well. The soundtrack, made up of his six sessions with her, contains her contemptuous dismissals of the way he was working, or wanted to work, with occasional outbursts of real fury, and calmer moments when she reminisced, these often recorded after she thought the equipment had been turned off (and she had had a couple of cups of whisky-laced Earl Grey).

To give himself images to work with, Maximilian reconstructed a replica of her apartment in a studio, and filmed himself in the distance as if interviewing Marlene, giving the impression that she was just out of sight behind a half-open door. He filmed scenes of himself and his editors struggling to cut together what footage they had of her films and shows, and of places connected with her.

All in all, it turned out a fascinating picture of a fascinating woman, although in a way it did her a slight disservice in presenting her as the cantankerous old woman she had become (her ill-temper born out of rage and disappointment at her age and impotence), rather than as the witty and charming (although tempestuous) woman she had been in her prime.

When she saw the finished film, Marlene loathed it, to the extent of trying to prevent it from being shown. But as years passed she did rather soften in her attitude towards it, especially after it was nominated for an Oscar for Best Feature-Length Documentary.

Also, of course, she could not afford to stop it from being shown. If it was not shown she would get no money for it, and she needed money badly. In 1982, even as she was working with Maximilian, she was starting to get behind in her rent, and two years later, in June 1984, her landlords began sending her letters demanding payment, eventually serving her with eviction papers.

The case came to court, and she managed to get the order for eviction quashed. The publicity drew her plight to the attention of the Paris authorities. She was, after all, a Chevalier of the Légion d'Honneur, and the pride of Paris would not permit a holder of that award to be turned out into the street. They not only arranged to take care of her rent, they also upgraded her award, promoting her from a Chevalier to a Commandeur. Proudly she hung the new medal on her wall of awards.

She continued to keep a maternal eye on her family. By 1986 the New York house that she had bought for the Rivas was occupied by her third grandson, John Paul, now twenty-eight and with a young French wife, and by his younger brother John David, now twenty-five. John Michael, the eldest grandson, had taken after his father and was now achieving success as an art director in Hollywood.

Still money was tight for Marlene. In November 1987, in spite of wanting to keep everything associated with her in store, on the grounds that it would be even more valuable after she was gone, she allowed Christie's to auction a few items of her jewellery, abstracted from a bank vault she kept in Geneva – with each she offered a letter of provenance, signed by herself. They were a set of diamond and sapphire cufflinks, several gold cigarette cases encrusted with diamonds, a diamond-studded gold compact presented to her by Vittorio de Sica and so inscribed, and a necklace of seventy diamonds from Van Cleef & Arpels.

She also found that she could make money by allowing herself to be interviewed (though not seen), and duly allowed the German *Die Welt* to interview her over the telephone, and the German *Der Spiegel* to send her a list of a hundred questions, quite a few of which she briefly answered. And she used her voice to recite the verses of two Frederick Hollander songs, for use on a nostalgic album by the German pop-singer Udo Lindenberg – they were 'When I Thirst For What I Wish', which she had recorded, with Hollander at the piano, in Berlin in 1930, and 'Illusions', which she had sung, again with him at the piano, in *A Foreign Affair*. These were recorded at her apartment without her leaving her bed.

Some projects using her voice never came into being. One was to record the poems of Rilke for a German radio station. Another was to record for talking books, a medium which fascinated her. One recording she did make, but which brought in no money, was a short acceptance speech she gave in 1989, after she was awarded a European Film Award for Lifetime Achievement.

And all the time her world kept contracting as people died. Ginette Spanier (to whom she had not spoken for years), Margo Lion (who had refused to answer her phone calls for years in case she wanted to borrow money), and, on 15 April 1990, Greta Garbo (to whom she had hardly spoken at all, but who had been such an important influence on her life).

Towards the end of 1990, on 3 October, the Berlin Wall came down. West and East Germany were at last reunited, and this so uplifted her that she allowed the *New York Times* a brief interview, telling them over the phone, 'Of course I'm happy. Anything that brings people together and encourages peace always makes me happy. Happiness is so rare in this troubled world.'

On 27 December 1991, on her ninetieth birthday, the media of the recently unified Germany united to pay her tribute. It had been only at the beginning of that year, in January, that she had protested on German television (by phone) at a plan to demolish the old UFA studios at Babelsberg, south of Berlin. Now UFA, having had a new cash injection, had renovated the stage where she had filmed *The Blue Angel*, and in honour of her birthday they named it Marlene-Dietrich-Halle.

When she was young, she had wanted to be a film star, although she could not have imagined then the superstar that she would eventually become. In a way it entailed a much more consuming lifestyle than she had ever bargained for. But when it happened she rose to it. She was seduced by it.

The image she constructed of herself, for herself, of the legendary Marlene, the most beautiful woman in the world, gave her the biggest role of her life, a persona that as the years went by would replace the real person who had been a shy schoolgirl and a teenager who feared she was not beautiful. A person who had sustained so many losses. The father and stepfather she barely knew. The mother who, with the best motives in the world, withheld affection. The young soldier who gave her her first kiss and then went off to be killed in the Great War. The nation that, by voting in the Nazis, lost her her language and the city she had so much enjoyed in the flower of her youth. The only other thing in her life that gave her so much feeling of 'being herself' was her war record.

All her losses and her feelings of uncertainty and inadequacy were replaced, with firm determination, by a constructed personality so magnificent that it was beyond praise or blame. A total perfection, adored by men and woman alike.

And it was a personality that people could adore. Seizing the stage, she gave to millions of people, for one night in their lives, the illusion of beauty. That they were part of it, and part of her. Making them for the moment feel as beautiful as she appears to them. A woman with secrets, aloof and mocking, but at the same time letting all the members of her audience feel they share those secrets.

Early in May 1992, she phoned all her remaining friends to say goodbye to them, telling them she was now sure she was dying. After that she took her phone off the hook and retired to her bedroom, refusing to let anyone enter and flying into a rage if they tried. This distressed her secretary, who explained the situation to her second grandson, Peter, when he arrived at the apartment next morning.

Peter managed to get Marlene to let him carry her from her bed and lay her on the sofa in her living-room, where he placed round her reassuring treasured possessions – mostly books and photographs. It was his intention to get her bed replaced by an orthopaedic one, and to get a perpetual medical-surveillance order from a magistrate. But the following afternoon, sleeping peacefully on the sofa after being given a bowl of soup by her housekeeper, Marlene died. It was 6 May 1992.

Her funeral service took place at L'Eglise de la Madeleine, in the centre of Paris. There her coffin was draped in the French tricolor, her medals resting on it. Then it was draped in an American stars-and-stripes and flown to Berlin, where it was in turn draped in the red, black and gold of reunified Germany. Then there was another ceremony, as she was interred at Friedenau next to her mother.

She wouldn't have been pleased. She had often declared that she wished to be buried in Paris, with maybe her heart in England, but nothing in Germany. And a few Germans felt the same. When the hole for her grave was dug, several made the trip there to spit in it, and during the following ten years her gravestone was frequently defaced, once with words describing her, in German, as a 'slut in furs'.

But the old hostility is fading. On 16 May 2002, almost the tenth anniversary of her death, the Berlin legislature declared her an honorary citizen, calling her, 'an ambassador for a democratic, freedom-loving and humane Germany.'

She was all that and more.

Bibliography

BOOKS ABOUT MARLENE

Bach, Steven: *Marlene Dietrich: Life And Legend* [HarperCollins (UK) 1992]
Bret, David: *Marlene Dietrich, My Friend* [Robson Books (UK) 1993]
Dietrich, Marlene: *My Life* [Weidenfeld & Nicholson (UK) 1989]
Frewin, Leslie: *Dietrich: The Story Of A Star* [Coronet Books (UK) 1974]
Higham, Charles: *Marlene: The Life Of Marlene Dietrich* [Norton (USA) 1977]
Riva, Maria and Naudet, Jean-Jacques: *Marlene Dietrich* [Thames & Hudson (UK) 2001]
Spoto, Donald: *Dietrich* [Bantam Press (UK) 1992]
Walker, Alexander: *Dietrich: A Celebration* [Pavilion (UK) 1998]

OTHER BOOKS

Agate, James: *Around Cinemas* [Home & Van Thal (UK) 1946]
Agate, James: *Around Cinemas (Second Series)* [Home & Van Thal (UK) 1948]
Arnold, Eve: *Film Journal* [Bloomsbury (UK) 2002]
Bankhead, Tallulah: *Tallulah* [Victor Gollancz (UK) 1952]
Bloom, Ken: *Hollywood Song: The Complete Film & Musical Companion* (three volumes) [Facts On File (US) 1995]
Brunelin, André: *Gabin* [Robert Laffont (France) 1987]
Dewey, Donald: *James Stewart* [Warner Books (UK) 1998]
Evans, David: *Glamour Blondes* [Britannia Press Publishing (UK) 1995]
Ford, Selwyn: *The Casting Couch* [Grafton Books (UK) 1990]
Green, Abel and Laurie, Joe Jr: *Show Biz, From Vaude To Video* [Permabooks (US) 1953]
Holmstrom, John: *The Moving Picture Boy* [Michael Russell (UK) 1996]
Hotchner, A E: *Hemingway And His World* [Vendome (US) 1989]
Madsen, Axel: *Billy Wilder* [Secker & Warburg (UK) 1968]
McBride, Joseph: *Hawks On Hawks* [Faber & Faber (UK) 1996]

McCarthy, Todd: *Howard Hawks: The Grey Fox Of Hollywood* [Grove Press (US) 1997]

McGilligan, Patrick: *Fritz Lang: The Nature Of The Beast* [Faber & Faber (UK) 1997]

McIntosh, Elizabeth P: *Sisterhood Of Spies: The Women Of The OSS* [Dell (US) 1999]

Manvell, Roger: *Film* [Penguin Books (UK) 1944]

Manvell, Roger: *Chaplin* [Hutchinson (UK) 1975]

Marx, Groucho: *The Groucho Phile* [Galahad Books (US) 1976]

Maurois, André: *The Life Of Sir Alexander Fleming* [Jonathan Cape (UK) 1959]

Niven, David: *The Moon's A Balloon* [Coronet Books (UK) 1965]

Pallot, James and Levich, Jacob: *The Fifth Virgin Film Guide* [Virgin Books (UK) 1996]

Perry, George: *The Films Of Alfred Hitchcock* [Dutton Vista (UK) 1965]

Renoir, Jean: *My Life And My Films* [Collins (UK) 1974]

Rhode, Eric: *A History Of The Cinema* [Pelican Books (UK) 1978]

Rust, Brian and Debus, Allen G: *The Complete Entertainment Discography* [Da Capo Press (US) 1989]

Short, Ernest: *Fifty Years Of Vaudeville* [Eyre & Spottiswoode (UK) 1946]

Stallings, Penny, with Mandelbaum, Howard: *Flesh And Fantasy* [Macdonald & Jane's (UK) 1978]

Sternberg, Josef von: *Fun In A Chinese Laundry* [Macmillan (USA) 1965]

Taylor, John Russell: *Hitch: The Life And Work Of Alfred Hitchcock* [Faber & Faber (UK) 1978]

Thomson, David: *A Biographical Dictionary Of Film* [Andre Deutsch (UK) 1995]

Thomson, David: *Movie Man* [Secker & Warburg (UK) 1967]

Truffaut, François: *Hitchcock* [Panther (UK) 1969]

Whiting, Charles: *Patton* [Pan/Ballantine (UK) 1973]

Zolotow, Maurice: *Billy Wilder In Hollywood* [Putnam (USA) 1977]

Index